RUSSIAN GRAMMAR

RUSSIAN GRAMMAR

BY

NEVILL FORBES

THIRD EDITION
REVISED AND ENLARGED BY
J. C. DUMBRECK
University of Manchester

OXFORD
AT THE CLARENDON PRESS
1964

Oxford University Press, Amen House, London E.C.4

GLASGOW NEW YORK TORONTO MELBOURNE WELLINGTON
BOMBAY CALCUTTA MADRAS KARACHI LAHORE DACCA
CAPE TOWN SALISBURY NAIROBI IBADAN ACCRA
KUALA LUMPUR HONG KONG

PRINTED IN GREAT BRITAIN

EDITOR'S PREFACE

DR. NEVILL FORBES, Reader in Slavonic Languages at Oxford from 1910 until his untimely death in 1929, was one of the pioneers of Russian studies in Britain. His *Russian Grammar* has been valued by successive generations of students both as a textbook and as a work of reference. The book is particularly useful to those who have completed an elementary course of Russian and are continuing their studies—either in classes leading to a G.C.E. or university examination, or on their own with the aid of a Russian novel or a special reader. As this is a practical rather than a theoretical Grammar, philological comparisons, historical comments, and etymological explanations have generally been avoided, in order not to discourage the beginner.

This third edition is set in the latest Soviet orthography, with the exception of a few religious terms (Бог, Тро́ица, &c.), which have been given capital initial letters. The paragraphs (apart from the section on pronunciation) bear the same numbers as the corresponding paragraphs in the second edition, but many of them have been substantially revised and extended, especially those dealing with the use of the genitive with a negatived verb, impersonal statements, the use of the tenses, numerals, prefixes, and interjections. The lists of irregular verbs, irregular comparatives, prepositions, and prefixes are now, for practical purposes, complete. The modes of address, the terms for relationships, currency, weights, and measures have been brought up to date. The section on pronunciation has been entirely rewritten in the light of advances made by phoneticians since the first edition appeared, but

Forbes's homely method of relating Russian sounds, wherever possible, to the nearest sounds in English has been retained, as being the most helpful to the student who is not a specialist in phonetics; for the same reason, the English alphabet has been used for the phonetic transcription of Russian words, in preference to special symbols. A short bibliography of reference works and annotated texts, selected by the editor, will be found at the end of the book, together with an English subject index and an index of the Russian words dealt with in the text.

I am indebted to the late Professor D. P. Costello and Professor S. Konovalov for their valuable observations and to Mr. Michael Beresford for his careful reading of the proofs and many helpful suggestions. I should also like to express my thanks to Mr. G. V. Adamovitch and the other Russian friends, in Britain and the Soviet Union, who helped me with opinions on points of usage and style, and to Mrs. O. A. Narkiewicz for reading the revises.

J. C. D.

CONTENTS

CONTENTS

INTRODUCTION

§1. The Russians and the Russian Language

RUSSIAN, like English and most of the other languages of Europe, is a member of the great Indo-European family of languages. It belongs to the Slavonic branch of that family, just as French belongs to the Romance and German to the Germanic branch.

The Slavonic languages are divided into three groups—Western, Southern, and Eastern. The Western group includes Polish, Czech, Slovak, and Lusatian (sometimes called Wendish, and still spoken by about 150,000 inhabitants of the Spree valley in Eastern Germany). Bulgarian and the languages of Yugoslavia (Serbo-Croat, Slovene, and Macedonian) form the Southern group. The Eastern group, the most important numerically, comprises Russian, Ukrainian, and Belorussian.

The original Indo-European sounds developed in the Slavonic languages along different lines from those of the other European languages, so that the affinity of Russian with these languages is not always directly apparent even in the many words that have a common origin. But one has only to look at such primitive words as сестра (sestra), брат (brat), сын (syn), дочь (doch'), бровь (brov'), борода (boroda), молоко (moloko), гусь (gus'), иск- (isk-) to see their close connexion with our *sister, brother, son, daughter, brow, beard, milk, goose, ask*. Other words, such as мать (mat'), дом (dom), вера (vera), око (oko), виде- (vide-), immediately recall cognate words in Greek and Latin. Many, as вдова (vdova) *widow*, have equivalents which are closely similar in most of the Indo-European languages.

At the last census (1959) the population of the Soviet Union was nearly 209 millions, speaking well over a hundred different languages. Approximately 160 millions are descendants of the Eastern Slavs who, in historic times, fell under different foreign influences and became divided into three nationalities: Russian, Ukrainian, and Belorussian.

There are over 115 million Russians. They form 83 per cent. of the population of the R.S.F.S.R. (Russian Soviet Federative Socialist Republic) which stretches some 7,000 miles from the Baltic eastwards, to Kamchatka and the Bering Strait, and 2,000 miles from Murmansk southwards, to the foothills of the Caucasus. In the fourteen other Soviet Socialist Republics the percentage of Russians among the inhabitants varies between 43 per cent. (in the Kazakh Republic) and 3·2 per cent. (in the Armenian Republic).

Russian (formerly also termed Great Russian) is the native language of more than 99 per cent. of these Russians. In addition, some 10 million non-Russians now consider Russian their first language. Russian is therefore the normal means of communication of nearly 125 million Soviet citizens.

Of the remaining Slavs in the Soviet Union, about 37 millions are Ukrainians, inhabiting mainly the Ukrainian Soviet Socialist Republic and also parts of the R.S.F.S.R., the Kazakh S.S.R. (including southern Siberia) and the Moldavian S.S.R. Their language, Ukrainian, is sometimes referred to as Ruthenian, formerly also as Little Russian.

There are some 8 million Belorussians (or White Russians), whose language differs rather less from Russian than Ukrainian does; they live mostly in the Belorussian S.S.R. (lying between Smolensk and the Polish frontier) and in neighbouring areas of the R.S.F.S.R. and the Ukrainian S.S.R.

Some two-and-a-half million Russians, Ukrainians, and Belorussians have settled outside the U.S.S.R., principally in the U.S.A. and Canada.

In Soviet schools the Russian language is a compulsory subject for all non-Russians. Russian is an official language, beside the local language, of law-courts throughout the Soviet Union; it is also the *lingua franca* in which Soviet citizens of different nationalities (e.g. a Georgian and an Uzbek) converse with one another, and it has had a very marked influence in recent years on the other languages of the U.S.S.R., especially on the vocabularies of the languages spoken by the less highly developed nationalities.

§ 2. The Alphabet

The alphabet used by the Russians and, in slightly different versions, by the Ukrainians, Belorussians, Bulgarians, Serbians, and Macedonians, is known as the Cyrillic (кири́ллица). It was given this name because it was thought to have been invented by St. Cyril (826–69), otherwise known as Constantine the Philosopher, an inhabitant of the Greek port of Salonika, who spoke both Greek and the Slav dialect of neighbouring Macedonia. In 862 the prince of Moravia, Rostislav, requested the Byzantine emperor to send missionaries to convert his subjects to Christianity. The emperor, Michael II, entrusted this task to Cyril and his brother, Methodius. No previous attempt had been made to write down a Slav tongue, and in order to translate the Gospels for the Moravians St. Cyril was obliged to devise an alphabet which would accurately represent the sounds of the Slavonic vernacular. The Slavonic dialect for which he composed his alphabet is generally considered to have been Old Bulgarian or, more precisely, Old Macedonian, which was probably readily understood by the Moravians, since at that time the Slavonic dialects had not yet become sufficiently differentiated for them to be considered as separate languages. It is now thought that St. Cyril was the author not of the alphabet called Cyrillic but of the cognate Glagolitic alphabet (глаго́лица), which is still used in a few isolated parts of Dalmatia. The Glagolitic alphabet has been proved to be older than the Cyrillic; it was possibly founded on the Greek minuscule script of the ninth century and, owing to the complexity and confusing similarity of its letters, it was later supplanted almost everywhere by the Cyrillic, which was based mainly on the Greek majuscule script and was much more legible than the Glagolitic.

The Cyrillic is the only alphabet the Russians have ever used, and it is not unnatural that its origin should have been attributed to the man who was the first to record any Slavonic dialect in black and white and who has ever since been regarded by all Slavs of the Orthodox faith as the fountain of their enlightenment. Books and the art of writing were introduced into Russia with Christianity in 988. Old Bulgarian immediately established itself in the Russian lands as the language of the Church, a position which, with minor modifications, it still holds. It became the approved medium of expression for all literary work, although it could not remain absolutely free from the influences of the Russian vernacular, especially in works of a secular nature. Mention will be made later of the influence of Old Bulgarian, also called Old Church Slavonic, on Russian grammatical forms and vocabulary. The Cyrillic alphabet took such firm root in Russia that no attempt to supplant it has been successful. Indeed, its use has been extended recently to many languages of non-Slavonic nationalities in the Soviet Union.

The influence of Church Slavonic and the fact that the Cyrillic alphabet was not originally devised for Russian, account for the discrepancies between Russian as it is written and Russian as it is spoken, for the illogicalities of the orthography, which is based on morphology and historical tradition and recalls that of our own language, and, consequently, for many of the difficulties which we experience in mastering modern Russian. It is necessary in every language to submit to certain conventions, and it is doubtful whether those that regulate the orthography of Polish, Czech, Slovene, and Croatian, which use adaptations of the Latin alphabet, are more rational and less formidable than those governing Russian.

The Cyrillic alphabet is based on the majuscule characters of the Greek alphabet, but it contains important additional signs, representing sounds which did not exist in Greek. Its direct derivation from the Greek is apparent in the incorporation in it, until the spelling reform of 1917, of the three letters eta (и), iota (i), and ypsilon (v), all of which had exactly the same value in ninth-century Greek, viz. *i*, and in the necessity of inventing a sign for *b* (Б б), because by the ninth century the Greek β was pronounced *v* while Old Bulgarian had both the sounds *v* and *b*.

The Cyrillic characters were originally very plain, but by the eighteenth century they had assumed somewhat complicated and unwieldy shapes. In drawing up his Civil Script (гражда́нский шрифт), to meet the requirements of the printing-press, Peter the Great simplified the characters and discarded several redundant letters. A reformed spelling was introduced in 1917, and its use was enforced by the decree of 10th October 1918, issued by the Council of People's Commissars; the letters i and v were replaced by и, which had an identical sound; ѣ and ѳ were similarly

replaced by e and ф respectively; ъ was omitted at the
end of words, a final consonant being considered 'hard'
unless followed by the 'soft sign' (ь); and certain other,
minor changes were made towards phonetic spelling. In
their normal printed form, the Russian small letters have
the same shape as the capitals, with the exception of a, б,
e, and ё.

The Russian printed alphabet now has the following
appearance:

NORMAL[1]	CURSIVE[2]	TRANS-LITERATED	NAME
А а	*А а*	*a*	а
Б б	*Б б*	*b*	бэ
В в	*В в*	*v*	вэ
Г г	*Г г*	*g*	гэ
Д д	*Д д*	*d*	дэ
Е е	*Е е*	*e*[3]	е (i.e. йэ)
Ё ё	*Ё ё*	*ё*[4]	ё (i.e. йо)
Ж ж	*Ж ж*	*zh*	жэ
З з	*З з*	*z*	зэ
И и	*И и*	*i*	и
Й й[5]	*Й й*	*y*[6]	и кра́ткое
К к	*К к*	*k*	ка
Л л	*Л л*	*l*	эль
М м	*М м*	*m*	эм
Н н	*Н н*	*n*	эн
О о	*О о*	*o*	о
П п	*П п*	*p*	пэ
Р р	*Р р*	*r*	эр
С с	*С с*	*s*	эс
Т т	*Т т*	*t*	тэ
У у	*У у*	*u*	у
Ф ф	*Ф ф*	*f*	эф

NORMAL[1]	CURSIVE[2]	TRANS-LITERATED	NAME
X x	*X x*	*kh*	ха
Ц ц	*Ц ц*	*ts*	цэ
Ч ч	*Ч ч*	*ch*	че
Ш ш	*Ш ш*	*sh*	ша
Щ щ	*Щ щ*	*shch*	ща
Ъ ъ[7]	*Ъ ъ*	omitted[8] (see §14)	твёрдый знак[9]
Ы ы[7]	*Ы ы*	*y* (see §6)	ы
Ь ь[7]	*Ь ь*	omitted[8] (see §13)	мягкий знак
Э э	*Э э*	*e*	э[10]
Ю ю	*Ю ю*	*yu*	ю
Я я	*Я я*	*ya*	я

[1] Known technically as прямо́й шрифт *upright type*.

[2] The cursive letters fulfil the same function as our italics.

[3] To help the general reader who is ignorant of the pronunciation of Russian e, in isolated Russian names in an English text this letter is best transcribed *ye* when it occurs at the beginning of a word or after ъ, ь, or a vowel, e.g. *Yesenin* or *Esenin* for Есенин, *Andreyev*, or *Andreev* for Андреев.

[4] For the general reader ё may be transcribed *yo* or (after ж, ч, ш, or щ) *o*.   [5] Never initial in words of pure Russian origin.

[6] The sign *ĭ* is the most satisfactory way of transliterating this letter, although it is still seldom employed. Philologists use *j* and write, for instance, *Chajkovskij* for Чайковский; but this is misleading to the uninitiated English-speaking reader. More common in works of a general nature are *y* and (not recommended, because it is ambiguous in some positions) *i*, e.g. *Tolstoy* (or *Tolstoi*) for Толсто́й, *Maykov* (or *Maikov*) for Ма́йков, *geroy* for геро́й *hero* (the spelling *geroi* is best reserved for the plural геро́и *heroes*).

The common adjectival ending -ый in an isolated name or title in an English book intended for the general reader is customarily transcribed by *-y*, since the more precise transliteration *-yy* (or *-yi*) is misleading to those who do not know Russian; so Но́вый мир is rendered by *Novy mir*. For the same reason the ending -ий is usually transcribed *-y* (or *-i*), as in *Mirsky* or *Mirski* for Ми́рский.   [7] The three letters ъ, ы, ь, are never initial.

[8] Omitted when transcribing isolated Russian words in an English text for the general reader; in linguistic works the hard sign (ъ) is best transliterated by a double apostrophe (") and the soft sign (ь) by a prime (ʹ) or a single apostrophe (ʹ), e.g. *Gogol"* or *Gogolʹ* for Го́голь.

[9] Sometimes called раздели́тельный знак *separating sign*.

[10] Occasionally called э обор́отное (i.e. *reverse* є).

THE WRITTEN ALPHABET

А а	*К к*	*Х х*
Б б	*Л л*	*Ц ц*
В в в	*М м*	*Ч ч*
Г г	*Н н*	*Ш ш*
Д д	*О о о*	*Щ щ*
Е е	*П п*	*ъ ъ*
Ё ё	*Р р*	*ы*
Ж ж	*С с*	*ь ь*
З з	*Т т*	*Э э э*
И и	*У у*	*Ю ю ю*
Й й	*Ф ф ф*	*Я я*

Where two forms of a small letter are given in the table, the second is to be used at the end of a word, and before the hooked letters *ᴧ ᴧ ᴧ*. The letter *ᴃ* should not be joined to any following letter.

Although pupils in Soviet schools are taught to write the letters in the above manner, other forms of some of the letters are still found, especially in rapid writing; the most important are given here, to aid recognition: *ᴅ ᴅ ᴦ ᴦ* (д), *ᴈᴧ ᴈᴧ ᴧᴧ* (ж), *ᴈ ᴈ ᴈ ᴈ* (з), *ᴋ ᴋ ᴋ* (к), *ᴎ ᴎ* (н), *ᴨ* (п), *ᴩ ᴩ ᴩ ᴩ* (р), *ᴄ* (с), *ᴛ ᴛ ᴛ* *ᴛ ᴛ ᴛ* (т), *ᴔ* (ф), *ᴑ ᴑ* (х), *ᴧ ᴧ* (ц), *ᴕ* (ч), *ᴣᴧ* (ш), *ᴣᴧ ᴣᴧ* (щ), *ᴃ ᴃ* (ь), *ᴙ ᴙ* (я), *ᴈ ᴈ ᴩ* (final я).

HOW LETTERS ARE ADDRESSED IN RUSSIAN

с. Воронино, Московской обл.,
Клинского района,
2-я Советская, д. 7, кв. 4,
Давыдову,
Фёдору Никитичу.

Москва, К-57,
Цветной бульвар,
д. 19/6, кв. 11,
Надеждину, Михаилу Павловичу,
для Соколова А. В.

г. Сочи,
Главпочтамт
до востребования,
Первомайской,
Нине Антоновне.

PRINTED VERSION OF FOREGOING ADDRESSES

с. (= село) Воро́нино, Моско́вской обл. (= о́бласти),
Кли́нского райо́на (*or* р-на),
2-я Сове́тская (*sc.* у́лица), д. (= дом) 7¹, кв. (= кварти́ра) 4,
Давы́дову,
Фёдору Ники́тичу.

Москва́, К-57,
Цветно́й бульва́р,
д. 19/6 (= дом № 19, подъе́зд № 6), кв. 11,
Наде́ждину, Михаи́лу Па́вловичу,
для Соколо́ва А. В.

г. (= го́род) Со́чи,
Главпочта́мт (= гла́вный почта́мт),
до востре́бования,
Первома́йской,
Ни́не Анто́новне.

ENGLISH TRANSLATION

village Voronino, Moscow oblast (= region) (*gen.*),
Klin rayon (= district) (*gen.*),
Second² Soviet (Street), house 7, flat 4,
Davydov, Fyodor Nikitich (*dat.*, surname first)

Moscow, K-57 (postal district)
Tsvetnoy Boulevard
house (building) 19, entrance 6, flat 11,

Nadezhdin, Mikhail Pavlovich (*dative case*),
for Sokolov, A. V. (*genitive*)
(i.e. to A. V. Sokolov, c/o M. P. Nadezhdin.)

---

¹ Notice crossed fig. 7.
² In some Soviet towns there are groups of neighbouring streets with the same name; such streets are distinguished from one another by an ordinal numeral.

town Sochi,
Head post-office (G.P.O.),
to be called for (Poste Restante),
Pervomayskaya, Nina Antonovna (*dat*., surname first)[1].

---

[1] A comma is placed after the surname if the person's other names (not merely initials) follow.

A LETTER IN RUSSIAN

Уважаемый товарищ Соколов!

Спасибо за Ваше письмо от 1-го августа, которое я получил сегодня. Я очень рад, что Вы благополучно доехали до Москвы, и надеюсь скоро с Вами познакомиться. Буду Вас ждать у себя завтра в 11 часов утра. Если же это Вас не устраивает, то я могу прийти к Вам. Прошу только назначить день и час, которые Вам удобны.

Желаю Вам всего хорошего,

А. М. Петров.

FOREGOING LETTER IN PRINTED FORM

Уважа́емый[1] това́рищ Соколо́в!

Спаси́бо за Ва́ше[2] письмо́ от 1-го а́вгуста, кото́рое я[2] получи́л сего́дня. Я о́чень рад, что Вы благополу́чно дое́хали до Москвы́, и наде́юсь ско́ро с Ва́ми познако́миться. Бу́ду Вас ждать у себя́ за́втра в 11 часо́в утра́. Е́сли же э́то Вас не устра́ивает, то я могу́ прийти́ к Вам. Прошу́ то́лько назна́чить день и час, кото́рые Вам удо́бны.

Жела́ю Вам всего́ хоро́шего,

А. М. Петро́в.

---

[1] When writing to a very eminent or important person, глубо̀коуважа́смый *deeply respected* may be used.

[2] In letters it is usual to begin all forms of вы and ваш with a capital letter. Unless it begins a sentence, я *I* must be written with a small letter.

ENGLISH TRANSLATION

Respected comrade Sokolov,

Thank you for your letter of 1st August, which I received today. I am very glad that you have reached Moscow safely, and hope soon to make your acquaintance. I shall expect you at my house tomorrow at 11 a.m. If, however, this does not suit you, then I can come to [see] you. I request you only to fix a day and time that are convenient to you.

I wish you everything good,

A. M. Petrov.

In letters to officials who are not known personally by the sender, no equivalent of *Sir* or *Dear Sir* is used in Russian; the text stands immediately below some such heading in the dative case, as:

Дире́ктору Автомоби́льного заво́да
и́мени Лихачёва
в Москве́.

or:

Управля́ющему колхо́зом «Кра́сное зна́мя»
Пско́вской о́бласти.

A person with whom the writer is acquainted is addressed with уважа́емый *respected* or дорого́й *dear* followed by first name and patronymic (formed from the father's first name by means of a suffix, see p. 116):

Уважа́емый Алекса́ндр Никола́евич   *Dear Alexander Nikolaevich*

Дорого́й Ива́н Гео́ргиевич   *Dear Ivan Georgievich*

A relative, close friend, or young child is addressed with дорого́й followed by the first name in its basic form or, more intimately, by one of its diminutives of endearment:

Дорогóй Ивáн (*or* Вáня, Ваню́ша, *etc.*) *Dear John* (*Jack, Johnny*).

Rather more intimate than дорогóй for *dear* is ми́лый (used mostly by women); somewhat more formal is любéзный.

Letters usually end with a very simple greeting, such as:

С уважéнием *or* С почтéнием *Yours respectfully*
Искренне Ваш *Yours sincerely*/*truly*/*faithfully*.

Less formal endings include:

[Желáю Вам] всегó хорóшего   [*I wish you*] *all the best*
С привéтом   *With greetings, regards*
[Крéпко] жму Вáшу рýку   *I shake your hand* [*firmly*].

Only the date is put at the head of a private letter; the writer's address goes at the bottom of the envelope, preceded by Отпр. (= Отправи́тель) *sender*, and followed by his name and initials in the nominative case.

In a letter from an official, the signature is customarily placed beneath the indication of his status; the official's initials and name may be typed below the signature.

PRONUNCIATION

§ 3. The Vowels

There are ten vowel-letters in the Russian alphabet: five hard and, corresponding to these, five soft.

The soft vowel-letters serve two purposes. First, when a soft vowel-letter (except и) is the first letter of a word, or when it stands after ь, ъ (see §§ 13, 14) or another vowel-letter, the vowel-sound is iotated, i.e. preceded by the sound of *y* in the English word *yet*. For example, the sound represented by the English words *you* and *yew* is an iotated *u*, similar to the Russian ю in юг *south*; the German word ja *yes* is an iotated a, similar to the Russian я of я *I* and ясно *clearly*. Secondly, when it stands after a consonant, a soft vowel loses this iotation, since the *y*-element coalesces with the consonant, which thereby becomes softened, or palatalized, i.e. it is pronounced with the middle of the tongue raised towards the hard palate, in the position for *y* of English *yet*. Palatalization affects some consonants much more than others. In the process of palatalization the *y* is lost as a separate sound, but between the palatalized consonant and the following vowel-sound there is a very brief glide, like a fleeting *y*. This glide must be kept as short as possible. There is a similar palatal glide between the consonants ч, щ (which are always soft) and any following vowel.

The pronunciation of the vowel-letters is influenced by the position of the stress, which in Russian is mobile, i.e. it may fall on different syllables in words from a common root or in different forms of the same word. There are certain rules for determining the position of the stress, but as they are positively riddled with exceptions, it is probably less difficult to pick up the correct stress by ear or by reading accented texts. The rules are therefore not given in this book, but the stressed syllable is marked by an acute accent on all polysyllabic words, unless they are enclitic, in which case their stress is taken over by the preceding word (which is accented, even if monosyllabic).

Russian stressed vowels are of medium length, like English *ee* and *oo* when followed by a voiceless consonant (as in *feet, boots*); they are shorter than the English long vowels of *feed* and *boom*, but longer than the English short vowels of *fit* and *foot*. Russian unstressed vowels are short.

The Hard Vowels

The five hard vowel-letters are

а э ы о у

§ 4. A a = a

When stressed and not followed by a soft consonant or soft vowel, this vowel-letter is pronounced somewhat as in English *father*, but shorter. More exactly, it is intermediate in quality between the *a* of *father* and that of *apple*, and is similar to those of the French *la nappe*, the German *das Land*, and the Northern English and Scottish pronunciation of *bad lad*, e.g. да *yes*, ра́но *early*, а́лый *scarlet*.

When it occurs in the syllable immediately before the stress (and is not followed by a soft consonant or vowel), it has much the same quality, but is shorter and less tense, like the Southern English pronunciation of the *u* in *up*, *rub*, e.g. рабо́та *work*.

Initial a is rare in truly Russian words but is common in loan-words; unless it is stressed, it is always pronounced like the *u* in *up*, e.g. апте́ка *dispensary*, апостро́ф *apostrophe*.

When it occurs in the stressed syllable or the syllable before the stress and is followed by a soft consonant or a soft vowel, a sounds 'sharper' (i.e. less open, more like the *a* in the French word *Espagne*), e.g. in such words as Ита́лия *Italy*, даю́ *I give*; between the vowel-sound and a following soft consonant there is a very short *i*-like glide, so that the vowel-sounds of сталь *steel*, бра́ни *of abuse*, and мани́ *beckon!* approach those of English *stile*, *briny*, and *my knee*. This tendency towards a diphthong should not be exaggerated, and the glide must be kept so short as not to be heard as a separate sound.

For the pronunciation of a after ч and щ, see §§ 33, 34.

When a stands in any other position, it sounds like the English neutral (or 'obscure') vowel, i.e. like the *a* in

barometer, ago, china, solar, e.g. папиро́са *cigarette,* о́блако
cloud, до́ма *at home.* This neutral vowel is represented in
phonetic transcription by the sign *ə,* e.g. *pəp'iró́sə.* (Note:
p′ = palatalized *p.*)

§ 5. Э э = *e*

occurs in only two or three genuinely Russian words (in
which it is always stressed) as a demonstrative prefix, but
it is more common in words of foreign origin. Its pronunciation depends on whether it is followed by a hard or a
soft consonant. If the following consonant is hard, e.g. in
the word э́то *this* (n.), э represents an open vowel-sound
followed by a very short glide with the quality of the *a* in
china; the whole sound approaches the Southern English
pronunciation of *air* in *air, hair, fair,* &c. If the following
consonant is soft, э is closer, i.e. produced with the tongue
nearer to the hard palate, so that the sound resembles the
Scottish and Northern English pronunciation of *a* in *hate*
or *ei* in *eight* and the French *é* of *été,* e.g. э́ти *these* (т is soft
owing to the following и).

In foreign words, stressed э is liable to the same changes,
e.g. поэ́т *poet* with э open, as in э́то, but поэ́те *poet* (locative case) with the close variety of э, as in э́ти. Unstressed э
in words of foreign origin is similar to *e* in the English word
end, e.g. эрмита́ж *hermitage,* экземпля́р *copy, specimen,*
Эдуа́рд *Edward.*

§ 6. Ы ы = *y*

This is the vowel which causes most difficulty to foreigners, but less to those whose native language is English than
to Germans or Frenchmen, because a rather similar sound
exists in English. Its approximately correct pronunciation
is best attained by saying with clenched teeth the syllables
containing *i* or *y* in the following English words: *bill,*

twenty, Amy, rill, sin, dim. Russian words with similar syllables are: был *he was*, ты *thou*, мы *we*, рыл *he dug*, сын *son*,
дым *smoke*. Between б, в, м, or п and a following ы there is
a slight glide, like a very brief and lax English *w*; but it is
better to omit this glide altogether than to exaggerate it.

The pronunciation of ы is comparatively little affected
by its being unstressed or followed by a soft consonant. For
example, the ы in была *she was* scarcely differs from that in
был; the ы in были *they were* (where it is followed by л
which is palatalized by the subsequent и) is pronounced
not quite so thickly, i.e. not so far back in the mouth, but
it is affected much less noticeably than is э (§ 5).

The letter ы is never initial, and cannot stand after к, г,
х, ж, ш, ч, or щ, after which letters its place is taken by и. It
should be noted that after the consonants ж, ш, and ц (which
are always hard) the letter и is pronounced as if it were ы.

It is important not to confuse the various uses of the
letter *y* in the transliteration of Russian words. When used to
transliterate ы it is a vowel, e.g. был — *byl*, мы — *my*; elsewhere *y* may be a consonant, indicating iotation, e.g. ясно —
yásnə, or a semi-consonant, e.g. бой (*a fight*)—*boy* (cf. § 21).

In works on the history of the Russian language this
letter is often called еры́.

§ 7. О о = *o*

When stressed, this vowel-letter represents a sound like
the *aw* of English *saw*, but shorter and pronounced with
rounded lips, e.g. он *he*, до́ма *at home*. Unstressed o is pronounced in exactly the same way as Russian unstressed a
in the same position (cf. § 4), i.e. like the *u* of rub if it
stands in the syllable immediately preceding the stress,
and elsewhere like ə, the neutral vowel represented by *a* in
the English words *ago, china*. This peculiarity of Russian as
spoken in Moscow and to the west and south of that city

explains the first vowel of the old English word *Muscovy*, based on Москва́ *Moscow*.

As with a, when o stands in the stressed syllable or the syllable immediately before the stress, there is an *i*-like glide before a following soft consonant, which is especially noticeable if ь follows the consonant. Thus, the vowels in the Russian words конь *steed*, со́лью *with salt*, проси́ *ask!*, хочу́ (ч is soft, cf. § 33) *I want*, боле́ть *to ache*, approach the sounds of the English vowels in the syllables *coin*, *soil-you*, *pry-see*, *high-chew*, *by-late*, but the Russian glide is much shorter than the second element of the English diphthongs and must not be exaggerated.

§ 8. У у = *u*

When stressed, this vowel sounds like *u* in German tun (*to do*), being pronounced with more lip-rounding than the English *oo* in *boot*, e.g. у́тка *duck*, могу́ *I can*, у́мный *clever*; when unstressed it is shorter, like the English *oo* in *book*, e.g. мо́гут *they can*, туда́ *thither*. Its quality is not affected by a subsequent soft consonant to the same extent as are a, э, and o, although a slight anticipation of the palatal sound does take place.

The reason why Russian *u* is written y is that in Greek the sound could only be represented by ov, which was incorporated in the Cyrillic alphabet as oy and was long written thus; these two letters were later combined to form the letter ȣ, which in its turn became gradually assimilated to the Western European y, but with a different value.

The Soft Vowels

The five corresponding soft vowel-letters are

я е и [ё] ю

§ 9. Я я = *ya* or *'a*[1]

is the soft vowel-letter corresponding to a.

[1] The prime (′) indicates the palatalization of a preceding consonant.

When not preceded by a consonant, я is an iotated vowel and has one of five sounds, depending on its position:

(i) stressed я, if final or followed by a hard consonant, sounds approximately as *ya* in English *yard*[1], e.g. моя́ *my* (f.), я *I*, я́сно *clearly*;

(ii) stressed я is similar to *ya* in *yap* (in phonetic transcription—*yæ*) if it is followed by a soft consonant or vowel, e.g. я́сень *ash-tree*, объя́тие *embrace*, сия́я *shining*;

(iii) when standing in the syllable before the stress, я resembles the *ya* of *Yale*, but is closer and shorter, e.g. язы́к *tongue, language*, but very many speakers pronounce it here almost as in position (v), i.e. as *yi*;

(iv) when unstressed я occurs in the endings -я, -ям, -ями, -ях, -ят, it sounds like the consonant *y* plus *ə* (the neutral vowel, like *a* in *china*), i.e. like *ia* in the English pronunciation of *Sonia*, e.g. ста́рая *old* (f.), ду́я *blowing*, учи́теля *of the teacher*, стоя́т *they cost*, на гобо́ях *on oboes*;

(v) elsewhere, unstressed я has the sound of *yi* in *Yiddish*, e.g. языково́й *linguistic*, по́яс *belt*.

When preceded by a consonant, я represents the same vowel-sounds as in (i)–(v) above, but the *y*-element is lost as a separate sound, since it coalesces with the consonant, which becomes softened, or palatalized, as explained in § 3. Between the softened consonant and the vowel-sound there is a very short *y*-like glide which must not be allowed to become as strong, or as long, as the *y* of *yet*.

Examples of я after a consonant:

(i) with я́сно (*yásnə*) compare ряд *rank, row* which is pronounced *r'at*, i.e. soft *r*+*a* as in *father*[2]+hard *t* (see § 18);

(ii) with объя́тие (*abyǽt'iyə*) cf. мять *to crumple*, pron. *m'æt'*, i.e. soft *m*+*a* as in *apple*+soft *t* (see § 29);

---

[1] More precisely, like the *y* of *yet* plus an *a* like those of French *la flamme* or German *das Land*.

[2] More precisely, as in French *la flamme* or German *das Land*.

(iii) with язы́к (*yezýk*) cf. ряды́ *ranks, rows*, pron. *r′edý*, i.e. soft *r*+*e* like *a* in Scottish *ale*;

(iv) with ста́рая (*stárәyә*) cf. Ва́ря *Barbara* (dim.), pron. *vár′ә*, i.e. soft *r* and *ә* like *a* in *china*; also де́тям *to the children*, но́сят *they carry*, при́нят (m. sing.) *accepted*;

(v) with языково́й (*yizykavóy*) cf. рядово́й *ordinary*, pron. *r′idavóy*, i.e. soft *r* and *i* as in *it*; also па́мять (f.) *memory*, при́няты (pl.) *accepted*, вы́тянуть *to pull out*.

The quality of the stressed vowel я before a soft consonant is so distinctive that the foreigner may ignore the slight *i*-glide between я and the consonant.

я never occurs after г, к, х, ж, ш, ц, ч, or щ.

§ 10. E e = *ye* or *′e*

is the soft counterpart of the hard vowel э. It denotes (like я) either that a preceding consonant is palatalized and followed by slight *y*-glide and a simple vowel or, when not preceded by a consonant, that the same simple vowel is iotated (i.e. preceded by the sound of *y* in *yet*).

1. The exact quality of the vowel depends on the position of e in relation to the stress. When stressed e is final or before a hard consonant, it represents an open e-sound[1] followed by a slight off-glide like a very short *ә* (the neutral vowel, as *a* in *china*). The vowel + glide resemble the Southern English pronunciation of *air* or (when e is iotated) of the river *Yare*, but it must be noted that the neutral vowel used instead of rolled *r* in the English words is much longer and more prominent than the Russian off-glide in such words as нет *no*, мне *to me*, and ел *he ate*.

2. When stressed e stands before a soft consonant or soft vowel, it denotes a close e-sound[2] followed by a very slight *i*-glide. This vowel + glide are somewhat similar to the diphthong represented by *a* in the Southern English pronunciation of *ale* or (when e is iotated) the *ya* of *Yale*. How-

---

[1] In phonetic transcription—*ɛ*.   [2] In phonetic transcription—*e*.

ever, the lips are much closer together for the e-element of
the Russian sound, which is more like the Scottish pronunciation of *ay* in *day* or the French *é* in *été*, and the Russian
i-glide is shorter than the second element of the Southern
English diphthong. For example, сеть *net*, бей *hit!*, éли
they ate, имéют *they possess*.

3. In the syllable immediately before the stress, e sounds
rather like the *a* in *ale* (when iotated—the *ya* in *Yale*) though
it is closer and much shorter; but very many speakers pronounce it almost as in other unstressed positions (see below).
Thus, in лесá *forests* (transcribed *l'esá*) e is pronounced
somewhat as *a* in *ale* or as the first sound of *event* and *exist*.

4. In other unstressed positions, e has a sound close to
that of *i* in *it* (when iotated—the *yi* in *Yiddish*), e.g. в пóле
(*fpól'i*) *in the field* (loc. case), кóмнате (*kómnət'i*) *room* (dat.
& loc.), европéец (*yivrap'éyits*) *European*, переводúть
(*p'ir'ivad'ít'*) *to translate*.

While it is now permissible to pronounce unstressed e always in this manner, there are certain endings in which e is
still often pronounced ə (as it was in most endings in
Moscow in the nineteenth century). These endings are:

(i) the -ое or -ье of the nom. and acc. sing. of neuter
adjectives: молодóе (*məladóyə*) *young*, стáрое (*stárəyə*) *old*,
врáжье (*vrázhyə*) *enemy's*;

(ii) the -ое of the collective numerals двóе (*dvóyə*) *two*
and трóе (*tróyə*) *three*.

(iii) the -ем of the instrumental sing. of masc. and neut.
nouns: с товáрищем (*stavár'ishch'əm*), перед учúтелем
(*p'ir'iduch'ít'il'əm*) *in front of the teacher*, над пóлем (*natpól'əm*)
above the field.

(iv) the -его, -ему,-ем, of soft masc. and neut. adjectives:
сúнего (*s'ín'əvə* or *s'ín'ivə*) *blue*, &c.

(v) the -ьев of the gen. plur. of masc. and neut. nouns:
стýльев (*stúl'yəf*) *chairs*, дерéвьев (*d'er'év'yəf*) *trees*.

(vi) the -e of the nom. and acc. (never locative!) sing. of neuter nouns: по́ле (*pól'ə* or *pól'i*) *field*—cf. в по́ле (always *fpól'i*) *in the field* (loc. case); ущéлье (*ushch'él'yə* or *ushch'él'yi*) *gorge*, знáние (*znán'iyə* or *znán'iyi*) *knowledge.*

(vii) in the -ee of the comparative form of adjectives: умнéе (*umn'éyi* or *umn'éyə*) *more intelligent.*

5. The consonants ч, щ are always soft and cannot be further palatalized by a following e.

6. The consonants ж, ш, ц are always hard and are not softened by a following e. The combinations же, ше, and це, when stressed, have the sound that жэ, шэ, and цэ would have in the same position; when standing in the syllable immediately before the stress, they sound like жы, шы, and цы, as in желéзо *iron*, шестóй *sixth*, цена́ *price*; in other unstressed positions, e after ж, ш, and ц is a type of neutral vowel (*ə*), e.g. женихи́ (*zhən'ikh'í*) *suitors*, шел-ко́вица (*shəlkav'ítsə*) *mulberry*, целико́м (*tsəl'ikóm*) *completely*, полотéнце (*pəlat'éntsə*) *towel*, тóже (*tózhə*) *also.*

7. In many foreign words that have not yet been fully assimilated into Russian, e is identical with э: it has the sound of *e* in *end* and does not palatalize a preceding consonant, e.g. шоссé *high-road*, кабарé *cabaret*, диéта *diet*, пастéль *pastel*, детекти́в *detective*. The velar consonants г, к, and х are always softened by a following soft vowel.

[Ё ё = *yo* or *'o*]

8. It is a peculiarity of Russian that stressed e before a hard consonant or when final, although in certain categories of words pronounced as above, changes its quality in the majority of cases and is pronounced like a Russian stressed o (cf. § 7) preceded by iotation or a palatalized consonant. This vowel, which is really the soft counterpart of o, is not usually counted as a separate letter of the alphabet and has here therefore been placed in brackets. As

Russians know when to pronounce e as yo/ʹo, ё is seldom used, except in dictionaries, in books intended for non-Russian readers, and to distinguish всё (n. sing.) *all, everything* from все (pl.) *all, everybody*. In this book ё is used throughout. Since only stressed e can be pronounced ё, the accent is omitted in these cases and its place taken by the diaeresis (¨). For example, село *village* (pron. *s'eló*) but сёла *villages* (pron. *s'ólə*); весело *cheerfully* (pron. *v'és'ilə*), where the c is palatalized by the following e and therefore the first e retains its original value, but весёлая *cheerful* (f.) (pron. *v'es'óləyə*), where the л is hard, being followed by the hard vowel a; смесь *mixture*, where c is palatalized by ь, but нёс *he carried*, where c is final and therefore hard.

Final stressed e is always pronounced yo/ʹo, except in the Russian words уже *already*, те *those* (pronoun), все (pl.) *all, everybody*, сие *this* (n.), бытие *existence*, житие *vita* (*biography of a saint*), in loan-words like портье, купе, and кафе, and in the endings of the locative and dative singular. Thus, её *her* (acc. and gen. of она) is pronounced yeyó; моё *my* (nom. and acc. neut. of мой) is pronounced *mayó*; питьё *beverage* (nom. & acc.) is *p'it'yó*, but the locative case is питье, pronounced *p'it'yé*.

Stressed e before a hard consonant is not pronounced yo/ʹo in such common words as бегать *to run*, бедный *poor*, белый *white*, ехать *to travel*, железо *iron*, лес *forest*, лето *summer*, место *place*, свет *light, world*, снег *snow*, хлеб *bread*, человек *person*, and many others, in which e is derived from an earlier ѣ, nor in the very numerous borrowings from Church Slavonic.

Conversely, e is pronounced yo/ʹo in many cases where it is not to be expected, i.e. although followed by a soft consonant or a soft vowel. In this position the vowel-sound of ё is somewhat different from that of Russian o: it is centralized, i.e. approaches the Southern English *ur* of *fur*, and resembles the *o* of French *l'homme*; it is followed by a slight *i*-glide. These exceptions to the rule are due to the influence of analogy, e.g. ведём we are leading (pron. *v'ed'óm*) has by analogy caused ведёте *you are leading* to be pronounced ведёте (*v'ed'ót'i*) although the stressed e is here followed by a palatalized т; by analogy with all the other cases (which have hard endings), the locative singular of nouns like утёс *cliff* is утёсе (pron. *ut'ós'i*), &c., although the final letter is here softened by the e of the ending; by analogy with тётка *auntie*, тётя *aunt* is pronounced *t'ót'ə* despite the following soft т; the instrumental singular ending of nouns of the feminine declension in -a (e.g. горóй or горóю from горá *hill*)has influenced the declension of feminine nouns with soft endings, like земля́ *earth*, the instrumental singular of which is землёй or землёю, pronounced *z'eml'oy*[*u*], in spite of the following soft й/ю. Where there is no influence from other forms, stressed e before a soft consonant or soft vowel will retain its original sound, as in моéй, твоéй (the instrumental singular feminine of the pronoun-adjectives мой *my* and твой *thy*) and in ножéй (the genitive plural of нож *knife*).

The consonants ж and ш are always hard and are not softened by a following ё, the combinations жё and шё having the same sound as stressed жо and шо.

The consonants ч and щ are always soft and are not palatalized further by a following ё. The combinations чё and щё sound like stressed чо and що.

§ 11. И и = *i* or *'i*

is the soft vowel corresponding to ы. Stressed и sounds like the *i* of Italian *vino* and French *il dit*; the nearest English vowel is the half-long *ee* of *meet* and *beet*. и always palatalizes a preceding consonant, but the *y*-glide between them, having a quality similar to that of и itself, is not so clearly audible as in the case of the other soft vowels.

The consonants most noticeably affected by a following и are т (*t*), д (*d*), н (*n*), and л (*l*): these consonants are strongly palatalized by и, and the following *y*-glide is especially clear after т and д, cf. the pronunciation of артист *performer* (almost like the English words *art* and *yeast* run together, with the stress on *ea* and the *r* rolled), один *one* (rather like *add* followed without a break by the syllable *yeen*), они *they* (like *Ann* + *ye* fused together), and молитва *prayer* (pron. *mal'ítvə*, with *l'i* as Italian *gli*, Spanish *lli*). When speaking a foreign language, Russians have great difficulty in producing a 'clean' *i*-sound after the letters *t* and *d*; they tend to insert the short *y*-glide of their own language, so that, for instance, their pronunciation of *tea, din, need* may sound to our ears like *tyea, dyin, nyeed*.

The position of the word-stress has little effect on the quality of и, nor is its pronunciation altered appreciably by the presence of a following soft consonant or soft vowel. Unstressed и in the flexional endings of words or in the syllable immediately before the stress is rather shorter than stressed и, but they are almost identical in quality. With артист and один compare эти (*ét'i*) *these*, тиран (*t'irán*) *tyrant*, and диван (*d'iván*) *settee*. Unstressed и in other positions is even shorter and less tense; it tends towards the sound of English short *i* in *bit, him*.

It should be noted that и after the hard consonants ж, ш, and ц, is always pronounced as if it were ы, i.e. it has become hard, e.g. жир *fat, grease* (pron. *zhyr*), наши *our* (pl.) (pron. *náshy*), мотоцикл *motor-cycle* (pron. *mətatsýkl*).

Initial и is not iotated, i.e. if и is the first letter of a word it is pronounced *i*, and not *yi* as one might expect, e.g. ива *willow* is pronounced *ívə*, never *yívə*. The only possible exceptions to this rule are three forms of the personal pronouns, which may be pronounced without or with initial iotation, viz. им (pron. *im* or *yim*) *by him, by it, to them,* ѝми *by them,* and их *them, of them, their.*

Initial и is pronounced ы by some people when the word is closely connected in speech and in sense with a preceding word ending in a hard consonant. This is quite usual when the first word is a preposition without a stress of its own, e.g. под ѝвой *under a willow,* без ѝмени *without a name,* в исто́рии *in history* sound as though they were written подѝвой, безы́мени, высто́рии. When the first word is not a preposition, the student should pronounce such an и as an и, although such pronunciations as братывáн for брат Ивáн *brother Ivan* and дáлым for дал им *gave to them* are heard in rapid speech.

и must not be confused with the consonant й (§ 21).

и is never part of a diphthong: it always has the sound of a full vowel. If и stands after another vowel, it begins a new syllable, e.g. бои́мся *we fear* is pronounced *ba-ím-s'ə* (three syllables). Notice that the plural of мой *my* (pron. *moy*) is мои́, which must be pronounced as two syllables: *ma-í* (with stressed *i* like the *ee* in *meet*). Many other words form their plural in this way.

The form of this letter is derived from the Greek *H* (eta); it is curious to note that, whereas the Greek *H* has become И in Russian, the Greek *N* appears in Russian as Н (see § 25).

For **Ё ё** = *yo* or *'o*—see Е е.

§ 12. Ю ю = *yu* or *'u*

is the soft vowel corresponding to Russian у.

When not preceded by a consonant, stressed ю represents an iotated vowel which sounds like English *you,* i.e. the *y* of *yet* plus the *oo* of *boot.* When stressed ю stands after a consonant, the consonant is palatalized and followed by a slight *y*-glide and the half-long *oo* of *boot*.

When unstressed, ю is pronounced as in the preceding paragraph, but the *oo*-sound is shorter and less tense, fairly close to that of Standard English *foot*.

Although, for practical purposes, the types of English *oo* described above render ю adequately, the Russian sound, when final or followed by a hard consonant, is articulated a little farther back in the mouth than the English and, when followed by a soft consonant, is articulated further forward.

Examples of iotated ю: ю́мор (*yúmər*) *humour*, даю́ (*dayú*) *I give*, ста́рую (*stáruyu*) *old* (acc. sg. fem.), побью́ (*pab'yú*), i.e. almost as English *pub + you* with *y* clearly heard) *I shall beat*.

Examples of ю after a consonant: этю́ды (*et'údy*, cf. *Tud* of English *Tudor*) *studies, sketches*, дя́дю (*d'äd'u*, cf. English *dew*) *uncle* (acc.), пюпи́тр (*p'up'ítr*, cf. English *pew*) *reading-desk*.

§ 13. The Soft Sign (ь)

Originally this letter, called soft sign (мя́гкий знак), re-presented an ultra-short vowel sound, as also did the hard sign (ъ). Some eight centuries ago these sounds were re-placed in certain cases by the full vowels e and o; in other cases they ceased to be pronounced at all and were no longer written unless they served some orthographic pur-pose in a particular position. In technical works on the Russian language the soft and hard signs are often referred to by their old names: ерь and ер, respectively. The soft sign (ь) now has the following functions:

1. When it stands after a consonant (other than ж, ш) at the end of a word or before another consonant, ь

indicates that the preceding consonant is to be given its palatalized (or 'soft') sound. For example: брат (*brat*) means *brother*, but брать (*brat'*), with ь to show that the т is to be pronounced as the *t* in English *tube*, means *to take*. There are several pairs of words distinguished in this way.

2. When ь stands between a consonant (other than ж, ш) and a soft vowel (я, е, ё, ю, or и), it denotes that the consonant is to be palatalized and followed by a fully iotated vowel. For instance, the first syllable of дядя (*d'éd'ə*) is pronounced with a palatalized *d* followed by the vowel of English *add*; whereas дьяк (*d'yak*) *scribe* is pronounced with the same palatalized *d* but it is followed by a sound like *ya* of English *yard*.

3. Since ж and ш are always unpalatalized and ч and щ are always palatalized, a soft sign following them does not affect their quality.

The combination -шь, -жь, -чь, or -щь at the end of a noun indicates that the noun is of feminine gender and must be declined accordingly (§ 42), e.g. ночь (f.) *night* but мяч (m.) *ball*, рожь (f.) *rye* but нож (m.) *knife*.

The same combinations can also indicate that a word is the second person singular of the imperative, e.g. ешь *eat!* вырежь *cut out!* плачь *weep!* The second person plural of such imperatives is formed regularly, by adding -те, thus: éшьте, вырежьте, плáчьте. Cf. плач *lament*, a masculine noun.

The ending -шь also indicates the second person singular of the present tense (future in the case of perfective verbs).

A soft sign is written after ш and ч at the end of adverbs and particles, and also after ж in the adverb нáстежь *wide open*.

In the ending of the infinitive, ч is always followed by a soft sign, even when the reflexive suffix -ся follows, e.g. стричь *to cut (someone's hair)*, стрúчься *to have one's hair cut*.

A soft sign between а ж, ш, ч, or щ and a soft vowel (я, е, ё, ю, and и) indicates only that the vowel is to be fully iotated, e.g. ружьё (*ruzh*+*yó*) *rifle*, ночью (*nóch'*+*yu*) *by night*, чьи газеты (*ch'*+*yi gaz'éty*) *whose newspapers?*

In some foreign loan-words, under the influence of the original spelling, -ьо- is used instead of -ьё-, e.g. серьёзно (*s'er'yóznə*) *seriously*, but бульон (*bul'yón*) *broth* (cf. French *bouillon*).

§ 14. The Hard Sign (ъ)

For many centuries this letter, which was no longer pronounced, was used at the end of a word to indicate that the preceding consonant was to be given its unpalatalized (or 'hard') sound; but since this was adequately shown by the absence of a soft sign, final ъ was sometimes omitted in private correspondence even before 1917, when it was officially abolished. The hard sign is now limited to the following useful function.

Both in words of purely Russian origin and in foreign loans, the hard sign is used to separate a prefix which normally ends in a hard consonant from a root beginning with я-, е-, ё-, or ю-; similarly, it separates the hard ending of the first element of a compound word from a second element commencing with a soft vowel. In this way the letter before ъ remains unpalatalized and is followed by a fully iotated vowel, as in отъехать (*at*+*yékhət'*) *to depart*, подъём (*pad*+*yóm*) *lifting*, предъявит (*pr'ed*+*yáv'it*) *he will show*, субъект (*sub*+*yékt*) *subject*, трансъевропейский *trans-European*.

Compare, for instance, объеду *I shall drive round* (pron. *ab*+*yédu*, in which hard *b* is followed by *yé*) with обеду *to dinner* (pron. *ab'édu*, in which *b* is palatalized and followed by *é*).

Despite the hard sign in the spelling, the preceding

consonant has sometimes come under the influence of the iotated vowel and is palatalized. This happens always to the prefixes в- and с-, usually to из-, and may happen also to раз-, e.g. въéхать (*v'yékhət*) *to drive in*, изъя́н (*iz'yán*) *defect*. Compare съел *he ate* (pron. *s'yɛl*, in which *s* is palatalized and followed by the sound of English *yell*) with сел *he sat down* (pron. *s'ɛl*, where the palatalized *s* is followed by the sound of English *ell*).

The prepositions об, в, под, над, без, из, с, от, and usually also перед and через, form a phonetic unit with the following word (see §§ 15, 16, 18, 20, 29). When considering the pronunciation of their last consonant before a word commencing with я, е, ё, or ю, it is helpful to remember that up to 1917 they all ended in -ъ, hence над я́русом *above the gallery*, под ёлкой *under the fir sapling*, от епи́скопа *from the bishop* are pronounced as if written надъя́русом, (i.e. *nad + yárusəm*, not *nad'árusəm*), подъёлкой (*pad + vólkəy*), отъепи́скопа (*at + yep'ískəpə*).

The final sound of the prepositions в, с, and usually also of из, без, and че́рез, is palatalized before a word commencing with я, е, ё, or ю, despite the theoretically intervening hard sign; for instance в я́му (*v'yámu*) *into the pit*, с ю́га (*s'yúgə*) *from the south*, без ю́мора (*b'ez'yúmərə*) *without humour*.

When any of the foregoing prepositions stands before a word beginning with и-, the last sound of the preposition is always hard, the theoretical hard sign and и combining to give the sound ы (see § 11).

The Consonants

§ 15. Б б = *b*

1. Standing immediately before a hard vowel (а, о, у, ы, or э) б sounds like the *b* of *ball* or *boot*, e.g. бой *battle* pro-

nounced approx. as English *boy*, бук *beech*, pron. *buk* (*bu* as *boo* in *boot*). A б pronounced in this way is called a hard б.

2. At the end of a word, б is voiceless (i.e. uttered without vibrating the vocal cords) and is pronounced as hard Russian п (see § 26), e.g. лоб *forehead*, pron. *lop*.

Note that, for phonetic purposes, the preposition об and the following word form one unit, so об э́том *about this* = *abétəm*, not *op étəm*.

3. Before a soft vowel (я, е, ё, ю, or и) or non-final soft sign (ь), б is softened or palatalized (i.e. during its pronunciation the middle portion of the tongue is arched towards the hard palate, in the position for *y* of *yet*, see § 3); consequently, when the lips part after their closure for the б, a very brief *y*-like glide is emitted before the tongue takes up its position for the following vowel-sound. This glide occurs after *all* the soft consonants. Also, there is a very slight *i*-like glide between a stressed vowel (apart from и) and *any* following soft consonant; it is especially noticeable before a soft consonant at the end of a word or syllable. These two glides have been dealt with in §§ 3, 9–14, and will not be described in detail in subsequent paragraphs. In the transcription of Russian words a prime (′) indicates the palatalization of the preceding sound and the *y*-glide before the following vowel. For the sake of simplicity, the prepalatal *i*-glide is normally not indicated in the transcription; besides, it is far better for the beginner to omit it than to exaggerate it.

This soft б (transcribed *b*′), is not unlike the *b* of *Bute*, *beauty*, *to abuse* (cf. *boot*, *booty*, *to a booze*) but is more palatalized than the English sound. It occurs in such words as бюро́ *office*, pron. *b'uró*, i.e. as *bu* in *abuse* + *ro* as Eng. *raw*; бес *devil*, pron. *b'εs*, i.e. like the English vocable *byess* (one syllable; *y* representing a fleeting glide). In words like добью́ *I shall obtain*, ь softens б and also separates it from the soft vowel, which therefore is fully iotated; it is transcribed *dab'yú* and pronounced as English *dub + you* with the *y* quite distinct, not merely a glide.

In unstressed syllables, owing to the complete closure of the lips for this consonant, the palatalization is sometimes scarcely noticeable, especially in the case of the preposition без *without*, which in the rapid speech of some Russians sounds like *bez*. It is never wrong, however, to palatalize a soft б clearly; it is better to over-palatalize than to under-palatalize any Russian soft consonant.

4. Before a final soft sign (-ь), б sounds like Russian soft п (see § 26), e.g. го́лубь *pigeon*, pron. *gólup'* (*p'* as the *p* of English *pew*); Обь *Ob* (Siberian river), pronounced with noticeable prepalatal *i*-glide (see 3, above)—approx. *o^i p'*.

5. Before another voiced consonant, б has the sound of:
hard б (as in 1, above)—before г, д, ж, з, л, н, р, hard б, hard в, or hard м;
soft б (as in 3)—before soft б, в, or м.
Before a following voiceless consonant, б has the sound of:
hard п (as in 2)—before к, с, т, х, ц, ч, ш, щ, or a hard п or ф;
soft п (as in 4)—before soft п or ф.
For example: о́бласть (*óbləs't'*) region, but ро́бко (*rópkə*) *timidly*.

Note that the б of the preposition об and the prefix об- remains hard, e.g. обме́н (*abm'én*) *exchange*.

Since Greek *B* (beta) was pronounced *v* by the time the Cyrillic alphabet was being devised, a new sign (Б, an adaptation of B) was invented to represent the sound *b*.

§ 16. В в = *v*

1. Before a hard vowel or a voiced consonant (apart from soft в and soft м), в sounds as English *v* in *van* and

vow, e.g. вот (*vot*) *here is*, снóва (*snóvə*) *anew*, врач (*vrach'*) *physician*, взор (*vzor*) *gaze*.

2. Before a voiceless consonant or as the last letter of a word, в is voiceless and pronounced as English *f* in *far*, e.g. лáвка (*láfkə*) *bench, shop*; ковш (*kofsh*) *ladle*, ров (*rof*) *ditch*. Note Пáвлов (*pávləf*) (*Mr.*) *Pavlov*, but Пáвлова (*pávləvə*) (*Mrs.* or *Miss*) *Pavlov*.

Notice that the sound represented by the preposition в *in, into* depends on the first letter of the following word, and that the two words form a phonetic unit: в ýгол (*vúgəl*) *into the corner*, в дом (*vdom*) *into the house*, в сад (*fsat*) *into the garden*.

3. Before a soft vowel, a non-final soft sign (ь) or soft в and м, в is softened or palatalized (see § 3 and § 15, 3), rather like *v* in English *view*. The extent to which the palatalization is heard depends on whether the following soft vowel is stressed or not, e.g. in вéра *faith* (with stressed e) the palatalization is clearly heard (= *v'érə*), whereas веснá *spring* may be pronounced *v'esná*, but in rapid conversation often sounds like *visná*. This weakening of the palatal *y*-glide is especially noticeable when в is followed by unstressed и: Лéвин (a surname) in rapid speech sounds like *l'évin*.

In words like вью *I wind*, the ь softens the в and also separates it from the iotated vowel, so that вью = *v'yu*, i.e. like the last four letters of English *of you*, not as English *view*.

4 Before final ь, в is soft and voiceless, identical with Russian soft ф, i.e. it is similar to the *f* of English *few*. For instance, кровь *blood* is pronounced *kro^if'* (with distinct *i*-glide before the palatal *f*).

In the Russian forms of foreign words beginning with eu- and auto-, the Greek *v* is represented by в, e.g. Еврóпа (*yevrópə*) *Europe*, автомобúль (*aftəmabíl'*) *motor-car*.

§ 17. Г г = g

1. Before a hard vowel or a voiced consonant, г sounds like *g* in English *go* and *good* (never like those in *George*), e.g. Волга (*vólgə*) *the Volga*, горы (*góry*) *mountains*, когда (*kagdá*) *when*, где (*gd'ɛ*) *where*.

Exceptions:

(*a*) In the adjectival and pronominal ending -ого/-его, г is pronounced *v*, e.g. его (*yevó*) *him, it* (acc. & gen.), also *his*; моего (*məyevó*) *of my* . . .; нового (*nóvəvə*) *of the new*; Толстого (*talstóvə*) *of Tolstoy*; сегодня (*s'evódn'ə*) *today*, lit. *of this day*.

Note that the adverb много *much* is not a genitive, and the г is therefore pronounced as written (*mnógə*).

(*b*) In the exclamations ага! ого! эгé! and гоп!, as well as words ending in -галтер and -гальтер, г has the sound of voiced Russian x, like the fricative *g* sometimes heard in German *Wagen*, &c. This same sound is still often used in the vocative Господи! *Lord!*; but its use in the other forms of Господь [*our*] *Lord*, in the oblique cases and derivatives of Бог *God*, in благо *goodness* and its derivatives, and in the words когда *when*, тогда *then*, &c., is obsolescent: the student is advised to pronounce г in these words as *g*.

Except in a few words of foreign origin, ы and э can never follow г. In Russian words the combination гы has been supplanted by ги.

2. A soft vowel 'fronts' a preceding г, i.e. the arching of the middle of the tongue causes the tongue to make contact with the roof of the mouth further forward than it does for a hard or English *g*; the usual palatal glide follows. Examples: на ноге (*nənag'ɛ́*) *on the leg*, по Волге (*pavólg'i*) *along the Volga*, георгин (*g'iarg'ín*) *dahlia*.

In purely Russian words, the soft vowels ё, ю, я, and the the soft sign (ь) cannot occur after г.

3. In standard Russian, г is voiceless and has the sound of English *k* when it stands before a voiceless consonant (apart from к and ч) or at the end of a word (except Бог), e.g. когти (*kókt'i*) *claws*, лёгши (*l'ókshy*) *having lain down*, враг (*vrak*) *enemy*, снег (*sn'εk*) *snow*.

4. г is pronounced as Russian х (= *ch* of Scottish or German *Loch*) in the nominative Бог *God* (for its other cases— see 1*b*) and in мягкий *soft*, мягче *softer*, лёгкий *light, easy*, лёгче *lighter, easier* and all their derivatives.

> In many dialects г is pronounced as Russian х at the end of every word and before any unvoiced consonant, and as a voiced х (see sect. 1*b*) in all other positions; this pronunciation is not uncommon even amongst educated speakers.

In the Russian forms of foreign words and names, г is very often employed to represent an original *h*. This results in rather bizarre (to the foreigner) effects: Виктор Гюго *Victor Hugo*, Гаага *The Hague*, готтентот *Hottentot*, гигиена *hygiene*; the port of Hull is shown on Soviet maps as Гулль or Халл, while Гул represents Goole.

The form of this letter is derived from the Greek *Γ* (gamma).

§ 18. Д д = *d*

Russian д and т, like their French and Italian counterparts, are truly dental; they are pronounced with the tip of the tongue touching either the top teeth alone or both top and bottom teeth. The acoustic effect is very different from that of English *d* and *t*, which are, of course, not dental at all, but alveolar, the tip of the tongue being placed against the ridge behind the top teeth. It is also important for the Englishman to notice that Russian д and т followed by a, о, у, ы, or э are uttered with more force than English *d* and *t* in (say) *day, too*. The explosion produced is also 'cleaner' (shorter and sharper) and followed immediately by the vowel: there is no aspiration—that h-like puff of breath which is especially audible between English *k*, *p* or *t* and a vowel, e.g. *tar* (pron. tʰar), or *paw* (pron. pʰaw).

1. д is pronounced as described above when it is followed by a 'hard' vowel, e.g. дýма (*dúmə*) *thought*, домá (*damá*) *houses*, тогдá (*tagdá*) *then*.

2. When final, д is voiceless and sounds as Russian hard т (see above and § 29), e.g. сад (*sat*) *garden*, Ленингрáд (*l'in'ingrát*) *Leningrad*. For phonetic purposes, the prepositions над, под, из-под, and usually also перед, combine with the following word to form a single unit, so над дóмом *nadómэm* (where *d̄* represents a prolonged *d*), над окнóм *nэdaknóm*, над столóм *nэtstalóm*, &c.

3. Soft д (followed by a 'soft' vowel or non-final ь) is dental and strongly palatalized, i.e. the tip of the tongue lies against the teeth and the middle of the tongue is raised towards the roof of the mouth. Apart from its more dental quality, Russian soft д (transcribed *d'*) is similar to the *d'y* of English *d'you know* and the *d* of *dew* or *due*; care must be taken not to go so far as to pronounce it as English *j*. Examples: дядя (*d'ǽd'ə*) *uncle*, Нáдю (*nád'u*) *Nadya* (girl's name, acc.), дéло (*d'élə*) *matter*, дивáн (*d'iván*) *couch*.

This explains why Russians, although generally good linguists, often mispronounce *d* in many foreign words, so that their pronunciation of the English words *deep*, *Dickens*, &c., sounds to us like *dyeep*, *Dyickens*, &c. Medial д followed by ь + consonant is difficult for foreigners to pronounce, e.g. седьмóй *seventh* is only a disyllable, pron. *s'ed'mój*, in which *d'* has the same quality as the *d'y* of *d'you know*; it is important to remember that it is neither English *d* nor English *j*.

4. д is soft and voiceless, like Russian soft т (see § 29), before a final ь, e.g. in the imperatives будь (*but'*) *be!* and сядь (*s'ét'*) *sit!* Note that the д in the plural of these words (бу́дьте, ся́дьте) is unvoiced by the following soft т and is also pronounced *t'*; the words may be transcribed *buĭ'i*, *s'éĭ'i*, the *ĭ'* denoting a prolonged soft *t*.

5. Before another voiced consonant, д has the sound of:

hard д (as in 1)—before г, ж, л, р, or hard б, в, д, з, м, or н;

soft д (as in 3)—before soft б, в, д, з, м, н, and sometimes л (as in ме́дленно *slowly*).

Before a following voiceless consonant, д has the sound of:

hard т (as in 2, above)—before к, х, ц, ш, or hard п, с, т, or ф;

soft т (as in 4)—before soft п, с, т, ф, ч, or щ.

For example: друг (*druk*) *friend*, дверь (*d'v'er'*, with soft *dv*) *door*, ло́дка (*lótkə*) *boat*, идти́ (*iĭ'i*, with long soft *t'*) *to go*.

Note that the final -д of prepositions and prefixes usually softens only before a soft д or т.

In the Russian transliteration of foreign words, the sound of English *j* is rendered by дж, as Джон *John*, джентльме́н *gentleman*, бридж *bridge* (card game).

The form of the letter is derived from Greek *Δ* (delta).

§ 19. Ж ж = *zh*

1. When it stands before a vowel or voiced consonant, ж is pronounced like *s* in the English words *measure* and *pleasure*, e.g. ко́жа (*kózhə*) *skin*, жду (*zhdu*) *I wait*, уже́ (*uzhé*) *already*, мужи́к (*muzhýk*; see below) *peasant*.

2. Standing before a voiceless consonant, at the end of a word, or before final ь, ж becomes voiceless and sounds like English *sh*, e.g. муж (*mush*) *husband*, ло́жка (*lóshkə*) *spoon*, рожь (*rosh*) *rye*.

While the beginner may be satisfied to use the English sounds nearest to ж, as described above, and will be readily understood, more advanced students should note that the English sounds *zh* (i.e. the *s* of *measure*) and *sh* (as in *ship*, *sheet*) are somewhat palatalized; a sound nearer to Russian (non-palatalized) ж and ш will be obtained if the middle of the tongue is kept as low as possible and the tip curled slightly back. When the Russian sounds are whispered, they are markedly lower in pitch than the English ones.

For historical reasons, the only vowels that may follow ж and its voiceless counterpart (ш) in words of pure Russian origin are а, е, ё, и, о, у; and since ж and ш are always hard, a following е, ё, or и is pronounced as if it were the hard vowel-letter э, о, or ы respectively (see §§ 10, 11). In native words ю and я can never follow ж or ш; жю and шю are found in words borrowed from foreign languages, especially French (ю renders French *u*), but in all such words which have become assimilated in Russian the жю/шю is pronounced жу/шу, e.g. брошю́ра *brochure*, парашю́т *parachute*.

The ending -жь is pronounced with hard ж, the ь being silent and merely an orthographic device to show that the word belongs to the feminine declension (e.g. рожь *rye*, gen. ржи) or is an imperative (e.g. режь *cut!*, plural ре́жьте); it is also used in на́стежь (adv.) *wide open*.

The double-length жж in words like во́жжи *reins* and сожжёт *he will burn* may be palatalized, but there is an increasing tendency among the younger generation to pronounce it as a long hard ж.

For the combination зж see § 21, 1.

ж is used to represent French *j*, as in журна́л *magazine* (cf. French *journal*) and Жан-Жак Руссо́ *Jean-Jacques Rousseau*; English *j* is rendered by дж (see § 18).

The form of this letter is of uncertain origin.

§ 20. З з = *z*

1. Before a hard vowel or a voiced consonant, з is pronounced as *z* in English *ozone* and *razor*, e.g. взор (*vzor*) *gaze*, за́пад (*zápət*) *west*, берёзы (*b'er'ózy*) *birch trees*.

2. Before a soft vowel or non-final soft sign, з is palatalized and has the sound of *z* in *Zeus*, e.g. зима́ (*z'imá*) *winter*, зе́ркало (*z'érkələ*) *mirror*, зюзю́кать (*z'uz'úkət'*) *to lisp*, возьму́ (*vaz'mú*) *I shall take*.

3. At the end of a word з is voiceless, sounding like Russian с (*s*) in the same position, e.g. воз (*vos*) *cart*, он вёз (*on v'os*) *he was transporting*.

For phonetic purposes the prepositions без, из, and usually also через, form one unit with the following word, e.g. без вас (*b'ezvás*) *without you*, без труда́ (*b'istrudá*) *without effort*, из я́мы (*iz'yámy*) *out of a pit*, из кни́ги (*iskn'íg'i*) *from the book*, из журна́ла (*izhurnálə*) *from a magazine*, без ша́пки (*b'eshápk'i*) *without a cap*.

4. Final -зь is palatalized and voiceless, like soft Russian с (*s'*), e.g. и́зморозь (*ízmərəs'*) *hoar-frost*, мазь *ointment* (pron. ma*i*s', with noticeable prepalatal *i*-glide, so that it approaches the sound of the English word *mice*).

5. In the combination зж, the з is assimilated to the ж in normal speech, the resulting sound being a long ж ($\bar{zh}$), which may usually be either soft or hard; but if the з is the the last letter of a prefix, it is always pronounced hard. For example, е́зжу *I ride* is pronounced *yéz̄h'u* or *yéz̄hu*, but разжёчь *to kindle* is always *raz̄hech'*.

6. Before ш, з sounds like ш (*sh*), e.g. влéзши *having got in* and из шкóлы *from school* are pronounced *vl'éshy, ishkóly*, with long, hard *sh*.

7. Before ч, з has the sound of soft ш (*sh'*), so that зч is identical with the Leningrad type of щ (*shch'*, see § 35), e.g. грýзчик (*grúshch'ik*) *stevedore*, без числá (*b'ishch'islá*) *without number*.

8. Before another voiced consonant (except ж, see 5, above), з has the sound of:

> hard з (as in 1 above)—before г, р, or hard б, в, д, з, л, м, or н;
>
> soft з (as in 2)—before soft б, в, д, з, л, м, or н.

Russian з is voiceless before a voiceless consonant (for ш, see 6; for ч, see 7, above); it has the sound of:

> hard с (as in 3, above)—before к, х, ц, or hard п, с, т, or ф.
>
> soft с (as in 4)—before soft п, с, т, or ф.

It should be noted that whenever the prefixes без-, воз-, из-, низ-, раз-, and через- are used before a root beginning with a voiceless consonant, they are actually *written* бес-, вос-, &c., to indicate that their final sound is voiceless.

Note that prefixes ending in з/с soften this letter in accordance with the rules set out above. It is usual for the prepositions из, без, and через to follow these rules, but some speakers do not soften their last sound except before soft з or soft с.

The form of this letter is derived from the Greek *Z* (zeta).

§ 21. Й й = *y* (consonant)

The English sound nearest to Russian й is the consonant *y* of *yet, yard, beyond*. It is sounded forcefully before a stressed vowel, as in майóр (pron. *ma + yór*) *major*, райóн (*ra+yón*) *region, district*, Йорк *York*. In this position this sound is represented by й only in foreign loan-words: in words of Russian origin it is indicated by an iotated vowel or a soft or hard sign, e.g. ёж (= йож) *hedgehog*, приют (= прийу́т) *shelter*, друзья́ (= друзйа́) *friends*, отъе́зд (= отйе́зд) *departure*.

The student must be careful not to substitute for this sound the English weak short i represented by *i* or *y* in *toil*, *boy*, &c. The ой of the Russian words бой *battle*, той *of that* (f.), рой *swarm* differs from the English diphthong *oy* of *boy*, *toy*, *Roy* in that its second element (й) is a consonant and the passage of the air through the mouth is almost completely obstructed by the tongue, so that friction is distinctly heard. To make the Russian sound the tip of the tongue is pressed against the bottom teeth, its sides are pressed against the side top teeth, and the middle of the tongue is arched until it is even nearer the top palate than for the vowel и. The breath is forced out through the narrow channel running from back to front down the middle of the tongue.

Students who experience difficulty in producing this sound after a vowel, should repeat 'raw *youth*' slowly several times, then say it again eliminating *-outh*. The resulting sound (*raw+y*) should be a good approximation to Russian рой *swarm*. Then, using the same *y*-sound, they should try the combination май *May*, бей *strike!*, но́вый *new*, жуй *chew!*, ру́сский *Russian*, над землёй *above ground*, плюй *spit!* and э́той зимо́й (*étǝy z'imóy*) *this winter*.

A similar, though rather less tense, sound occurs, but is indicated in the normal spelling not by й but by an iotated vowel: (i) between stressed and unstressed vowels, as in мо́ю (= мо́йу) *I wash*; (ii) between two unstressed vowels, as in ру́сская (= ру́сскайа) *Russian* (f.). The same sound is indicated (iii) by a soft or hard sign between a consonant and an unstressed vowel, e.g. ли́стья (= ли́стйа) *leaves*, объясни́ть (= обйасни́ть) *to explain*; and also (iv) by an initial unstressed я, е, or ю—as in ему́ (= йему́) *to him* and юри́ст (= йури́ст) *lawyer*.

§ 22. К к = *k*

1. This is pronounced as in English before a hard vowel or any consonant except б, г, д, ж, з, or at the end of a word,[1] e.g. ко́шка (*kóshkə*) *cat*, рука́ (*ruká*) *hand, arm*, потоло́к (*pətalók*) *ceiling*, как (*kak*) *how*.

For historical reasons ы and э cannot occur after к in purely Russian words.

Latin (and hence Italian, English, and German) *qu* is rendered by кв, e.g. кво́рум *quorum*, квинте́т *quintet*, outline. ква́кер *Quaker*.

The Latin x and Greek ξ are usually represented in Russian by кс, e.g. экспеди́ция *expedition*, аксио́ма *axiom*, but the prefix *ex-* before a vowel occurs most frequently in the form экз-, e.g. экзога́мия *exogamy*, экза́мен *examination* (see below).

2. Before a soft vowel (only е and и are possible in words of Russian origin) к is palatalized and 'fronted', i.e. the arching of the tongue causes it to make contact with the roof of the mouth at a point considerably further forward than that for hard к. The nearest English sound is the *k* in *Kew*. For example, кедр (*k'ɛdr*) *cedar*, в руке́ (*vruk'έ*) *in the hand*, ру́ки (*rúk'i*) *hands, arms*, кит (*k'it*) *whale*.

3. к becomes voiced, sounding like *g* in English *go*, when it is immediately followed by one of the voiced sounds б, г, д, ж, or з, e.g. экза́мен (*egzám'in*). This may also happen to final к before a closely connected word beginning with б, г, д, ж, or з, e.g. ка́к же? (*kágzhə*) *how then? really?*

---

[1] See also 3, below.

The preposition к *towards*, forming a phonetic unit with the following word, is naturally governed by this rule: к окну́ (*kaknú*) *to the window*, к вам (*kvam*) *to you*, but к до́му (*gdómu*) *to the house*, к заво́ду (*gzavódu*) *to the factory*.

The soft sign follows к only in a few words of foreign origin, as кья́нти *chianti*.

The form of the letter was taken from the Greek *K* (kappa).

§ 23. Л л = *l*

is pronounced in two very distinct ways, depending on whether it is hard or palatalized.

1. Before a consonant, a hard vowel, or when final, л sounds like the 'dark' *l* of English *bottle*, *fall*, or *cold*. When final or before a consonant, this sound will cause the student no difficulty, e.g. мол (*mol*) *pier* is close to the sound of English *maul*; гул (*gul*) *rumble* is almost identical with English *Goole*; and тыл (*tyl*) *rear* (mil.) is very like English *till*. Волк *wolf* and толпа́ *crowd* are pronounced *volk* and *talpá*, with *l* as it would be if the words were English.

However, unless the student comes from Scotland or North America, he may experience considerable difficulty in pronouncing this same sound *before a vowel*, as in ла́мпа (*lámpə*) *lamp*, лоб (*lop*) *forehead*, and луна́ (*luná*) *moon*. If so, he should say aloud several times the English word *awl*, prolonging the *l*-sound and finally isolating it; he will then be able to add to it a Russian hard vowel to form a syllable (viz. ла, лы, ло, or лу), and can then pass on to whole words. Another way to master initial hard л in (say) ла́мпа is to repeat '*awl*+а́мпа' many times and, while keeping the *l* as 'dark' as possible, reduce the initial *aw*-sound until it is lost entirely and ла́мпа, correctly pronounced, is left.

2. Before a soft vowel or ь, on the other hand, л is strongly palatalized, like Italian *gl* in *degli* or Spanish *ll* in *llamar*. It is formed by pressing the whole front part of the tongue against the teeth and hard palate. Before a soft vowel, л is much softer (more liquid) than English *l* + vowel in (say) *long* or *leave*: the nearest English sound is the *l* of *lewd*, e.g. лю́ди *people*, pron. *l'úd'i* (approx. as English *lewd* + *ye* fused together). Compare лук *onion* and клык *tusk* (pron. *luk* and *klyk*, with hard *l*) with люк *hatch* and клик *call* (pron. *l'uk* and *kl'ik*, with soft *l* and *y*-glide).

ль before a soft vowel indicates that the л is soft and the vowel iotated, so налью́ (*nal'yú*) *I shall pour out* is pronounced somewhat as English *null* + *you* but with soft *l*.

ль frequently occurs at the end of words and before consonants; it requires special care, as English *l* is always 'dark' in these positions. For example: учи́тель (*uch'it'il'*) *teacher*; льда (*l'da*), gen. of лёд *ice*. In cases like the last, pronunciation is often facilitated by a preceding word ending in a vowel, e.g. на льду *on ice*, pron. *nal'dú*.

The prepalatal *i*-glide is noticeable in a stressed syllable ending with л + soft vowel and, especially, with ль, e.g. боль (*bo'l'*) *pain* sounds not unlike English *boil*, except that it has a soft *l'*; дра́ли *they tore* and да́ли *they gave* sound rather like English *dry* + *lee* and *die* + *lee* respectively.

Most foreign words ending in -*l* are written in Russian with -ль, as ве́ксель *bill of exchange* and Брюссе́ль *Brussels*; some (usually more common or recent words) end in -л, as капита́л *capital* (financial), футбо́л *football*, гол *goal*; with others, particularly in proper nouns borrowed from English, usage fluctuates, e.g. Ливерпу́ль and (less common but gaining popularity) Ливерпу́л for Liverpool, Гулль and (more recent) Халл for Hull.

The form of this letter is derived from the Greek *Λ* (lambda).

§ 24. М м = *m*

Hard м (before a hard vowel and most consonants) is pronounced as *m* in English *man* or *moon*, e.g. там (*tam*) *there*, мо́ю (*móyu*) *I wash*.

м is palatalized by a following soft vowel, soft sign (ь) or soft б, п, or м. It then sounds like the *m* of English *music*, e.g. мя́со (*m'ásə*) *meat*, в до́ме *in the house*, имби́рь (*m.*) *ginger*.

The pronunciation of final -мь causes some foreigners difficulty. Although the palatal quality of the sound may be hard to detect in rapid conversation, its influence on the quality of a preceding е is marked. Compare тем *by that* (pron. *t'ɛm*, with the vowel of *yet*) with темь *darkness* (pron. *t'em'*, with *e* as *ai* in English *aim*).

The form of the letter was taken from Greek *M* (mu).

§ 25. Н н = *n*

Before hard vowels and most consonants, н is hard and sounds like English *n* in *noon* or *hand*, but its quality is slightly different, since it is articulated with the tip of the tongue against the teeth (as for д, see § 18). For example: нам (*nam*) *to us*, он (*on*) *he*. It must be noted that н never has the sound of the *n* in English *bank* and *angle*; apart from the difference in vowel quality, банк *bank* (for money) is pronounced as English *ban+k*, А́нглия *England* as *án + gl'iyə*.

Soft н (followed by a soft vowel, soft sign, ч, щ, or soft д, т, н, з, or с) is not dissimilar to English *n* in *new*, but it is closer to the *gn* of Italian *ogni* and French *Boulogne* (which is written Було́нь in Russian), e.g. виню́ (*v'in'ú*) *I blame*, они́ (*an'í*) *they*, нет (*n'ɛt*) *no*, меня́ (*m'en'á*) *me*.

Between a stressed vowel and soft н, the prepalatal *i*-glide may often be quite distinct. Thus, конь (*ko'n'*) *steed* with many speakers approaches the sound of English *coin*, though, of course, the *i*-sound is much shorter and the *n'* soft; similarly Таню *Tanya* (acc. case) may approach the sound of the English words *tie + new*.

The Russian H is derived from the Greek *N* (nu). Whereas the middle stroke of English N has remained sloping, those of Cyrillic N (= *n*) and H (= *i*) have moved round anticlockwise through 45° in the course of the centuries.

§ 26. П п = *p*

Before a hard vowel and most consonants, п is hard and sounds like *p* in French *papa*. Apart from there being no aspiration before the following sound (cf. § 18), this hard п is like English *p* in *pooh!* and *poor*, e.g. па́лка (*pálkə*) *stick*, топо́р (*tapór*) *axe*, пусто́й (*pustóy*) *empty*, ла́пы (*lápy*) *paws*, лапша́ (*lapshá*) *noodles*.

Palatalized п (i.e. standing before a soft vowel, soft sign, or a soft п, м, в, or ф) sounds like *p* in English *pew* and *pure*, e.g. пюпи́тр (*p'up'ítr*) *music-stand*, перо́ (*p'eró*) *feather, pen*, пя́тка (*p'átkə*) *heel*. Compare цеп *flail* (pron. *tsɛp*, with hard *p* and open *ɛ*, the vowel of English *sell*) with степь *steppe* (pron. *s't'ep'*, with soft *p'* and close *e*, the vowel of *sail*).

When пь is followed by a vowel, the п is to be palatalized and the vowel iotated, as in попью́ *I shall have a drink*, which is pronounced *pap'yú*, very like English *pup + you*.

The form of this letter is derived from the Greek *Π* (pi).

§ 27. Р р = *r*

is trilled with the tip of the tongue, as in Scotland and Wales, but not strongly. The tip of the tongue is raised loosely towards the ridge behind the teeth and vibrates as the breath passes over it. In most positions one or two flaps of the tongue against the teeth-ridge are sufficient, but after a consonant, and especially at the end of a word, p is stronger and the tongue should make three or four flaps.

Care must be taken not to substitute the English fricative *r* or the French or German guttural *r* for the Russian trill.

Example of hard р: рука́ (*ruká*) *arm, hand*, па́ра (*pára*) *pair*, ры́нок (*rýnək*) *market*, бюро́ (*b'uró*) *office*; stronger in двор (*dvor*) *court-yard*, дар (*dar*) *gift*, дра́ма (*drámə*) *drama*.

A following soft vowel or soft sign palatalizes р, which is then produced by arching the middle of the tongue towards the roof of the mouth and vibrating the tip slightly. This sound is heard in ряд (*r'at*) *row, series*, рю́мка (*r'úmkə*) *wine-glass*, на дворе́ (*nədvar'é*) *outside*, &c.

It is particularly difficult for the Englishman to bring out the palatal quality of medial and final рь; however, its presence is usually made clear either by the prepalatal glide, e.g. Ха́рьков *Kharkov* is pronounced *khá'r'kəf* (i.e. approximately as English *hire + cuff*, but with a slightly rolled *r*) or by the quality of the vowel, as in дверь *door* (pron. *d'v'er'*, with soft *r'* and therefore close *e*, like the *ai* of *aim*). Compare the last example with its diminutive form две́рка *small door* (pron. *d'v'érkə*), with hard *r* and therefore open *ε*, like the *ai* or Eng. *air*).

The form of this letter is derived from the Greek *P* (rho).

§ 28. С с = *s*

1. The normal sound of Russian hard с is similar to that of English voiceless *s* in *say* or *saw* (not that of *s* in *rose* and *ways*). This sound occurs when Russian с is final or is followed by a hard vowel or by most consonants (namely: any р, к, х, or ц, or a hard л, м, н, п, с, т, ф, or в). For example: со́рок (*sórək*) *forty*, стул (*stul*) *chair*, роса́ (*rasá*) *dew*, нос (*nos*) *nose*, до́ски (*dósk'i*) *boards*, с су́пом (*šúpəm*, with long hard *s*) *with soup*.

2. с is voiceless and palatalized when it stands before a soft vowel, a soft sign, or a soft л, м, н, п, с, т, ф, or в. For example: си́ла (*s'ílə*) *force*, в росе́ (*vras'é*) *in the dew*,

сюрприз (s'urpr'ís) surprise, ось (o^{i}s') axle (o^i almost as oi in voice), Ва́ська (vá^{i}s'kə) Basil (dim.) (a^i almost as i in English vice), с тем (s't'ɛm, with soft s and soft t) with that, спи (s'p'i) sleep!, с си́лой (š'íləy) with force.

Note that the reflexive suffixes -ся and -сь are often pronounced (as written) with soft c, but sometimes with hard c. The pronunciation depends on the place of birth, generation, and education of the speaker. Many young people use a soft c in these suffixes unless they are preceded by a hard consonant, -шь-, or -ть-; others use a soft c except when the word ends in -сся, -тся, or -ться. Notice that -сся is always pronounced -šə, with long hard s, and that -тся and -ться are both pronounced -t̄sə, with long hard t.

On the stage and among Russians of the older generation, the reflexive suffixes may be heard pronounced as if spelt -ca and -c in all positions except present gerunds ending in stressed -а́сь and -я́сь.

3. A following г or a hard б, д or з causes the voicing of c, which then has the sound of з (z), e.g. сдам (zdam) I shall hand over, с год (zgot) about a year, сза́ди (z̄ád'i) from behind.

4. Soft б, д, and з palatalize and voice a preceding c into soft з (i.e. z'); this also occurs in the rare combination -сьб-. For example: сде́лать (z'd'élət', with soft z and soft d) to do, с би́твой (z'b'ítvəy) with the battle, про́сьба (pró^{i}z'bə) request.

5. The combination сж has the sound of long hard ж (z̄h), e.g. сжа́ла (z̄hálə) she squeezed, сжёг (z̄hok) he burnt, с журна́лом (z̄hurnáləm) with a magazine. Note: сейча́с же (s'eych'áz̄hə or s'ich'áz̄hə) immediately.

6. The combination сш has the sound of long hard ш (sh, see § 34), e.g. сшил (s̄hyl) he sewed, с шу́мом (s̄húməm) with noise.

7. c has the sound of palatalized sh, as in English sheep, when it stands before ч (ch'), e.g. расчи́стка (rashch'ístkə)

clearing away. In the words счёт *account* and счáстье *happiness* and all their derivatives, сч has the same sound as щ (i.e. *shch′* or *s͞h′*, according to region).

8. c is silent in the combination сщ, as in расщéлина *crevice*, and often before another c + consonant, as in рýсский *Russian*.

The form of the letter is derived from Ϲ, the form of Greek uncial sigma at the time when the Cyrillic alphabet was being devised.

§ 29. Т т = *t*

1. As has already been explained (§ 18), in the articulation of Russian hard т the tip of the tongue touches the teeth; on its release there is a forceful and sharp explosion, followed immediately by the vowel-sound. Russian hard т sounds like the French *t* of *ta tante*, very different from the English (aspirated and alveolar) *t*, as in *tar* (pron. *tʰar*).

т has the sound described above when it stands at the end of a word, before a hard vowel, or before most consonants, (namely, any к, л, р, х, ц, ш, or a hard в, м, н, п, с, т, or ф), e.g. тот (*tot*, somewhat like English *taught*), труп (*trup*) *corpse*, твори́т (*tvar′ít*) *creates*, ты (*ty*) *thou*.

2. A soft vowel, soft sign, ч, щ, or a soft м, н, п, с, т, ф, or в palatalizes a following т strongly, so that it sounds like the *t* in a careful pronunciation of English *tube* and *Tudor*. Consider: тéло (*t′élə*) *body*, хотя́ (*khat′á*) *although*, э́ти (*ét′i*) *these*, дари́ть (*dar′ít′*) *to present*, тьма (*t′ma*, one syllable!) *darkness*.

Students who find it difficult to pronounce ть at the end of a word or before a hard consonant can try the following exercise. Say '*eat you*' quickly several times in a rather slovenly fashion—without, however, softening the *t* so much that it becomes '*eechew*'. It should then be possible to stop short before the *oo*-sound, having pronounced correctly Russian -ить, which is the ending of a great many infinitives, as говори́ть *to speak*. Next, try the endings -ать and -ять, as in игра́ть *to play* and поня́ть *to understand*. Then attempt the same sound before a hard consonant, as in во тьму (*vat′mú*) *into the darkness*. The importance of attaining a tolerably good pronunciation of ть can be seen in the fact that only the quality of the т distinguishes говори́ть *to speak* from говори́т (*he*, *she*, *it*) *speaks*, and брать *to take* from брат *brother*, &c.

3. Since б, д, з, г, and ж cause the voicing of a preceding voiceless consonant:

т becomes hard д (*d*) before г, ж, and hard б, д, or з;
т becomes soft д (*d′*) before soft б, д, or з; and
ть becomes soft д (*d′*) before any б, д, з, г, or ж.

For example: о́тзвук (*ódzvuk*) *echo*, отде́л (*ad̄′él*, with long soft *d*) *department*, молотьба́ (*məlad′bá*) *grinding*.

The preposition от *from* forms a phonetic unit with the following word, and its т is voiced by a following б, д, з, г, or ж, e.g. от окна́ (*atakná*) *from the window*, от вас (*atvás*) *from you*, but от бра́та (*adbrátə*) *from the brother*, от до́ктора (*ad̄óktərə*) *from the doctor*.

The preposition от and the prefix от- are usually pronounced with hard *t/d*, except before soft т or soft д.

The form of this letter is derived from the Greek *T* (tau); the cursive form *m* (which is also the form of the written capital and small letter) is the result of the gradual lengthening downwards of the serifs at the ends of the bar across the top of the letter: T > Т > ᛖ .

§ 30. Ф ф = *f*

1. When final or followed by a hard vowel or a consonant, ф has the sound of English *f* in *food*, e.g. фото́граф (*fatógrəf*) *photographer*, телефо́н (*t′il′efón*) *telephone*.

2. When the following letter is a soft vowel or ь, ф is palatalized and sounds similar to the *f* of *feud* and *future*, e.g. фюзеляж (*f'uz'el'ásh*) *fuselage*, тюфяк (*t'uf'ák*) *mattress*, физика (*f'íz'ikə*) *physics*, Фёдор (*f'ódər*) *Theodore*.

This letter occurs only in words of non-Russian origin.

As can be seen in the foregoing examples, Russian ф renders both Greek φ (*ph*) and θ (*th*). Its form is derived from the Greek Φ (phi).

§ 31. X x = *kh*

is very similar to the Scottish or German pronunciation of *ch* in *Loch*, but it is articulated further forward in the mouth and is not so strongly vibrated. The nearest English sound is *h*, but a better approximation to the Russian sound will be obtained by putting the tongue loosely in the position for *k* and pronouncing *h*. For example: хо́лодно (*khóladnə*) *coldly*, на нога́х (*nənagákh*) *on the feet*, хвасту́н (*khvastún*) *braggart*.

Like г and к, this sound is 'fronted' (see §§ 17, 22) by a following soft vowel; it then approaches the sound of *h* in *huge*, e.g. хи́мия (*kh'ím'iyə*) *chemistry*, хи́тро (*kh'ítrə*) *slily*, херуви́м (*kh'iruv'ím*) *cherub*.

In words of purely Russian origin, x cannot be followed by ы or ь.

The form of the letter was borrowed from the Greek X (chi).

§ 32. Ц ц = *ts*

This letter represents the sound *t* followed immediately by a very short *s*; it has the same sound as German *z* in *zu* and *zwei*, e.g. цвет (*tsv'ɛt*) *colour*, отéц (*at'ɛ́ts*) *father*, цыга́н (*tsygán*) *gipsy*.

In literary Russian ц is never palatalized and cannot be followed by a soft vowel-sound. Accordingly, и after ц is pronounced as ы, stressed e as ə; e in the syllable before the stress has the sound of ы, elsewhere unstressed e after ц sounds like the neutral vowel (ə). Examples: цирк (*tsyrk*) *circus*, центр (*tsɛntr*) *centre*, ценá (*tsyná*) *price*, целикóм (*tsəl'ikóm*) *wholly*.

As can be seen from these examples and from words like Цицерóн *Cicero*, цивилизáция *civilization*, Цéзарь *Caesar*, and целлюлóза *cellulose*, ц renders Latin and neo-Latin c before e, i, and ae.

The form of this letter is based on the Hebrew צ (tsadeh).

§ 33. Ч ч = *ch'*

is pronounced as *ch* in English *church*, except that the Russian sound is rather more fully palatalized. For example: чѝсто (*ch'ístə*) *purely*, Чéхов (*ch'ɛ́khəf*) *Chekhov*.

By an orthographic convention, the letters я and ю after ч are replaced by a and y, but this does not indicate that the ч is hard: the slight *y*-glide between consonant and vowel is still there, although it may be clearly discernible only in stressed syllables and in slow, deliberate utterance. Thus, чýдо *wonder*, *miracle* has the sound *ch'údə*, whereas in normal speech the *y*-glide is hardly audible in the plural form чудесá.

Note that the a in чай (*ch'æy*) *tea*, мяч (*m'æch'*) *ball*, &c., stands between two palatal sounds and is therefore like *a* in *apple*.

In unstressed syllables, ча has the sound *ch'i* except in the endings -ча, -чам, -чах, and -чат, where it is *ch'ə*, e.g. часовóй (*ch'isavóy*) *sentry*, часы́ (*ch'isý*) *hours*, тóтчас (*tótch'is*) *immediately*, мóлча (*mólch'ə*) *in silence*, дáча(*dách'ə*) *summer residence*.

The letter ы can never stand after ч.

A following soft sign cannot soften ч further; it is used merely as an indication that the word belongs to the feminine declension, e.g. ночь *night*, to the imperative mood, as плачь *weep!*, or is an infinitive, as течь *to flow*.

The form of the letter is of uncertain origin.

§ 34. Ш ш = *sh*

is the voiceless equivalent of ж and, like ж (see § 19), is not palatalized. It is pronounced much as *sh* in English *bush* and *shoo!*, never as in *sheep*. Examples: шáшка (*sháshkə*) *sword*, наш (*nash*) *our*, шум (*shum*) *noise*, шоколáд (*shəkalát*) *chocolate*, шкóла (*shkólə*) *school*.

ш is always hard, and consequently a following e, ё, or и is pronounced as if it were э, о, or ы, e.g. шест (*shɛst*), *pole*, шёлк (*sholk*) *silk*, шúна (*shýnə*) *tyre*. For the sound of ше in unstressed positions, see § 10, 6.

ш is never followed by я or ю in native Russian words, their place being taken by a and y (see § 19).

A following ь does not soften ш; final -шь is now merely a conventional indication of the second person singular or of the feminine declension, as in знáешь *thou knowest*, мышь (f.) *mouse* (cf. ковш (m.) *ladle*).

The form of the letter was borrowed from the Hebrew 𝔚 (shin).

§ 35. Щ щ = *shch'*

is pronounced in one of two ways, depending on the speaker. The variant used in Moscow, and spreading rapidly into other areas, is a prolonged *palatalized* ш, like *shsh* in *Danish sheep*. The type of щ used in Leningrad and many other parts is easier for the Englishman to imitate. It sounds like *shch* in *Ashchurch* and *fresh chill*. This sound is really a palatalized шч (composed of soft *sh'* + soft *t* of English type + soft *sh'*; the *t* should be kept weak).

Both variants are palatalized, no matter what vowel

follows; as with ч, there is a slight *y*-glide, often not clearly audible, between щ and a following vowel.

The letters я, ю, ы, and э cannot follow щ, being always replaced by a, y, и, and e, respectively.

Examples of щ: щи *cabbage soup* (a Russian national dish) is pronounced *shch'i* by some speakers, and *s͞h'i* by others; ча́ща *thicket* is *ch'æshch'ə* or *ch'æs͞h'ə*—the stressed a, being between soft consonants, has the sound of *a* in *apple*.

ща before the stress sounds as щи, e.g. in щади́ть *to spare*.

The soft sign is used after щ merely as an indication of feminine declension, e.g. по́мощь (f.) *help*, cf. борщ (m.) *beetroot soup*.

The form of this letter in Old Bulgarian was щ (i.e. ш superposed on т), which represented the sound *sht*, as it still does in modern Bulgarian.

PHONETIC TRANSCRIPTION

§ 36. In the foregoing, §§ 4–35, the ordinary English letters have been employed to render the pronunciation of the Russian consonants and vowels, with the addition only of ε to represent the open e of нет, &c., æ to represent a sound like the *a* of *apple*, and the sign ə, to represent the neutral vowel. This has been done for the sake of the general student who has no specialized knowledge of phonetics. For the benefit of those students who are already acquainted with the alphabet of the International Phonetic Association, the I.P.A. symbols, as used for the transcription of Russian by the late Professor S. C. Boyanus, are listed below:

The symbols p b m f v t d n l s z r k g x (= Russian x) ɣ (= voiced Russian x) represent 'hard' consonantal sounds, while the corresponding 'soft' or palatalized sounds are represented by appending ، (part of the letter j)

to these, thus: p̦, b̦, m̦, f̦, v̦, ț, d̦, n̦, l̦, ș, z̦, r̦, k̦, g̦, x̦, ɣ̦; ts
ʃ ʒ ʒ̦ʒ̦ tʃ ʃtʃ (țʃ̦) represent the sounds of ц ш ж жж ч щ
respectively; j renders the sound of й and of the first element of я [ja] *I*.

The vowel symbols are:

    i for the sound of stressed и in и́ва *willow*
    ɪ for the sound of unstressed и/е in зима́ *winter*,
        леса́ *forests*
    ɨ for the sounds of ы in вы *you*, во́ды *waters*
    ɛ for the sound of stressed e in нет *no*
    e for the sound of stressed e in день *day*
    a for the sound of stressed a in да *yes*
    a (or ʌ) for the sound of a/o in сады́ *gardens*,
        дома́ *houses*
    ə for the sound of a/o in кни́га *book*, котелки́ *pots*.
    æ for the sound of stressed я in пять *five*
    o for the sound of stressed o in дом *house*
    ö for the sound of ё in тётя *aunt*
    u for the sounds of у in стул *chair*, куда́ *whither*
    ü for the sounds of ю in тюль *tulle*, тюрьма́ *prison*.

For more detailed descriptions of the sounds represented
by these symbols, for texts in this phonetic script, and for
information on Russian intonation, the student is referred
to *Russian Pronunciation: the Russian System of Speech Habits in
Sounds, Stress, Rhythm, and Intonation, together with a Russian
Phonetic Reader* by S. C. Boyanus.

In the Soviet Union, the Cyrillic alphabet is frequently
used for phonetic transcriptions; the softness of a consonant
is indicated by a following apostrophe, the sound [ə] is
rendered by ъ, [ɪ] by ь, и, and иᵉ. For example, а́втор,
хорошо́, я́сная, перево́дить are transcribed [а́фтър], [хъра-
шо́], [йа́снъйъ], [п'ьр'ьвад'и́т']. This system is also used
by D. Ward in his *Russian Pronunciation: a Practical Course*.

58   § 37

WORD STRESS

§ 37. As has already been remarked, the stress in Russian may fall on the first, second, or any other syllable, depending on the word. Thus, it falls on the first syllable in ко́мната *room*, on the second in газе́та *newspaper*, on the third in борода́ *beard*, on the fourth in сковорода́ *frying-pan*, and so on. There are certain rules which govern the stress in certain cases, but their value is discounted by the existence of numerous exceptions. Correct stress is one of the greatest difficulties that Russian presents to the foreigner, as a misplaced stress may lead to disconcerting error; at the best, a foreigner who puts the stress on the wrong syllable will merely not be understood at all. The difficulty is increased by the fact that neither in writing nor in print is the stress marked, and also by the fact that in many cases words, though spelt identically, have quite different meanings according to where the stress is placed, e.g. мука́ means *flour*, but му́ка is *torment*; плачу́ *I pay*, but пла́чу *I weep*; во́ды *waters* (nom. pl.), but воды́ *some water* (gen. sing.), and many others.

The stressed syllable in Russian is always *very* strongly emphasized, and the unstressed syllables are much weaker and consequently lose in some cases the full value of their vowels, e.g. in the syllable immediately preceding the stress unstressed o always sounds like unstressed a in the same position (i.e. like our *u* in *rub*), as in вода́ *water* (pron. *vadá*); o and a in other unstressed positions are pronounced like the *a* in *ago* and *china* (represented by the phonetic symbol *ə*), so ко́мната *room* is pronounced *kómnətə* and борода́ *beard* is *bəradá*. It should be mentioned that a number of words are often stressed differently by different but equally well-educated Russians, e.g. высоко́ and высо́ко *highly*, ина́че and и́наче *otherwise*, о́бух and обу́х *butt*, and also that the stress is sometimes withdrawn altogether from

the noun by a preposition which governs it, e.g. за́ руку
by the hand (ру́ку is acc. sing. of рука́ *hand*), на́ голову *on
to the head* (го́лову is acc. sing. of голова́ *head*), во́время *in
good time* (written as one word to distinguish it from во
вре́мя (+gen.) *during*), and sometimes from the past tense
of a verb by the negative particle, e.g. не́ было (*it*) *was not*,
не́ дал (*he*) *did not give*, though such cases, both with nouns
and with verbs, are the exception rather than the rule.

Although the vast majority of Russian words have only
one stressed syllable, there are certain words which have
or may have a secondary stress also. Such words are mostly
technical terms and always combine two roots, each of
which is emphasized; the secondary (weaker) stress falls
on the first element, the main stress on the last element.
The secondary stress is indicated here by a grave accent (ˋ)
over the vowel (other than ё). For example, во̀донепрони-
ца́емость *impermeability to water, watertightness* and срѐдне-
годово́й [дохо́д] *average yearly* [*income*] are normally pronounced with secondary stress on the first element (viz.
vòdən′iprən′itsáyiməst′, sr′èdn′igədavóy), whereas машино-
строе́ние *engineering* (lit. *engine-building*) may have a
secondary stress (*mashỳnəstrayén′iyə*), but is more often pronounced without (viz. *məshynəstrayén′iyə*).

Compound words having as first element a numeral
(see pp. 137–8), the prefix после- or сверх-, or a foreign
prefix (see pp. 390–1) often have a secondary stress:
трѐхле́тний *three-year-old*, пятѝдесятиле́тие *fiftieth anniver-
sary*, девяно̀стокопе́ечный *ninety-copeck*, сто̀грамм́овый
weighing 100 grammes, по̀слереволюцио́нный *post-revolu-
tionary*, про̀италья́нский *pro-Italian*.

Most hyphenated words have secondary stress on the first
element: ю̀го-за́пад *south-west*, давны̀м-давно́ *long, long
ago*, ма̀ло-пома́лу *little by little*, but there is usually only
one stress in кто́-нибудь *anyone*, когда́-то *at one time*, &c.

Failing the help *viva voce* of a competent teacher, beginners are recommended to read only accented texts, of which many have been published, in order to get used to the stress, and also to read poetry, where the position of the stress can usually be determined from the metre.

A list of accented texts is given in the bibliography at the end of this book. By observing carefully the accents on the most commonly used cases and parts of the most commonly used nouns, verbs, &c., the student will learn where to place the stress far more quickly than by learning rules and exceptions which always contain forms that are rarely used. The stress of a word is invariably marked by an acute accent in all Russian dictionaries, even in those printed in the U.S.S.R. for the use of Russians.

THE DECLENSION OF THE NOUNS

§ 38. There are three genders in Russian—Masculine, Feminine, and Neuter; and two numbers—Singular and Plural, though traces of the old Dual number are to be found in the declensions.

There is no definite or indefinite article in Russian corresponding to our *the, a, an*. The context is usually sufficient to indicate whether *the* or *a* is meant; otherwise recourse must be had to the demonstrative or indefinite pronouns. The demonstrative pronoun is sometimes used as a definite article after the noun which it qualifies, though only in the colloquial language (see § 48).

There are six cases in Russian—Nominative, Genitive, Dative, Accusative, Instrumental, and Locative. This last is sometimes called the Prepositional, because it is never used except after one of the five prepositions: o *concerning*, в *in*, на *on*, при *in the presence of*, по *after*. The Instrumental can be used without a preposition, when it denotes the instrument or agent by means of which something is done. It is also used after certain prepositions and then it loses the meaning which the name implies. For the remains of the Vocative in modern Russian see § 39, Obs. 10.

§ 39. Masculine Nouns

Almost all masculine nouns end in a consonant, or -ь. All nouns that end in a consonant (including й) are masculine.

Some masculine nouns (including certain diminutives and augmentatives) end in -a and -я; these are dealt with in § 40, Obss. 2 and 8, and § 45. The few masc. nouns in -o and -e are mentioned in §§ 41, 44, 45, indeclinable nouns —at the end of § 44, and the noun путь in § 42, Obs. 5.

All nouns that end in a consonant (except й) are called *hard* and belong to the *hard* type of declension, in which most of the endings consist of or begin with a *hard* vowel (see § 4); nouns ending in -ь and -й are said to be *soft* and belong to the *soft* type of declension, in which the case-endings usually begin with the corresponding *soft* vowel (see § 9); otherwise the endings are usually similar for both hard and soft nouns. Note that the soft sign (ь) and the consonant й disappear in the oblique cases, since their function is fulfilled by the soft vowel of the ending (cf. §§ 13, 21).

Examples: (hard) стол *table*, дед *grandfather*; (soft) сарáй *shed*, словáрь *dictionary*, писáтель *writer*—

Singular

N.	стол	дед	сарáй	словáрь	писáтель
G.	столá	дéда	сарáя	словаря́	писáтеля
D.	столу́	дéду	сарáю	словарю́	писáтелю
A.	стол	дéда	сарáй	словáрь	писáтеля
I.	столóм	дéдом	сарáем	словарём	писáтелем
L.	столé	дéде	сарáе	словарé	писáтеле

Plural

N.	столы́	де́ды	сара́и	словари́	писа́тели
G.	столо́в	де́дов	сара́ев	словаре́й	писа́телей
D.	стола́м	де́дам	сара́ям	словаря́м	писа́телям
A.	столы́	де́дов	сара́и	словари́	писа́телей
I.	стола́ми	де́дами	сара́ями	словаря́ми	писа́телями
L.	стола́х	де́дах	сара́ях	словаря́х	писа́телях

OBSERVATIONS

1. The acc. sing. and pl. of all masculine nouns is the same as the nom. sing. and pl. in the case of inanimate objects, and the same as the gen. sing. and pl. in the case of animate beings: thus the acc. sing. of стол is стол, but the acc. sing. of дед is де́да.

2. Nouns in -ий (like ге́ний *genius*, Гео́ргий *George*, сана-то́рий *sanatorium*) have loc. sing. in -ии, i.e. as nom. pl.

3. The masculine nouns in -ь have borrowed the ending of the gen. pl. (-ей, e.g. словаре́й) from another declension.

4. The nom. pl. (and acc. pl. also if inanimate) of masculine nouns in -к, -г, -х, -ч, -щ, -ж, -ш, ends in -ки, -ги, -хи, -чи, -щи, -жи, -ши (i.e. takes -и instead of -ы), because ы cannot stand after these letters, e.g. ма́льчик *boy*, nom. pl. ма́льчики; нож *knife*, nom. pl. ножи́; ключ *key*, nom. pl. ключи́.

5. Nouns in -ч, -щ, -ж, and -ш originally belonged to the soft type of declension, relics of which can still be seen in their instr. sing., which ends in -ем (-ом if stressed), and their gen. pl. in -ей, e.g. това́рищ *friend, comrade*, instr. sing. това́рищем, gen. pl. това́рищей, but плащ *cape, raincoat*, instr. sing. плащо́м, gen. pl. плаще́й; матч *match (game)*, instr. sing. ма́тчем, gen. pl. ма́тчей, but ключ *key*, instr. sing. ключо́м, gen. pl. ключе́й.

In the same way, nouns ending in -ц were originally soft; now those which are stressed on the last syllable take the hard endings throughout (e.g. отéц *father* has instr. sing. отцóм and gen. pl. отцóв), while those which are not stressed on the last syllable have instr. sing. in -ем, and gen. pl. in -ев (e.g. мéсяц *month*, instr. sing. мéсяцем and gen. pl. мéсяцев).

6. A large number of words which contain e or o (often stressed) in the last syllable of the nom. sing. lose this vowel in the oblique cases. These disappearing vowels are termed бéглые in Russian and 'mobile', 'fleeting', or 'unstable' in English. If the stress falls on a 'mobile' e or o in the nom., it falls on the case-endings in the oblique cases; the emphasis on the stressed syllable is so strong that the weak vowel of the unstressed adjacent syllable has disappeared, e.g. отéц *father*, gen. sing. отцá, dat. sing. отцý, nom. pl. отцы́; дворéц *palace*, gen. sing. дворцá; песóк *sand*, пескá; кусóк *piece*, кускá; день *day*, gen. sing. дня; зáмок *castle*, зáмка.

In лев *lion*, лёд *ice*, лён *flax*, пáлец *finger*, &c., e becomes ь to show that the л remains soft, e.g. лёд *ice*, gen. sing. льда; cf. лоб *forehead* with hard л, gen. sing. лба.

The e is retained in cases where its omission would cause an excessive accumulation of consonants, e.g. мертвéц *corpse* has gen. sing. мертвецá; игрóк *gambler* has gen. sing. игрокá.

A few words in -ей have gen. sing. in -ья, dat. in -ью, nom. pl. in -ьи, &c., e.g. ручéй *stream*, gen. sing. ручья́, nom. pl. ручьи́, also воробéй *sparrow*, муравéй *ant*, соловéй *nightingale*, &c.

Words in -ец after a vowel have gen. sing. in -йца, &c., e.g. боéц *fighter*, *soldier*, gen. бойцá; by analogy, зáяц *hare* has gen. зáйца, &c.

Two words ending in -ем after a vowel have gen. sing. in -йма, dat. sing. in -йму, &c.: заём *loan*, gen. sing. зáйма, and наём *hire*, gen. sing. нáйма.

In some cases where the same process apparently occurs, the e or o was inserted centuries ago in the nom. sing. to facilitate pronunciation, e.g. ве́тер (formerly ветр) *wind*, gen. sing. ве́тра; ого́нь *fire*, огня́; у́гол *corner*, угла́; у́голь *coal*, у́гля.

7. Many masculine nouns denoting divisible matter have a gen. sing. in -y (-ю) when the genitive is used in a partitive sense, e.g. стака́н ча́ю (or ча́я) *a glass of tea*, but *the flavour of tea* can be only вкус ча́я; ма́ло наро́ду *few people* (lit. *little of people*), but мне́ние наро́да *the opinion of the people*.

This genitive has become usual in a number of cases where there is no idea of partition, e.g. с ви́ду *by sight*, бе́з то́лку *without sense*, сни́зу *from below*, све́рху *from above*, о́троду *from birth*, и́з дому *out of the house* (or *from one's home*), and many other similar adverbial expressions.

8. Several nouns have a loc. sing. in -ý (-ю́), always stressed, which is used to express actual location in space after the prepositions в *in*, and на *on*, e.g. в саду́ *in the garden*, на мосту́ *on the bridge*, в ... году́ *in the year ...*, в лесу́ *in the forest*, на берегу́ *on the bank, shore*, на лугу́ *in the meadow*, на краю́ *on the edge* (from край), в углу́ *in the corner* (nom. у́гол), на полу́ *on the floor*, and others. See § 68.

N.B. The locative in -ý is never used after the prepositions о *concerning*, по *after*, при *near*, nor after в and на when they do not indicate actual location, nor when the noun is used in a specialized, technical sense, e.g. ско́лько гра́дусов в прямо́м угле́? *how many degrees are there in a right angle?*, он понима́ет толк в ле́се *he is an expert on timber*, он игра́л в «Вишнёвом са́де» *he acted in 'The Cherry Orchard'*.

9. Several nouns have nom. pl. in -á (-я́), which is always stressed. This is really the old nom. dual, but its use has extended from the dual to the plural: глаз *eye*, nom.

pl. глаза́; бе́рег *bank, shore*, nom. pl. берега́ *the two banks of a river* and also *the shores of an ocean*; рог *horn*, nom. pl. рога́; бок *side*, nom. pl. бока́; also ве́чер *evening* has nom. pl. вечера́; дом *house*, дома́; го́лос *voice*, голоса́; ко́локол *bell*, колокола́; го́род *town*, города́; край *region, country*, края́; до́ктор *doctor*, доктора́; профе́ссор *professor*, профессора́; учи́тель *teacher*, учителя́; век *age, century* has both века́ and (in phrases) ве́ки; год *year* has both го́ды and (poet.) года́. A few have two forms of the nom. pl. with different meanings: о́браз *form, manner, holy image* has образа́ *holy images* and о́бразы *forms*; хлеб *grain, bread, loaf* has хлеба́ *the crops* and хле́бы *loaves*; цвет *colour, blossom* has цвета́ *colours* and цветы́ *flowers* (for the sing. the diminutive цвето́к is used in the sense of a single *flower*); мех *fur, bellows* has nom. pl. меха́ *furs* and мехи́ [*pairs of*] *bellows*.

Nouns in -ёнок (-онок) denoting young creatures have their nom. pl. in -ята (-ата) and decline in the plural like the neuter сёла *villages* (see § 41, Obs. 4).

Several masculine nouns have nom. pl. in -ья, which was originally a (feminine) collective singular. Thus, брат *brother* has nom. pl. бра́тья; зять *brother-in-law* or *son-in-law* has nom. pl. зятья́; стул *chair*—сту́лья; лист *leaf* or *sheet of paper* has nom. pl. ли́стья *leaves, foliage* and (regularly) листы́ *sheets of paper*; друг *friend*—друзья́; муж *husband*—мужья́; князь *prince*—князья́. The last three have gen. pl. in -е́й, like слова́рь, e.g. друзе́й; while бра́тья has gen. pl. бра́тьев, зятья́ has зятьёв, and сту́лья has сту́льев, like some other, less common nom. pl. in -ья; all, however, from the dat. pl. onwards, go alike, e.g. dat. pl. друзья́м, instr. pl. друзья́ми, loc. pl. друзья́х.

Сын *son* has nom. pl. сыновья́, gen. pl. сынове́й, dat. pl. сыновья́м, &c. Сосе́д *neighbour* and чёрт *devil* decline in the plural like слова́рь throughout: nom. pl. сосе́ди and че́рти; gen. pl. сосе́дей and чертей, &c.

A number of masculine nouns in -ин denoting individuals drop the suffix -ин- in the plural and have nom. pl. in -e (a few in -ы) and in the gen.-acc. pl. have no ending: гражданин *citizen* has nom. pl. гра́ждане, gen. pl. гра́ждан; англича́нин *Englishman* has nom. pl. англича́не *the English*, gen. pl. англича́н. From the dat. pl. onwards such nouns take the regular hard endings: гра́жданам, гра́жданами, гра́жданах; англича́нам, англича́нами, англича́нах. So also: тата́рин *Tartar*, nom. pl. тата́ры, gen. pl. тата́р; болга́рин *Bulgarian*, болга́ры; датча́нин *Dane*, датча́не; ри́млянин *Roman*, ри́мляне; славяни́н *Slav*, славя́не; дворяни́н *nobleman*, дворя́не; крестья́нин *peasant*, крестья́не, and (not to be confused with the last, though of identical derivation) христиани́н *Christian*, христиа́не, and others.

Господи́н *Mr* has nom. pl. господа́ *Messrs*, 'Gentlemen' (also 'Ladies and Gentlemen'), gen. pl. госпо́д, dat. pl. господа́м, &c.; note that in the Soviet Union these forms of address are only used to and by foreign visitors. Хозя́ин *host, householder, master* has nom. pl. хозя́ева *hosts* or *host and hostess*, &c., gen. pl. хозя́ев, dat. pl. хозя́евам, &c.

Several masculine nouns with regular nom. pl. have gen. pl. without any ending, as the above; this is really the old gen. pl. of this declension, while the form now termed 'regular' (in -ов, -ев) was borrowed from another declension. Thus, во́лосы *hair* (collective) has gen. pl. воло́с; раз *time, once*, gen. pl. раз; солда́т *soldier*, gen. pl. солда́т; глаз *eye*, gen. pl. глаз; арши́н *Russian yard* (old measure, = 28 inches), gen. pl. арши́н.

The gen. pl. of челове́к *human being, person* is челове́к, which is used only after numerals, e.g. сто челове́к *a hundred people*, but мно́го люде́й *many people*. The other cases of the plural of челове́к are rarely used, being replaced by those of лю́ди *people*. For the declension of лю́ди see § 42, Obs. 2.

The gen. pl. of год is годóв, except after cardinal numerals, when лет (gen. pl. of лéто *summer*) is used instead.

10. Бог *God* has a special form for the voc. sing.: Бóже. Otherwise it is declined regularly, like стол, e.g. gen. sing. Бóга, &c. Госпóдь *the Lord* has a special voc. sing. Гóсподи *Lord*, and, though soft in the nom., is declined from the gen. sing. onwards like стол, viz. Гóспода, &c. Христóс *Christ* drops the -ос from the gen. sing. onwards and declines like стол, viz. Христá, &c. The old vocative form of отéц *father* occurs in the phrase Óтче наш *Pater noster*.

11. (*a*) Most masculine nouns are stressed on the same syllable in all their forms, e.g. нарóд *people, nation*:

sing. нарóд	нарóда	нарóду	нарóд	нарóдом	нарóде
pl. нарóды	нарóдов	нарóдам	нарóды	нарóдами	нарóдах

but in a large number of words of one syllable, some of two syllables, and a few of more than two syllables, the stress shifts to another position in certain cases. Such words can be divided into four groups:

(*b*) Words like сад *orchard, garden*, in which the stress falls on the stem in the singular (apart from the special locative in -ý, see Obs. 8), but on the endings throughout the plural:

sing. сад	сáда	сáду	сад	сáдом	сáде (but в садý)
pl. садьí	садóв	садáм	садьí	садáми	садáх

(*c*) Words like зуб *tooth*, where the stress falls on the stem in the singular and in the nom.-acc. plural, but elsewhere on the endings:

sing. зуб	зýба	зýбу	зуб	зýбом	зýбе
pl. зýбы	зубóв	зубáм	зýбы	зубáми	зубáх

(*d*) Words like стол *table*, in which the stress falls on the endings throughout:

sing. стол	столá	столý	стол	столóм	столé
pl. стольí	столóв	столáм	стольí	столáми	столáх

This is the pattern followed by all nouns with stressed 'mobile' ó, é, or ё, and nearly all with the stressed suffixes -а́к, -я́к, -и́к, -у́к, -у́х, -у́н, -а́ч, and -и́ч;

(e) Words like гвоздь *nail*, where the stress falls on the ending, except in the nom.-acc. pl.:

sing.	гвоздь	гвоздя́	гвоздю́	гвоздь	гвоздём	гвозде́
pl.	гво́зди	гвозде́й	гвоздя́м	гво́зди	гвоздя́ми	гвоздя́х

§ 40. Feminine Nouns with nom. sing. in -a, -я

Almost all nouns ending in -a and -я are feminine. All those which end in -a are called *hard*; those ending in -я are called *soft*; those case-endings which begin with a *hard* vowel when the noun is *hard*, begin with the corresponding *soft* vowel when the noun is *soft*; otherwise the endings are similar for both hard and soft nouns.

As regards the accusative case, the acc. sing. of all nouns in -a and -я is quite different from the nom. sing., whether the noun be animate or inanimate; but the acc. pl. is the same as the nom. pl. in the case of inanimate objects and the same as the gen. pl. in the case of animate beings. This feature of the plural is due to the influence of the masculine declension.

Examples: (hard) же́нщина *woman*, черта́ *line, feature, trait;*

(soft) неде́ля *week*, а́рмия *army*:

Singular

N.	же́нщина	черта́	неде́ля	а́рмия
G.	же́нщины	черты́	неде́ли	а́рмии
D.	же́нщине	черте́	неде́ле	а́рмии
A.	же́нщину	черту́	неде́лю	а́рмию
I.	же́нщиной	черто́й	неде́лей[1]	а́рмией
L.	же́нщине	черте́	неде́ле	а́рмии

[1] This ending becomes -ёй when stressed, e.g. земля́ *land*, instr. sing. землёй.

Plural

N.	же́нщины	черты́	неде́ли	а́рмии
G.	же́нщин	черт	неде́ль	а́рмий
D.	же́нщинам	черта́м	неде́лям	а́рмиям
A.	же́нщин	черты́	неде́ли	а́рмии
I.	же́нщинами	черта́ми	неде́лями	а́рмиями
L.	же́нщинах	черта́х	неде́лях	а́рмиях

OBSERVATIONS

1. The instr. sing. of nouns in -a and -я has two forms—the short (-ой, -ей, or -ёй), and the long (-ою, -ею, or -ёю). The latter is the older form, but it is now used mainly for rhetorical effect and in poetry when an additional syllable is required.

2. The gen. pl. of all nouns ending in a vowel + я, which would end in ь if the last letter of the stem were a consonant, is always written with an й and is a diphthong, e.g. а́рмия *army* and ше́я *neck* have gen. pl. а́рмий and шей.

The gen. pl. of nouns (some masc.) ending in -ья ends in -е́й (N.B. never -ёй), e.g. статья́ *article* (*printed*), gen. pl. стате́й. Дя́дя *uncle* and до́ля *share* also have gen. pl. in -ей (дя́дей, до́лей); судья́ *judge* has gen. pl. суде́й (судья́ is otherwise declined like неде́ля, viz. gen. sing. судьи́, nom. pl. су́дьи, &c.); ю́ноша *young man, youth* has gen. pl. ю́ношей; го́стья (*female*) *guest* has gen. pl. го́стий.

3. The dat. and loc. sing. of nouns ending in -ия end in -ии, like the gen. sing., e.g. а́рмия *army*, dat. and loc. sing. а́рмии; рели́гия *religion*, рели́гии; Росси́я *Russia*, Росси́и; А́нглия *England*, А́нглии.

Many feminine Christian names are spelt in two ways in the nom. sing.—either -ия (the more formal) or -ья (colloquial); when spelt in the former way, the dat. and loc. sing. end in -ии, and when in the latter way, they end

in -ье. For example, София *Sophia* has dat. and loc. sing.
Софи́и, but the more colloquial form Со́фья has dat. and
loc. Со́фье.

4. The gen. sing. and nom. pl. (also acc. pl. of inani-
mates) of all nouns in -ка, -га, -ха, -ча, -ща, -жа, -ша end
in -ки, -ги, -хи, -чи, -щи, -жи, -ши because ы cannot
stand after a velar consonant or after ч, щ, ж, or ш.

5. The instr. sing. of all nouns ending in -ца, -ча, -ща,
-жа, -ша ends in -ой when the stress falls on the ending,
and in -ей when the stress falls on the stem, e.g. душа́ *soul*
has instr. sing. душо́й, but больни́ца *hospital* has instr.
sing. больни́цей.

6. A number of words with stems ending in two or more
consonants have a vowel before the last consonant in the
gen. pl. The inserted vowel is generally -e-, but -o- is usual
after a velar and between two consonants (other than ж, ш,
ц) that are hard in the nom. sing., e.g. земля́ *land* has gen.
pl. земе́ль; ко́шка *cat*—ко́шек; ло́дка *boat*—ло́док; ви́лка
fork—ви́лок; ку́хня *kitchen*, дере́вня *village*, and ба́рышня
young lady have gen. pl. ку́хонь, дереве́нь, and ба́рышень
respectively, but note that other nouns in consonant + ня
have hard н in the gen. pl., as пе́сня *song*—пе́сен, ба́сня
fable—ба́сен, ба́шня *tower*—ба́шен.

Some nouns with ь or й in the stem replace this with e
in the gen. pl., e.g. судьба́ *fate*—су́деб (but про́сьба *request*—про́сьб), копе́йка *copeck* (coin)—копе́ек.

7. (*a*) Most nouns in -а/-я are stressed on the stem
throughout their declension, as си́ла *force*:

| sing. | си́ла | си́лы | си́ле | си́лу | си́лой | си́ле |
| pl. | си́лы | сил | си́лам | си́лы | си́лами | си́лах |

(*b*) In many others the stress falls on the endings throughout (in the gen. pl.—on the last syllable of the stem), as in
черта́ *line, feature*:

sing. черта́   черты́   черте́   черту́   черто́й   черте́
pl.   черты́   черт   черта́м черты́   черта́ми черта́х

but there are many nouns (mostly of two syllables) which have mobile stress and belong to the following classes:

(*c*) The stress falls on the endings, except in the nom.-acc. pl., as in губа́ *lip* :

sing. губа́   губы́   губе́   губу́   губо́й   губе́
pl.   гу́бы   губ   губа́м гу́бы   губа́ми губа́х

(*d*) The stress falls on the endings of the singular and on the stem of the plural, as in война́ *war* :

sing. война́ войны́ войне́ войну́ войно́й войне́
pl.   во́йны войн   во́йнам во́йны во́йнами во́йнах

(*e*) In the singular the stress falls on all the endings except the accusative, the plural being stressed as in (*d*) or (*c*), as in вода́ *water* and рука́ *arm* :

sing. вода́   воды́   воде́   во́ду   водо́й   воде́
pl.   во́ды   вод   во́дам во́ды   во́дами во́дах

sing. рука́   руки́   руке́   ру́ку   руко́й   руке́
pl.   ру́ки   рук   рука́м ру́ки   рука́ми рука́х

N.B. голова́ *head* has acc. sing. го́лову, nom.-acc. pl. го́ловы, but gen. pl. голо́в, dat. pl. голова́м. Other words with -оло- and -оро- in the stem are stressed in the same way.

8. It is to be noted that the great majority of nouns in -a and -я are feminine, but that a few masculine nouns, including a number of names (mostly diminutives), also have these endings and are declined in the same way as the feminines, although any adjectives associated with them take the *masculine* endings. Among such nouns are дя́дя *uncle,* ю́ноша *youth, young man,* судья́ *judge,* слуга́ *male servant* (N.B. the collective noun прислу́га *male* or *female*

servant(s) is feminine), Алёша (diminutive of Алексе́й *Alexis*), Ва́ня (dim. of Ива́н *John*), Воло́дя (dim. of Влади́-мир *Vladimir*), Ко́ля (dim. of Никола́й *Nicholas*), Ми́ша (dim. of Михаи́л *Michael*), Пе́тя (dim. of Пётр *Peter*), Са́ша (dim. of Алекса́ндр *Alexander*), Серёжа (dim. of Серге́й *Sergius*), and many others; notice also the names Ники́та *Nikita* and Илья́ *Elias*. уби́йца *murderer*, пья́ница *drunkard*, у́мница *clever chap*, and сирота́ *male orphan* are masc. only when they refer to male beings.

§ 41. Neuter Nouns with nom. sing. in -o and -e

Almost all neuter nouns end in -o or -e. All nouns which end in -o and -e are neuter, except подмасте́рье *apprentice* (masc.), masculine nouns with the suffixes -ище and -ишко (e.g. доми́ще (masc.) *big [ugly] house*, доми́шко (masc.) *wretched [little] house*), and a few indeclinable loanwords, like мае́стро *maestro* (masc., denoting male being), цеце́ *tsetse fly* (fem., since му́ха *fly* is fem.), and ко́фе *coffee* (masc.).

Neuter nouns, even when denoting animate beings, have acc. sing. identical with nom. sing., but the acc. pl. of лицо́ in the sense of *person* is identical with gen. pl. (лиц).

All nouns which end in -o are called *hard*, those ending in -e (except after ж, ш, ч, щ, or ц; see Obs. 2) are called *soft*.

Example: (hard) село́ *village*; (soft) мо́ре *sea*, зда́ние *building*, уще́лье *ravine*:

Singular

N.	село́	мо́ре	зда́ние	уще́лье
G.	села́	мо́ря	зда́ния	уще́лья
D.	селу́	мо́рю	зда́нию	уще́лью
A.	село́	мо́ре	зда́ние	уще́лье
I.	село́м	мо́рем	зда́нием	уще́льем
L.	селе́	мо́ре	зда́нии	уще́лье

Plural

N.	сёла	моря́	зда́ния	уще́лья
G.	сёл	море́й	зда́ний	уще́лий
D.	сёлам	моря́м	зда́ниям	уще́льям
A.	сёла	моря́	зда́ния	уще́лья
I.	сёлами	моря́ми	зда́ниями	уще́льями
L.	сёлах	моря́х	зда́ниях	уще́льях

OBSERVATIONS

1. The neuter nouns in -e have borrowed the ending of the gen. pl. (-ей, e.g. море́й) from another declension; this -ей can never become -ёй.

Abstract nouns in -ие can also be spelt -ье, especially in poetry when one syllable less is desired, e.g. жела́ние or жела́нье *wish*; in the former case such nouns have loc. sing. in -ии, and in the latter—in -ье.

Nouns in -ье formerly had loc. sing. in -ьи; this ending, though very rare, is still found in poetry and in the phrase в забытьи́ *in a daze* (from забытьё).

Nouns in -ье (unstressed) usually have gen. pl. in -ий, as уще́лье *ravine*, gen. pl. уще́лий, but пла́тье *dress* has gen. pl. пла́тьев and подмасте́рье (masc.) *apprentice* has gen. pl. подмасте́рьев; similarly, у́стье *mouth (of a river)* and a few others.

Nouns in -ьё as a rule have gen. pl. in -е́й, but ружьё *rifle* has gen. pl. ру́жей, and копьё *spear* has gen. pl. ко́пий.

The noun острие́ *sharp point* or *edge* has loc. sing. острие́ and gen. pl. острие́в.

2. Nouns in -че, -ще, -же, -ше, -це follow the hard declension, but have instr. sing. in -ем, e.g. зре́лище *sight*, instr. sing. зре́лищем, but gen. sing. зре́лища, gen. pl. зре́лищ; ло́же *couch*, gen. pl. лож. A few of the neuter diminutives in -це have gen. pl. in -цев, instead of the regular -ц.

Masculine augmentatives in -ище have nom. pl. in -ища and (colloq.) -ищи, e.g. домúще *great big [ugly] house* (masc.) has nom. pl. домúща and домúщи, and gen. pl. домúщ.

3. A number of hard neuter nouns with stems ending in two consonants insert a vowel between the two consonants in the gen. pl. in order to facilitate their pronunciation, e.g. окнó *window*, gen. pl. óкон; письмó *letter*, gen. pl. пúсем.

Яйцó *egg* has gen. pl. яúц (two syllables), while the nom. pl. is яúца.

4. Some nouns in -o have unexpected forms in the plural.

Nouns in -ко have nom. pl. in -кá when the ending is stressed, otherwise in -ки, e.g. вóйско *army*, nom. pl. войскá *troops*, but яблоко *apple*, nom. pl. яблоки, gen. pl. яблок; note also плечó *shoulder*, nom. pl. плéчи, gen. pl. плеч; колéно meaning *knee* has nom. pl. колéни, gen. pl. колéней; ýхо *ear*—ýши, ушéй; óко *eye* (poetic)—óчи, очéй. The endings in -и are relics of the old neuter dual, the eyes, ears, and shoulders being naturally mentioned in the dual more often than in the plural. In the dat., instr., and loc. pl. all these words follow the declension of стол, e.g. instr. pl. яблоками, ушáми, плечáми.

The diminutive ýшко (or ушкó) *little ear* (from ýхо) has nom. pl. ýшки and gen. pl. ýшек, according to the rule formulated above; but ушкó meaning *eye of a needle* (and in other specialized senses) and очкó *pip, point, hole* (from óко) are treated in the plural as masculine nouns: ушкú and очкú, gen. ушкóв and очкóв. The plural очкú in the sense of [*a pair of*] *glasses, spectacles* (gen. очкóв) has no singular.

Нéбо *sky, heaven* has nom. pl. небесá, gen. pl. небéс; чýдо *miracle*—чудесá, чудéс; these have dat. pl. небесáм, чудесáм, &c.; óблако *cloud* has nom. pl. облакá, gen. pl. облакóв; сýдно *vessel* has nom. pl. судá *vessels (ships)* and сýдна *vessels (containers)*, with gen. plur. судóв and сýден respectively.

Дéрево *tree* has nom. pl. дерéвья, gen. pl. дерéвьев, dat. pl. дерéвьям, &c.; similarly, перó *feather, pen* has пéрья, пéрьев, &c.; крылó *wing*—крылья, &c.

There is a whole category of words that are neuter in the plural, but masculine in the singular. These are all names of young living creatures, e.g. котя́та (gen. pl. котя́т) *kittens*, sing. котёнок (dim. of кот); цыпля́та *chickens*, sing. цыплёнок; жеребя́та *foals*, sing. жеребёнок; теля́та *calves*, sing. телёнок; порося́та *sucking-pigs*, sing. поросёнок; ребя́та *lads* (see § 43), cf. ребёнок *child*. In the singular all these words come under Obs. 6 of § 39, i.e. gen.-acc. котёнка, &c. N.B. щеня́та *puppies* has nom. sing. щенóк (gen. sing. щенкá) and бесеня́та *little devils* has nom. sing. бесёнок.

5. (*a*) Most neuter nouns are stressed on the same syllable of the stem in all cases, as болóто *marsh*, здáние *building*, ущéлье *ravine*.

(*b*) A few neuters are stressed on all the endings (where there is no ending—on the last syllable of the stem), as существó *substance*, nom. pl. существá, gen. pl. существ.

Quite a large number of neuters, mostly words of two syllables, have a stress-shift in the plural; of these there are two types:

(*c*) The stress falls on the stem in the singular, but on all the endings in the plural, as in мóре *sea* (see table above) and слóво *word*:

sing.	слóво	слóва	слóву	слóво	слóвом	слóве
pl.	словá	слов	словáм	словá	словáми	словáх

(*d*) The stress falls on the endings in the singular, but on the stem in the plural, as in село́ *village* (see table above) and окно́ *window*:

sing. окно́ окна́ окну́ окно́ окно́м   окне́
pl. о́кна о́кон о́кнам о́кна о́кнами о́кнах

Note also ружьё *rifle*, nom. pl. ру́жья.

§ 42. Feminine Nouns with nom. sing. in -ь

A number of feminine nouns, especially abstract nouns derived from adjectives, such as ра́дость *joy* from рад *glad*, end in -ь in the nom. and acc. sing. and form a distinct class, sometimes called the *i*-declension.

Example: метéль *snow-storm*

	Singular	*Plural*
N.	метéль	метéли
G.	метéли	метéлей
D.	метéли	метéлям
A.	метéль	метéли
I.	метéлью	метéлями
L.	метéли	метéлях

OBSERVATIONS

1. The acc. sing. of all nouns in this declension is like the nom. sing., but the acc. pl. of the names of animate beings is the same as the gen. pl.; e.g. ло́шадь *horse* has nom. pl. ло́шади, gen. and acc. pl. лошадéй, whereas the inanimate кость *bone* has gen. pl. костéй, acc. pl. ко́сти. The -ей of the gen. pl. of this declension is borrowed by soft masculine and neuter nouns (see § 39, Obs. 5 and 9, and § 41, Obs. 1); note that this -ей of the gen. pl. can never become -ёй when stressed.

2. The former ending of the instr. pl. of this declension was -ьми́; this has been retained as the normal ending only

by ло́шадь *horse*, instr. pl. лошадьми́ (or лошадя́ми) and by the two plural nouns лю́ди *people* (instr. pl. людьми́) and де́ти *children* (instr. pl. детьми́). A few other nouns (кость *bone*, плеть *whip*, дверь *door*) still have a form in -ьми́ besides the more usual instr. pl. in -я́ми; it is used mostly in idioms, e.g. лечь костьми́ *to die, fall (in battle)*.

The declension of the very common plurals лю́ди *people* and де́ти *children* is so important that it is given here in full:

N.	лю́ди	де́ти
G.	люде́й	дете́й
D.	лю́дям	де́тям
A.	люде́й	дете́й
I.	людьми́	детьми́
L.	лю́дях	де́тях

Лю́ди is employed as the normal plural of челове́к *person, human being* (see § 39, Obs. 9); the singular люд means *[a certain class of] people*. Де́ти is the normal plural of ребё- нок *child*; its own singular дитя́ is dealt with in § 43.

3. Those nouns which end in -чь, -щь, -жь, and -шь, as well as це́рковь *church* (see also Obs. 4), have dat. pl. in -ам, instr. pl. in -ами, and loc. pl. in -ах; e.g. ночь *night*— ноча́м, ноча́ми, ноча́х; вещь *thing*—веща́м, веща́ми, веща́х; це́рковь — церква́м, церква́ми, церква́х.

4. The five nouns це́рковь *church*, любо́вь *love*, рожь *rye*, ложь *lie*, and вошь *louse* lose the o in all the oblique cases except the instr. sing. Thus, gen. sing. це́ркви, любви́, ржи, &c., but instr. sing. це́рковью, любо́вью, ро́жью. When, however, Любо́вь is used as a name, it retains the o; gen. sing. Любо́ви, &c.

5. The masculine noun путь *way (road and means)* is declined exactly as мете́ль, except that the instr. sing. is путём.

6. The noun сажéнь *seven feet* (old measure of length) has gen., dat., loc. sing., and nom. pl. сажéни, and gen. pl. сажéней; the alternative сáжень has gen. sing. сáжени, gen. pl. сáжен or саженéй, with stress on the endings in the dat., instr., and loc. pl.

7. The two nouns мать *mother*, and дочь *daughter* are declined as follows:

	Singular	*Plural*
N.	мать	мáтери
G.	мáтери	матерéй
D.	мáтери	матеря́м
A.	мать	матерéй
I.	мáтерью	матеря́ми
L.	мáтери	матеря́х

The instr. pl. of дочь is дочерьми́ or дочеря́ми. In the colloquial language, the word мать is often replaced by мáма or the affectionate diminutives мамáша, мамýся, мамýля, &c.; and дочь by the diminutive дóчка; all of these follow the ordinary feminine declension.

8. The stress on feminine nouns in -ь is usually constant, but several—e.g. кость *bone*, часть *part*, вещь *thing*—have the stress on the endings of the gen., dat., instr., and loc. pl., and a few have irregular stress in the singular.

9. After в *in* or на *on* used in a purely spatial sense, some two dozen feminine nouns in -ь have a special locative in stressed -и́ (cf. masculines in -ý, § 39, Obs. 8); they include глубь, горсть, грудь, грязь, даль, дверь, кость, кровь, мель, ночь, печь, пыль, связь, степь, тень, тишь, цепь, честь, the place-names Русь and Тверь, and some others.

Sometimes when an adjective intervenes, and always when в and на do not indicate location, the ordinary locative in unstressed -и is used, e.g. в связи́ с э́тим *in connexion with this,* but в непреры́вной свя́зи с ним *in constant touch with him;* likewise: ключ в двери́ *the key is in the door,* but ему́ отказа́ли в но́вой две́ри *they refused him a new door.*

§ 43. Neuter Nouns with nom. sing. in -я

Ten neuter nouns end in -мя in the nom. and acc. sing. and form a distinct class, sometimes called the *n*-declension.

Example: вре́мя *time*

	Singular	*Plural*
N.	вре́мя	времена́
G.	вре́мени	времён
D.	вре́мени	времена́м
A.	вре́мя	времена́
I.	вре́менем	времена́ми
L.	вре́мени	времена́х

The only other common words in this declension are: и́мя (*Christian*) *name,* пле́мя *tribe,* пла́мя *flame(s)* (no pl.), бре́мя *burden,* зна́мя *banner* (nom. pl. знамёна), се́мя *seed* (irreg. gen. pl. семя́н), and стре́мя *stirrup* (irreg. gen. pl. стремя́н).

The word дитя́ *child* is all that remains of another class of neuter nouns; it is declined in the singular as follows:

N.	дитя́
G.	дитя́ти
D.	дитя́ти
A.	дитя́
I.	дитя́тею
L.	дитя́ти

The singular form дитя́ is very seldom used except in a figurative sense and in poetry; the other singular forms are obsolete. The plural дети is the normal word for *children*; its declension is given on p. 77.

The normal singular word for *child* is ребёнок, whose own plural (ребята, see § 41, Obs. 4) rarely means *children* but is often used colloquially in the sense of *lads, fellows, fellow students, work-mates*, &c.

§ 44. Note on the Terminations of Nouns

Nouns ending in a consonant or -й are masculine.

Nouns ending in -о or -е are neuter (for the few exceptions see § 41 and the note on indeclinable loan-words on p. 82).

Nouns ending in -ь are either masculine or feminine, e.g. день *day* (masc.), but ночь *night* (fem.).

Most nouns in -а and -я are feminine, but a few are masculine, e.g. слуга (*man-*)*servant* and судья *judge*, and eleven nouns in -я are neuter, as время *time*.

Common terminations denoting male and female agents are:

masc.: -ик, -ник, -тель, -ец, -ин, -янин, -чанин, -ич, -ун, -чик, -щик, and others;

fem.: -ица, -ница, -иха, -ка, -янка, -чанка, -унья, -чица, -ша, and others; for example:

Masculine	*Feminine*
помощник *assistant* (male)	помощница *assistant* (female)
переводчик *translator*	переводчица
штукатурщик *plasterer*	штукатурщица
учитель *teacher*	учительница
большевик *Bolshevik*	большевичка
земляк *fellow countryman*	землячка *fellow countrywoman*
рыбак *fisherman*	рыбачка *fisherman's wife* or *woman doing fisherman's job*

коммуни́ст *Communist*	коммуни́стка
спортсме́н *sportsman*	спортсме́нка *sportswoman*
стаха́новец *Stakhanovite*	стаха́новка
певе́ц *singer*	певи́ца
купе́ц *merchant*	купчи́ха *merchant's wife* or *woman merchant*
вдове́ц *widower*	вдова́ *widow*
болту́н *chatterbox*	болту́нья
библиоте́карь *librarian*	библиоте́карша
до́ктор *doctor* (male or female)	до́кторша *doctor's wife* (colloq.), also *woman-doctor* (pop.)
генера́л *general*	генера́льша *general's wife* (obs.)
граждани́н *citizen* (male)	гражда́нка *citizen* (female)
господи́н[1] *gentleman, Mr*	госпожа́[1] *lady, Mrs, Miss*
боя́рин *boyar*	боя́рыня *boyar's wife*
царь *tsar, czar*	цари́ца *tsaritsa, czarina*
коро́ль *king*	короле́ва *queen*
князь *prince*	княги́ня *princess* (*prince's wife*) and княжна́ *princess* (*prince's sister* or *daughter*)

Notice that молоде́ц *brave fellow, clever chap* (a very common word of praise), друг *friend*, това́рищ *comrade, friend*, челове́к *person*, до́ктор *doctor*, инжене́р *engineer*, and the designations of those engaged in many other professions and trades, are used both of males and females, but any attributive adjective preceding them is always masculine; сирота́ *orphan*, пья́ница *drunkard*, уби́йца *killer*, у́мница *clever chap* can be applied to a man or a woman and an accompanying adjective will be respectively masculine or feminine. If one wants to be specific, the feminine of до́ктор or врач, meaning *doctor*, and of инжене́р *engineer*, &c., is же́нщина-врач *woman-doctor*, же́нщина-инжене́р *woman-engineer*, &c.

---

[1] In the Soviet Union, used only to and by foreign visitors.

These suffixes are also used in nouns denoting the inhabitants of countries, towns, &c., as англича́нин *Englishman* (see p. 66)—англича́нка *Englishwoman*, не́мец *German* —fem. не́мка (pl. не́мцы—fem. не́мки), сибиря́к *Siberian*—fem. сибиря́чка. Other names of this type include америка́нец *American*, голла́ндец *Dutchman*, ирла́ндец *Irishman*, испа́нец *Spaniard*, италья́нец *Italian*, лито́вец *Lithuanian*, норве́жец *Norwegian*, украи́нец *Ukrainian*, шотла́ндец *Scot*, and швейца́рец *Swiss*; all these turn -ец into -ка for the feminine and end in -цы/-ки in the nom. pl. and -цев/-ок in the gen. pl.; португа́лец *Portuguese* has fem. португа́лка and nom. pl. in -льцы/-лки; австри́ец *Austrian* has fem. австри́йка and nom. pl. австри́йцы/австри́йки; бельги́ец *Belgian* has fem. бельги́йка and nom. pl. бельги́йцы/бельги́йки; швед *Swede*, fem. шве́дка, серб *Serb*, fem. се́рбка, венгр *Hungarian*, fem. венге́рка, белору́с *Belorussian*, fem. белору́ска, францу́з *Frenchman*, fem. францу́женка, грек *Greek*, fem. греча́нка; ту́рок *Turk* (fem. турча́нка) has nom. pl. ту́рки and irreg. gen. pl. ту́рок; грузи́н *Georgian* (fem. грузи́нка) has irreg. gen. pl. грузи́н; поля́к *Pole* (fem. по́лька) has gen. pl. поля́ков (fem. по́лек); чех *Czech* (fem. че́шка) gen. pl. че́хов (че́шек). A person born or living in Moscow is a москви́ч (fem. москви́чка), in Kiev—киевля́нин (fem. киевля́нка), in Rostov—ростовча́нин (fem. -ча́нка), in Odessa—одесси́т(ка), in Leningrad—ленингра́дец (fem. -дка), and in Baku—баки́нец (fem. баки́нка).

INDECLINABLE NOUNS

There are several indeclinable neuter nouns, such as пальто́ (from Fr. *paletot*) *overcoat*, шоссе́ (Fr. *chaussée*) *highroad*, такси́ *taxi*, меню́ *menu*, амплуа́ *role*, *line*, all of foreign origin and all ending in vowels; such nouns referring to male beings are masculine, as маэстро *maestro*, дэнди *dandy*, those referring to female beings are feminine, as лэ́ди *lady* (title), Ки́ти *Kitty*. The indeclinable names of animals and birds, e.g. кенгуру́ *kangaroo* and колибри *humming-bird* are normally masculine, but are feminine when a female is specifically denoted.

Indeclinable also are surnames in -о, -ых, and -их, such as Черны́х, Дурново́, and Жива́го; masculine surnames in -ко (of Ukrainian origin), as Шевче́нко, Короле́нко, Франко́, are usually not declined, but may be declined like a feminine in -ка in the gen., dat., instr., and loc.

Surnames in -о, -ых, -их, and -ич, and common nouns used as surnames (like Го́голь, Бонда́рь), as well as surnames of non-Slavonic origin, have no special feminine forms and, when they refer to a woman, are indeclinable.

§ 45. Diminutives, Augmentatives, &c.

The extensive use of diminutives in Russian is one of the first things that strike the beginner. Some words are only used in their diminutive forms, e.g. ло́дка *boat*, from which a further diminutive has had to be formed, viz. ло́дочка *little boat*. In many cases the diminutives are really meant to imply smallness, but very frequently they are used merely as a means of expressing affection, politeness, or good humour, and then they are difficult, if not impossible, to translate into English. For example, a waiter usually refers to plates and spoons as таре́лочки and ло́жечки irrespective of their size, and the guard on a train asks to see your биле́тики *little tickets*; this does not imply that the tickets are small, but merely expresses the good humour of the guard and the fact that he would not refuse a drink if you offered him one.

The commonest diminutive endings that express smallness or endearment, or a combination of both, are:

Masculine

-ик	e.g. до́мик *small house, cottage*
-чик	e.g. чемода́нчик *small suit-case*
-ьчик	e.g. колоко́льчик *little bell*
-ек	e.g. вну́чек *grandson*
-ёк	e.g. ручеёк *small stream, rivulet*
-ок	e.g. дружо́к *friend*
-ец	e.g. бра́тец *brother*
-ёнок	e.g. котёнок *kitten* (cf. § 41, Obs. 4)
-онок	e.g. медвежо́нок *young bear*

Masculine 'double' diminutives end in -очек, -ечек, and
-ичек, for instance лист *leaf* has dim. листо́к and 'double'
dim. листо́чек *tiny little* (or *dear little*) *leaf*; the 'double' dim.
дружо́чек (from друг *friend*) is even more affectionate
than the dim. дружо́к; василёчек *little cornflower* is diminutive of василёк *cornflower*, which is itself a diminutive form
derived from Васи́лий *Basil*; нож (dim. но́жик) has
'double' dim. но́жичек *little knife*.

Feminine

-ка	e.g. кни́жка	*small book, booklet*
-ица	e.g. части́ца	*particle* (from часть *part*)
-ушка	e.g. де́вушка	*young woman, girl*
and -ца (rare)	e.g. крепостца́	*small fort*

Feminine 'double' diminutives end in -очка, -ечка, -ичка.
For example, шля́па *hat* usually refers to a man's hat; the
dim. шля́пка refers to a woman's hat, while the 'double'
dim. шля́почка denotes a woman's small and elegant hat.
The diminutive of кни́га *book* is кни́жка which denotes
a book which is small or has few pages, as a bank-book
or identity card, while its 'double' diminutive implies
extreme smallness or affection—кни́жечка *tiny little book*

or *dear little book*. Сестра́ *sister* has 'double' dim. сестри́чка, which is more affectionate than the dim. сестри́ца.

Neuter

-ко	e.g. о́блачко	*small cloud*
-цо́	c.g. письмецо́	*short letter*
-це	e.g. блю́дце	*small dish, saucer*
-ошко	e.g. око́шко	*small window*
-ышко	e.g. пёрышко	*little feather*
-юшко	e.g. по́люшко	*little field*

'Double' diminutives in -ечко can be formed from some neuter nouns, but very few are in common use, e.g.

сло́во — словцо́ — слове́чко *word*.

As an example of the varieties of diminutives that can be formed from one word, take the word де́ва *virgin* (only used in such expressions as Орлеа́нская де́ва *the Maid of Orleans*, or ста́рая де́ва *an old maid*):

деви́ца *spinster*; also де́вица (in folk poetry) *maiden*
де́вка *girl* (sc. *common girl, wench*, a very derogatory term)
де́вочка *girl* (up to about 16 years)
де́вушка *girl* (from 16 till marriage, or till about 30)
девчо́нка *young girl, slut* (contemptuous)
девчу́рка ⎱ *little girl* (affectionate)
девчу́шка ⎰

The following terminations imply good humour or affection specifically:

-ушка, -ушко, -юшка, -юшко, -енька, -онька.

The following terminations are usually derogatory:

-ишка, -ишко, -ёнка, -онка, -ашка, -ёшка, and some times -ка (esp. masc.).

The following suffixes are called augmentative, as they usually imply largeness, often combined with ugliness or clumsiness:

-ище (m.,n.), -ища, -ина (m.,f.)

The following suffixes are called singulative; they single out one individual from a group:

-ин, -ина, -инка,

as	англича́нин	*Englishman*	from англича́не	*the English*
	роси́нка	*dew-drop*	from роса́	*dew*
	жемчу́жина	*pearl*	from же́мчуг	*pearls* (coll.)

THE DECLENSION OF THE PRONOUNS

§ 46. The inflexions of these are for the most part different from those of the nouns, though there are a few points of similarity, e.g. the dat. pl. always ends in -м and the instr. pl. always in -ми.

Personal Pronouns

я *I*, ты *thou*, он *he*, она́ *she*, оно́ *it*, мы *we*, вы *you*, они́ *they*

Singular

N.	я	ты	он	она́	оно́
G.	меня́	тебя́	его́	её	его́
D.	мне	тебе́	ему́	ей	ему́
A.	меня́	тебя́	его́	её	его́
I.	мной	тобо́й	им	е́ю	им
L.	мне	тебе́	нём	ней	нём

Plural

N.	мы	вы	они́
G.	нас	вас	их
D.	нам	вам	им
A.	нас	вас	их
I.	на́ми	ва́ми	и́ми
L.	нас	вас	них

OBSERVATIONS

1. There is a reflexive personal pronoun, себя, which has no nominative and is declined alike in the singular and plural:

G.	себя
D.	себе́
A.	себя
I.	собо́й
L.	себе́

i.e. just like тебя

The peculiarity of its use is that it can be applied to any of the three persons; e.g. я люблю́ себя *I love myself*, ты лю́бишь себя *thou lovest thyself*; он or она́ лю́бит себя *he or she loves himself or herself*. It also occurs in a few very common idioms, e.g. само́ собо́ю разуме́ется *that is understood* (lit. *itself understands itself by itself*); она́ хороша́ собо́й *she is a good-looking woman* (lit. *she [is] nice by (in respect of) herself*); он живёт себе там . . . *he goes on living there* (here the unstressed себе implies that he goes on living in his own way, paying little attention to others, but not necessarily that he is a recluse); та́к себе *fairly, averagely*.

When joined to an ordinary transitive verb (making it reflexive), the form себя is replaced by -ся or -сь; e.g. разуме́ется *of course* (lit. *it understands itself*), э́то не де́лается *that is not done*; нахожу́сь *I am [situated]* (lit. *I find myself*). But the addition of the reflexive pronoun by no means always makes the word passive; Russian has many reflexive verbs which are middle in meaning, e.g. боя́ться *to fear*, бою́сь *I fear*; нра́вится *it pleases*, мне нра́вится *(it) pleases me, I like (it)*; он мо́ется *he is washing* (sc. *himself*), я оде́нусь *I shall dress* (sc. *myself*). Cf. §§ 100, 110.

2. The nominatives он, она́, оно́, они́ did not belong

originally to eró, &c., and were originally not personal pronouns at all, but demonstrative pronouns, meaning *yonder*, which went out of regular use as demonstrative pronouns and were borrowed to supply the place of the lost nominatives of eró, &c.

3. It is important to notice that the acc. sing. of он and of онó is always eró, i.e. the gen. sing., even when the thing to which it refers is inanimate. Similarly the acc. pl. of они́ is always их.

4. The initial и- in им, их, and и́ми is pronounced *yi*- by some Russians.

5. The genitives of the personal pronouns (eró, её, and их) are used also to express *his*, *her*, and *their*, and, not being adjectives in Russian, they do not decline, e.g. *his father* in Russian is eró отéц (or отéц eró), *to her father* is её отцý, &c. See also § 47, Obs. 2.

6. The oblique cases of он, онá, and они́, when directly governed by a preposition,[1] are always prefixed by the letter н; the reason is that certain prepositions originally ended in н, and this letter was borrowed by other preposiitons which did not end in it. Subsequently, when the prepositions lost their final н, it stuck to the pronouns beginning with a vowel, where it has remained. As the locative case in Russian is never used without a preposition, the locative of this pronoun is always prefixed by н. When a preposition precedes eró, её, or их in their meaning of *his*, *her*, or *their*, and therefore does not directly govern the pronoun, the н is omitted.

Examples: с ним *with him*, от них *from them*, о нём *about him*, but от их отцá *from their father*, о eró брáте *about his brother*, &c.

---

[1] This rule does not apply to most prepositions derived from other parts of speech (благодаря́, вопреки́, всле́дствие, навстре́чу, согла́сно, &c.) nor does it apply to prepositional phrases.

7. For the instr. sing. мной, тобóй, and собóй the longer forms мнóю, тобóю, and собóю are sometimes used, especially when they are not preceded by a preposition. When preceded by a preposition, the instr. sing. fem. is more often ней than нéю.

8. In correspondence all cases of the pronoun вы are always spelt with an initial capital for politeness.

9. The unstressed particle же (or ж) often follows the personal pronouns and expresses identity, or gives emphasis to the pronoun; e.g. я твой брат, я́ же и твой друг *I am thy brother, I too am thy friend*; кто вам дал э́то? он — а э́то? óн же *who gave you this? he [did] — and this? he [did] too.* Егó же printed in front of titles means *by the same author*.

же can also mean *but* and *after all*, e.g. онá сидéла дóма, óн же пошёл в кинó *she stayed at home, but he went off to the pictures*, вы́ же знáете э́то *after all, you know that*.

10. The particle -то affixed to the personal pronouns also expresses identity or gives emphasis, e.g. óн-то э́то сдéлал *it was he who did it*.

§ 47. Possessive Pronouns

The declension of these resembles that of он: мой, моя́, моё; мой *my, mine*; твой, твоя́, твоё; твой *thy, thine*; свой, своя́, своё; свой *one's own*; наш, нáша, нáше; нáши *our, ours*; ваш, вáша, вáше; вáши *your, yours*.

	Singular			Plural
	Masc.	Fem.	Neut.	All Genders
N.	мой	моя́	моё	мой
G.	моегó	моéй	моегó	мойх
D.	моемý	моéй	моемý	мойм
A.	= N./G.	мою́	моё	= N./G.
I.	мойм	моéй	мойм	мойми
L.	моём	моéй	моём	мойх

	Singular			*Plural*
N.	наш	на́ша	на́ше	на́ши
G.	на́шего	на́шей	на́шего	на́ших
D.	на́шему	на́шей	на́шему	на́шим
A.	= N./G.	на́шу	на́ше	= N./G.
I.	на́шим	на́шей	на́шим	на́шими
L.	на́шем	на́шей	на́шем	на́ших

OBSERVATIONS

1. Твой and свой are declined exactly like мой, and ваш exactly like наш.

2. Свой can be used of any of the three persons, but it can only be used when it refers to possession by the subject of the clause; e.g. я люблю́ своего́ отца́ can only mean *I love my father* (though it is also possible to say я люблю́ моего́ отца́), whereas я люблю́ его́ отца́ means *I love his father*. Again, он лю́бит свою́ сестру́ = *he loves his (own) sister*, свою́ referring to possession by the subject of the clause, whereas он лю́бит его́ сестру́ = *he loves his* (i.e. *someone else's*) *sister*.

3. The acc. sing. masc. and the acc. pl. of all three genders of these pronouns follow the rule of the masculine nouns: when referring to an animate being, the acc. is like the gen., otherwise it is the same as the nom.

4. For the instr. sing. fem. мое́й, твое́й, свое́й, на́шей, and ва́шей, the longer forms мое́ю, твое́ю, свое́ю, на́шею, and ва́шею are also used, but much less often.

5. It is important to notice that the nom. pl. мои́ (also твои́ and свои́) is a disyllable, pronounced *ma-í*; the nom. sing. masc. мой (as also твой and свой), on the other hand, is a diphthong, pronounced as one syllable, *moy*, to rhyme with English *boy* (but see § 21).

6. In correspondence all cases of the pronoun ваш are spelt with an initial capital for politeness.

7. The particle же (or ж) following the possessive pronouns expresses identity of ownership, e.g. чей э́тот дом? мой — а чьё э́то по́ле? моё же *whose is this house? mine — and whose is this field? also mine.*

8. The particle -то emphasizes the pronouns, e.g.

мо́й-то дом? [*do you mean*] my *house?*

§ 48. Demonstrative Pronouns

The declension of these is similar for the most part to that of the possessive pronouns, though differing from it in some important particulars.

тот, та, то; те that (yonder)

	Singular			*Plural*
	Masc.	Fem.	Neut.	All Genders
N.	тот	та	то	те
G.	того́	той	того́	тех
D.	тому́	той	тому́	тем
A.	= N./G.	ту	то	= N./G.
I.	тем	той	тем	те́ми
L.	том	той	том	тех

э́тот, э́та, э́то; э́ти this (or that)

	Singular			*Plural*
	Masc.	Fem.	Neut.	All Genders
N.	э́тот	э́та	э́то	э́ти
G.	э́того	э́той	э́того	э́тих
D.	э́тому	э́той	э́тому	э́тим
A.	= N./G.	э́ту	э́то	= N./G.
I.	э́тим	э́той	э́тим	э́тими
L.	э́том	э́той	э́том	э́тих

сей, сия́, сие́ (or сё); сий *this*[1]

	Singular			Plural
	Masc.	Fem.	Neut.	All Genders
N.	сей	сия́	сие́	сий
G.	сего́	сей	сего́	сих
D.	сему́	сей	сему́	сим
A.	= N./G.	сию́	сие́	= N./G.
I.	сим	сей	сим	си́ми
L.	сём	сей	сём	сих

OBSERVATIONS

1. For the instr. sing. fem. той, э́той, and сей the longer forms то́ю, э́тою, and се́ю are also used occasionally.

2. Of these three pronouns э́тот is the most often, сей the most seldom used. Э́то is frequently used where we should say *that* in English, e.g. in very common phrases such as:

что э́то тако́е?	*what's that?* (lit. = *what this such?*)
кто э́то тако́й?	*who's that?* (lit. = *who this such?*)
э́то бы́ло давно́	*that was long ago*
э́то о́чень хорошо́	*that's very nice*
э́то наш дом	*that is our house*

Э́то can also mean *these* or *those* when it is the subject of a sentence and very frequently has this meaning, e.g.:

э́то мои́ де́ти *these* (or *those*) [*are*] *my children*

The neuter pronoun то is often used as an enclitic particle affixed to a noun or another pronoun, irrespective of gender or number, to emphasize or to differentiate, e.g.

[1] See Obs. 9.

в то́м-то и де́ло or то́-то и есть *that's just the point*; до́мто мой *the house is mine* (sc. *even if something else is not*).

(The first of these is not to be confused with the similar idiom in Obs. 6.)

In some dialects this pronoun can be affixed to any noun (but only in the nom.) agreeing with it in gender and number, thus acquiring the value of a definite article.

3. Тот is used specially frequently in argument, e.g. то, что . . . *that which . . .*; it is also used as a definite article before a relative clause, e.g. тот ма́льчик, кото́рому я дал де́ньги *the boy to whom I gave the money*. In conversation, however, even *that (yonder)* is frequently rendered by э́тот (with or without the addition of там *there*), e.g. э́тот дом [там] — наш *that house over there is ours*.

4. Тот is especially common in composition with prepositions, e.g. пото́м *then* (lit. *upon that*), зате́м *then* (lit. *behind that*), потому́ *therefore* (lit. *according to that*), кро́ме того́ *besides* (lit. *outside that*), зато́ *on the other hand* (lit. *for that*).

5. Тот and э́тот are often used for *the former* and *the latter* respectively.

6. It is important to notice the very common idiom то и де́ло (lit. *and that's the thing*), which means *incessantly, constantly*.

7. The expression не то́ is used in the following idioms:

я не то́ хоте́л сказа́ть	*I didn't mean that*
э́то уже́ не то́	*that's quite different*
не то́..., не то́...	*not exactly . . ., nor quite . . .*
не то́, что́бы...	*not exactly . . .*

(+ adj., noun, or past tense)

не то́, or а то́, used by itself at the beginning of a sentence means *or else, otherwise*.

Notice also:

э́то не тóт дом	*that's the wrong house*
я принёс не тý кни́гу	*I've brought the wrong book*

8. Тот followed by the enclitic же means *the same* and is very common, e.g. в тóм же дóме *in the same house*, тогó же áвтора (gen.) *by the same author*, с тéм же мáльчиком *with the same boy*; the words оди́н и *one and* often precede, e.g. в однóм и тóм же гóроде *in one and the same town*, в однó и тó же врéмя *at one and the same time*. The phrase тóже, written as one word, means *also*, e.g. мы тóже *we also*. Э́тот же *this same* and такóй же *of the same kind, similar*, are also common.

9. Сей is seldom used except in a few phrases, in which it is extremely common, e.g. сейчáс *presently, at present, just now* (lit. *this instant*, though the noun час has changed its meaning and in modern Russian means *hour*), сейчáс же *immediately*; сию́ минýту *this minute, this instant*; сегóдня *today* (lit. *of this day*); до сих пор *till now* (lit. *till these times*); то да сё *this and that*; ни то, ни сё *neither one thing nor the other*; при сём 'enclosed' (lit. *in the presence of this*).

10. The pronouns такóй and таковóй (also э́такий, colloq.) *such* are declined like adjectives, see § 53.

11. The pronoun óный *that (yonder)*, whose short forms supplied the personal pronouns он, &c., is now obsolete and only common in the phrase во врéмя óно *in days of yore* (lit. *into that time*).

§ 49. Relative and Interrogative Pronouns

кто *who*; что *what*

N.	кто	что
G.	когó	чегó
D.	комý	чемý
A.	когó	что
I.	кем	чем
L.	ком	чём

Russian has a special pronoun for *whose* which is declined throughout : чей, чья, чьё; чьи :

	Singular			*Plural*
	Masc.	Fem.	Neut.	All Genders
N.	чей	чья	чьё	чьи
G.	чьего́	чьей	чьего́	чьих
D.	чьему́	чьей	чьему́	чьим
A.	= N./G.	чью	чьё	= N./G.
I.	чьим	чьей	чьим	чьи́ми
L.	чьём	чьей	чьём	чьих

кото́рый *which*, како́й and (now rare) каково́й *of what sort*, are declined like adjectives, q.v. Кто is grammatically masculine singular, although it may refer to a female or to more than one animate being, e.g. те, кто пришёл, получи́ли пре́мии *those who came received prizes.*

OBSERVATIONS

1. The pronoun чей is of course most frequently used in the nominative, e.g. чей э́то дом? *whose house is this?* But the other cases are not uncommon, e.g. чью жену́ он лю́бит? *whose wife does he love?*

2. Что is used to introduce a subordinate clause in all those cases where in English we use the conjunction *that*, i.e. after all verbs of asserting, denying, believing, thinking, perceiving, feeling, &c., e.g. я говорю́, что он дура́к *I say that he [is] a fool.* It is also used in the expressions for *why* and *because*, e.g. отчего́? *why?* (lit. *from what*), оттого́ что *because* (lit. *from that what*), почему́? *why?* (lit. *according to what*), потому́ что *because* (lit. *according to that what*). It is important to notice the difference in meaning between these two expressions: отчего́ = *from what natural cause*, e.g.

отчего́ сего́дня так темно́? *why is it so dark today?* отчего́ вы так бле́дны? *why are you so pale?* but почему́ = *on what ground, for what reason,* e.g. почему́ вы говори́те э́то? *why do you say this?* почему́ он жела́ет ви́деть меня́? *why does he wish to see me?* Of course there are many questions in which either of the two words could be used indifferently, and the answer to both is usually introduced by потому́ что, which is far commoner than оттого́ что. There is yet another expression for *why,* viz. заче́м? which means *after what?, trying to get what?* or *with what object?* e.g. заче́м вы пришли́? *why* (sc. *with what object*) *have you come?* The answer to such a question is introduced by зате́м, что́бы (or more often merely by что́бы) *in order that,* which is followed by the past tense or the infinitive; the particle бы affixed to что was once part of the verb быть *to be.* Что́бы (sometimes written чтоб) means *in order that,* and is also used to introduce wishes, when it is always followed by the past tense, e.g. что́бы э́то бы́ло так! *[would] that it were so!* Что as a conjunction (= *that*) is an enclitic and has no stress, being pronounced *shtə*; что́бы may have a slight stress on the first syllable or be pronounced without stress, as a proclitic.

3. Кто is often used by itself to express *whoever* or *anyone who,* e.g. кто уме́ет говори́ть по-норве́жски, тот понима́ет и по-да́тски *anyone who knows Norwegian can also understand* (lit. *that one also understands*) *Danish,* кто говори́т э́то, врёт *whoever says that, lies.* Another very common way of expressing *whoever* and *whatever* is to add бы ни to кто and что, which are then always followed by the past tense; it is important to notice that the particle ни does not imply negation. Note that бы is placed immediately after кто/что and ни immediately before the verb, e.g. кто́ бы мне ни говори́л э́то, я ему́ не пове́рю *whoever should tell me this, I shall not believe him;* что́ бы вы ни де́лали, я не бу́ду вас

слу́шать *whatever you do, I shall not listen to you*; and the following common idioms may be mentioned: кто́ бы то ни́ был *whoever it may be*, что́ бы то ни́ было *whatever it may be*, and во что́ бы то ни ста́ло *cost what it may* (lit. *into whatever it should become*). This use of бы must be carefully distinguished from that mentioned in the preceding paragraph. *Whoever . . . not* can only be translated by кто не . . ., e.g. кто не вида́л Москвы́, не зна́ет Сове́тского Сою́за *anyone who has not seen Moscow, does not know the Soviet Union*. Other common ways of expressing *whoever* and *whatever* are paraphrases such as *everyone who, all that*, &c.

4. Кто . . ., кто . . . is commonly used to express *some . . . others . . .*, e.g. все уе́хали, кто на маши́не, кто по желе́зной доро́ге *they all left, some by car, some by train*.

5. The emphatic particle же or ж very frequently follows кто, что, чей, and како́й, and gives these pronouns the meaning *who then? &c.*; e.g. кого́ же вы ви́дели? *who then was it you saw, whom then did you see?* что́ же случи́лось? *what then has happened?* Что ж by itself, as an exclamation, is commonly used with concessive force to introduce a statement and means approximately *well, then*. Another very common idiom is ну, так что ж? *well, what about it?* Yet another is что ж де́лать? *what's to be done? que voulez-vous?*

Отчего́ же? and почему́ же? are also common in argument, meaning *but why?*

6. Что (or что ж) is also frequently used in colloquial speech to introduce a question; in this use it is never strongly stressed; e.g. что, вы пое́дете в э́том году́ за грани́цу? *well, will you go abroad this year?* что and чего́ may also (colloquially) mean *why?*, e.g. что мне са́хару не даёшь? *why haven't you given me some sugar?* чего́ ты кричи́шь? *why are you shouting?*

§ 50. Determinative Pronouns

сам, сама́, само́; са́ми *self*

	Singular			Plural
	Masc.	Fem.	Neut.	All Genders
N.	сам	сама́	само́	са́ми
G.	самого́	само́й	самого́	сами́х
D.	самому́	само́й	самому́	сами́м
A.	= N./G.	самоё[1]	само́	= N./G.
I.	сами́м	само́й	сами́м	сами́ми
L.	само́м	само́й	само́м	сами́х

весь, вся, всё; все *all, the whole*

	Singular			Plural
	Masc.	Fem.	Neut.	All Genders
N.	весь	вся	всё	все
G.	всего́	всей	всего́	всех
D.	всему́	всей	всему́	всем
A.	= N./G.	всю	всё	= N./G.
I.	всем	всей	всем	все́ми
L.	всём	всей	всём	всех

OBSERVATIONS

1. Вся́кий and ка́ждый *every, each*, ино́й *some*, and друго́й *other*, are declined like adjectives, q.v. For оди́н *only, alone* (lit. *one*) see Numerals, § 60.

---

[1] Colloquially also саму́.

2. *One another* is expressed in Russian by the phrase друг друга, which is the nom. and acc. sing. of the word друг, which originally meant *second* or *other*, but in modern Russian has acquired the meaning of *friend*; e.g. они́ о́чень лю́бят друг дру́га *they love one another very much*, мы пошли́ друг с дру́гом *we went [there] together* (lit. *we went one with the other*), они́ зна́ли друг о дру́ге *they knew about each other*.

3. Сам can be used either before or after the noun it qualifies, e.g. я сам *I myself* (masc.), я сама́ *I myself* (fem.), сам мини́стр *the minister himself*, я ви́дел самого́ мини́стра *I saw the minister himself*, он мне самому́ сказа́л э́то *he told this to me myself, to me personally* (sc. *not through anybody else*), мы са́ми *we ourselves*, он сам or сам он *he himself*, само́ собо́ю *by* or *of itself*, also *of course*, я сам себе́ купи́л э́то *I bought this for myself*, она́ сама́ себе́ купи́ла э́то *she [herself] bought this for herself*.

4. It is not difficult to distinguish the use of сам from that of the reflexive pronoun себя́, but сам is very easily confused with the longer form of the same word (са́мый *the very*, which is declined like an adjective), e.g. тот же са́мый челове́к *the very same man*, but сам челове́к *the man himself*; в са́мом це́нтре го́рода *in the very centre of the town*, but в само́м го́роде *in the town itself*. Са́мый is also used in the formation of the superlative degree of adjectives, see § 59.

5. The use of весь does not present any difficulties, e.g. весь го́род *the whole town*, весь день (acc.) *all day long*, всю ночь (acc.) *all night long*, она́ вся в чёрном *she [is] all in black*. It is important to notice a few very common idioms in which the word occurs: совсе́м *quite* (lit. *with all*), всё равно́ *it's all the same* (lit. *all even*), всего́ хоро́шего, всего́ лу́чшего! (*I wish you*) *everything good, all the best!* (gen. after implicit verb of wishing), всего́ *altogether, in all*, e.g. всего́

пять мест багажа́ *five pieces of luggage in all*, всё or всё вре́мя *continually* (this is an adverbial use of the neuter acc.), e.g. она́ всё пла́кала *she kept on crying all the time*, он всё кричи́т *he keeps on shouting, he is always shouting*, я всё пишу́ *I am always writing*, он всё хо́дит в теа́тр *he is always going to the theatre*. It is important to be sure of pronouncing весь with a soft c and close e, as there is another word вес having the open e-sound and hard c, meaning *weight*.

N.B. весь год = *the whole year* (sc. *Jan. to Dec.*), whereas *a whole year* (sc. *any 365 days*) = це́лый год, &c.

§ 51. Indefinite Pronouns
никто́ *no one*, ничто́ *nothing*

These are declined exactly like кто and что, but it is to be observed that the nom. and acc. ничто́ is rarely used, the genitive being almost always required by the associated negative verb, either expressed or implied, e.g. ничто́ не ве́чно *nothing lasts for ever*, что с ва́ми? ничего́! *what is the matter with you? nothing!* э́то ничего́ *it doesn't matter*. When the verb associated with either of these pronouns is expressed, it must always be negatived, since the ни- of the pronouns is not a true negative and the не before the verb is required to complete the negation, e.g. никто́ не пришёл *no one has come*, я никому́ не сказа́л *I have told no one*, он мне ничего́ не́ дал *he has given me nothing*.

The following common idioms may be noticed: никого́ не вида́ть *there is no one to be seen*, ничего́ не вида́ть *there is nothing to be seen*, никого́ (or ничего́) не слыха́ть *no one (or nothing) can be heard*.

There is an idiomatic adverbial use of the word ничего́ in which it means *tolerably, fairly well*, e.g. как вы себя́ чу́вствуете? ничего́ *how do you feel [yourself]? fairly well*. This can also be used with a verb, e.g. он игра́ет ничего́ *he plays fairly well*, but of course with a negatived verb the meaning would be negative, e.g. он ничего́ не игра́ет *he is not playing anything*.

When никто́ and ничто́ are used with a preposition, the latter is inserted between the ни- and the pronoun, and the expression written as three words, e.g. ни с ке́м *with no one*, ни о чём *about nothing*, ни за что́ *not for anything*, как бу́дто ни в чём не быва́ло *quite unruffled, as if nothing had happened*.

никако́й   *of no kind*

is declined like an adjective, see § 53.

ниче́й   *nobody's, no one's*

is declined like чей, чья, чьё; see § 49. The acc. fem. is used in the adverb вничью́, e.g. кома́нды сыгра́ли вничью́ *the teams drew, it was a draw, a dead heat*.

не́кого   *there is no one to . . .*
не́чего   *there is nothing to . . .*

не- can be prefixed to any case of кто and что except the nominative, and the words thus formed are written as one word, except when used with a preposition, which, just as in the case of никто́, is inserted between the two elements; they are always followed by the infinitive. It is important to remember that the stress is always on the не-, while in никто́ and ничто́ it is always on the last syllable; e.g. не́чего де́лать! or де́лать не́чего! *there is nothing to be done!* (lit. *to do*; a common idiom), говори́ть не́чего! *there is nothing more to be said! there's no denying it!* не́кому сказа́ть *there is no one to tell*, не́ с кем говори́ть *there is no one to talk to* (lit. *with*), не́ о чем писа́ть *there is nothing to write about*, and the common idioms: не́ за что *don't mention it* (cf. the French *il n'y pas de quoi*), не́зачем (written as one word) + infin. *there is no object, no point in . . .*

не́кто *someone* (nom.), не́что[1] *something* (nom. & acc.)

are only used in this form and have no other cases; e.g. я слы́шал не́что стра́нное о нём *I have heard something strange about him,* он мне не́что сказа́л *he told me something,* вошёл не́кто в си́нем костю́ме *someone in a blue suit came in,* не́кто Ша́нцев *a certain Shantsev, someone called Shantsev.*

It is important not to confuse these two words with не́кого and не́чего. Much commoner expressions for *someone* and *something* are those mentioned below.

не́который *a certain, some,* is declined like an adjective, see § 53.

кто́-то *someone,* что́-то *something,* кто́-нибудь *someone or other, anyone* (lit. *whoever it be*), что́-нибудь *something or other, anything,* кто́-либо *anyone,* что́-либо *anything.*

These are all declined exactly like кто and что. The difference in meaning between кто́-то and кто́-нибудь is slight but very important. Кто́-то is the more definite of the two and can never mean *anyone;* кто́-нибудь is less definite and means *someone* or *anyone.* The difference is best illustrated by examples: кто́-то идёт *someone* (*a definite person*) *is coming,* кто́-то пришёл *someone has come,* кто́-то сказа́л мне *someone told me,* кто́-то там [*there is*] *someone there,* кто́-то позвони́л *someone has rung,* я дал кому́-то кни́гу, но не по́мню кому́ *I gave the book to someone* (*a definite person*), *but I don't remember to whom,* она́ сказа́ла мне что́-то о нём *she told me something about him* (sc. *a definite thing, but I am not telling you what*), я ви́жу что́-то там *I see something there,* он написа́л что́-то на бума́жке *he wrote something on the piece of paper,* рубль с чём-то *a rouble with something* (i.e. *over a rouble, I forget how much*), говя́дина с чём-то *beef with something* (i.e. *something with it, I forget what*), я куплю́ вам что́-то *I shall*

---

[1] Pronounce *n'échtə,* not *n'ɛshtə.*

buy you something (sc. *I know what, but I am not telling you*), but спроси́те кого́-нибудь *ask someone* (*anyone at all*), до́ма-ли кто́-нибудь? or кто́-нибудь до́ма? *is anyone at home?* я спрошу́ у кого́-нибудь сове́та *I shall ask advice from someone,* я куплю́ вам что́-нибудь *I shall buy you something or other* (sc. *I don't know myself exactly what*), на́до сде́лать что́-нибудь *something must be done* (sc. *I don't know what*), наде́ньте что́-нибудь тепле́е *put something warm[er] on* (sc. *it doesn't matter what*), ску́шайте что́-нибудь ещё *eat something more,* скажи́те мне что́-нибудь о себе́ *tell me something about yourself,* сыгра́йте нам что́-нибудь! *do play us something!*

Кто́-либо and что́-либо are still more indefinite, e.g. спроси́те кого́-либо, а он ска́жет вам . . . *ask anyone you like, and he will tell you . . .*, да́йте кому́-либо *give [it] to anyone you like.*

Ко̀е-кто́ *a few people,* ко̀е-что́ *a little, a few things.* These are also declined exactly like кто and что; they imply indefiniteness of number or quantity, e.g. я спра́шивал ко̀е-кого́ *I have been asking one or two people,* он сказа́л мне́ ко̀е-что́ о себе́ *he told me a few things about himself,* я узна́л ко̀е-что́ о нём *I have found out a thing or two about him.* A governing preposition must be placed between the two parts and the expression written as three words, e.g. я ко̀е с ке́м говори́л об э́том *I have been talking to one or two people about this.*

Любо́й *any you like* and ко̀е-како́й *some . . . or other* (mostly used in pl., *a few*) are declined like adjectives, see § 53. The oblique cases of ко̀е-како́й may be preceded by a preposition or the preposition may be placed between the two parts, e.g. с ко̀е-каки́ми веща́ми or ко̀е с каки́ми веща́ми *with a few things.*

ко̀е-кто́, ко̀е-что́, and ко̀е-како́й are sometimes written with кой- instead of ко̀е-.

DECLENSION OF THE ADJECTIVES

§ 52. The adjective in Russian has two forms, the shorter and the longer; the shorter is called the predicative, the longer the attributive form.

The predicative form of the adjective is used almost solely when the adjective is the predicate of a sentence; in form it is exactly like a noun, and except in popular poetry it occurs only in the nominative, e.g. дом хорош *the house* [*is*] *nice* (cf. German: *das Haus ist schön*), моя сестра больна *my sister* [*is*] *ill*, море глубоко *the sea* [*is*] *deep*, они живы *they* [*are*] *alive*, я очень рад *I* [*am*] *very glad*, он счастлив *he* [*is*] *happy*, она здорова *she* [*is*] *well*, я виноват *I* [*am*] *to blame*, я виновата *I* [*am*] *to blame* (if a woman is speaking). But whenever an adjective qualifies a noun, the longer or attributive form must be used; this is an amalgamation of the shorter form with the pronominal endings. There is a hard and a soft declension, as in the case of nouns.

§ 53. Hard Declension

Example: белый *white*

	Singular			*Plural*
	Masc.	Fem.	Neut.	All Genders
N.	белый	белая	белое	белые
G.	белого	белой	белого	белых
D.	белому	белой	белому	белым
A.	=N./G.	белую	белое	= N./G
I.	белым	белой	белым	белыми
L.	белом	белой	белом	белых

Hard Declension when the ending is stressed

Example: молодой *young*

	Singular		
	Masc.	Fem.	Neut.
N.	молодой	молодая	молодое

after which it is declined exactly like бе́лый, except that
the stress is always on the ending, and on the first syllable
of the ending when this is disyllabic, e.g.

G.　молодо́го　　　молодо́й　　　молодо́го

OBSERVATIONS

1. The rule with regard to the acc. sing. masc. and acc.
pl. of the adjective is the same as that which governs the
acc. sing. of masc. and the acc. pl. of all nouns, i.e. for an
animate being it is always the same as the genitive and for
an inanimate object the same as the nominative.

2. There is an alternative longer form for every fem. instr.
sing., e.g. бе́лой or бе́лою.

3. The nom. sing. and pl. of the attributive form of the
adjective arose through the affixing of the lost pronominal
nominatives (which are given in scientific works as jь ja je,
pronounced *i ya ye*, whose place in the pronominal declension has been taken by он она́ оно́) to nominatives of the
predicative form, thus бе́лый (until 1917 spelt бѣ́лый) is
derived from the old predicative бѣлъ+и (< jь), бе́лая <
бѣла+я (< ja), бе́лое < бѣло + e (< je). The form of the
nom. sing. masc. is really of Old Bulgarian origin and has
forced its way not only into Russian orthography but also
into the living language, thanks to the influence of the Old
Bulgarian ecclesiastical tradition on the Russian language;
the truly Russian form of the nom. sing. is -ой, which is still
retained in adjectives which are stressed on the ending, e.g.
молодо́й *young*.

The other cases were formed analogously, though the
process is clearer in some than in others, e.g. бе́лого <
бѣла+его, бе́лую < бѣлу+ю (< ju, an old acc. of the
pronoun ja), бе́лому < бѣлу+ему; in the other cases more
drastic changes by analogy or contraction have occurred.

4. Several common adjectives (including surnames) are

stressed on the ending and declined like молодо́й, e.g. передово́й *foremost*, золото́й *golden*, больно́й *ill*, седо́й *grey-haired*, большо́й *big*, Толсто́й *Tolstoy* (while the adjective то́лстый *thick, fat*, is declined like бе́лый). It may be mentioned that almost all Russian surnames are adjectives and must be declined adjectivally (see also § 55), e.g. сочине́ния Толсто́го *the works of Tolstoy*, я знал Толсто́го *I knew Tolstoy*, я зна́л графи́ню Толсту́ю *I knew Countess Tolstoy*, Толсты́е *the Tolstoys*, у Толсты́х *at the house of the Tolstoys*. Also the ordinals второ́й *second*, шесто́й *sixth*, седьмо́й *seventh*, восьмо́й *eighth*, and сороково́й *fortieth*.

5. Many adjectives ending in -ый and -о́й are used substantivally, e.g. столо́вая (sc. ко́мната) *dining-room*, гости́ная *drawing-room*, кладова́я *store-room*, насеко́мое[1] *insect*, живо́тное[1] *animal*, портно́й *tailor*, полице́йский *policeman*, рядово́й *private (soldier)*, ломово́й *carter*, больно́й *the patient, the invalid* (fem. больна́я), чужо́й *stranger*, мясно́е *meat-course, joint*, борза́я *wolf-hound* (lit. *swift*), and very commonly the names of streets, e.g. Не́вский[2] (sc. проспе́кт) *the Nevsky* (broad avenue in Leningrad), Морска́я (sc. у́лица) *Sea Street*.

6. (*a*) Adjectives with nom. sing. masc. in **-кий, -гий**, and **-хий** are declined like кре́пкий *strong*, viz.:

	Singular			Plural
	Masc.	Fem.	Neut.	All Genders
N.	кре́пкий	кре́пкая	кре́пкое	кре́пкие
G.	кре́пкого	кре́пкой	кре́пкого	кре́пких
D.	кре́пкому	кре́пкой	кре́пкому	кре́пким
A.	= N./G.	кре́пкую	кре́пкое	= N./G.
I.	кре́пким	кре́пкой	кре́пким	кре́пкими
L.	кре́пком	кре́пкой	кре́пком	кре́пких

[1] Neut. adjectives used substantivally and denoting animate beings have acc. sing. as nom. sing., but acc. pl. as gen. pl.

[2] See Observation 6 below.

The ы of the case-endings of all adjectives whose stems both end in к, г, or х, and are unstressed, became и, e.g. кре́пкий, кре́пким, кре́пкие, &c. (but кре́пкая, кре́пкое, кре́пкого, &c.). So also: ма́ленький *little*, вели́кий *great*, широ́кий *broad*, ди́кий *wild*, стро́гий *severe*, ти́хий *quiet*, у́зкий *narrow*, коро́ткий *short*, сла́дкий *sweet*, and many others; this category includes nearly all adjectives derived from the names of towns and countries, e.g. моско́вский *of Moscow, Muscovite*, ленингра́дский *of Leningrad*, ки́евский *of Kiev, Kievan*, ри́жский *of Riga*, ру́сский *Russian*, неме́цкий *German*, францу́зский *French*, англи́йский *English*, and innumerable surnames (which are often derived from the names of places), e.g. Чайко́вский *Chaikovski*, Достое́вский *Dostoyevski*, Го́рький *Gorki*, &c. It must not be forgotten that all such surnames are declined throughout, e.g. the wife, unmarried daughter, or sister of a man called Оболе́нский is Оболе́нская, and his whole family together are the Оболе́нские, &c.

(*b*) When an adjective whose stem ends in к, г, or х, is stressed on the ending, then it is declined like молодо́й, except that ы changes to и in the masc. and neut. instr. sing. and throughout the plural, e.g. городско́й *belonging to the town, municipal* (nom. pl. городски́е), дорого́й *dear* (instr. sing. дороги́м, nom. pl. дороги́е, &c.); also those surnames of this category, as well as adjectives derived from place-names, which are stressed on the ending, e.g. Трубецко́й *Trubetskoy* (nom. pl. Трубецки́е *the Trubetskoys*), Шаховско́й *Shakhovskoy* (fem. Шаховска́я), тверско́й *of Tver'*, &c.

In this category are included those adjectives whose stems end in ж and ш, and which are stressed on the ending, e.g. the very common words большо́й *big* (большо́й дом *a large house*, большо́й люби́тель иску́сства *a great lover of art*, больши́е *the big ones, the grown-ups*), чужо́й *strange* (sc. *not known*), *someone else's* (чужи́е *strangers*, у чужи́х *among strangers*, в чужо́м до́ме *in another person's house*).

To sum up, adjectives with nom. sing. masc. in **-ко́й, -го́й, -хо́й, -жо́й,** and **-шо́й** are declined like большо́й, viz.

		Singular		*Plural*
	Masc.	Fem.	Neut.	All Genders
N.	большо́й	больша́я	большо́е	больши́е
G.	большо́го	большо́й	большо́го	больши́х
D.	большо́му	большо́й	большо́му	больши́м
A.	= N./G.	большу́ю	большо́е	= N./G.
I.	больши́м	большо́й	больши́м	больши́ми
L.	большо́м	большо́й	большо́м	больши́х

7. The pronouns that are declined like adjectives all belong to the hard declension: ка́ждый *every*, кото́рый *which*, не́который *a certain, some*, are declined exactly like бе́лый; вся́кий *of every kind, every*, не́кий (g.s. masc. не́коего) *a certain*, and э́такий *such, like that*, go like кре́пкий; тако́й *of such a kind, such, like that*, тако́й же *of the same kind*, како́й *of what kind*, никако́й *of no kind, no sort of*, друго́й *other*, and ко̀е-како́й *some, a few* decline like большо́й; and любо́й *any* [*you like*], ино́й *some*, and the nearly obsolete каково́й *of what kind* and таково́й *of such a kind*—like молодо́й.

These words are so common that a few examples of their use are added: ка́ждый день (acc.) *every day*, на ка́ждом шагу́ *at every step*, ка́ждую мину́ту (acc.) *every minute*, ка́ждый зна́ет *everyone knows*, кото́рый но́мер? *which number?* кото́рый час? *what time is it?* (lit. *which hour?*), в кото́ром часу́? *at what time (hour)?* кото́рое (or како́е) сего́дня число́? *what date is it today?* не́которые нахо́дят, что . . . *some consider* (lit. *find*) *that . . .*, не́кий (or не́кто) Ивано́в *a certain* [*man called*] *Ivanov*, до не́которой сте́пени *to a certain extent*, в не́котором ро́де *in a certain way, in some ways*, вся́кий вздор *all sorts of rubbish*, вся́кая кни́га *each book*, вся́кие кни́ги *all sorts of books*, вся́кая вся́чина *odds and ends*, он тако́й ми́лый! *he is such a nice man!* (N.B. Russians never say так ми́лый for *so nice*; так cannot be used with the attrib. form of an adjective), она́ така́я ми́лая *she is such a nice woman*, они́ таки́е ми́лые *they are such nice people*, в таку́ю пого́ду *in such weather*, в тако́е вре́мя *at such a time*, таки́м о́бразом *in this way* (lit. *by such manner*), which often comes to mean *by doing this*, до тако́й сте́пени *to such an extent*, тако́го ро́да *of such a sort* (e.g. тако́го ро́да пье́са *a play of this sort*; the nominative often follows the genitive, but can also precede it), в тако́м слу́чае *in such a case*, which comes to mean *since this is so, therefore*, в тако́м ро́де *in that manner, of that sort*, тако́го же ро́да, в тако́м же ро́де *of the same kind, in the same manner*, како́й он интере́сный! *how interesting he is!* кака́я интере́сная кни́га! *what an interesting book!* како́й краси́вый ма́льчик! *what a handsome boy!* кака́я хоро́шая пого́да! *what nice weather!* кака́я плоха́я (скве́рная) пого́да! *what bad (nasty) weather!* каки́м о́бразом? *in what manner?* каки́е но́вости сего́дня? *what news is there today?* како́го ро́да? *of what sort?* (e.g. э́то како́го ро́да пье́са? *what sort of a play is this?*), како́й вздор! *what rubbish!* така́я кни́га, каку́ю вы написа́ли *a book of the sort which you have written*, друго́й раз *another time*, друго́го ро́да *of another sort*, на друго́й день *the next day*, други́м о́бразом *in another way*, други́е говоря́т *others say*, никаки́м о́бразом *in no way*, ни в како́м слу́чае *in no case, in no eventuality*, which comes to mean *whatever happens*, ни за каки́е ко́-ври́жки *not for anything in the world* (lit. *not for any sort of little cakes*), в кото́рой кварти́ре (or в кото́рой из кварти́р) вы живёте? *in which flat do you live?* кото́рый час? *what is the time?* ко̀е-каки́е но́вости *some items of news*, ино́й раз *sometimes*, ины́е говоря́т *some say* (originally ино́й meant *one*, cf. German *ein* and the old word иноро́г (now единоро́г) *unicorn*, but it acquired the meaning *other*, e.g. иностра́нцы *people of another country,* i.e. *foreigners,* ко̀е-каки́е кни́ги *a few books of sorts, some books or other,* в любо́й час *at any hour,* в любо́м го́роде *in any town you like to mention,* в любо́й день [*on*] *any day you like.*

There is a strange idiomatic use of каково́й as an interjection, usually expressing admiration of somebody's performance, and it is always used in the predicative form, even though it precedes the noun, e.g. каков ру́сский бале́т! *well, what do you think of the Russian ballet? isn't it fine!* какова́ певи́ца! *isn't she a splendid singer!* како́в урожа́й! *what a fine harvest!*

The difference between како́й and како́в is this: како́й means *of what kind, which sort,* e.g. э́то како́е вино́? *what kind of wine is that?* како́в means *of what quality, how do you like?,* e.g. каково́ вино́? *how do you like this wine?*

The pronoun тако́в (short forms only) is used in the idiom . . . и был тако́в! *and off he went (disappeared)!*

The full forms каково́й and таково́й are seldom used; in meaning they are similar to како́й and тако́й, but they are used rather as pure pronouns, referring to a noun in a previous sentence, and not as adjectives. Тако́й-то means *such and such, a certain,* see pp. 108-9.

Како́й-нибудь and како́й-то correspond in meaning to кто́-нибудь, кто́-то, ка́к-нибудь, ка́к-то, e.g. како́й-нибудь го́род *any town* [*you like to mention*], в како́м-то ца́рстве *in a certain kingdom* (as the opening of a fairy-tale).

8. It is not absolutely true that all adjectives have both predicative and attributive forms. The two words рад (fem. ра́да) *glad* and гора́зд *capable* have only the predicative form. To render their meaning when used attributively synonyms such as ра́достный *joyful,* спосо́бный *capable* must be used.

Conversely, большо́й *big* has no predicative form, and if used predicatively the synonym вели́кий takes its place,

e.g. Россия велика *Russia is large*; further, all words with
the suffixes -ск- and -ов-, e.g. русский *Russian*, городской
of the town, деловой *concerning business*, and adjectives denoting materials, e.g. золотой *of gold*, каменный *of stone* or
brick, have only the attributive form, e.g. *he is Russian* он
русский, *my ring is gold* моё кольцо золотое, *this bridge is
made of stone* этот мост каменный. Otherwise most adjectives have both forms, though sometimes only one form is
appropriate in a given sense. Generally, however, the long
form relates an object to others of its kind and denotes its
particular and permanent quality; whereas the short form
denotes its quality (especially a temporary state) without
reference to other objects of its class. The short form must
be used when the quality is limited by another word, as in
the last two examples below.

Examples: глубокая река *a deep river*, река глубока *the
river is deep* (sc. *now*), река глубокая *the river is a deep one* (sc.
as rivers go), он [так] мил *he is [so] nice*, он [такой] милый
he is [such] a nice (sc. man), эта книга интересная *this book
is an interesting one*, эта книга интересна [для детей] *this
book is interesting [for children]*, он был болен ангиной *he was
ill with tonsillitis*.

To form a short from a long adjective it is only necessary
to cut off the endings -ый (or -ой), -я, and -e for the sing.
and -e for the pl., e.g. милый *nice* has short forms мил,
мила, мило, милы. The only difficulty in forming the
short form occurs in the masc. sing. when, after -ый is cut
off, a group of consonants would be left. A 'mobile' e (ё
when stressed) is frequently inserted, e.g. больной *ill*—
болен, умный *clever*—умён, спокойный *calm*—спокоен;
but note достойный *worthy*—достоин. Before -к the mobile
vowel is o, e.g. крепкий *strong*—крепок; лёгкий *light*—
лёгок (except when unstressed after ж and ш, when it is e,
e.g. тяжкий *heavy*—тяжек). 'Mobile' o also occurs in a few

other words: злой *bad-tempered, wicked*—зол; по́лный *full*—
по́лон. Adjectives in -анный have a short masc. sing. form
in -ан, e.g. образо́ван *educated* (fem. образо́ванна); as regards adjectives in -енный, the short masculine of some
ends in -ен, as легкомы́слен *frivolous* (fem. легкомы́сленна)
while that of most ends in -енен, as соверше́нен *perfect*
(fem. соверше́нна). In many other cases, however, groups
of consonants are left without any vowel being inserted,
e.g. до́брый *good-natured*—добр; мёртвый *dead*—мёртв;
чёрствый *hard* (especially *stale*, of bread)—чёрств.

9. It has been pointed out that in the language as it is
spoken and written the predicative form of the adjective
only occurs in the nominative; in folk-poetry, however,
the other cases are also found, usually as fixed epithets for
certain things, and recur with great frequency.

10. When the first element of a compound adjective has
a stem ending in a hard consonant (except ж, ш, and ц) it
is linked to the second element by the vowel -о-, e.g. бѣло-
ка́менный *of white stone*, свѣтлозелёный *light-green*, тёмно-
се́рый *dark-grey*, ру́сско-неме́цкий слова́рь *a Russian-German
dictionary*, Во́лго-донско́й кана́л *the Volga-Don Canal*.

§ 54. Soft Declension

There is also a soft declension of adjectives, though the
number of adjectives belonging to it is small.

Example: си́ний, си́няя, си́нее *dark blue*

	Singular			Plural
	Masc.	Fem.	Neut.	All Genders
N.	си́н**ий**	си́н**яя**	си́н**ее**	си́н**ие**
G.	си́н**его**	си́н**ей**	си́н**его**	си́н**их**
D.	си́н**ему**	си́н**ей**	си́н**ему**	си́н**им**
A.	= N./G.	си́н**юю**	си́н**ее**	= N./G.
I.	си́н**им**	си́н**ей**	си́н**им**	си́н**ими**
L.	си́н**ем**	си́н**ей**	си́н**ем**	си́н**их**

It will be observed that all the soft vowels in the endings of the soft declension correspond to the hard vowels in those of the hard declension, i.e. и to ы, я to a, ю to y, e to o.

OBSERVATIONS

1. The rule with regard to the acc. sing. masc. and acc. pl. of all genders is the same as for the hard adjectives.

2. There is an alternative longer form for every instr. sing. fem., e.g. си́ней or си́нею.

3. The predicative form of the soft adjectives is practically never used.[1]

4. There are no soft adjectives with the stress on the ending.

5. There are a few soft adjectives which are used substantively, e.g. ле́ший *wood-demon*, пере́дняя (sc. ко́мната) *ante-room, entrance-hall*, го́нчая (sc. соба́ка) *sporting-dog* (cf. Obs. 7), бу́дущее (sc. вре́мя) *future*.

6. Common adjectives that decline like си́ний are only a few in number, and are therefore given here: и́скренний *sincere*, дома́шний *domestic*, ли́шний *superfluous*, вну́тренний *internal*, вне́шний *external*, зде́шний *belonging to this locality, local*, та́мошний *belonging to that place*, за́дний *rear*, пере́дний *front*, ве́рхний *upper*, сре́дний *middle, average*, ни́жний *lower*, сосе́дний *neighbouring*, да́льний *distant*, кра́йний *extreme*, после́дний *last*, ны́нешний *of nowadays, present*, тепе́решний *present* (lit. *of now*), тогда́шний *former* (lit. *of then*), пре́жний *former*, дре́вний *ancient*, ра́нний *early*, по́здний *late*, у́тренний *morning*, вече́рний *evening*, вчера́шний *yesterday's*, сего́дняшний *today's*, за́втрашний *tomorrow's*, весе́нний (and ве́шний) *vernal*, ле́тний *summer*, осе́нний *autumnal*, зи́мний *winter*.

---

[1] Except the very common forms: хоро́ш, хороша́, хорошо́, pl. хороши́; горя́ч, -ча́, -чо́, -чи́; свеж, -жа́, -жо́, -жи́; похо́ж, похо́жа, похо́же похо́жи, see Obs. 7.

7. Adjectives ending in **-жий, -ший, -чий,** and **-щий** are declined somewhat differently from си́ний, since the laws of Russian spelling do not allow я and ю to follow ж, ш, ч, or щ, and they are replaced by the hard vowels a and y. As some of these adjectives are very common, one is given here in full:

хоро́ший *nice, good*

	Masc.	Fem.	Neut.	Plural All Genders
		Singular		
N.	хоро́ший	хоро́шая	хоро́шее	хоро́шие
G.	хоро́шего	хоро́шей	хоро́шего	хоро́ших
D.	хоро́шему	хоро́шей	хоро́шему	хоро́шим
A.	= N./G.	хоро́шую	хоро́шее	= N./G.
I.	хоро́шим	хоро́шей	хоро́шим	хоро́шими
L.	хоро́шем	хоро́шей	хоро́шем	хоро́ших

The following common words are declined in the same way: горя́чий *hot* (as in горя́чей воды́ (gen.) *some hot water*), све́жий *fresh*, похо́жий *like*, ме́ньший *lesser, smaller*, бо́льший *greater, bigger*, вы́сший *higher*, ни́зший *lower*, лу́чший *better*, as well as superlatives in -ший and participles in -чий and -щий.

8. When the first element of a compound adjective has a stem ending in a soft consonant or in ж, ш, or щ, it is linked to the second element by the vowel -e-, e.g. средневеко́вый *medieval* (cf. сре́дние века́ *the Middle Ages*), древнегре́ческий *ancient Greek*, огнеупо́рный *fireproof*, большегла́зый *large-eyed* (cf. большо́й глаз).

The adjective derived from Ни́жний Но́вгород, the former name of the city now called Го́рький, was нижего́родский.

9. Special attention must be called to the plurals мно́гие *many*, and немно́гие *few*, which are declined like хоро́шие; the respective singulars are adverbs, мно́го *much* and нем-

нóго *a little*; нéсколько *some* is similarly used except in the nom. pl., for which нéкоторые is invariably substituted (cf. p. 102), e.g.

мнóгие нахóдят, что ... *many people consider* (lit. *find*) *that* ... (it would be impossible to use the adverb here), тóлько у (óчень) немнóгих свой самолёты *only a (very) few have their own aeroplanes*, в нéскольких слу́чаях *in several cases*. The neuter singular мнóгое *many things* is also used, e.g. во мнóгом э́та кни́га мне нрáвится *there is much in this book that pleases me* (lit. *this book in much*).

§ 55. Declension of Possessive Adjectives

There are a large number of these adjectives in Russian, and as the declension is different from that of the ordinary adjective, an example is given in full:

Петрóв belonging to Pyotr (Peter)

	Masc.	Singular Fem.	Neut.	Plural All Genders
N.	Петрóв	Петрóва	Петрóво	Петрóвы
G.	Петрóва	Петрóвой	Петрóва	Петрóвых
D.	Петрóву	Петрóвой	Петрóву	Петрóвым
A.	= N./G.	Петрóву	Петрóво	= N./G.
I.	Петрóвым[1]	Петрóвой	Петрóвым[1]	Петрóвыми
L.	Петрóвом[2]	Петрóвой	Петрóвом[2]	Петрóвых

Петрóв may mean *belonging to Pyotr*, as in Петрóв дом *Pyotr's house*, or it may be the surname *Petrov*, which is an ellipse standing for Петрóв сын *Pyotr's son* (cf. *Peterson*); Петрóва may mean *belonging to Pyotr* (fem.), as in Петрóва

[1] When used as a place-name, the instrumental ends in -ом, as под Петрóвом *near Petrovo*; cf. also за Ки́евом *beyond Kiev*.

[2] When used as a noun (surname or place-name) the locative ends in -е. as in о Петрóве *about Petrov or Petrovo*.

сестрá *Pyotr's sister*, or, by itself, it means *Miss* or *Mrs Petrov* (cf. *Mrs Peterson*); Петрóво may mean *belonging to Pyotr* (neut.), or it may be the name of a village originally called after Pyotr, in which case the word селó is understood; Петрóвы may mean *belonging to Pyotr* (pl.), or it may mean, by itself, *the Petrovs*. Surnames and names of places formed in this way are endless, e.g. Пáвлов *belonging to Pavel (Paul)* or [*Mr*] *Pavlov*, Пáвлова *Mrs* or *Miss Pavlov*, Ивáнов[1] *Ivan's (John's)*, Попóв *Popov* (from поп *priest*; a common surname); they include many fantastic surnames of sometimes curious origin, e.g. Абрикóсов (lit. *apricot's*), Филосóфов (*philosopher's*), Грибоéдов (*mushroom-eater's*). There are also a number of possessive adjectives formed (by the suffix -ев; -ёв if stressed) from soft stems, e.g. Андрéй *Andrew* makes Андрéев; Васúлий *Basil*—Васúльев; Сергéй *Sergius*—Сергéев; note Яковлев from the hard stem Яков *James*. Possessive adjectives from stems ending in -ц, -ж, -ш, -ч, and -щ have the -ев suffix when the suffix is not stressed; when the word-stress falls on the suffix the spelling will be -óв or -ёв, e.g. Стáрцев, Подъячев, Мáлышев, but Кузнецóв, Шишóв, Чижóв, Пугачёв, Хрущёв. In this category are included names of not purely Russian origin, such as Лéрмонтов *Lermontov* and Тургéнев *Turgenev*.

It is from these words that the well-known Russian patronymics are formed, by adding to them -ич (which is a suffix with the meaning *son of*) for the masculine and -на for the feminine; and it must be remembered that it is by the first (or Christian) name, together with the patronymic that all Russians address one another, unless they are strangers, or intimate friends or relations. For example, if

---

[1] As a possessive adjective proper, Ивáнов is stressed on the second syllable; but the majority of people with this surname now call themselves Иванóв, Иванóва.

a man's surname is Попо́в, his father's first name Пётр
(*Peter*), and his own first name Па́вел (*Paul*), his friends
will call him Па́вел Петро́вич; let us say that his wife's
name is А́нна (*Anne*) and her father's first name Ива́н
(*John*), then her full name will be А́нна Ива́новна Попо́ва,
and her friends will call her А́нна Ива́новна. In speech
the suffix (-ов- or -ев-) of most patronymics is not pronounced unless it bears the word-stress; -ович is pronounced
as -ыч, -евич as -ич, -овна as -на, and -евна as -(ь)на; note
that -е́евич sounds like -е́ич, and -е́евна as -е́вна. Other
contractions take place in fast speech, of which the following pronunciations are typical: 'а́нныва́нна' for А́нна
Ива́новна, 'па́лыва́ныч' for Па́вел Ива́нович, 'ве́ран-
дре́вна' for Ве́ра Андре́евна, 'васи́лья́колич' for Васи́лий
Я́ковлевич, алекса́налекса́ныч for Алекса́ндр Алекса́н-
дрович.

Besides, there are a large number of names and words
which form their possessive adjectives in -ин, -ын, instead
of in -ов (the case-endings are exactly the same), e.g.
Фома́ (*Thomas*) makes Фоми́н (*Thomas's*), fem. Фомина́,
and patronymics Фоми́ч (*Thomas's son*) and Фоми́нична
(*Thomas's daughter*); Илья́ (*Elias*)—Ильи́н (patronymics
Ильи́ч, fem. Ильи́нична); Ники́та (*Nikita*)—Ники́тин
(patronymics Ники́тич, fem. Ники́тична). This category
includes such words as же́нин *wife's* (from жена́ *wife*),
му́жнин *husband's* (муж), се́стрин *sister's* (сестра́), бра́тнин
brother's (брат), and those derived from diminutives, e.g.
Серёжин from Серёжа = Серге́й *Sergius*, Са́шин from
Са́ша = Алекса́ндр *Alexander* or Алекса́ндра *Alexandra*.

These and the innumerable Russian surnames and
place-names formed with this suffix take the same endings
as Петро́в, e.g. о Ники́тином до́ме *about Nikita's house*, о
Ники́тине *about [Mr] Nikitin*. Пу́шкин (the name of the
poet and of the town called after him) has instr. Пу́шки-

ным (the man) and Пу́шкином (the town); its locative is Пу́шкине (man and town). Similarly, с Ле́ниным *with Lenin* (the man) but под Ле́нином *near Lenino* (a village).

Госпо́дь *the Lord* makes Госпо́день, Госпо́дня, Госпо́дне; and Христо́с *Christ* makes Христо́в, &c.

All these possessive adjectives have the predicative (short) form for some of their cases, but they can always be used attributively, as се́стрина ко́мната [*my*] *sister's room*.

Finally there is a large category of possessive adjectives formed mostly from names of animals, but including some others; these have only the attributive form. As the declension is rather different from the others, an example is given:

ры́бий fish's (from ры́ба fish)

	Masc.	Fem.	Neut.	Plural All Genders
	Singular			
N.	ры́бий	ры́бья	ры́бье	ры́бьи
G.	ры́бьего	ры́бьей	ры́бьего	ры́бьих
D.	ры́бьему	ры́бьей	ры́бьему	ры́бьим
A.	= N./G.	ры́бью	ры́бье	= N./G.
I.	ры́бьим	ры́бьей	ры́бьим	ры́бьими
L.	ры́бьем	ры́бьей	ры́бьем	ры́бьих

Common words belonging to this category are во́лчий *wolf's* (волк), ли́сий *fox's* (лиса́), соба́чий *dog's* (соба́ка), коша́чий *cat's* (ко́шка), медве́жий *bear's* (медве́дь), пти́чий *bird's* (пти́ца), Бо́жий *God's* (Бог), челове́чий *man's, human* (челове́к), and the ordinal тре́тий *third*, e.g. тре́тьего кла́сса *of the third class*, в тре́тьем кла́ссе *in the third class*, and the idiom тре́тьего дня *the day before yesterday* (lit. *of the third day*).

§ 56. Note on the Terminations of Adjectives

Adjectives ending in -оватый or -еватый correspond in meaning to English adjectives in *-ish*, e.g. желтоватый *yellowish* (жёлтый *yellow*).

Those ending in -áстый often imply largeness of the attribute, бородáстый *with a big beard* (бородá *beard*, бородáтый *bearded*). Those in -истый imply possession of a certain attribute: душистый *fragrant* (духи (pl.) *scent*).

The terminations -енький and -онький are diminutive and affectionate (cf. Eng. *nice little . . .*), e.g.

маленький *little, small* (from мáлый, which is seldom used except in the sense of *brief, concise*)

бéленький *nice white little . . .* (cf. бéлый)

слáденький *nice and sweet* (cf. слáдкий)

N.B. хорóшенький means *pretty* (cf. онá хорошá собóй *she is good-looking*)

The terminations -ёхонький, -óхонький, -ёшенький are used in popular style to imply completeness; very often the adjective in its original form precedes the other; these forms are generally used predicatively:

сыт-сытёхонек *absolutely satiated* (*with food*)

один-одинёшенек *quite alone*

THE COMPARISON OF ADJECTIVES

§ 57. The Predicative Comparative

The comparative is formed by cutting off the -ый or -ой of the attributive form of the adjective and adding -ее (or -ей) to the stem.

The word thus formed is indeclinable and can only be used predicatively or postpositively (see § 58).

In the case of words of more than three syllables the comparative can be formed by using the positive preceded by the adverb бóлее *more*, as in English, e.g. *more intelligible*.

Comparison can be expressed in three ways:

(1) by the conjunction

чем[1] (instr. sing. of что) or ⎫
нéжели[1]   ⎬ *than*
                     ⎭

followed by the nominative,[2]

and (2) by the genitive of comparison (but never after a form compounded with бóлее), e.g.

длúнный *long*, comparative длиннéе

эта пáлка длиннéе, чем та *this stick* [*is*] *longer than that*

красúвый *beautiful*, comp. красúвее

мой цветы́ красúвее вáших (gen.) *my flowers* [*are*] *more beautiful than yours*

прямóй *straight*, comp. прямéе

эта дорóга прямéе той (gen.) *this road* [*is*] *straighter than that*

or (3) purely predicatively:

эта пáлка длиннéе *this stick* [*is the*] *longer*

When the comparative is followed by the pronouns егó *his*, её *hers*, or их *theirs*, a conjunction should be used, e.g.

мой дом красúвее, нéжели егó *my house* [*is*] *more beautiful than his* (красúвее егó could mean *more beautiful than he* [*is*]).

An example of an adjective of more than three syllables:

образóванный *cultured*; predic. comp. бóлее образóван (fem. бóлее образóванна) or образóваннее, e.g.

мы бóлее образóванны, чем онú *we* [*are*] *more cultured than they* [*are*]

To express *less* the adverb мéнее is used, followed where necessary by чем or нéжели, e.g.

---

[1] These words are always preceded by a comma.

[2] But note such constructions as емý лéгче, чем мне *it is easier for him than for me* and у негó пáлка длиннéе, чем у меня́ *he has a longer stick than I have.*

они́ ме́нее образо́ванны, чем мы *they are less cultured than we [are]*

After a form compounded with ме́нее (as with бо́лее), the genitive of comparison cannot be used.

A large number of adjectives, however, form their comparatives by adding -e, not -ee, to their stems. Most of these have stems ending in consonants (к, г, х, т, д, ск, ст) which are liable to be changed by a following e into ч, ж, ш, or щ. A few lose a syllable in the comparative or have a corresponding comparative with unrelated stem (cf. English bad—worse, good—better).

Many of these adjectives are extremely common but, for the sake of completeness, the following list contains also a few that are little used or colloquial.

бли́зкий	*near*	бли́же
бога́тый	*rich*	бога́че
бо́йкий	*lively, glib*	бо́йче[1]
большо́й⎫ вели́кий[2]⎭	*big*	бо́льше
высо́кий	*high*	вы́ше
вя́зкий	*glutinous*	вя́зче
га́дкий	*nasty*	га́же
ги́бкий	*flexible*	ги́бче
гла́дкий	*smooth*	гла́же
глубо́кий	*deep*	глу́бже
глухо́й	*deaf*	глу́ше
го́рький	*bitter* (taste) *bitter, cruel* (misfortune)	го́рче го́рше
гро́мкий	*loud*	гро́мче
густо́й	*dense; thick* (liquid, gas)	гу́ще

[1] Also бойче́е (colloq.).

[2] But вели́кий in the sense of [*morally*] *great* has only the compound comparative: бо́лее вели́к[ий].

далёкий ⎫ да́льний ⎭	*distant*	да́льше
дешёвый	*cheap*	деше́вле
до́лгий	*long* (of time)	до́льше
дорого́й	*dear*	доро́же
дурно́й	*bad, evil* *ugly, doltish*	ху́же дурне́е
е́дкий	*caustic*	е́дче
жа́ркий	*hot*	жа́рче
жёсткий	*hard*	жёстче
жи́дкий	*liquid; thin* (liquid, gas)	жи́же
зво́нкий	*sonorous*	зво́нче[1]
коро́ткий	*short*	коро́че
кра́ткий	*brief*	кра́тче
кре́пкий	*strong*	кре́пче
круто́й	*steep*	кру́че
лёгкий	*light, easy*	ле́гче
ло́вкий	*adroit*	ло́вче[2]
ма́ленький ⎫ ма́лый ⎭	*small, little*	ме́ньше
ме́лкий	*small, petty, shallow*	ме́льче
молодо́й	*young*	моло́же
мя́гкий	*soft*	мя́гче
ни́зкий	*low*	ни́же
отло́гий	*gently sloping*	отло́же
пло́ский	*flat*	пло́ще
плохо́й	*bad*	ху́же[3]
поло́гий	*gently sloping*	поло́же
просто́й	*simple*	про́ще
пры́ткий	*nimble*	пры́тче
ре́дкий	*rare, sparse*	ре́же
ре́зкий	*sharp*	ре́зче

[1] Also звонче́е (colloq.).   [2] Also ловче́е (colloq.).
[3] Also пло́ше (pop., rare).

сла́дкий	*sweet*	сла́ще
ста́рый	*old* (of animate beings)	ста́рше
	old (of things)	старе́е
стро́гий	*strict, severe*	стро́же
сухо́й	*dry*	су́ше
твёрдый	*hard*	твёрже
те́рпкий	*astringent*	те́рпче
ти́хий	*quiet, still*	ти́ше
то́лстый	*thick, stout*	то́лще
то́нкий	*thin, slender*	то́ньше
туго́й	*tight, taut*	ту́же
у́зкий	*narrow*	у́же[1]
хлёсткий	*scathing*	хлёстче
хоро́ший	*good, nice*	лу́чше
худо́й	*bad*	ху́же
	lean, thin	худе́е
ча́стый	*frequent;* *thick* (hair, &c.)	ча́ще
чи́стый	*clean, pure*	чи́ще
ши́бкий	*brisk*	ши́бче
широ́кий	*wide*	ши́ре
я́ркий	*bright*	я́рче

As can be seen from the table, a few adjectives have two forms of the simple comparative; in four cases the form depends on the meaning it is desired to convey.

Го́рький has comparative го́рче in reference to taste, but го́рше in connexion with fate or disaster.

Дурно́й *bad* borrows its comparative ху́же from худо́й, but in the meaning of *ugly* the 'regular' form дурне́е is used.

Ста́рше is normally used when referring to the age of persons and animals, as Ива́н ста́рше Ви́ктора *Ivan is older than Victor*; it can also refer to seniority, as in полко́вник

---

[1] Not to be confused with уже́ *already*.

ста́рше майо́ра *the colonel is senior to the major*. When referring to things, the usual form is the 'regular' comparative старе́е, which may also be applied to animate beings in advanced old age, as: его́ дед старе́е и седе́е моего́ *his grandfather is older and greyer than mine*.

Худо́й has two meanings: (1) *thin* (of human beings and animals) and (2) *bad*; the comparative in the first meaning is худе́е and in the second ху́же. *Fat* (of human beings and animals) is usually rendered by по́лный (comp. полне́е) *full*, though то́лстый is also used, less politely, of human beings.

As regards the stress, the following rule may be mentioned: all so-called irregular comparatives (ending in -e, not -ee) are stressed on the penultimate. Of the others, adjectives of two syllables are stressed on the -е́е in the comparative; also the monosyllabic злой *wicked*—зле́е. Adjectives of more than two syllables keep the stress in the comparative where it was in the positive, e.g. краси́вый *beautiful*—краси́вее; to this rule there are a few exceptions:

здоро́вый	*healthy*	comp.	здорове́е
холо́дный	*cold*	,,	холодне́е
горя́чий	*hot*	,,	горяче́е

(горя́чий is used of substances, e.g. water, food, and of the emotions; жа́ркий is used especially of the weather; тёплый *warm* (comp. тепле́е) can be applied to anything.

Many adjectives have no simple form for the predicative comparative, only a compound (analytical) comparative formed with бо́лее, e.g. Ива́н бо́лее горд, чем Пётр *Ivan is prouder* (lit. *more proud*) *than Pyotr*.

Besides го́рдый *proud*, рад *glad*, and гора́зд *clever*, such adjectives include all those ending in -ский, -ско́й, -овый, -ово́й, -жий; many, formed from verbs, ending in -чий, -ший, -щий, -лый, and -ло́й; also ра́нний *early*, по́здний

late, ли́шний *superfluous*, вели́кий in the sense of *great,*
больно́й *ill,* кро́вный *thoroughbred, vital,* and others.

Adjectives in -кий (not suffix -ский), -гий, and -хий,
apart from those included in the table above, usually form
their comparatives with бо́лее; however, by analogy with
such words as гро́мкий and кре́пкий, simple comparatives
(in -че, -же, and -ше) are occasionally found in colloquial
and popular speech, e.g. де́рзкий (comp. бо́лее де́рзкий,
бо́лее де́рзок, or де́рзче) *impudent,* жа́лкий (жа́льче) *piti-
ful,* жу́ткий (жу́тче) *terrible,* кро́ткий (кро́тче) *meek,*
мы́лкий (мы́льче) *lathering easily,* ро́бкий (ро́бче) *timid,*
хо́дкий (хо́дче and (pop.) ходче́) *swift; marketable,*
хру́пкий (хру́пче) *frail,* чу́ткий (чу́тче) *sensitive;* ве́тхий
decrepit makes бо́лее ве́тх[ий] or, very rarely, ве́тше.

Ме́рзкий *vile* has comp. мерзе́е.

§ 58. The Attributive Comparative

When the comparative is used not for purposes of strict
comparison, but as an attributive adjective expressing a
higher degree of a quality than is expressed by the positive, the form in -ee, &c., cannot be employed. Instead, it
must be expressed either by using бо́лее with the positive
form of the adjective, or by another special form which
some adjectives possess; this form ends in -ший, -шой, or
-е́йший and is declined like хоро́ший (or like молодо́й).

As only a few adjectives are commonly used in this form
a full list is given:

высо́кий *high, tall,* comp. вы́сший, e.g.

　вы́сшее образова́ние *higher education*
　вы́сшее ка́чество *superior quality*

ни́зкий *low,* comp. ни́зший, e.g.

　ни́зшие це́ны *lower prices*
　ни́зший эта́ж *a lower floor*

ста́рый *old*, comp. ста́рший, e.g.

   ста́рший брат *elder* (or *eldest*) brother
   ста́рший лейтена́нт *Senior Lieutenant*

молодо́й *young*, comp. мла́дший (from the cognate stem млад-), e.g.

   мла́дшая дочь *younger* (or *youngest*) daughter

хоро́ший *good, nice*, comp. лу́чший (from another stem), e.g.

   лу́чшие магази́ны *superior shops*
   лу́чшее ка́чество *better* (or *best*) quality

худо́й, плохо́й *bad*, comp. ху́дший, e.g.

   ху́дшие сорта́ *inferior sorts*

большо́й *big*, comp. бо́льший, e.g.

   бо́льшей ча́стью *for the most (greater) part*
   бо́льшие города́ *the larger towns*

ма́лый, ма́ленький *little*, comp. ме́ньший *lesser* and меньшо́й *younger*, e.g.

   ме́ньшая часть *the lesser (smaller) part*
   меньшо́й сын *the younger* (or *youngest*) son

да́льний *distant*, comp. дальне́йший, e.g.

   дальне́йшее разви́тие *the subsequent (further) development*

(There is no attributive comparative formed from далёкий apart from бо́лее далёкий.)

The form in -е́йший and -а́йший possessed by several other adjectives is a superlative, see § 59.

In almost all cases except those mentioned above, the attributive comparative can be and is usually expressed by бо́лее with the positive form, e.g.

э́то бо́лее краси́вая шля́па *this is the prettier hat*
в бо́лее удо́бном кре́сле   *in a more comfortable arm-chair*

Rather + the positive or comparative is expressed by по-
with the predicative comparative form; this compound
form is placed *after* the noun it describes and is indeclinable, e.g.

мне нужна́ па́лка подлинне́е	*I need a rather long[er] stick*
я хочу́ что́-нибудь полу́чше	*I want something [rather] better*
покажи́те мне шля́пы подо-ро́же	*show me [rather] more expensive hats*
у нас нет ничего́ подеше́вле	*we have nothing cheaper*
он лю́бит чай посла́ще	*he likes his tea [rather] sweet*

§ 59. The Superlative

The superlative can be expressed in several ways; the
commonest way is to use the pronoun са́мый with the positive. In the case of an adjective with a special comparative
form in -ший (see § 58), this form may be used alone as a
superlative, or са́мый may be used either with this form or
with the positive.

са́мый краси́вый	*most beautiful*
са́мый некраси́вый	*ugliest*
са́мый кре́пкий	*strongest*
са́мый сла́бый	*weakest*
са́мый большо́й	*biggest*
са́мый ма́ленький	*smallest*
са́мый плохо́й ⎫ [са́мый] ху́дший ⎬ са́мый скве́рный ⎭	*worst*
[са́мый] лу́чший	*best*
[са́мый] ста́рший	*eldest*
[са́мый] мла́дший	*youngest*
[са́мый] вы́сший	*highest*
[са́мый] ни́зший	*lowest*, &c.

These can be used either attributively or predicatively, e.g.

са́мый лу́чший магази́н	*the best shop*
э́то бу́дет са́мое лу́чшее	*that will be the best* (sc. *way*)

Another way of forming the superlative is by means of the prefix наи-, but only a few adjectives (always comparatives) are treated in this way and even they are seldom used, the form being considered archaic and pedantic. The commonest are:

наилу́чший	*best*
наибо́льший	*biggest*
наиме́ньший	*smallest*

Another way of expressing *very* is by means of the prefix пре-, which is compounded with the positive; this form is quite common in colloquial Russian, e.g.

прехоро́шенький	*very pretty*
прескве́рный	*very bad*
преподо́бный	*very reverend*

The termination -ейший (-айший after ч, ж) is added to some adjectives with the meaning of a superlative; the commonest are:

высо́кий	*high*, superl. высоча́йший
вели́кий	*great*, superl. велича́йший
ма́лый	*small*, superl. мале́йший
глубо́кий	*deep*, superl. глубоча́йший
ни́зкий	*low*, superl. нижа́йший
чи́стый	*clean*, *pure*, superl. чисте́йший
бли́зкий	*near*, superl. ближа́йший
любе́зный	*amiable*, *kind*, superl. любе́знейший

Note:

дорого́й *dear,* superl. дража́йший (from stem драг-)
коро́ткий *short,* superl. кратча́йший (from stem
кратк-)

and

тя́жкий *grave,* superl. тягча́йший (from stem тягк-)

These forms are used only attributively. They may indicate
a relative superlative quality, in comparisons with other
similar objects, as in:

Эльбру́с высоча́йшая гора́ на Кавка́зе *Elbrus is the highest
mountain in the Caucasus*
Пу́шкин велича́йший из ру́сских поэ́тов *Pushkin is the
greatest of Russian poets*

but more frequently in modern Russian they are used as
absolute, or intensive, superlatives, i.e. to indicate that the
quality is present to a high degree; they then often correspond to the English *very . . ., most . . .,* e.g.

он зле́йший челове́к	*he is a most wicked man*
без мале́йшего сомне́ния	*without the slightest doubt*
Пу́шкин велича́йший ру́сский поэ́т	*Pushkin is a very great Russian poet*

Yet another way of expressing the superlative predicatively is by the predicative comparative followed:

(*a*) by всех, gen. of все *all* (sc. *things, persons*), e.g.
э́то ме́сто лу́чше всех *this place is the best of all* (sc.
places)
он поёт лу́чше всех *he sings best of all* (sc. *people*);

or (*b*) by всего́, gen. of всё *everything,* e.g.

он бо́льше всего́ лю́бит рисова́ть *he likes drawing most
of all, more than anything else*

THE NUMERALS

§ 60. The Cardinal and Ordinal Numerals

1	оди́н, одна́, одно́	пе́рвый
2	два (m. & n.), две (f.)	второ́й
3	три	тре́тий
4	четы́ре	четвёртый
5	пять	пя́тый
6	шесть	шесто́й
7	семь	седьмо́й
8	во́семь	восьмо́й
9	де́вять	девя́тый
10	де́сять	деся́тый
11	оди́ннадцать	оди́ннадцатый
12	двена́дцать	двена́дцатый
13	трина́дцать	трина́дцатый
14	четы́рнадцать	четы́рнадцатый
15	пятна́дцать	пятна́дцатый
16	шестна́дцать	шестна́дцатый
17	семна́дцать	семна́дцатый
18	восемна́дцать	восемна́дцатый
19	девятна́дцать	девятна́дцатый
20	два́дцать	двадца́тый
21	два́дцать оди́н/одна́/одно́	два́дцать пе́рвый
22	два́дцать два/две	два́дцать второ́й
23	два́дцать три	два́дцать тре́тий
30	три́дцать	тридца́тый
40	со́рок	сороково́й
50	пятьдеся́т	пятидеся́тый
60	шестьдеся́т	шестидеся́тый
70	се́мьдесят	семидеся́тый
80	во́семьдесят	восьмидеся́тый
90	девяно́сто	девяно́стый
100	сто	со́тый

101	сто один/одна/одно	сто первый
125	сто двадцать пять	сто двадцать пятый
200	двести	двухсотый
300	триста	трёхсотый
400	четыреста	четырёхсотый
500	пятьсот	пятисотый
600	шестьсот	шестисотый
700	семьсот	семисотый
800	восемьсот	восьмисотый
900	девятьсот	девятисотый
1 000	тысяча	тысячный
2 000	две тысячи	двухтысячный
5 000	пять тысяч	пятитысячный
10 000	десять тысяч	десятитысячный
100 000	сто тысяч	стотысячный
1 000 000	миллион	миллионный

Note that in Russian printed numbers (except dates) a small space or a full-stop (never a comma) usually follows the number of thousands, millions, &c., to facilitate reading.

N.B. миллиард (or биллион) = *milliard* (Britain), *billion* (U.S.A.)

триллион = *billion* (Britain), *trillion* (U.S.A.)

61. Declension and Use of the Numerals

Один is declined as follows:

	Masc.	*Singular* Fem.	Neut.	*Plural* All Genders
N.	один	одна	одно	одни
G.	одного	одной	одного	одних
D.	одному	одной	одному	одним
A.	= N./G.	одну	одно	= N./G.
I.	одним	одной	одним	одними
L.	одном	одной	одном	одних

The plural of один is used in several ways, e.g.

одни́ . . ., други́е . . .	*some . . ., others . . .*
одни́ же́нщины	*women only, nothing but women*
мы одни́	{ (1) *only we, we alone* { (2) *we are alone*
одни́ми рука́ми	*with the hands only*
but одно́й руко́й	*with one hand*
одни́ми слова́ми	*by words alone*
but одни́м сло́вом	*in a* (lit. *one*) *word*
оди́н Бог зна́ет	*God alone knows*
одно́ и то́ же	*one and the same thing*
одни́ но́жницы	*one pair of scissors*

оди́н, одна́, одно́ are used in all numbers compounded with 1 according to the gender of the noun that follows, which is always in the singular, e.g.

два́дцать оди́н год	*twenty-one years*
со́рок одна́ копе́йка	*forty-one copecks*
я купи́л сто одну́ ма́рку	*I bought 101 stamps*
«Ты́сяча и одна́ ночь»	*«The Thousand and One Nights»*

	два, две *two*			о́ба, о́бе *both*		
	Masc.	Neut.	Fem.	Masc.	Neut.	Fem.
N.	два	два	две	о́ба	о́ба	о́бе
G.		двух			обо́их	обе́их
D.		двум			обо́им	обе́им
A.		= N. / G.			= N. / G.	= N. / G.
I.		двумя́			обо́ими	обе́ими
L.		двух			обо́их	обе́их

	три *three*	четы́ре *four*
N.	три	четы́ре
G.	трёх	четырёх

D.	трём	четырём
A.	= N. / G.	= N. / G.
I.	тремя́	четырьмя́
L.	трёх	четырёх

Nouns of any gender which follow два, три, and четы́ре, as well as all numerals compounded with these three, are invariably in the gen. sing., not in the nom. pl. The reason for this is that два originally took the dual and the nom. dual masc. ended in -a, i.e. it was identical with the gen. sing. When the dual became obsolete the ending -a still continued to be used after два but came to be looked on as the gen. sing. Subsequently, by analogy, the gen. sing. of neuter nouns was used with два and the gen. sing. of feminine nouns after две, and also the gen. sing. of nouns of all genders came to be used after три and четы́ре.

два бра́та	*two brothers*
три стола́	*three tables*
две сестры́	*two sisters* (nom. pl. сёстры)
четы́ре села́	*four villages* (nom. pl. сёла)
два́дцать два го́да	*twenty-two years*
сто три рубля́	*one hundred and three roubles*, &c.

The old neuter dual is still apparent in the word две́сти 200.

If an adjective comes between the numeral and the noun, it can be in either the gen. pl. or the nom. pl., not in the singular as might be expected; the nom. pl. is rare before masculine and neuter nouns.

две краси́вые (or краси́вых) де́вочки	*two pretty little girls*
три больши́х (or больши́е) дома́	*three large houses*

The effect of putting the numeral after the noun is to make the former approximate:

дня два	*about two days, two or three days*
го́да четы́ре	*about four years*

When the numeral is used in any form other than the nominative, both numeral and noun (and when there is an adjective, that also) agree, the regular cases of the plural being used, e.g.

N.	два ма́леньких ма́льчика	*two little boys*
G.	двух ма́леньких ма́льчиков	*of two little boys*
D.	двум ма́леньким ма́льчикам	*to two little boys*, &c.

N.	три сестры́	*three sisters*
G.	трёх сестёр	*of three sisters*
D.	трём сёстрам	*to three sisters*, &c.

Both о́ба and о́бе take the gen. sing.

о́ба бра́та	*both* [*the*] *brothers*
о́ба села́	*both villages* (nom. pl. сёла)
о́бе сестры́	*both sisters* (nom. pl. сёстры)
о́бе руки́	*both arms* (nom. pl. ру́ки)

Some speakers, mostly of the older generation, still use the nominative plural of certain nouns after the feminine form о́бе, e.g.

о́бе сто́роны for о́бе стороны́ *both sides*
but such usage is obsolescent and not recommended.

пять *five*, and all numerals ending in -ь up to and including три́дцать, decline as follows:

N.	пять
G.	пяти́
D.	пяти́
A.	пять
I.	пятью́
L.	пяти́

N.B. во́семь has G. D. L. восьми́ and I. восьмью́ (or восемью́).

пятьдеся́т *fifty*, шестьдеся́т *sixty*, се́мьдесят *seventy*, во́семьдесят *eighty*:

N.	пятьдеся́т
G.	пяти́десяти
D.	пяти́десяти
A.	пятьдеся́т
I.	пятью́десятью
L.	пяти́десяти

The numbers from пять onwards are really feminine nouns, which are equivalent, for example, to the French *une cinquaine*. The numbers from 11 to 19 are composed of the single numerals and -дцать (a corruption of the old loc. of де́сять) joined by на *on*, e.g. трина́дцать (< три на деся́те, lit. *three on ten*). Два́дцать and три́дцать are *two-tens* and *three-tens*. In пятьдеся́т, шестьдеся́т, се́мьдесят, and во́семьдесят the -десят is an old gen. pl. and пятьдеся́т might be translated in French *une cinquaine de dizaines*.

со́рок *forty*, девяно́сто *ninety*, and сто *one hundred* are nom. and acc.; they have only one ending for all the other cases, viz. -a, e.g.

со ста рубля́ми	*with a hundred roubles*
в сорока́ слу́чаях	*in forty cases*
к девяно́ста гра́дусам	*towards 90°*
в ста шести́ дома́х	*in one hundred and six houses*

две́сти 200, три́ста 300, четы́реста 400, пятьсо́т 500, &c.

N.	две́сти	три́ста	четы́реста	пятьсо́т
G.	двухсо́т	трёхсо́т	четырёхсо́т	пятисо́т
D.	двумста́м	трёмста́м	четырёмста́м	пятиста́м
A.	две́сти	три́ста	четы́реста	пятьсо́т
I.	двумя́ста́ми	тремя́ста́ми	четырьмя́ста́ми	пятьюста́ми
L.	двухста́х	трёхста́х	четырёхста́х	пятиста́х

тысяча *one thousand* is declined as a feminine noun in -ча:

1 000	2 000	5 000
N. тысяча	две тысячи	пять тысяч
G. тысячи	двух тысяч	пяти тысяч
D. тысяче	двум тысячам	пяти тысячам
A. тысячу	две тысячи	пять тысяч
I. тысячей[1]	двумя тысячами	пятью тысячами
L. тысяче	двух тысячах	пяти тысячах

миллио́н, миллиа́рд, биллио́н, and триллио́н are declined like стол, but with the stress always on the stem.

Nouns which follow all numerals ending in -ь (except compounds of 1, 2, 3, and 4, such as 21, 32, 43, &c.) are always in the gen. pl., provided the numerals are in the nom. or acc. The reason for this is that, as has already been stated, numerals in -ь are really feminine nouns, and so the noun following is naturally put in the gen. pl. This can be seen in the word пятьдеся́т *50*, which is really a nom. sing. (пять) followed by a (now obsolete) gen. pl. (десят), lit. *a five of tens*. When a numeral in -ь is in any other case than the nom. or acc., both numeral and noun agree, as in the case of два, три, &c. Besides the numerals which end in -ь, со́рок *40*, сто *100*, две́сти *200*, три́ста *300*, &c., come under the above rule:

	пять рубле́й	*five roubles*
	де́сять дне́й	*ten days*
but N.B.	с пятью детьми́	*with five children*
	в семи́ дома́х	*in seven houses*
	к двумста́м солда́там	*towards 200 soldiers*

A noun dependent on the form тысяча (nom.), тысячу (acc.), or тысячи (gen.) is always in the gen. pl.; a noun

---

[1] When a noun follows, the form тысячью is often used, e.g. с тысячью солда́т[ами] *with a thousand soldiers*.

dependent on any other form of the singular of тысяча should also be in the genitive but is sometimes found in the same case as the numeral, provided that the numeral is not qualified by an adjective, e.g.

у него была тысяча солдат	*he had a thousand soldiers*
я видел там тысячу книг	*I saw a thousand books there*
с тысячью рублей (or рублями)	*with a thousand roubles*
с одной тысячей рублей	*with one thousand roubles*
в тысяче случаев (or случаях)	*in a thousand cases*
в каждой тысяче случаев	*in each thousand cases*

After any form of миллион, миллиард, биллион, &c., or any whole number of thousands above 1,000, the noun is *always* in the genitive plural:

я видел две тысячи солдат	*I saw two thousand soldiers*
в миллионах звёзд	*in millions of stars*
с тремя тысячами рублей	*with three thousand roubles*

Nought (zero) is ноль (or нуль), a masc. noun which takes the stress on all its endings. A following noun goes into the gen. pl.

§ 62. Cardinal Numbers in Composition

один makes одно-, e.g. односторонний *one-sided*.

два makes двух-, sometimes дву-, e.g. двухэтажный *two-storied*, двухлетний *two-year-old*, двухместный *two-seater*, двухсотый *two-hundredth*, двуглавый *double-headed*, двусмысленный *ambiguous*.

три makes тре- in треугольник *triangle*, треножник *tripod*, and a few other technical words, otherwise трёх-, e.g. трёхлетний *three-year-old*, трёхкомнатный *three-roomed*, трёхтонка *three-tonner* (lorry), трёхтысячный *three-thousandth*.

четыре makes четверо- in четвероногий *four-legged* and a few other terms, but usually четырёх-, e.g. четырёхлистный *four-leaved*, четырёхчасова́я речь *four-hour speech*, четырёх-уго́льный *four-cornered*, *quadrangular*, четырёхэта́жный *of four floors*.

со́рок makes сорока- and сорока̀- (with secondary stress; see § 37), e.g. сорока̀мину́тная бесе́да *forty-minute chat*, сорокале́тний англича́нин *forty-year-old Englishman*, соро-ка̀копе́ечная ма́рка *forty-copeck stamp*.

девяно́сто and сто do not change, e.g. девяно̀сто-мину́тная па́уза *ninety-minute pause*, сто̀рублёвая бума́жка *hundred-rouble note*. The grave accent indicates a secondary stress; see § 37.

All others end in -и. Note particularly во́семь *eight*, which makes восьми-, and пятьдеся́т, шестьдеся́т, се́мь-десят, and во́семьдесят, in which both elements take и: пятѝдесяти-, шестѝдесяти-, семѝдесяти-, восьмѝдесяти-.

Notice the forms:

двою́родный брат	*first cousin* (male)
двою́родная сестра́	*first cousin* (female)
трою́родный брат	*second cousin*, &c.

More examples of numerals in composition will be found in the section on money-values, § 69.

§ 63. Ordinal Numbers

The ordinal numbers are declined like attributive adjec-tives: второ́й, шесто́й, седьмо́й, восьмо́й, and сороково́й like молодо́й, тре́тий like ры́бий, and the rest like бе́лый. The ordinals have no short or predicative forms, hence

I am the first is я пе́рвый

The following idiomatic uses of the ordinals may be observed:

во-пе́рвых	*firstly, in the first place*
во-вторы́х	*secondly*
в-тре́тьих	*thirdly*

он сам-третéй   *he and two others*
я сам-четвёрт   *I and three others*, &c.

For the multiplicative use of сам-третéй, &c., see p. 142.
For the use of the ordinals in the expression of time see
§ 68.

§ 64. Distributive Numbers

These are expressed by placing the preposition по before
the cardinal numbers. Два, три, четы́ре, двéсти, три́ста,
четы́реста, полторá, полторы́, and the collective numerals
(see § 66) from двóе to дéсятеро remain in the nom.-acc.
form and the following noun in the gen. sing. or pl., but all
the other numbers are put in the dative with the noun in the
dative after оди́н, and in the gen. pl. after all the others, e.g.

он подари́л нам по однóй кни́ге *he gave us one book each*
у нас пó две, у вас пó три, а у них по четы́ре собáки
   we have two, you have three, and they have four dogs each
у обóих по пяти́ лошадéй *they both have five horses*

Note that only the first element of the numerals 500, 600,
700, 800, 900 goes into the dative, so по пятисóт, по
шестисóт, &c.
In colloquial style the use of the accusative form after
по in this meaning has spread to all numerals except оди́н.
For the use of the distributives in the expression of
money-values see § 69.

§ 65. Multiplicative Numerals

These are expressed as follows:

раз   *once* (lit. *a blow*)
два рáза   *twice* (lit. *two blows*)
четы́ре рáза   *four times*
пять раз   *five times*, &c.
ты́сячу раз   *a thousand times*

In пять раз, &c., раз is the old gen. pl., still used in a few phrases of this kind where it had become crystallized; the gen. pl. in -ов originally belonged to only a few nouns, but gradually became general.

The four words однáжды *once*, двáжды *twice*, трúжды *thrice*, and четы́режды *four times* are almost obsolete except as multipliers; однáжды is still sometimes used for *one fine day*, or *once upon a time*, but раз or одúн раз is more usual.

In the multiplication of two numbers, the multiplier is expressed:

1. By двáжды, трúжды, четы́режды, as

двáжды три — шесть	*twice three* = 6
трúжды четы́ре — двенáдцать	*three fours* = *12*
четы́режды пять — двáдцать	*4*×*5* = *20*

2. By the instrumental case of the numerals from пять to дéсять, and also of двáдцать and трúдцать, e.g.

пя́тью шесть — трúдцать	*5*×*6* = *30*
шéстью семь — сóрок два	*6*×*7* = *42*
двáдцатью двáдцать — четы́реста	*20*×*20* = *400*

Note that when these instrumentals are used as multipliers the stress falls on the first syllable.

3. By the use of the noun раз (gen. pl. — раз) after all other numerals, as

одúннадцать раз . . .	*eleven times* . . .
двáдцать одúн раз . . .	*21*× . . .
двáдцать два рáза . . .	*22*× . . .
двáдцать пять раз . . .	*25*× . . .
сóрок раз девянóсто	*40*×*90*

Note:

помнóжить пятьдеся́т нá пять	*to multiply 50 by 5*
вóсемь мéтров нá шесть	*8 metres by 6 (of size)*
мúнус на мúнус даёт плюс	*minus* × *minus* = *plus*

In counting objects and in counting for games, music, &c., the formula is: раз, два, три, четы́ре *one, two, three, four,* and so on.

Notice the following idioms in which раз occurs:

ско́лько раз (gen. pl.)	*how many times, how often*
мно́го раз	*many times*
не́сколько раз	*several times*
не раз	*time and again, more than once*
в два ра́за бо́льше	*twice as big* (lit. *by two times bigger*)
в два ра́за ме́ньше	*half as big*
в ты́сячу раз я́рче	*a thousand times brighter*
сра́зу (adv., old gen. sing.)	*at once; at the same time*
раз навсегда́	*once and for all*

and especially the difference between:

не ра́з *more than once*

e.g. я не ра́з говори́л . . . *I have said more than once* . . . and

ни ра́зу не . . . *not* [*even*] *once*

e.g. он ни ра́зу не́ был у нас *he has not once been at our house.*

The expression *twice as* may also be rendered by вдво́е (i.e. в + the collective numeral дво́е) with the comparative, e.g.

э́то вино́ вдво́е лу́чше того́ *this wine is twice as good as that*

similarly:

э́то перо́ втро́е доро́же моего́ *this pen is three times as expensive as mine*

For numbers above 10, раз must be used, e.g.

э́та карти́на в ты́сячу раз краси́вее, чем та *this picture is a thousand times more beautiful than that one*

Expressions such as *tenfold*, used predicatively, are

rendered by в де́сять раз or вде́сятеро, &c., *a hundredfold* by во́ сто раз. Note: урожа́й сам-пя́т *the crop has increased fivefold (is five times the amount sown).*

The adjectival multiplicatives двойно́й *double, twofold,* тройно́й *treble, threefold,* and стокра́тный *a hundredfold* (cf. the archaic во́ сто крат for во́ сто раз) are quite common.

The word for *simple, single* is просто́й.

§ 66. Collective Numerals

These are used for the numbers from 2–10, but only those for 2, 3, and 4 are common.

2	дво́е	*6*	ше́стеро
3	тро́е	*7*	се́меро
4	че́тверо	*8*	во́сьмеро
5	пя́теро	*9*	де́вятеро
	10	де́сятеро	

дво́е and тро́е are declined as follows:

N.	дво́е
G.	двои́х
D.	дво́им
A.	= N. / G.
I.	двои́ми
L.	двои́х

the others as че́тверо:

N.	че́тверо
G.	четверы́х
D.	четверы́м
A.	= N. / G.
I.	четверы́ми
L.	четверы́х

These numerals may refer to groups of persons (but not to females only) and are used in such phrases as:

нас тро́е *there are three of us*, оста́лись то́лько мы тро́е *just we three are* (or *were*) *left* (it would be wrong to say мы три), у меня́ че́тверо дете́й: два сы́на и две до́чери *I have four children*: *two sons and two daughters*, их бы́ло ше́стеро *there were six of them*.

Owing to their overtone of casualness, the collective numerals seldom refer to persons of high rank. For instance, one may say:

дво́е студе́нтов	*two* (*a couple of*) *students*
but only два премье́р-мини́стра	*two prime-ministers*

Another use for the collective numerals is the counting of things denoted by nouns which are used only in the plural, e.g.

час *hour* — три часа́	*three hours*
часы́ *watch, clock* — тро́е часо́в	*three watches, clocks*
са́ни *sledge* — че́тверо сане́й	*four sledges*
су́тки *24 hours* — дво́е су́ток	*two days* (*and nights*)

but for *five days* (and above) the cardinal is usual: пять су́ток (or дней); and where confusion might arise the word шту́ка *piece* or па́ра *pair* must be employed:

оди́ннадцать часо́в	*eleven hours, eleven o'clock*
оди́ннадцать штук часо́в	*eleven clocks*

In conversation the oblique forms of the collective numerals are now generally avoided, being replaced by the appropriate cardinal form:

у него́ тро́е дете́й	*he has three children*
у меня́ дво́е но́жниц	*I have two pairs of scissors*

but:

я ви́дел его́ трёх дете́й	*I have seen his three children*
коро́бка с двумя́ но́жницами	*a box containing two pairs of scissors*

N.B. вдвоём   *alone together, tête-à-tête*
     втроём   *à trois*

Some other collective numerals:

па́ра	*a pair*
две па́ры рук ⎫ дво́е рук ⎭	*two pairs of hands*
Тро́ица	*the Trinity*
дю́жина	*a dozen* (never of people)
деся́ток	*ten*, e.g. деся́тки ты́сяч *tens of thousands*
со́тня	*a hundred* (often sc. *roubles* or *soldiers*)
близнецы́	*twins*

For the use of the collectives as multiplicatives see § 65.

Notice the curious idiom он сам-дру́г *he and another*, я сам-пя́т *I and four others*, &c. (see § 63).

The names of the figures 0–10 are—

ноль (нуль) (m.)	*nought*	пятёрка	*a five*
едини́ца	*a one*	шестёрка	*a six*
дво́йка	*a two*	семёрка	*a seven*
тро́йка	*a three*	восьмёрка	*an eight*
четвёрка	*a four*	девя́тка	*a nine*
		деся́тка	*a ten*

This set of numerals can also indicate any object bearing one of the numbers 1–10. For instance, дво́йка may indicate a playing card with two pips, a bus or tram on route No. 2, a disk or tally with the figure 2 on it, &c.

ма́ленькая шестёрка *a small 6* (figure)

тро́йка *a set of three* (often *a team of three horses* or *a carriage* or *sledge drawn by three horses*)

деся́тка *a ten-rouble note*, *a 'tenner'*

«больша́я тро́йка» *the Big Three* (states)

он получи́л четвёрку по геогра́фии *he got 4 for geography* (in Russian schools marks are given out of 5)

§ 67. Fractions

половѝна *a half* is declined regularly, as a hard fem. noun, with the stress fixed on the third syllable.

$2\frac{1}{2}$ = два/двѣ с половѝной ($+$ gen. sing.)
$5\frac{1}{2}$ = пять с половѝной ($+$ gen. pl.)

The word полъ *half a* . . . is used only in composition with the gen. sing. of a noun, e.g. пòлмèтра *half a metre, a half-metre*, пòлминýты *half a minute*.

In declension such compounds are treated as follows:

N. A.	пòлмèтра	пòлминýты
G.	полумèтра	полуминýты
D.	полумèтру	полуминýте
I.	полумèтром	полуминýтой
L.	полумèтре	полуминýте

The plurals (полумèтры, полуминýты) take the regular endings.

For пòлдень *noon* and пòлночь *midnight* see § 68.

When the second element begins with л, a vowel, or a capital letter, a hyphen is used: пòл-лѝтра *half a litre*, пòл-оборòта *half a turn*, пòл-яˊблока *half an apple*, пòл-Москвыˊ *half Moscow*.

In colloquial style the first element may remain unchanged (пòл-) in all cases.

The form полу- (equivalent to English *semi-, hemi-, half-*) is combined with a nominative case to form compound nouns which follow the regular declensions: полукрýг *semicircle* (g.s. полукрýга), полумèсяц *half-moon*, полушаˊрие *hemisphere*.

For $1\frac{1}{2}$ there is a special word:

полтораˊ (made up of пол- and the old short gen. form of вторòй, lit. *half of the second*) for the masculine and neuter, and полторы́ for the feminine, e.g.

N. A. полтора́ ме́тра (gen. sing.) $1\frac{1}{2}$ *metres*

N. A. полторы́ мину́ты (gen. sing.) $1\frac{1}{2}$ *minutes*

For all the other cases the form полу́тора is used for both genders, the noun being declined in the plural, e.g. с полу́тора ме́трами, о́коло полу́тора мину́т.

For 150 полтора́ста may be used:

N. A. полтора́ста + gen. pl.

G. D. I. L. полу́тораста + G. D. I. L. pl.

$\frac{1}{3}$ треть (f.) $\frac{1}{4}$ че́тверть (f.)

$\frac{2}{3}$ две тре́ти $\frac{3}{4}$ три че́тверти

Other fractions are expressed as follows:

$\frac{1}{5}$ одна́ пя́тая (sc. часть *part* or до́ля *fraction*)

$\frac{2}{5}$ две пя́тых $\frac{3}{10}$ (or 0,3)[1] три деся́тых

$6\frac{7}{100}$ (or 6,07)[1] шесть [це́лых] и семь со́тых

§ 68. Expressions of Time

hour	час (N.B. часы́ = *hours* or *clock*)
what time is it?	кото́рый час?
at what time . . .?	в кото́ром часу́? . . . (see § 39, Obs. 7)
1 o'clock	час
at 1 o'clock	в час
[*at*] *about 1 o'clock*	о́коло ча́су
1.15	че́тверть второ́го (lit. $\frac{1}{4}$ *of the 2nd*)
1.5	пять мину́т второ́го
1.30	полови́на второ́го (*half past one*)
	or час три́дцать (*one thirty*)
at 1.30	в полови́не второ́го
1.45	без че́тверти два (lit. *2 without* $\frac{1}{4}$)
at 1.45	без че́тверти два (*at a quarter to two*)
	or в час со́рок пять (*at one forty-five*)

[1] Note that in Russian a comma is used where we should write a decimal point.

2 o'clock	два часá
at 2 o'clock	в два часá
at about 2 o'clock	часá в два
2.10	дéсять минýт трéтьего
2.30	половúна трéтьего
3 o'clock	три часá
3.50	без десятú [минýт] четы́ре
4 o'clock	четы́ре часá
5 o'clock	пять часóв
11.30	половúна двенáдцатого
12 o'clock	двенáдцать часóв
12.15	чéтверть пéрвого
12.30	половúна пéрвого
12.45	без чéтверти час
12.55	без пятú [минýт] час
half an hour	полчасá
2 hours	два часá
2½ hours	два часá с половúной
1½ hours	полторá часá

Notice especially the word сýтки (nom. pl. fem.) meaning *24 hours, a day and night*, e.g.

цéлые сýтки	*a whole 24 hours*
трóе сýток (gen. pl.)	*72 hours*
чéтверо сýток	*4 days and nights*
пять (or пя́теро) сýток, &c.	*5 days and nights*, &c.

minute	минýта
'one minute'	однý минýту, минýточку
'this minute'	сию́ минýту
second	секýнда
this instant	сию́ секýнду or
	сейчáс же
in one minute	в однý минýту (*within a minute*)
in five minutes	чèрез пять минýт (*5 minutes later*)

in two hours   чѐрез два́ часа́ (*after 2 hours have passed*)

N.B. чѐрез can also give the meaning *every other*:

чѐрез ча́с (1) *in an hour's time*
            (2) *every other hour*

Notice:

о́коло двух часо́в   (1) *about two hours*
                     (2) *about two o'clock*

помину́тно   *every minute* (*incessantly*)

по́лдень (m.) *midday, noon*
Gen. полу́дня (or по́лдня)
Dat. полу́дню (or по́лдню), &c.

Russian has no single word for *afternoon*. In expressions of time from noon to evening the adverb пополу́дни (*after noon*) was employed formerly, but дня (gen. of день *day*) is now preferred:

at 4 p.m.   в 4 часа́ дня
in the afternoon (1) днём (instr. of день)
                    (2) во второ́й полови́не дня
                    (3) по́сле за́втрака

по́лночь (f.) *midnight*
Gen. полу́ночи (or по́лночи), &c.

N.B. *half a day*   полдня́
     half a night полно́чи
     daily (adj.) ежедне́вный
            (adv.) ежедне́вно

The days of the week are:

понеде́льник *Monday* (lit. *after the holiday*)
вто́рник   *Tuesday* (cf. второ́й)
среда́   *Wednesday* (lit. *middle*)
четве́рг   *Thursday* (cf. четвёртый)
пя́тница   *Friday* (cf. пя́тый)

суббо́та   *Saturday* (cf. *Sabbath*)
воскресе́нье   *Sunday* (lit. *resurrection*)

N.B. *on Monday*   в понеде́льник
      on Tuesday   во вто́рник
      on Wednesday   в сре́ду
      on Thursday   в четве́рг
      on Friday   в пя́тницу
      on Saturday   в суббо́ту
      on Sunday   в воскресе́нье
      on Mondays   по понеде́льникам, &c.
      week   неде́ля
      fortnight   две неде́ли
      last week   на про́шлой неде́ле
      this week   на э́той неде́ле
      next week   на бу́дущей неде́ле
          (Note на той неде́ле = *last* or *next week*)
      every week   ка́ждую неде́лю
      for a week   на неде́лю (expresses intention)
      for a week   неде́лю or за неде́лю (duration
                            of a past action)
      weekly (adj.) еженеде́льный

The months are:

янва́рь	*January*	ию́ль	*July*
февра́ль	*February*	а́вгуст	*August*
ма́рт	*March*	сентя́брь	*September*
апре́ль	*April*	октя́брь	*October*
ма́й	*May*	ноя́брь	*November*
ию́нь	*June*	декабрь	*December*

they are all masculine.

In the words for the first two and the last four months
the stress is always on the ending, in the others it remains
throughout where it is in the nominative, e.g. *in January*
в январе́, *in May* в ма́е.

month	ме́сяц
monthly (adj.)	ежеме́сячный
the date (including year)	да́та
the date (day of month)	число́
January 1st	пе́рвое[1] января́
on February 2nd	второ́го февраля́
on March 3rd	тре́тьего ма́рта
of the 5th of April (e.g. letter)	от пя́того апре́ля
from November 6th (*onwards*)	с шесто́го ноября́
on May 21st	два́дцать пе́рвого ма́я
on June 30th	тридца́того ию́ня
on July 31st	три́дцать пе́рвого ию́ля
what date is it today?	како́е (or кото́рое) сего́дня число́?

year	год
six months	полго́да
two years	два го́да
three years	три го́да
four years	четы́ре го́да
but *five years*	пять лет (lit. *summers*)
six years	шесть лет
till *twenty years*	два́дцать лет
then *twenty-one years*	два́дцать оди́н год
twenty-two years	два́дцать два́ го́да
twenty-five years	два́дцать пя́ть лет
&c.	
how old are you?	ско́лько вам лет?
twenty-three	два́дцать три го́да
this year	в э́том году́
last year	в про́шлом году́
last year's	прошлого́дний
next year	в бу́дущем году́

---

[1] neuter, agreeing with число́ *number, day of the month.*

in 1899	в [ты́сяча восемьсо́т] девя-но́сто девя́том году́ (i.e. only the last numeral is an ordinal)
in 1914	в [ты́сяча] девятьсо́т че-ты́рнадцатом году́
of 1900	ты́сяча девятьсо́того го́да
August 1961	а́вгуст ты́сяча девятьсо́т ше́стьдеся́т пе́рвого го́да
the twenties	двадца́тые го́ды
of the thirties	тридца́тых годо́в
in the forties	в сороковы́х года́х

(but only of historical periods, not of personal age)

century	век, столе́тие
in a year's time	чѐрез го́д
every other year	(1) чѐрез го́д
	(2) ка́ждые два го́да
every year	ка́ждый год
yearly	ежего́дный, ежего́дно
per annum	в год
he lived here for two years	он жил здесь два го́да
he went away for two years	он уе́хал на́ два го́да
during the last 2 years	за после́дние два го́да

ago is expressed by тому́ наза́д (*to it back*), or наза́д by itself, e.g. *five years ago* пять лет [тому́] наза́д.

time	вре́мя
from time to time	вре́мя от вре́мени
in time, gradually	со вре́менем
opportunely, in time	во́время
during	во вре́мя (+ gen.)
at times	времена́ми, по времена́м
it is time (to . . .)	пора́ (+ infin.)
at times	поро́й, иногда́

from then on, since then	с тех пóр
till then	до тех пóр
till now	до сих пóр
since when?	с какѝх пóр?

§ 69. Expression of Money-values

рубль	*a rouble (= 100 copecks; about 8s. 4d.)*
полторá рубля́	*1½ roubles*
два рубля́	*2 roubles*
пять рублéй	*5 roubles*
копéйка	*a copeck (= 1d.)*
две копéйки	*2 copecks*
пять копéек	*5 copecks*
дéсять копéек	*10 copecks*
два рубля́ двáдцать копéек	*2 roubles 20 copecks*
три рубля́ сóрок	*3 r. 40 c.*
пять рублéй пятьдеся́т or (rare) пять с полтѝ́ной	*5½ roubles*

The amounts 60, 70, 80, and 90 *copecks* are sometimes expressed colloquially as 6, 7, 8, 9 грѝвен, from the word грѝвна, now obsolete except in the oblique cases of the plural.

The following are the colloquial names of the coins and notes:

копéйка	*a copeck piece*	
двухкопéечная монéта	*2-copeck piece*	
трёхкопéечная монéта	*3-copeck piece*	(copper)
пятачóк or пятáк	*5-copeck piece*	
грѝвенник	*10-copeck piece*	
пятиалты́нный	*15-copeck piece*	
двугрѝвенный	*20-copeck piece*	(nickel)
полтѝ́нник	*50-copeck piece*	
рубль or целкóвый	*a rouble piece*	

рублёвка or [одно-] рублёвая бумáжка	*a rouble note*	⎫ Officially termed Госудáрствен-
трёхрублёвая бумáжка or трёхрублёвка	*3-rouble note*	⎬ ные казначéй- ские билéты
пятирублёвая бумáжка or пятирублёвка	*5-rouble note*	*State Treasury Notes* ⎭
десятирублёвая бумáж-ка or десятирублёвка	*10-rouble note*	⎫ Officially termed билéты Госу-
двадцатѝпятирублёвая бумáжка	*25-rouble note*	дáрственного Бáнка СССР
пятѝдесятирублёвая бумáжка	*50-rouble note*	*Notes of the State Bank of the*
стòрублёвая бумáжка or стòрублёвка	*100-rouble note*	*U.S.S.R.* ⎭

Note also

однокопéечная мáрка	*a one-copeck stamp*
двухкопéечная мáрка	*a two-copeck stamp*
трёхкопéечная мáрка	*a three-copeck stamp*
четырёхкопéечная мáрка	*a four-copeck stamp*
семикопéечная мáрка	*a seven-copeck stamp*
десятикопéечная мáрка	*a ten-copeck stamp*

When the cost of one article is mentioned, the preposition за + acc. is employed, e.g.

однó я́блоко зá шесть копéек *one apple at (for) six copecks, a sixpenny apple*

дáйте одѝн [билéт] зá пять копéек *give me one five-copeck [ticket]*

When several like articles of the same price are mentioned, the preposition по + dat. or acc. (see § 65) should be used:

двe мáрки по однóй копéйке *two one-copeck stamps*

пять мáрок пó двe копéйки *five stamps at 2 copecks each*

10 карандашéй по 8 копéек (or 10 восьмикопéечных карандашéй) *ten pencils at 8 copecks each*

Note that дéсять карандашéй за вóсемь копéек would mean *ten pencils for a total sum of 8 copecks*.

The price of articles is asked by скóлько стóит/стóят? (*how much costs/cost?*), or by the idiom по чём? (*at what [price]?*) with plural noun:

по чём э́ти гáлстуки? *how much [each] are these ties?*

The answer to по чём? should also contain по (+ dat. or acc., as explained in § 64):

пó два рубля́   *two roubles each*
по пяти́ рублéй   *five roubles each*

For the use of the preposition в with similar meaning see § 65.

THE ADVERB

§ 70. The adverb is generally the same as the nominative singular neuter of the predicative (short) form of the adjective, e.g.

ми́лый	ми́лая	ми́лое	*nice* (attributive adj.)
мил	мила́	ми́ло	*nice* (predicative adj.)
		ми́ло	*nicely* (adverb)
хорóший	хорóшая	хорóшее	*good, nice*
хорóш	хороша́	хорошó	*good, nice*
		хорошó	*well; all right*
Similarly:		плóхо	*badly*
		прия́тно	*pleasantly*
		печáльно	*sadly*
		отли́чно	*excellently*, &c.

Most adjectives in -ний form the adverb with -е, e.g.

| кра́йний | *extreme* | кра́йне | *extremely* |
| и́скренний | *sincere* | и́скренне | *sincerely* |

but some of them take -о, e.g.

да́вний	*former, distant*[1]	давно́	*long ago*
по́здний	*late*	по́здно	*late* (adv.)
ра́нний	*early*	ра́но	*early* (adv.)

и́скренний also makes и́скренно

Owing to the fact that the present tense of the verb *to be* is almost obsolete in Russian, the adverb (or, more accurately, the short neuter adjective) is very frequently used as an impersonal expression which may form a sentence by itself, e.g.

ра́но	*it is early* (often *too early*)
по́здно	*it is late* (often *too late*)
жа́рко	*it is hot*
тепло́	*it is warm*
бли́зко	*it is near*
хорошо́, что вы пришли́	*it is good* (or *nice*) *that you have come*
возмо́жно, что он придёт	*it is possible that he will come*
невозмо́жно, чтобы он пришёл	*it is impossible that he should come*

A few adverbs can be stressed in two ways, each equally correct, e.g.

далеко́ or далёко	*it is far*[2]
высоко́ or высо́ко	*it is high* (also *highly*)
глубоко́ or глубо́ко	*it is deep* (also *deeply*)

---

[1] Of time, events.   [2] But *far from* (*excellent*, &c.) is далеко́ не . . .

Adjectives in -ский form the adverb by changing -ский into -ски, e.g.

ирони́ческий	*ironical*
ирони́чески	*ironically*

similarly:

поэти́чески	*poetically*
дру́жески	*in a friendly way, warmly*
хрони́чески	*chronically*, &c.

The preposition по- prefixed to such adverbs gives the meaning *in the manner of*:

по-прия́тельски	*in a friendly way*
по-моско́вски	*in Moscow fashion*

and when the adverb is one formed from the name of a nationality it can also mean *in . . .*, e.g.

по-ру́сски	*in Russian*
по-англи́йски	*in English*
по-неме́цки	*in German*
по-францу́зски	*in French*

e.g. я говорю́ по-ру́сски *I speak Russian*
я не понима́ю по-неме́цки *I don't understand German*

Notice the colloquial idiom:

э́то по-каќовски? *in what language is it?*

Otherwise, adverbial expressions with по- are formed by using the dative singular of the adjective or pronoun, e.g.

по-но́вому	*in the modern manner*
по-ста́рому	*in the old way*
по-сво́ему	*in one's own way*
по-мо́ему	*in my own way* or *in my opinion*
по-ва́шему	*in your way* or *in your opinion*
по-вое́нному	*in military fashion*

(notice the stress)

See also § 73.

§ 71. Adverbs of Place

здесь } тут[1]	*here*
там	*there*
везде (по)всю́ду[1]	*everywhere*
где	*where*

нигде́ *nowhere*

> нигде́ нет ме́ста *there is no place* (or *room*) *anywhere*
> нигде́ никого́ нет *there is no one anywhere*

не́где *there is nowhere to . . .*
> нам не́где сесть *there is nowhere for us to sit*

где́-то *somewhere, in a certain place* (sc. *I don't remember or know where,* or *I don't wish to say where*)
> он где́-то в Росси́и *he is somewhere in Russia*

где́-нибудь *somewhere, anywhere*
> он проведёт зи́му где́-нибудь за грани́цей *he will spend the winter somewhere abroad* (sc. *the place is not yet fixed*)

где́ бы то ни́ было́ *wherever you like, anywhere at all*
там и сям *here and there*

The foregoing adverbs indicate position. Russian adverbs corresponding to *hither, thither, hence, whence,* &c., must be used when the action connotes motion from one place to another; such adverbs of direction include:

сюда́ *here* (= *hither, to this place*)
> иди́ сюда́ *come here*

туда́ *there* (= *thither, to that place*)
> я иду́ туда́ *I am going there*

---

[1] Rather more colloquial than literary.

куда́ *where* (= *whither*)
> куда́ вы положи́ли мою́ кни́гу? *where have you put my book?*

никуда́ *nowhere* (= *to no place*)
> я никуда́ не иду́ *I am not going anywhere, I am going nowhere*

не́куда *there is no place to which . . .*
> не́куда итти́ *there is nowhere to go to*

куда́-то *somewhere* (= *to a particular place*)
> он куда́-то ушёл *he has gone off somewhere*

куда́-нибудь *somewhere* (= *anywhere*)
> пойдём куда́-нибудь *let's go somewhere*

куда́ бы то ни́ было *wherever you like, anywhere at all*

отсю́да *from here*
> отсю́да до Москвы́ далеко́ *it is a long way from here to Moscow*

отту́да *from there*
> отту́да до нас пять киломе́тров *it is five kilometres from there to us* (i.e. *our house*)

отку́да *from where?*
> вы отку́да? *where do you come from?*

отку́да-то *from somewhere* (= *from a particular place*)
> он прие́хал отку́да-то далеко́ *he has arrived from somewhere distant*

отку́да-нибудь *from somewhere* (*from any place*)
> доста́ньте отку́да-нибудь *get it from somewhere* (*anywhere*)

отку́да бы то ни́ было *from anywhere at all*

Notice the following idiomatic uses of где and куда́ :

где мне э́то сде́лать! *I shall never be able to do that!*
где вам! *how can you think of it?*
э́тот го́род куда́ бо́льше того́ *this town is ever so much
    bigger than that*
э́то вино́ хоть куда́ *this wine is simply splendid*
где . . ., где . . . *in one place . . ., in another . . .*

and the common idiom with никуда́:

никуда́ не годи́тся *it is no good at all*

Notice: вверху́   *up above, on top*
        наверху́   *up above,* sc. *upstairs*
        внизу́   *down below* or *downstairs*
        вверх   *up[wards]*
        наве́рх   *upstairs* (motion)
        вниз   *down[wards]*
        снару́жи   *outside, outwardly*
        внутри́   *inside, inwardly*

§ 72. Adverbs of Time

            тепе́рь   *now*
            тогда́   *then*
            всегда́   *always*
            когда́   *when*

никогда́ *never*
    никогда́ не ем мя́са *I never eat meat*

не́когда (1) *there is no time to . . .*
    мне тепе́рь не́когда! *I've no time for that now!*

не́когда (2) *formerly, once upon a time*
    не́когда жи́ли-бы́ли дед да стару́ха *once upon a time
    there lived an old man and an old woman*

иногда́ *at times, sometimes*

когда́-то *formerly, a long time ago* (sc. *I don't remember* or *know exactly when*)

    он когда́-то был жена́т *he was married once* (sc. *his wife is now dead or divorced*)

когда́-нибудь *some time* (*any time*)

    загляни́те к нам когда́-нибудь! *look us up some time or other!*

        когда́ бы то ни́ было *at any time at all*

        ещё *still*

        нет ещё ⎫
                 ⎬ *not yet*
        ещё не . . . ⎭

        уже́ *already*

        уже́ нет ⎫
                 ⎬ *no longer*
        уже́ не . . . ⎭

        снача́ла *at first*

        наконе́ц *at last*

        пото́м *after that, later on*

        ско́ро *soon, quickly*

        сно́ва, опя́ть *again*

        поскоре́е *as quickly as possible, hurry up!*

        до́лго [*for*] *a long time*

        он до́лго не идёт *he is a long time in coming*

        давно́ ⎫
                      ⎬ *long ago, long since*
        давны́м-давно́ ⎭

        сейча́с *now, at present, just now, shortly*

        сейча́с же ⎫
        то́тчас [же] ⎬ *immediately*
        сию́ мину́ту ⎭

        позавчера́, тре́тьего дня *the day before yesterday*

        вчера́ *yesterday*

        сего́дня *today*

        за́втра *tomorrow*

        послеза́втра *the day after tomorrow*

ны́не, ны́нче *nowadays* (adj. ны́нешний *present*)
пока́ is often used adverbially in the sense of *for the present, for the time being*

§ 73. Adverbs of Manner

так   *thus, in this way*
как   *how, as, like*
ника́к (1) *in no wise, by no means*
    ника́к нет *not at all* (*no*, a military expression)
    ника́к нельзя́ *it is quite out of the question*

and, in popular speech,
    ника́к (2) *perhaps, as likely as not, it seems, I expect*:
    ника́к он придёт *perhaps he will come*

ка́к-то (1) *somehow, sort of, somehow or other*
    мне ка́к-то не хо́чется *somehow or other* (*I can't explain why*) *I don't want to*
    э́то стра́нно ка́к-то *it's queer somehow*

and, colloquially, ка́к-то (2) *once, at some time or other*:
    мы ка́к-то (or когда́-то) встре́тили его́ в теа́тре *we once met him at the theatre*

ка́к-нибудь *somehow or other, by hook or by crook*
    устро́йте э́то ка́к-нибудь *arrange this* (*matter*) *by some means or other*
    приезжа́йте к нам ка́к-нибудь ле́том *come and see us in the summer if you possibly can*
    э́то на́до сде́лать ка́к-нибудь (*we*) *must do this somehow or other*

ка́к бы то ни́ было *however that may be, may have been*
ина́че (or и́наче) *otherwise, differently*

э́то на́до устро́ить ина́че *this must be arranged differently*
учи́сь хороше́нько, ина́че тебя́ нака́жут *learn your lesson
    well, or else you'll be punished*

не та́к *differently* often means *wrong* (adv.); although
there is a word for *incorrectly*, viz. непра́вильно, the most
common way of saying *wrong* is не та́к, e.g.

вы не та́к сде́лали	*you have done it wrong*
он не та́к пое́хал	*he has taken the wrong road*
вы не та́к сказа́ли	*you have said it wrong*
я не та́к по́нял его́	*I misunderstood him*

though of course the same expression is often used literally
to mean *not like that, not in that way.*

Notice the common adverbs:

вдруг	*suddenly*
постепе́нно ⎫ ма́ло-пома́лу ⎭	*gradually*
напра́сно	*in vain* (often sc. *it is a pity that . . .*)
наро́чно	*on purpose*
нечáянно	*unintentionally*
случа́йно	*accidentally*
осо́бенно	*especially*
вообще́	*in general*
вме́сте	*together*
впро́чем	*however, moreover*
да́ром	*free, gratis; in vain*
сло́вно	*exactly like, just as if*
вероя́тно	*probably*
очеви́дно	*evidently*
и́менно	*namely*
действи́тельно	*actually, in very fact, indeed*
коне́чно	*of course*
наве́рно	*surely, certainly*

сле́довательно   *consequently*
обяза́тельно   *without fail*
беспреста́нно   *incessantly*
включи́тельно   *inclusively*
исключи́тельно   *exclusively*
безусло́вно   *absolutely*
обы́чно   ⎫
                 ⎬ *usually*
обыкнове́нно   ⎭
необыкнове́нно   ⎫
                 ⎬ *unusually, uncommonly*
чрезвыча́йно   ⎭

and the idioms:

[и] так и сяк *this way and that, either way*
та́к себе *so-so, fair, middling*
ничего́ *not bad, passably; never mind!*
так *correctly; unintentionally, with no particular purpose*
та́к ли я де́лаю? *am I doing it right?*
я э́то то́лько та́к сказа́л *I didn't mean it*
так и + verb *just as if, simply, in so many words*
глаза́ у него́ так и горя́т *his eyes are simply burning*
я так и не узна́л *I just never found out*
так и быть *so be it, all right, right you are*
и та́к *even so, as it is*
та́к-то та́к, но . . . *that may be, that's all very well, but . . .*
так то́чно *just so* (= *yes*, a military expression)
то́чно та́к *just like that, just in that way*
то́чно *it is just as if; exactly*
он то́чно в неё влюблён *you'd think he was in love with her*
у меня́ соба́ка то́чно така́я *I've got a dog just like that*
ро́вно *exactly, precisely*
ро́вно в два часа́ *at two o'clock prompt*
то̀чь-в-то́чь *exactly, an exact copy* (lit. *dot-to-dot*)

See also § 70.

Note on the use of -то after adverbs of place, time, and manner

It should be mentioned that -то is often used enclitically after interrogative adverbs, not to express indefiniteness, but as an emphatic particle or expletive, as much as to say, *I wonder*, e.g.

где́-то они́ тепе́рь!	*I wonder where they are now!*
когда́-то мы увиди́мся!	*I wonder when we shall meet again!*
ка́к-то он устро́ится!	*I wonder how he' ll settle his affairs!*

After definitive adverbs its use implies *surprise*, e.g.

тепе́рь-то я понима́ю! *now I understand!*

та́к-то вы по́няли меня́! *you understood me that way!* (i.e. *so that's what you thought I meant!*)

§ 74. Adverbs of Degree and Quantity

	мно́го	*much, a great deal*
	немно́го	⎱
dim.	немно́жко	⎰ *a little, some*
	ма́ло	*little, not much*

e.g. да́йте мне немно́го вина́ (gen.) *give me a little wine*

ещё немно́жко? *a little more?*

э́то ма́ло! *that's not much* (sc. *too little*)!

э́то мно́го! *that's a great deal* (sc. *too much*)!

в э́той кни́ге ма́ло хоро́шего *in this book there's little that is good*

у меня́ [есть] немно́го де́нег *I have a little money* (with emphasis on де́нег)

у меня́ ма́ло де́нег
у меня́ немно́го де́нег ⎱ *I have but little money*
у меня́ де́нег немно́го ⎰
(with emphasis on немно́го)

(for the declension of the plural мно́гие, &c., cf. § 54, Obs. 9)

ско́лько *how much, how many, as much*

>ско́лько э́то сто́ит? *how much does this cost?*
>я помога́ю ему́, ско́лько могу́ *I help him as much as I can*

сто́лько *so much, so many*

>он был сто́лько раз у меня́, что наконе́ц он мне надое́л *he has been to see me so many times that I've finally got sick of him*
>ско́лько голо́в, сто́лько умо́в [*so*] *many men,* [*so*] *many minds*

то́лько *only*

>не то́лько *not only*

Notice the idioms:

да и то́лько ⎫
то́лько и всего́ ⎭ *and that's all*

>не хочу́, да и то́лько *I don't want to, and that's all about it*

ниско́лько *not in the least* (always with не before verb)

>я ниско́лько не хочу́ *I don't want to in the least*

ско́лько-нибудь *at all, in the slightest degree*

>е́сли он ско́лько-нибудь поря́дочный челове́к *if he is at all a decent fellow*

не́сколько *some, a few, somewhat*

>не́сколько раз *several times*
>не́сколько рубле́й *a few roubles*
>у него́ не́сколько дете́й *he has several children*
>э́та шля́па не́сколько доро́же *this hat is rather dearer*

гора́здо [*ever so*] *much* (followed by the comparative)

>э́то изда́ние гора́здо деше́вле *this edition is ever so much cheaper*

дово́льно ⎫
доста́точно ⎭ *enough, rather, fairly*

дово́льно де́нег *enough money*
дово́льно хо́лодно *it is rather cold*
N.B. *not enough* is usually expressed by ма́ло (+gen.), e.g. ма́ло де́нег *not enough money*; otherwise by недоста́точно, e.g. здесь недоста́точно тепло́ *it's not warm enough here*

бо́льше *more*
у него́ бо́льше книг, чем у меня́ *he has more books than I*
бо́льше всего́ *most of all*
побо́льше *rather more, as much as possible, a good lot*
да́йте мне побо́льше (+gen.) *give me a good lot of* . . .

ме́ньше *less*
ме́ньше де́нег *less money*
ме́ньше всего́ *least of all*
поме́ньше *as little as possible*

скоре́е *rather* (sc. *sooner*)
я скоре́е дам вам, чем ему́ *I would rather give* (lit. *shall give*) *it to you than to him*

сли́шком[1]⎫
чересчу́р ⎭ *too, excessively*
э́то сли́шком мно́го *that is too much*
э́то сли́шком ма́ло *that is too little*
(N.B. *never* with немно́го)

о́чень *very, very much*
она́ о́чень мила́ *she is very nice*
я её о́чень люблю́ *I like her very much*
я о́чень хочу́ *I want to very much*
у него́ о́чень ⎰мно́го⎱ де́нег *he has* ⎰*a great deal of*⎱ *money*
　　　　　　 ⎱ма́ло ⎰ 　　　　　 ⎱*very little* ⎰
(N.B. *never* with немно́го)

---

[1] Not to be confused with с ли́шком (two words) *more than* (lit. *with excess*), e.g. ему́ с ли́шком со́рок лет or ему́ со́рок с ли́шком лет *he is over forty.*

весьма́ *very, exceedingly*

 я весьма́ благода́рен *I am exceedingly grateful*

во́все не *not in the least*

 я во́все не хочу́ *I don't in the least want to*

почти́ [что] *almost*

 почти́ темно́ *it is nearly dark*
 я почти́ что упа́л *I nearly fell down*

далеко́ не ⎱
совсе́м не ⎰ *far from, not nearly, not at all*

 он далеко́ не бога́тый челове́к *he is far from being a rich man*
 я совсе́м не понима́ю *I don't understand at all*

совсе́м *quite*

 мне совсе́м удо́бно *I'm quite comfortable*

не совсе́м *not quite*

вполне́ *entirely, completely*

сплошь *entirely, all over*

едва́, е́ле, е́ле-е́ле, чуть, чуть-чу́ть *scarcely, with difficulty*

 он едва́ уме́ет писа́ть *he scarcely knows how to write*
 она́ е́ле-е́ле хо́дит *she walks with the greatest difficulty*

едва́ не, чуть [ли] не, чуть-чу́ть не *almost*

 меня́ едва́ не уби́ли *they almost killed me*
 она́ чуть-чу́ть не упа́ла *she very nearly fell down*
 (чуть-чу́ть by itself means *the tiniest bit*)

по кра́йней ме́ре *at least*

отча́сти *partly*

итого́ *in all, total* (this curious word, pronounced *itavó*, is really и + того́ (gen. sing. of то) meaning literally *and of that*; it is put at the foot of a bill, summing up the items, and from it has been formed the noun итог *total*, e.g. подвести итог счёту *to reckon up the total of* (lit. *to*) *a bill*).

Strong colloquial equivalents of о́чень *very* are: бо́льно *extremely*, *terribly*, стра́шно *frightfully*, ужа́сно *awfully*, and здо́рово (not to be confused with здоро́во, § 119) *magnificently*; the negative не бо́льно means *not particularly*.

Note on the Use of Adverbs as Numerals

As will have been noticed in the foregoing examples, the adverbs of quantity мно́го, немно́го (and its dim. немно́жко), ма́ло, сто́лько (also сто́лько-то *a certain number of*), ско́лько, не́сколько, бо́льше, and ме́ньше may be used as **indefinite numerals** (either with or without a following noun in the genitive). These adverbial forms serve for both nominative and accusative cases, e.g.

в теа́тре бы́ло ма́ло (nom.) дете́й *there were few children in the theatre*

я сего́дня ви́дел мно́го (acc.) студе́нтов *I've seen a lot of students today*

у него́ ме́ньше (nom.) недоста́тков, чем у меня́ *he has fewer failings than I have*

мы купи́ли не́сколько (acc.) книг *we bought several books*

These indefinite numerals (apart from ма́ло, немно́жко, бо́льше, and ме́ньше) may be expressed in the other cases by borrowing the oblique forms of corresponding adjectives, provided always that the associated nouns are plural, e.g.

во мно́гих слу́чаях	*in many cases*
за немно́гими исключе́ниями	*with few exceptions*
сто́льким лю́дям	*to so many people*
от не́скольких студе́нтов	*from several students*

Since ма́ло, немно́жко, бо́льше, and ме́ньше are not

treated in this way, some periphrastic expression must be used, as:

в ма́леньком коли́честве слу́чаев ⎫
в ре́дких слу́чаях ⎭ *in a few cases*

ря́дом с небольшо́й гру́ппой студе́нтов *next to a few students*

насчёт бо́льшей су́ммы де́нег *concerning more money*

When the associated noun is singular, none of these indefinite numerals may be declined, and recourse must be had to a periphrasis, usually containing the word коли́чество *quantity.*

Compare о́чень ма́ло са́хару *very little sugar*
and с о́чень ма́леньким коли́чеством са́хару *with very little sugar*

Compare ско́лько рабо́ты? *how much work?*
and в како́м коли́честве рабо́ты? *in how much work?*

Note on the Degrees of Comparison of Adverbs

The comparative of the adverb is exactly the same as the predicative comparative of the adjective, e.g.

лу́чше *better* (adj. and adv.)
ху́же *worse* (adj. and adv.)

The comparative of ра́но *early* (adv.) is ра́ньше or ра́нее and that of по́здно *late* (adv.) is по́зже or позднее́.

Besides the comparatives бо́льше, ме́ньше, да́льше, and до́льше there exist the specifically adverbial forms бо́лее, ме́нее, да́лее, and до́лее, which are used principally in idioms, while the first two also help to form the analytical comparative of adjectives and adverbs, e.g.

бо́лее и́ли ме́нее   *more or less*
не бо́лее и не ме́нее[, как . . .] *neither more nor less [than . . .]*

всё бо́лее и бо́лее	*more and more* (+ adj. or verb)
бо́лее интере́сная кни́га	*a more interesting book*
де́йствовать бо́лее геро́йски	*to act more heroically*
одева́ться бо́лее по-но́вому	*to dress more in the modern style*
ме́нее хо́лодно	*less cold, less coldly*
и так да́лее	*and so on, and so forth*

Note the superlative forms:

| наибо́лее | (*the*) *most* (adv.) |
| наиме́нее | (*the*) *least* (adv.) |

Comparatives preceded by по- (see § 87) are commonly used adverbially, e.g.

повы́ше	[*a little*] *higher*
пони́же	[*somewhat*] *lower down*
пода́льше	[*a bit*] *farther along*
побли́же	[*rather*] *closer*

Adverbs in -ски and those of the по + dat. type (§ 70) can form comparatives only analytically, with бо́лее.

PARTICLES AND CONJUNCTIONS

§ 75. и, а, но, &c.

и *and* is often used to emphasize the preceding and following words, or with the meaning *just, moreover*, e.g.

я так и ду́мал! *I thought as much!*

я зате́м и пришёл сюда́ *it was for that very purpose* [*that*] *I came here*

в то́м-то и де́ло *that's just the point*

я и говори́л ему́ . . . *moreover I had told him* . . .

и не . . . *not in the least* . . .

я и не хотéл *I didn't in the least want to*, or *what's more I didn't want to*

In some cases, especially when things are mentioned in couples, да (pronounced *də*) may be used for *and*, e.g. муж да женá *husband and wife*

It is important to notice that expressions such as *you and I* are usually introduced by мы *we*, e.g.

мы с вáми	*you and I*
мы с ним	*he and I*
мы с сестрóй	*my sister and I*

Any antithesis can be introduced by 'a' *but*, *and*, e.g.

он хóчет, а я не хочý *he wants to, but* (or *and*) *I don't*

This a takes the place of и (*and*) when any antithesis is to be indicated. It can often be rendered in English by *but* or *while*, but at the beginning of a sentence it corresponds to *and* or *now*:

а что он сказáл? *and what did he say?*

но ⎫
да ⎭ *but*

A stronger antithesis is introduced by но (or да) *but, however*; still stronger are

однáко ⎫
однáко же ⎭ *nevertheless*
всё-таки   *however, after all*

(таки can be added as an enclitic after words in the sentence, e.g. óн таки постáвил на своём *he* (sc. *in spite of everything*) *would have his own way*)

ведь, *for, but, you know, of course, after all* (used as an expostulation at the beginning of a sentence, e.g. ведь вы знáли, что я не хочý *now look here, you knew that I didn't want to*)

и́ли *or*

и . . ., и . . .   *both . . . and . . .*

ни . . ., ни . . .   *neither . . ., nor . . .*

и́ли . . ., и́ли . . .   *either . . ., or . . .*

как . . ., так и . . .   *both . . . and . . .*

ита́к *and so* (mostly used in drawing an inference)

то́же *also, too*

та́кже[1] *also*

да́же *even*

вот *this is . . ., here is . . ., there is . . .* (like French *voici, voilà*)

вон *there (yonder) is . . .*

§ 76. Questions and Answers (see also § 49)

These are either introduced by some interrogative pronoun or adverb, or indicated by the use of the enclitic interrogative particle ли, e.g.

кто вы?	*who are you?*
вы́ ли э́то?	*is that you?*
до́ма ли Ива́н	*is Ivan at home?*

In ordinary conversation the ли is often omitted and the word-order not inverted,[2] the question being indicated merely by raising the voice at the end of the sentence, e.g. э́то вы? Ива́н до́ма? Colloquially, что is often used at the beginning of a question, instead of ли, e.g.

что мы пое́дем?   *shall we go, eh?*

This same question could also be put in the following ways:

а что, мы пое́дем?	*well then, shall we go?*
пое́дем, что́ ли?	*let's go, eh?*

[1] More literary and more restricted in use than то́же.

[2] Note that ли cannot be omitted from a negative question with *inverted* word-order.

If a negative answer is expected ра́зве is very often used:

ра́зве вы зна́ете его́? [*surely*] *you don't know him, do you?*

If an affirmative answer is expected, use ра́зве не:

ра́зве вы меня́ не узна́ли? *surely you recognized me?*

ра́зве вы не хоти́те? *do you mean you don't want to?*

Incredulity and amazement are expressed by неужёли:

неужёли э́то пра́вда! *can this possibly be true?*

Doubt by вряд ли (pronounced *vr'at l'i*) *scarcely*

вряд ли э́то так *I doubt whether this is so*

ли . . ., и́ли . . . *whether . . ., or . . .*

я не зна́ю, у́мер ли он и́ли нет *I don't know whether he is dead or not*

The affirmative answer is

да *yes*, and the negative is нет *no*

but, as often as not, a question can be answered by repeating a word contained in the question, e.g.

зна́ете ли вы его́? *do you know him?* — зна́ю *yes, I do*

до́ма ли учи́тель? *is the teacher at home?* — до́ма *yes, he is*

Other common expressions are:

коне́чно   *of course*

еще́ бы!   *I should say so! rather!*

§ 77. Negations

In negative sentences the negative particle не always comes immediately before the verb when the whole sentence is negatived, but before any particular word when only that word is negatived, e.g.

я не люблю́ его́   *I don't like him*

я люблю́ не его́, а её́ *I like her, not him*

The direct object of a negatived verb is usually put in the genitive, e.g.

<blockquote>
он не лю́бит му́зыки he doesn't like music
</blockquote>

(but note the important exceptions mentioned in § 81).

When a sentence contains a pronoun or adverb beginning with ни-, or the conjunction ни..., ни..., the negative particle не must be inserted before the verb, e.g.

никого́ не ви́жу	I [can] see no one
ничего́ не хочу́	I don't want anything
я ника́к не ожида́л	I didn't in the least expect it

There is not is translated by нет which always requires the genitive, e.g.

| нет наде́жды | there is no hope |
| до́ма никого́ нет | there is nobody at home |

Is there no . . . ? is rendered by нéт ли(+ gen.) ?

§ 78. Subordinating Conjunctions

чтóбы	in order that
чтóбы не	lest
éсли	if
хотя́	although
когда́	when
пока́	while
	&c.

(for the use of these see §§ 102–5)

[как] бу́дто	
бу́дто бы	} as it were, as though, allegedly
я́кобы	

are commonly used in reporting facts, incidents, or speeches of doubtful authenticity or credibility, e.g.

он как бу́дто не хóчет I fancy he doesn't want to

он говори́т, бу́дто не хо́чет *he makes out he doesn't want to*
она́ бу́дто бы нездоро́ва *she is supposed to be unwell*

Other particles used colloquially are

аво́сь   *may be*
небо́сь   *I expect*
мол ⎫
де́скать ⎭ *says he, said he* (in quoting another's words)

which are all very commonly used in dialect, but not much
in literature or the speech of educated people.

Until 1917 the particle -с was often affixed to some
word in the sentence, especially by servants and shop-
keepers and subordinate officials when addressing em-
ployers, customers, or superiors, to indicate subservience;
it is supposed to be an abbreviation of the words суда́рь
sir and суда́рыня *madam*. Apart from the speech of some
old people, its use in the Soviet Union expresses sarcasm.

A subordinate clause in Russian is often preceded by the
correlative pronoun то in the principal clause, which is
not needed in English and is puzzling at first sight, e.g.

де́ло в том, что я не могу́ прийти́ *the point is that I can't
come*

Analogously:

мѐжду те́м, как   *while, whereas*
по́сле того́, как   *after*
до того́, как ⎫
пѐред те́м, как ⎬ *before*
(but пре́жде, чем) ⎭
cf. с тех по́р, как   *since*
до тех по́р, пока́ не   *until*
(or simply пока́ не)

Sometimes the correlative may be omitted, as in [для того], чтобы and [с тем], чтобы *in order that, so that*.

When что beginning a clause means *what* (not *that*) it is sometimes accented (чтò).

THE PREPOSITIONS AND THE USE OF CASES WITH AND WITHOUT PREPOSITIONS

§ 79. Alphabetical List of Prepositions

excluding normal gerunds used as prepositions and prepositional phrases (e.g. adverb + simple preposition, simple preposition + noun) other than those conventionally written as one word.

	Basic meaning	*Followed by*
без (безо)	*without*	Gen.
благодаря́	*thanks to, owing to*	Dat.
близ[1]	*near*	Gen.
в (во)	*into, in*	Acc. Loc.
вверху́	*at the top of*	Gen.
ввиду́	*in view of, seeing*	Gen.
вдоль	*along*	Gen.
вме́сто	*instead of*	Gen.
вне	*outside* (position)	Gen.
внизу́	*at the foot, bottom of*	Gen.
внутри́	*inside* (position)	Gen.
внутрь	*inside* (direction)	Gen.
во́зле	*beside*	Gen.
вокру́г	*around*	Gen.
вопреки́	*despite, contrary to*	Dat.
впереди́	*in front of, ahead of*	Gen.
вро́де	*like*	Gen.
вслед	*after, following*	Dat.
всле́дствие	*owing to, on account of*	Gen.
до	*up to, before*	Gen.

[1] Pronounced as if written близь.

	Basic meaning	*Followed by*
для	*for, for the use of*	Gen.
за	*for, behind*	Acc.Instr.Nom.[1]
из (изо)	*out of*	Gen.
из-за	*from behind, because of*	Gen.
из-под	*from under*	Gen.
к (ко)	*towards; to* (a person)	Dat.
кро́ме	*besides, except*	Gen.
круго́м	*around*	Gen.
ме́жду (меж)	*between*	Instr. Gen.
ми́мо	*past*	Gen.
на	*on to, on*	Acc. Loc.
навстре́чу	*towards, to meet*	Dat.
над (надо)	*above*	Instr.
напереко́р	*in defiance of*	Dat.
наподо́бие	*like, similar to*	Gen.
напро́тив	*opposite*	Gen.
насчёт	*about, as regards*	Gen.
несмотря́ на	*in spite of*	Acc.
о (об, обо)	*about, against*	Loc. Acc.
о́коло	*about, near*	Gen.
от (ото)	*away from; from* (a person)	Gen.
пе́ред пе́редо, (пред, пре́до)	*in front of, [just] before*	Instr.
по	*according to, along, till, after*	Dat. Acc. Loc.
пове́рх	*over, on top of*	Gen.
под (подо)	*under*	Acc. Instr.
по́дле	*beside, by*	Gen.
позади́	*behind, at the back of*	Gen.
поми́мо	*besides, apart from*	Gen.

[1] See § 80.

	Basic meaning	Followed by
поперёк	across	Gen.
после	after	Gen.
посреди	in the middle of	Gen.
посредством	by means of	Gen.
прежде	before	Gen.
при	in the presence of, at, near	Loc.
про	about, concerning	Acc.
против	against, opposite	Gen.
противно	contrary to	Dat.
путём	by means of	Gen.
ради	for the sake of	Gen.
с (со)	with, down from, about	Instr. Gen. Acc.
сбоку	at the side of	Gen.
сверх	above, beyond, on top of	Gen.
свыше	over, more than	Gen.
сзади	behind, at the back of	Gen.
сквозь	through	Acc.
согласно	according to	Dat.
соответственно	in compliance with	Dat.
спустя	after	Acc.
среди	amid, among	Gen.
у	near, in the possession of, at the house of	Gen.
через	through, across; in (time)	Acc.

§ 80. The Nominative

The nominative is used, as in other languages, for the subject and the predicate of the sentence, e.g.

я твой отец *I* [*am*] *your father*

though under certain conditions the predicate is in the instrumental, see § 84.

The nominative is used for the vocative, except in the three instances mentioned in § 39, e.g.

оте́ц мой!　　　　*oh, father!*
Cа́ша, иди́ сюда́!　*Sasha, come here!*

за + nom.

The nominative is used after the preposition за *for* in phrases such as:

что э́то за кни́га? *what book is that? what sort of book is that?* (lit. *what this for book*). Cf. German: *was ist das für ein Buch?*

however, the accusative is required in object-phrases, e.g.

что за кни́гу вы купи́ли? *what [sort of] book did you buy?*

§ 81. The Genitive

The genitive is used to denote:

1. Possession:

дом отца́ *the house of the father, the father's house*

In this sense it may be replaced by the possessive adjective, see § 55.

2. Qualities:

ма́льчик хоро́шего хара́ктера　*a boy of good character*
челове́к пожилы́х лет　　　　　*a man of advanced years*

3. Partition:

я хочу́ воды́　　　　　　　　*I want [some] water*
хле́ба, пожа́луйста!　　　　*[some] bread, please!*
кусо́к мя́са　　　　　　　　　*a piece of meat*

often with the meaning of *a lot* after verbs with the prefix
на-:

> накопи́лось пи́сем [*a lot of*] *letters have accumulated*

4. Quantity:

> стака́н ча́ю *a glass of tea* (tea in Russia is usually drunk
> out of glasses)
>
> кило́ са́хару *a kilogram of sugar*
> ма́сса люде́й *a mass (crowd) of people*

with adverbs of quantity:

мно́го дете́й	*many children*
ма́ло друзе́й	*few friends*
немно́го (dim. немно́жко) мя́са	*a little meat*
не́сколько лет	*some years*

for the genitive in -y see § 39, Obs. 6; for the other adverbs
of quantity, and also for their adjectival forms and use,
see § 74, and § 54, Obs. 9.

5. With numerals, except оди́н *one* (see § 60).

6. Time in certain expressions:

сего́дня	*today* (lit. *of this day*)
пе́рвого ма́рта	*on the first of March*

7. Comparison:

> он слабе́е меня́   *he* [*is*] *weaker than I*

8. The genitive is always used with certain verbs:

боя́ться ⎫ опаса́ться ⎭	*to be afraid* (*of*)
пуга́ться	*to be frightened* (*by*)
(note also береги́(те)сь	*beware of . . .*!)

сторони́ться ⎫ чужда́ться ⎬ дичи́ться ⎭	*to shun*
избега́ть	*to avoid*
стесня́ться	*to be shy (of)*
стыди́ться	*to be ashamed (of)*
жела́ть	*to desire, wish*
жа́ждать	*to crave, thirst (for)*
хоте́ть	*to wish, want*
иска́ть	*to seek, look (for)*
проси́ть	*to beg, ask (for)*
тре́бовать	*to demand*
ждать ⎫ дожида́ться ⎬ ожида́ть ⎭	*to wait (for), await*
добива́ться (ipf.)	*to strive (for), try (for)*
доби́ться (pf.)	*to obtain, achieve*
достига́ть	*to reach, attain*
слу́шаться	*to obey*
держа́ться ⎫ приде́рживаться ⎭	*to adhere (to), keep (to)*
каса́ться (pf. косну́ться)	*to touch, concern*
лиша́ть	*to deprive (of)*

and the impersonal verbs of lacking: недостава́ть, не-хвата́ть (more correctly: не достава́ть, не хвата́ть).

Note that the verbs проси́ть, тре́бовать, and иска́ть are followed by the accusative case of nouns denoting a particular material object or a person, e.g. я ищу́ (прошу́, тре́бую) сестру́, свою́ газе́ту; the verb ждать is followed by the accusative when the object denotes an animate being: жду сестру́, but жду по́езда, письма́. When the object of any of these verbs is an abstract noun, it will *always* be in the genitive.

Examples:

я боюсь мо́ря *I am afraid of the sea*

хоти́те ли вы вина́ *would you like some wine?* but я хочу́
э́ту кни́гу (acc.) *I want this book*

жела́ю вам счастли́вого пути́! *I wish you a safe journey!*

[жела́ю вам] всего́ хоро́шего (лу́чшего)! [*I wish you*]
everything good (all the best)! (common phrases on saying good-bye or ending a letter.)

я ищу́ рабо́ты *I am looking for work*

жду ва́шего приéзда *I am awaiting your arrival*

сто́ило ему́ жи́зни *it cost him his life* (but in prices the acc.
is used, as сто́ит ты́сячу рубле́й *it costs 1,000 roubles*)

э́то каса́ется вас *this concerns you*

что каса́ется меня́ *as far as I am concerned*

notice the idiom:

ми́лости про́сим! *please come and see us! welcome!* (lit. *we
crave the favour*, a common form of general invitation).

9. After certain adjectives in the shorter or attributive
form:

по́лон *full*
вагóн по́лон люде́й *the carriage is full of people*
досто́ин *worthy*
она́ досто́йна его́ *she is worthy of him*

10. After a negatived verb the direct object is, as a rule,
in the genitive case, e.g.

я не ви́жу ва́шего до́ма *I do not* (= *cannot*) *see your house*
он не слы́шит моего́ го́лоса *he cannot hear my voice*
я не зна́ю ва́шей сестры́ *I don't know your sister*

However, this rule is frequently broken in speech and, less
frequently, in writing:

(i) When the object is a specific animate being:

вы не пóмните Вáню и Мáшу? *don't you remember Vanya and Masha?*

он не уважáл женý *he didn't respect his wife*

онá не лю́бит свою́ дочь *she doesn't love her daughter*

(ii) When the negative is чýть не or едвá не *nearly, almost*, so that the underlying idea is affirmative:

онá едвá не пропустúла пóезд *she very nearly missed the train* (= *she caught it with difficulty*)

(iii) When the sentence contains a 'double' negative, so that the meaning is fundamentally affirmative:

я не мог не дать емý нагрáду *I couldn't help but give him a reward* (= *I gave . . . because I had to*)

(iv) When the object is dependent on an infinitive following a negatived auxiliary; the genitive in such a case is felt to be rather old-fashioned:

я не хочý (не мог и т. д.) читáть ромáны *I don't want to (couldn't, &c.) read novels*

(v) When it denotes one particular object (or group of objects), the whole of which is (or would be) affected by the action of the verb; the use of the genitive here is literary and may sound somewhat stilted in speech:

он ещё не читáл э́то письмó *he hasn't read this letter yet*

онá не бралá ваш карандáш *she didn't take your pencil*

я не покупáю э́ту газéту *I don't buy this newspaper*

я не пью э́то винó *I am not drinking this wine* (particular)

cf. я не пью винá *I don't drink wine* (in general)

It must be borne in mind that only the genitive is possible when the object denotes (*a*) an abstract noun, or (*b*) a partitive notion (*some, any*); and the genitive is preferred (*c*) when the negative idea is stressed by a word like никогда *never* and ни разу *not [even] once*, and (*d*) after the verbs не видеть and не слышать, e.g.

- (*a*) я не имею возможности . . . *I have no opportunity to . . .*
  это не играет роли *that doesn't matter (plays no part)*
- (*b*) он мне не даёт денег *he doesn't give me [any] money*
- (*c*) он никогда не читает романов *he never reads novels*
- (*d*) я раньше не видел этой картины *I haven't seen this picture before*

The genitive is also always used after нет *there is not*, не будет *there will not be*, and не было *there was not:*

у меня нет денег *I have no money*
сегодня не будет представления *today there will be no performance*
не будет дождя *there won't be any rain*
не было ничего *there was nothing*
не было мороза *it wasn't frosty*

11. Note that the genitive and accusative cases are identical in the singular of animate masculine nouns ending in a consonant or -ь, and in the plural of animate nouns of all genders. See § 83.

12. Notice the idioms:

дома *at home*
мало того, что . . . *it's not enough that . . .*
мало того, чтобы + infin. *not content with . . ., in addition to . . .*

The genitive is used after the following prepositions:
без (**безо** before certain groups of consonants) *without*

без меня *without me, in my absence*
безо всего *without anything*

notice без того, чтобы сказать вам *without telling you*

до *up to, till, before*

до того́ *to that* (sc. *extent*), *to such an extent, so*
до того́ вре́мени *up to that time*
до сих по́р *till now* (see § 68)
до конца́ *up to the end*
до рождества́ Христо́ва *before the birth of Christ*, B.C.
до на́шей э́ры B.C. (lit. *before our era*) (Soviet usage)
до вас *before your time, before your arrival*

notice the idioms:

мне не до э́того *I have no time* (or *no inclination*) *for this*
    (sc. *now*)
им не до нас *they can't be bothered with us* (sc. *they have*
    more important things to do)
до́сыта *to one's heart's content*

из (**изо** before certain groups of consonants) *from, out of, of*
я получи́л письмо́ из Москвы́ *I have received a letter*
    from Moscow
он прие́хал из А́нглии *he has arrived from England*
из воды́ *from out of the water*
из зо́лота *of gold*
из стекла́ *of glass*
изо дня в день *from day to day*

it is always used in the expressions *one of, two of,* &c., e.g.

в одно́м из больши́х домо́в *in one of the big houses* . . .

the gen. cannot be used in such cases without a preposition.
Notice the idiom:

и́з дому *from home, out of the house*

The following two compound prepositions also take the
genitive:

из-за *from behind, from beyond, from out of, on account of*
из-за забо́ра *from behind the fence*

из-за грани́цы *from beyond the frontier,* i.e. *from abroad*
из-за э́того *on account of, as a result of, this*
из-за мое́й боле́зни *because of, as a result of, my illness*

из-под *from under*
   из-под стола́ *from under the table*

от (**ото** before certain groups of consonants) *from, away from*

он уе́хал от нас	*he has gone away from us* (sc. *left us*)
я получи́л письмо́ от бра́та	*I have received a letter from* (sc. *my*) *brother*
от ра́дости	*from joy*
от ску́ки	*from tedium*
ото всего́ э́того	*from* (*as a result of*) *all this*
он у́мер от э́того	*he died from* (*of*) *this*
ва́ше письмо́ от двадца́того ма́я	*your letter of 20th May*

notice the idiom:

           о́троду *in all one's life*

Phrases are common in which both от and до are used:

от Ленингра́да до Москвы́	*from Leningrad to Moscow*
от нача́ла до конца́	*from beginning to end*
от вре́мени до вре́мени	*from time to time*

с (**со** before certain groups of consonants) *from, since, down from, off*

с головы́ до ног	*from head to foot* (lit. *feet*)
с утра́ до ве́чера	*from morning till evening*
с января́	*since January*
с пя́того ма́я	*from the 5th of May*
он упа́л с кры́ши	*he fell from the roof*

снять пальто́ с крючка́	*to take one's coat from a hook*
верну́ться с мо́ря	*to return from the sea-side*
с рабо́ты, с фа́брики	*from work, from the factory*
со ста́нции, с по́чты	*from the station, from the post-office*
ско́лько с вас взя́ли?	*how much did they take off you?* (e.g. in shops, cf. *how much did they rook you for?*)
с меня́ взя́ли о́чень до́рого	*they made me pay dear*
со дня на́ день	*from day to day*
со ску́ки	*from tedium*
с отча́яния	*from despair*
с ва́шего позволе́ния	*with your permission*
also с како́й ста́ти?	*to what purpose?*

Notice adverbs such as:

сра́зу	*at once*
я сра́зу узна́л его́	*I immediately recognized him*
сно́ва	*again*
сы́знова	*all over again*
снача́ла	*at first*

which are formed by the preposition с with the genitive of nouns and adjectives.

y *near, at the house of, in the possession of, from*

As the verb *to have* (име́ть) is very seldom used in Russian unless the object is an abstract noun, recourse has to be had to a paraphrase to express possession, temporary or permanent. This paraphrase consists of the preposition y followed by a noun or pronoun in the genitive and a part of the verb *to be* (быть); the part most commonly used is есть *is*, though of course бу́дет *will be*, and бы́ло *was* are also very frequent. It remains to be said that the word есть is very often omitted, especially in the spoken language, so that the commonest way of saying in Russian:

I have	is	у меня́
thou hast	,,	у тебя́
he, she has	,,	у него́, у неё
we have	,,	у нас
you have	,,	у вас
they have	,,	у них

For example:

у меня́ на́сморк *I have a cold in the head*

у бра́та просту́да (*my*) *brother has a chill*

у них мно́го де́нег *they have a lot of money*

у него́ моя́ кни́га *he has* my *book*

у кого́ моя́ кни́га ? *who has my book?*

ва́ша кни́га у него́ he *has your book*

у челове́ка два у́ха и два гла́за *man has two ears and two eyes*

како́й у вас большо́й сад! *what a big garden you have!*

есть is used when inquiring as to the existence or not of something in someone's possession, i.e. when the main idea of the sentence is 'have' as opposed to 'have not'. Replies to such questions as

есть у вас кни́га по ру́сской литерату́ре? *have you [got] a book on Russian literature?* (sc. *or haven't you?*)

should contain either есть or нет, and will often consist of one of these words alone:

да, есть [у меня́ така́я кни́га]   *yes, I have*

нет [у меня́ тако́й кни́ги[1]]   *no, I haven't*

Similarly, to the questions:

есть у вас де́ньги?   *have you any money?*

[1] For use of genitive after нет, see opposite, p. 189.

есть у вас сего́дня я́блоки? *have you any apples today?*

the reply could be: есть *yes* or нет *no.*

When in English the emphasis is on some word other than the verb *to have,* then есть will be omitted both from the question:

моя́ кни́га у вас? *have* you *got my book?* (sc. *or has some-one else got it?*)

and from the answer:

ва́ша кни́га не у меня́, а у него́ *I haven't your book — he has it* (lit. *your book is not in my possession, but in his*)

In the past and future tenses, of course, the appropriate form of the verb быть must never be omitted —

у меня́ был на́сморк	*I had a cold*
у них бу́дут де́ньги	*they will have money*
у него́ была́ ва́ша кни́га	*he had your book*
у меня́ бы́ли сёстры	*I had sisters*
была́ у вас така́я шля́па?	*did you have a hat like this?*

The negative of есть is нет (a contraction of не есть); unlike есть, нет can never be omitted. Hence:

I have not	is	у меня́ нет	
I had not	„	у меня́ не́ было	$\Big\}$ + gen.
I shall not have	„	у меня́ не бу́дет	

Notice that нет, не́ было, and не бу́дет are all impersonal expressions and, being negative verbs, demand that their 'object' shall be in the genitive case, e.g.

I haven't a cold	у меня́ нет на́сморка
they won't have money	у них не бу́дет де́нег
he hadn't your book	у него́ не́ было ва́шей кни́ги

Notice the idioms:

у вас хоро́ший вид *you look well* (lit. *you have a good aspect*)
у него́ был плохо́й вид *he looked ill*

A subtle distinction is expressed by the word-order; it is a way of conveying the same difference as that between the definite and indefinite articles in English.

When a nominative follows the expression with y + gen., it is usually to be translated with the indefinite article, as in

> у меня́ [есть] соба́ка *I have a dog*

whereas, when the nominative precedes, the object(s) denoted by it will have been mentioned before, and so the definite article will generally be appropriate, as in

> соба́ка у меня́ *I have the dog* (not necessarily *my* dog), *the dog is in my possession, at my house, in my room,* &c.

Similarly:

> у него́ автомоби́ль means *he has a motor-car*

but

> автомоби́ль у него́ means *the motor-car is at present in his possession, he has the motor-car* (probably not *his own*)

y often means *at the house of,* e.g.

> они́ у нас *they* [*are*] *at our house*
> у нас сего́дня бал [*there is*] *a dance at our house today*
> я обе́даю сего́дня у друзе́й *I am dining at the house of some friends today*

With the personal pronoun it also acquires the meaning of a possessive adjective, e.g.

> у меня́ зуб боли́т *my tooth aches, I have got toothache*
> голова́ у неё боли́т *her head aches, she has a headache*
> дом у нас гори́т *our house is burning*
> кошелёк у меня́ пропа́л *I have lost my purse*
> он был у меня́ в карма́не *it was in my pocket*
> у нас в до́ме больша́я ку́хня *there's a large kitchen in our house*

In exclamatory remarks y, when coupled with the personal pronoun, may acquire something of the nature of the Latin ethic dative, e.g.

она́ у меня́ хоро́шая ло́шадь! *that's a fine horse!* (sc. *of mine*)

ты у меня́ краса́вица! *you're a beauty !* (not ironically, sc. *you are mine, you are beautiful, and I'm proud of you*)

она́ у вас у́мница! *she's a clever one !* (sc. *your little girl*)

Curiously enough, after certain verbs y can also mean *from*, e.g.

он о́тнял у меня́ де́ньги *he took the money away from me*

я взял у него́ кни́гу *I took the (or a) book from him*

он заказа́л костю́м у э́того портно́го *he ordered a suit from this tailor*

There are a number of prepositions taking the genitive which were originally adverbs (some, marked below with an asterisk, are still used as such), or cases of nouns with or without other prepositions:

близ *near*

близ Москвы́ *near Moscow*

о́коло *around, about, near*

о́коло Ло́ндона   (1) *not far from London*
(2) *around London*

о́коло двадцати́ лет   *about 20 years*

*вокру́г ⎫
*круго́м ⎭ *round, around*

вокру́г све́та *round the world*

по́дле ⎫
*во́зле ⎭ *beside, alongside*

во́зле меня́ *beside me*

по́дле реки́ *by the side of the river*

вдоль *along, down, up*

вдоль у́лицы *down the street*

вне *outside*

вне ко́мнаты *outside the room*

*внутри́ *inside*

внутри́ ко́мнаты *inside the room*

*впереди́ *in front of*

впереди́ нас *ahead of us*

вме́сто *instead of*

вме́сто того́ *instead of that*

сверх *over, on top of*

сверх того́ *in addition to that*

сверх (or пове́рх) шу́бы *over one's fur coat*

(свѐрхъесте́ственный *supernatural*)

среди́ (and *посреди́) *in the middle of, among*

среди́ поле́й *in the middle of the fields*

(Средизе́мное мо́ре *the Mediterranean*)

*позади́ (and *сза́ди) *behind, to the rear of*

позади́ меня́ *behind me*

*по́сле *after*

по́сле обе́да *after dinner*

*ми́мо *past*

ми́мо до́ма *past the house* (cf. мимохо́дом *in passing*)

для *for*

для чего́? *what for?*

он сде́лал э́то для меня́ *he did this for me*

кро́ме *besides, except*

кро́ме э́того *besides this*

кро́ме понеде́льника *except Monday*

ра́ди *for the sake of*

ра́ди Бо́га! *for God's sake!*

про́тив *against, opposite*

про́тив неприя́теля *against the enemy*

про́тив холе́ры *against cholera*

про́тив нас (1) *against us*, (2) *opposite us*

ме́жду (and **меж**) *between* (usually with instr., but with gen. pl. in a few fixed expressions, as

ме́жду двух огне́й *between two fires*)

and several others (see § 79).

§ 82. The Dative

is used without a preposition to express the object of certain Russian verbs; these include:

(по)ве́рить *to believe*

я вам ве́рю *I believe you*

он ве́рит сообще́нию *he believes the message*

but N.B. ве́ровать or ве́рить в Бо́га *to believe in God*

удивля́ться, удиви́ться *to be astonished at*

я удивля́юсь э́тому *I am astonished at this*

(об)ра́доваться *to rejoice at*

ра́дуемся ва́шему прие́зду *we rejoice at your arrival*

кла́няться, поклони́ться *to greet* (lit. *to bow to*)

кла́няюсь всем *greetings to all*

кла́няйтесь им от меня́ *give them my regards*

улыба́ться, улыбну́ться *to smile at/on*

судьба́ улыба́ется ей *fortune smiles on her*

не улыба́йся ему́ *don't smile at him*

(по)смея́ться *to laugh at* (something amusing)

чему́ вы смеётесь? *what are you laughing at?*

(N.B. *to laugh at* (=*to mock*) is смея́ться над + instr.)

(по)моли́ться *to pray to*

    я молю́сь Бо́гу *I pray to God*

(по)зави́довать *to envy*

    я вам зави́дую *I envy you*

(по)льсти́ть *to flatter*

    она́ льстит ему́ *she flatters him*

(по)сове́товать *to advise*

    он нам посове́тует *he will advise us*

угрожа́ть and грози́ть, пригрози́ть *to threaten*

    грози́т нам беда́ *misfortune is threatening us*

(по)грози́ть *to make threatening gestures*

    он погрози́л нам пистоле́том *he threatened us with a pistol*

(ото)мсти́ть *to take vengeance on*

    мы отомсти́м врагу́ *we'll take vengeance on the enemy*

(на)учи́ть (+ acc. of person and dat. of thing taught) *to teach*

    чему́ он вас у́чит? *what is he teaching you?*

учи́ться, вы́учиться/научи́ться *to learn*

    я учу́сь ру́сскому языку́ *I am learning Russian*

подража́ть *to imitate*

    не подража́й ему́ *don't imitate him*

напомина́ть, напо́мнить *to remind*

    напо́мните мне об э́том *remind me about this*

    э́то мне напомина́ет Мари́ю *this reminds me of Mary*

веле́ть (ipf. and pf.) *to order*

    я вам велю́ молча́ть *I [shall] order you to keep silent*

прика́зывать, приказа́ть *to command, order*

    он нам приказа́л вы́йти *he ordered us [to go] out*

(по)нра́виться *to please*

она́ мне нра́вится *I like her* (lit. *she pleases me*)

они́ ему́ нра́вятся *he likes them*

насле́довать (ipf. and pf.), унасле́довать (pf.) *to succeed
(be heir) to*

он насле́довал своему́ дя́де *he was heir to his uncle*

some verbs indicating irritation, hindrance, and prohibition:

досажда́ть, досади́ть *to vex, annoy*

он всё досажда́ет сестре́ *he keeps on annoying his sister*

надоеда́ть, надое́сть *to tire, bore*

э́то де́ло нам надое́ло *we are sick of this business*

наску́чивать, наску́чить *to weary, bore*

э́то мне наску́чило *I am weary of it*

(па)груби́ть *to be rude to*

он нагруби́л всем нам *he was rude to us all*

изменя́ть, измени́ть *to betray, fail*

я измени́л друзья́м *I let down my friends*

(по)меша́ть *to disturb, bother*

я вам не меша́ю? *am I disturbing you?*

(вос)препя́тствовать *to impede*

э́то препя́тствовало ему́ в разви́тии *it hindered his
development*

and verbs expressing sympathy and co-operation, such as:

сочу́вствовать *to sympathize with*

мы вам сочу́вствуем *we sympathize with you*

помога́ть, помо́чь *to help, aid*

чем могу́ вам помо́чь? *how can I help you?*

посо́бствовать *to aid, further*

содействовать *to co-operate, assist*

покровительствовать *to patronize, protect*

благоприятствовать *to favour, assist*

сопутствовать *to accompany, go hand in hand with*

The indirect object of Russian verbs is expressed in the dative case, corresponding to English *to* and *for*; among the verbs commonly associated with this construction are:

давать, дать *to give*

    он дал ей деньги *he gave her* (i.e. *to her*) *money*

    я даю вам слово *I give you my word*

(по)дарить *to present*

    подарили председателю часы *they presented a clock to the chairman*

говорить, сказать *to tell*

    скажи мне, где ты был *tell me where you have been*

рассказывать, рассказать *to narrate, tell*

    он нам рассказал анекдот *he told us an anecdote*

(по)жаловаться *to complain*

    он жалуется им на вас *he complains to them about you*

(на)писать *to write*

    пишу письмо сестре *I am writing a letter to my sister*

посылать, послать *to send*

    она послала ему книгу *she sent him a book*

покупать, купить *to buy*

    он купил мальчику собаку *he bought the boy* (i.e. *for the boy*) *a dog*

записывать, записать *to write down*

    я вам запишу его адрес *I'll jot down his address for you*

рекомендова́ть (ipf. and pf.), порекомендова́ть (pf.) *to recommend*

он рекомендова́л нам гости́ницу *he recommended us a hotel*

(по)звони́ть *to ring up, telephone*

мы позвони́ли отцу́ *we rang father*

сообща́ть, сообщи́ть *to communicate*

он нам сообщи́л пла́ны *he informed us of the plans*

Also with impersonal verbs:

мне хо́чется+infin. *I feel like (doing something)*

мне пить хо́чется *I am thirsty* (lit. *I want to drink.* There is no adjective for *thirsty* in Russian)

ка́жется *it seems*

мне ка́жется *it seems to me* (sc. *I think*)

мне не спи́тся *I cannot sleep*

мне нездоро́вится *I am unwell*

Notice the curious idiom:

он прихо́дится мне дя́дей (instr.) *he is my uncle*, &c.

which is used to describe relationships (N.B. прихо́дится usually means *one has to* + infin.).

The dative is also used in the following common expressions:

мо́жно мне?	*may I?*
вам невозмо́жно	*you cannot*
вам нельзя́	*you must not, may not*
пора́ нам!	*it is time for us* (sc. *to go*)
я рад ва́шему прие́зду	*I am glad you have arrived*

After adverbs expressing pleasure, displeasure, heat, cold, &c., e.g.

уго́дно ли вам . . . ?	*would you like* (+ infin.)?

как вам уго́дно	*just as you like*
мне хо́лодно	*I am cold*
мне бы́ло тепло́	*I was warm*
мне бу́дет жа́рко	*I shall be hot*
мне неприя́тно + infin.	*it is unpleasant for me to . . .*
мне жаль	*I am sorry*

Also in expressing age:

ско́лько вам лет? *how old are you?* (lit. *how many to you of years?*)

мне два́дцать лет *I am twenty*

and in a few expressions such as:

э́та кни́га вам	*this book is for you*
э́то мне	*this is for me*
цена́ э́тим веща́м	*the value of these things*
он нам сосе́д	*he is our neighbour*
он мне враг	*he is an enemy of mine*
э́то не пришло́ мне в го́лову	*it didn't enter my head*

The dative is also used with the infinitive to express *is to, has got to*, e.g.

кому́ написа́ть э́то письмо́?	*who is to write this letter?*
э́тому не быть	*this is not to be*
быть беде́	*there's going to be trouble*

Notice the idioms:

та́к себе *fairly, so-so*

e.g. как э́то вам нра́вится? та́к себе! *how do you like that? — not bad!*

и тому́ подо́бное *and so on* (abbr. и т. п. = &c.) (lit. *and to that similar*: sometimes also in pl.)

домо́й (derived from an old dat. form) *homewards, [to] home*

The dative is used after the following prepositions:

к (**ко** before certain groups of consonants) *to*

я пришёл к вам	*I have come to you*
приходи́те к нам	*come to us*, sc. *come and see us*
приходи́те ко мне	*come and see me*
у меня́ к вам про́сьба	*I have a favour to ask you*
к ве́черу	*towards evening*
к о́сени	*towards autumn, by the autumn*
к нача́лу октября́	*by the beginning of October*
к концу́ ноября́	*by the end of November*
к пе́рвому а́вгуста	*by the first of August*
к пяти́ часа́м	*by five o'clock*

Notice the idioms:

к сожале́нию	*unfortunately, to my regret*
к несча́стью	*unfortunately, unhappily*
к моему́ удивле́нию	*to my surprise*
э́то вам к лицу́	*that suits you* (of clothes)
к мои́м нога́м	(*he fell*) *at my feet*
лицо́м к лицу́	*face to face*
кста́ти	*by the by; à propos*

вопреки́ *against, in spite of*

вопреки́ прили́чиям	*in defiance of decorum*

по *along, over, according to*

по у́лице	*along the street*
по́ морю	*over the sea, by sea*
по-мо́ему or по моему́ мне́нию	*in my opinion*
почему́?	*why?* (*on what grounds?*)
потому́ что	*because*
по-пре́жнсму	*as formerly*
по но́вому сти́лю по ста́рому сти́лю	*according to the new, old, style*

(the last two expressions were formerly used in dating letters, the old Russian (Julian) calendar being, in this century, thirteen days behind ours (Gregorian); the abbreviations are: ст. ст., н. ст.).

Notice the common idioms:

потихо́ньку *quietly, on the sly*
понемно́жку ⎫
ма́ло-пома́лу ⎭ *gradually, little by little*
по желе́зной доро́ге *by rail*
по слу́чаю + gen. *on the occasion of . . .*
поднево́ле *perforce*
по мое́й ча́сти *in my line, in my department* (lit. *part*)
това́рищ по шко́ле *a school-friend*
я уда́рил его́ по голове́ *I hit him on the head*
я уда́рил его́ по плеча́м *I hit him about the shoulders*
по возвы́шенным це́нам *at raised prices* (sc. *higher than usual*)

also distributively:

по ноча́м *at night* (sc. *frequently*)
по утра́м *in the morning* (sc. *every morning*)
по воскресе́ньям *on Sundays, every Sunday*
он дал всем нам по я́блоку *he gave us all an apple each*
по пяти́ рубле́й (dat. + gen. pl.) *at five roubles each*

and a few other prepositions (see § 79).

§ 83. The Accusative is used

1. To denote the object of a transitive verb, e.g.

я люблю́ свою́ ро́дину *I love my country*

It has already been remarked that the acc. sing. of masculine nouns ending in a consonant or -ь, and the acc. pl. of nouns of all genders, is the same in form as the genitive in the case of animate, and the same as the nominative in the case of inanimate, nouns. All nouns in -a and -я have

acc. sing. in -y and -ю; all feminine nouns in -ь have acc.
sing. like nom. sing.

The same rule applies to all adjectives and to all the
pronouns except the personal pronouns; the accusative of
the personal pronouns is always the same as the genitive,
even the accusative of the neuter pronoun оно́ *it* being the
same, not as the nom., but as the gen., viz. его́.

The following examples of accusatives will serve to illus-
trate this basic rule of Russian:

я ви́дел . . .	*I saw* . . .
стол и студе́нта	*the table and the student*
столы́ и студе́нтов	*the tables and the students*
большо́го медве́дя	*a big bear* (медве́дь, masc.)
большу́ю ло́шадь	*a big horse* (ло́шадь, fem.)
медве́дей и лошаде́й	*bears and horses*
но́вого судью́	*the new judge* (судья́, masc.)
но́вых суде́й	*the new judges*
ста́рую актри́су	*the old actress*
ста́рых актри́с	*the old actresses*
ва́ши кни́ги	*your books*
ва́ших соба́к	*your dogs*

It must be observed, however, that this was not always
so; the old accusative of nouns (apart from those in -а, -я)
was invariably the same as the nom., and this is still to be
seen in a few expressions which became crystallized before
the genitive came to be used for the accusative in the case
of animate beings; such phrases, amongst others, are:

вы́йти за́муж *to marry*

(**N.B.** said of the woman only; the phrase literally means
to go out behind a man or *a husband*)

его́ произвели́ в полко́вники *they have promoted him to be
a colonel* (lit. *into the colonels*)

звать в го́сти *to invite* (lit. *to call into guests*, sc. *as guests*)
поступи́ть в солда́ты *to enlist*

2. To express duration of time and distance:

це́лый день	*a whole day*
всё ле́то	*all summer*
э́ту зи́му	[*throughout*] *this winter*
про́шлую о́сень	[*all*] *last autumn*
бу́дущую весну́	[*all*] *next spring*
кру́глый год	*the whole year round*
оди́н год	(*for*) *one year* (duration, not intention)
це́лую неде́лю	(*for*) *a whole week* (ditto)
мы прошли́ два киломе́тра	(acc.+gen. sing., cf. § 61)
	we have walked two kilometres

3. With жаль *pity*, in expressing the person pitied (but N.B. не жаль requires gen., as also does жаль in the sense of [*be*]*grudge*).

ему́ жаль Ма́шу	*he is sorry for Masha*
мне жаль сестру́	*I am sorry for my sister*
but мне не жаль сестры́	*I am not sorry for my sister*
ему́ бы́ло жаль рубля́ для дру́га	*he begrudged his friend a rouble*

The accusative is used after the following prepositions:

В (**ВО** before certain groups of consonants) *into*

я е́ду в Ита́лию	*I am travelling to Italy*
я е́ду в Ло́ндон	*I am travelling to London*
в Крым	*to the Crimea*
он вошёл в ко́мнату	*he came into the room*

Notice the following idiomatic uses:

в понеде́льник	*on Monday*
во вто́рник	*on Tuesday*
в день моего́ рожде́ния	*on my birthday*

в два часá	*at two o'clock*
раз в день	*once a day*
два рáза в недéлю	*twice a week*
во чтó бы то ни стáло	*cost what it may*
в два рубля́	*costing two roubles*
в рубль	*at one rouble*
в два этажá	*two stories [high]*
в ты́сячу раз лу́чше	*a thousand times better*
в старину́	*in the old days*
в таку́ю погóду	*in such weather*
во врéмя + gen.	*during [the time of]*
вóвремя	*opportunely, in time*
э́то мне не впóру	*it doesn't fit me*
в гóру	*up-hill*
(cf. вверх	*upwards*
вниз	*downwards*)

Notice the common expressions:

в течéние + gen.	*in the course of*
вслéдствие + gen.	*as a result of, owing to*
в продолжéние цéлого гóда	*for a whole year*

за *behind, beyond* (implying direction); *for by*

я éду за грани́цу	*I am going abroad* (lit. *beyond the frontier*)
он поéхал зá город	*he has gone out of town*
он взял меня́ зá руку	*he took me by the hand*
ся́дем за стол	*let's sit down at the table*
ей за пятьдеся́т лет	*she is over 50*

It translates *for* (=*in return for*, *in support of*, or *instead of*) after verbs such as:

(по)благодари́ть	*to thank*
накáзывать, наказáть	*to punish*
покупáть, купи́ть	*to buy*

продава́ть, прода́ть	*to sell*
плати́ть, заплати́ть	*to pay*
дава́ть, дать	*to give*
брать, взять	*to take*
боро́ться сража́ться би́ться	*to fight*
заступа́ться, заступи́ться	*to stick up for*
(по)моли́ться	*to pray*
голосова́ть	*to vote*

in sentences like the following:

я благодарю́ вас за письмо́	*I thank you for your letter*
его́ наказа́ли за непослуша́ние	*he was punished for disobedience*
я купи́л э́то за рубль	*I bought this for a rouble*
он про́дал слова́рь за де́сять рубле́й	*he sold the dictionary for ten roubles*
они́ голосова́ли за меня́	*they voted for me*
солда́ты боро́лись за ро́дину	*the soldiers fought for their country*
мы за э́то предложе́ние	*we are in favour of that proposal*
[я пью] за ва́ше здоро́вье!	*[I drink] to your health!*

Notice the idioms:

мне сты́дно за вас	*I am ashamed of you*
я рад за него́	*I am glad for his sake*
за кого́ вы меня́ принима́ете?	*who do you take me for?*
он выдава́л себя́ за специали́ста	*he posed as a specialist*
выходи́ть вы́йти } за + acc.	*to marry* (of a woman)
она́ вы́шла за не́мца	*she married a German*
за кого́ она́ вы́шла?	*who did she marry?*

For the phrase вы́йти за́муж see p. 201.

Also in certain expressions of time and distance:

она умерла за два часа до вашего приезда *she died two hours before your arrival*

мы живём за пять киломе́тров от ста́нции *we live five kilometres from the station*

за четы́ре дня его́ пребыва́ния здесь *during the four days of his stay here*

за́ ле́то *in the course of the summer* (spoken when it is over)

Notice the idioms:

за хвост, за́ го́лову	*by the tail, by the head*
за́ руку, за́ ногу	*by the hand, by the leg* or *foot*
заодно́ (с + instr.)	*in concert (with)*
зато́	*on the other hand*

на *on to*

положи́те кни́гу на сто́л	*put the book on the table*
на коле́ни	*on to (one's) knees*
на зе́млю	*on to the ground*

Notice the following idiomatic uses:

на́ ночь	*for the night*
он прие́хал на це́лый ме́сяц	*he has come for a whole month*
дня на́ два	*for about two days*
на друго́й день	*(on) the next day*
на сле́дующий раз (or на друго́й раз)	*for next time*
на́ гору	*up the hill* (direction)
на́ море	*to the seaside*
е́хать на Кавка́з	*to travel to the Caucasus*
на́ два рубля́ доро́же	*dearer by two roubles*
на пятьдеся́т копе́ек деше́вле	*50 kopecks cheaper*
оди́н на ты́сячу	*one in a thousand*

он лёг на́бок	*he lay down on his side*
налицо́	*(to be) present*
наси́лу	*with great effort*
на́ново	*afresh*
на́скоро	*hurriedly, slapdash*
положи́ться⎫ на + acc.	*to have confidence in, rely on*
надея́тся ⎭	

ку́шайте на здоро́вье! *eat up! may it do you good!* lit. *eat it to your health* (a common phrase when showing hospitality)

на се́вер	*to the north*
на юг	*to the south*
на восто́к	*to the east*
на за́пад	*to the west*
э́то похо́же на вас	*that is like you* (of a portrait)
э́то ни на что́ не по-хо́же!	*that is not like anything!* (sc. *shocking, abominable*)
на па́мять	*from memory; as a keepsake*
напока́з	*for show*
наве́рх	*upstairs* (direction)
нале́во	*to* (or *on*) *the left*
напра́во	*to* (or *on*) *the right*
наконе́ц	*at last*
наизу́сть	*by heart* (e.g. recitations, &c.)

о (**об** before а, э, и, о, у) *against, about*

я уши́бся о стол	*I have hurt myself against the table*
я опёрся о коло́нну	*I leant against a column*
рука́ о́б руку	*arm in arm*
об э́ту по́ру[1]	*about this time*

---

[1] о and об expressing approximate time are still found in a few fixed expressions, but are otherwise obsolete in the literary language.

по *till, up to*

с пе́рвого (sc. числа́) по три́дцать пе́рвое (sc. число́)
   января́ *from 1st to 31st January (inclusive)*
по коле́ни в воде́   *up to the knees in the water*

Notice the idioms:

по ту́ сто́рону	*on the other (far) side (of river, &c.)*
по пра́вую ру́ку	*on the right-hand side*
по ле́вую ру́ку	*on the left-hand side*

For the use of по + acc. in expressing money-values see
§ 69.

под *under* (direction)

положи́те э́ту поду́шку   *put this pillow under your head*
   себе́ под го́лову
под руку (взять кого́)   *(to take someone) by the arm*
под гору   *down-hill*

про *concerning*

про кого́ вы говори́те?   *who are you talking about?*

Notice the idiom:

про себя́   *to oneself*

e.g. они́ смея́лись про себя́ *they were laughing to themselves*

сквозь *through*

ви́дно сквозь дым   *visible through the smoke*
сквозь лес *through the forest* (e.g. of something that is
   visible through the trees of the forest). Cf. че́рез
   лес *through the forest* (e.g. of walking through the
   forest)
смотре́ть на всё сквозь ро́зовые очки́ *look at everything
   through rose-coloured spectacles*. Cf. смотре́ть че́рез очки́
   which may mean *look over [the top of] one's glasses*
пройти́ сквозь ого́нь и во́ду *go through fire and water*

с (**со** before certain groups of consonants) *about, like*

он с меня́ (sc. ро́стом)	*he is about my size* (sc. *in height*)
с неде́лю	*about a week*

через[1] (or **чрез**) *through, across, via, over*

чѐрез забо́р	*over the fence*
чѐрез во́ду	*through the water*
чѐрез во́здух	*through the air*
чѐрез ле́с	*through the forest*
чѐрез ре́ку	*across the river*, or *through the river* (direction)
мост чѐрез Неву́	*a bridge across the Neva*
чѐрез Москву́	*across, through,* or *via Moscow*
чѐрез кого́?	*through whom?* (sc. *by whose agency?*)

In expressions of time:

чѐрез полчаса́	*in half an hour's time*
чѐрез неде́лю	*in a week*

It also can mean *every other*:

чѐрез ча́с	*in an hour's time* or *every other hour*
чѐрез де́нь	*every other day*

§ 84. The Instrumental

The instrumental case denotes primarily, as its name implies, the instrument or agent by which something is done, e.g.

писа́ть карандашо́м	*to write with a pencil*
э́то письмо́ напи́сано мной	*this letter [was] written by me*
рука́ми	*with [one's] hands*
ного́й	*with [one's] foot,* or *leg*

[1] Unstressed or with weak stress on the first syllable.

It denotes manner:

парохо́дом и по́ездом	*by steamer and by train (by rail)*
авто́бусом и самолётом	*by bus and 'plane*
я е́ду в Росси́ю самолётом	*I am travelling to Russia by air*
сухи́м путём	*overland* (lit. *by dry way*)
мо́рем	*by sea*
толпо́й	*in a crowd*
стрело́й	*like an arrow*
ле́сом	*by* (sc. *through*) *the forest*
доро́жкой	*by the path*
по́лем	*through the field(s)*
нало́женным платежо́м	*cash on delivery, C.O.D.*

Notice the idioms:

е́хать ша́гом	*to drive* (or *ride*) *at walking-pace, 'au pas'*
идти́ пешко́м	*to go on foot*

and especially:

е́хать верхо́м *to ride* (sc. *on horseback*) (верх = *top*, and the phrase literally means *to travel as the top*, sc. *the upper part*). The phrase ката́ться верхо́м *to go riding* (lit. *to roll along as the top*) is also used; these two phrases are the only means of saying *to ride* (*on horseback*) in Russian.

Notice also:

ря́дом	*side by side, abreast*
гусько́м	*in single file*
таки́м путём	*in this way*
каки́м о́бразом?	*in what manner, how?*
каки́м спо́собом?	*by what means?*

таки́м о́бразом *in this* (lit. *such*) *manner, like that,* and often means *consequently, therefore*

посре́дством + gen.	*by means of*
кото́рым or каки́м по́ездом?	*by which* or *what train?*
места́ми	*in places, here and there*

бо́льшей ча́стью	*for the most part, mainly*
ра́зом	*all at once, all together*
о́птом, гурто́м	(*sell by*) *wholesale*
целико́м	*wholly, completely, all*
лицо́м к лицу́	*face to face*
[одни́м] сло́вом	*in a word*
други́ми слова́ми	*in other words*
его́ слова́ми	*in his words*
само́ собо́й	*of its own accord, auto-matically*
само́ собо́ю [разуме́ется]	*it goes without saying, natur-ally*
во́лей-нево́лей	*willy-nilly*

In certain expressions of the time of day and the seasons :

весно́й	*in the spring*
ле́том	*in the summer*
э́тим ле́том	*this summer*
о́сенью	*in the autumn*
зимо́й	*in the winter*
про́шлой зимо́й	*last winter*
у́тром	*in the morning*
ве́чером	*in the evening*
днём	*by day*, and also very fre-quently *in the afternoon*
но́чью	*by night*

N.B. 1. *this morning* is сего́дня у́тром; 2. *this evening* is сего́дня ве́чером. Similarly, за́втра у́тром *tomorrow morning*, &c.

The 'instrumental of respect' is used:

in such expressions as
он о́чень высо́к ро́стом *he is very tall*

(where póстом = *in [respect of] stature, build*)

онá хорошá собóй   *she is good-looking*

(where собóй = *in respect of her person, in her appearance*)

чем богáты, тем и рáды *you're welcome to what we have*

(lit. *with (in) what we are rich, with that we are glad [to serve you]*)

to denote origin:

póдом англичáнин   *an Englishman by birth*

in some expressions of measurement:

рекá ширинóй в киломéтр *a river 1 km wide (in width)*

горá в тысячу мéтров вышинóй (or высотóй) *a hill 1,000 metres high (in height)*

also глубинóй *in depth*, длинóй *in length*, &c.

The instrumental is used in measuring differences, e.g.

я póдом стáрше егó *I am a year older than he [is]* though these phrases are more commonly expressed by на + acc. (see § 83) or в . . . раз (see §§ 65, 83)

тем лýчше   *all the better*

тем не мéнее   *nevertheless*

тем бóлее   *all the more*

The instrumental is always used with certain verbs, including:

любовáться *to admire* (but only literally *to gaze at*)

восхищáться *to admire* (= *be delighted with*)

пóльзоваться *to take advantage of, to make use of*

пóльзуюсь этим слýчаем + infin. *I am taking advantage of this opportunity to . . .*

гордиться *to be proud of*

я горжýсь вáми *I am proud of you*

хвалиться *to boast (about)*

пренебрегáть *to neglect*

злоупотребля́ть *to abuse, misuse*

дорожи́ть *to value highly*

занима́ться *to be engaged* (*in*)*, study*

интересова́ться *to be interested* (*in*)

увлека́ться *to be keen* (*on*)

облада́ть *to possess, own*

же́ртвовать *to sacrifice*

   он пож́ертвовал всем свои́м состоя́нием *he sacrificed the whole of his fortune*

владе́ть *to rule, command*

   А́нглия владе́ла И́ндией *England ruled India*

   он хорошо́ владе́ет ру́сским языко́м *he has a good command of the Russian language*

кома́ндовать *to be in command over* (*troops,* &c.)

руководи́ть *to lead*

управля́ть *to manage*

   он управля́ет большо́й фа́брикой *he manages a large factory*

заве́довать *to look after*

   она́ заве́дует до́мом *she looks after the house*

пра́вить *to drive, steer*

   он хорошо́ пра́вит автомоби́лем *he drives a car well*

дыша́ть *to breathe*

па́хнуть *to smell* (intrans.)

   чем э́то па́хнет? *what does this smell of* (*like*)?

A very common and at first sight puzzling use of the instrumental is that called *predicative*. The predicate is put into the instrumental instead of the nominative whenever any temporary or hypothetical condition is to be indicated, e.g.

   когда́ я был ма́льчиком *when I was a boy* (sc. *I'm now a man*)

cf. Шекспи́р был англича́нин *Shakespeare was an Englishman* (sc. *all his life*) он бу́дет вели́ким челове́ком *he is going to be a great man* (sc. *but we cannot be sure of the future*)

лежа́ние у него́ не́ было ни необходи́мостью, ни случа́йностью *lying down was in his case neither a necessity nor an accident*

The predicative instrumental is also used after the following verbs:

де́латься ⎫
станови́ться ⎭ *to become*

называ́ться *to be called*

звать, называ́ть *to call*

меня́ зову́т Ива́ном[1] *they call me Ivan*, i.e. *my name is Ivan*

служи́ть *to serve as*

э́то служи́ло мне предло́гом *this served me as an excuse*

счита́ть *to consider*

я счита́ю э́то справедли́вым *I consider it just*

счита́ться *to be considered*

э́то счита́ется хоро́шим за́работком *that is considered good pay*

он счита́ется неве́жливым *he is considered rude*

слыть *to have the reputation of*

роди́ться *to be born*

каза́ться *to seem*

де́ло каза́лось серьёзным *the matter seemed serious*

притворя́ться *to pretend to be*

явля́ться *to be*

The instrumental is used after the following prepositions:

за *behind, beyond, for,* or *after* (=*to get something*)

за грани́цей   *abroad* (lit. *beyond the frontier*)

за столо́м   *at table*

---

[1] The nom. is also possible with proper names after **звать**.

за обéдом	*at dinner*
зá городом	*out of town* (position)
я пришёл за деньгáми	*I have come for the money*
нáдо послáть за дóктором	*(we) must send for the doctor*
зачéм?	*why?* (sc. *with what object?*)
затéм чтóбы + infin.	*in order to . . .*
затéм	*after that, then*

It is used of a married woman (cf. за + acc., § 83):

| онá зáмужем | *she is married* |
| за кем онá зáмужем? | *who is she married to?* |

междуˡ (and **меж**) *between* (also with gen. pl., see p. 193)

мèжду Ленингрáдом и Москвóй *between Leningrad and Moscow*

мèжду нáми *between us* (both of concrete objects and of emotions), *amongst us*

мèжду прóчим *amongst other things; incidentally*

Notice the idioms:

| мèжду тéм | *meanwhile; whereas really* |
| мèжду тéм как | *while; whereas* |

над (надо before certain groups of consonants) *above*

| над головóй | *above (my) head, overhead* |
| надо мнóй | *above me* (literally) |

передˡ (передо before мнóй) *in front of, before* (place), [*just*] *before* (time)

пèред дóмом	*in front of the house*
пèредо мнóй	*in front of me*
пèред э́тим	*before this* (temporal)
пèред обéдом	[*just*] *before dinner*
пèред тéм как + inf.	*before* + verb (e.g. *going*)

ˡ Unstressed or with weak stress on the first syllable.

под (**подо** before certain groups of consonants) *under, near*

под землёй	*underground*
подо мной	*under me*
под э́тим усло́вием	*on this condition*
под каки́м предло́гом?	*on what pretext?*
под Москво́й	*near Moscow*

с (**со** before certain groups of consonants) *with*

со мной	*with me*
с больши́м удово́льствием	*with great pleasure*
с наслажде́нием	*with relish*
с трудо́м	*with difficulty*
со вре́менем	*in course of time*
с кем вы говори́ли?	*with whom were you talking?*
с како́й це́лью?	*with what object?*
Бог с ни́ми!	*never mind them!* (lit. *God be with them!*)

§ 85. The Locative is only used with prepositions, hence it is sometimes called the prepositional case.

The locative is used with the following prepositions:

в (**во** before certain groups of consonants) *in*

в Москве́	*in Moscow*
во мне	*in me*
во Фра́нции	*in France*
в Крыму́	*in the Crimea* (cf. § 39, Obs. 7)
в конце́	*at the end*
в нача́ле	*at the beginning*
во сне	*in one's sleep* or *dreams*

Notice the idioms:

в конце́ концо́в	*at long last, finally*
в са́мом де́ле	*indeed*
вообще́	*in general*

втáйне	*secretly*
впослéдствии	*subsequently*
вполнé	*completely, thoroughly*

In certain expressions of time:

в слéдующем годý	*the following year*
в такóм-то годý	*in such and such a year*
в пéрвом часý	*between 12 and 1*[1]
во вторóм часý	*between 1 and 2*[2], *getting on for 2*

For other similar expressions see § 68

на *on*

на столé	*on the table*
на берегý мóря	*on the sea-shore, at the seaside*
на бокý	*on (one's) side*
на сóлнце	*in the sun*
на ýлице	*in the street, outside*

(this and на дворé[3] are the commonest ways of saying *out of doors*)

на льду	*on the ice* (from лёд)
на мостý	*on the bridge*
на слýжбе	*in service, at work*
на нéбе	*in heaven, in the sky (of star)*
but в нéбе	*in the sky (of bird, aircraft)*
на свéжем вóздухе	*in the fresh air*
на свéте	*in the world*
на свобóде	*at liberty*

Notice the idioms:

на своём векý	*in one's time, in one's life*
на лошадя́х	*by carriage, driving* (lit. *on horses*)
наединé (adv.)	*alone, in solitude*
наявý (adv.)	*in reality* (as opposed to *in one's sleep*)

---

[1] Esp. between 12.30 and 1. [2] Esp. between 1.30 and 2.
[3] Mostly in descriptions of the weather or the season.

It is used of men marrying, after the verb жени́ться *to marry*:

> он жени́лся на ру́сской *he married a Russian*
> на ком он жена́т?   *who is he married to?*

Notice the compound adverb:

> накану́не(+ gen.) *on the eve (of)*

о (**об** before а, э, и, о, у, and occasionally before other vowels and consonants also; **обо** before certain groups of consonants) *concerning*

> обо мне   *about me*
> о чём вы говори́ли?   *what were you talking about?*
> об э́том, обо всём   *about this, about everything*

In certain expressions of number:

> па́лка о двух конца́х *a stick with two ends* (sc. *a double-edged weapon*)

по [*immediately*] *after, following*

> по прие́зде   *on* or *after arrival*
> по на́шем возвраще́нии   *on our return*

Notice the idioms:

> скуча́ть по ро́дине   *to be home-sick (for one's country)*
> почём?   *at what price? how much* [*each*]*?*
> почём метр?   *how much a metre?* (see § 69)

при *near, in the presence of, in the time of*

> при мне *in my presence*; *in my time* [*there*]; *on* (= *with*) *me*
> при цари́зме *under tsarism*; при дворе́ *at court*
> при Петре́ Вели́ком *in the reign of Peter the Great*
> при би́тве под Ле́йпцигом *at the battle of Leipzig*
> при све́те + gen. *by the light of* . . .

при ви́де Ива́на *at the sight of* (*on seeing*) *Ivan*
Бори́с при га́лстуке *Boris has a tie on*
я́сли при заво́де *the crèche attached to* (*run by*) *the factory*

Notice the idioms:

прито́м and при том *besides* [*that*]
при всём том *in addition to*, or *in spite of*, *all that*
при всём моём стара́нии *for* (*despite*) *all my efforts*
причём *in addition to which*
при чём тут мы? *how does this concern us?*
мы тут ни при чём *we are not involved* (*to blame*) *in this*

THE VERB

§ 86. The Russian verb consists of the following parts:

Present Past Future Conditional — Imperative — Infinitive — Present Gerund Past Gerund — Present Participle Past Participle	Active
Present Participle Past Participle	Passive

The present is the only tense which has personal endings. The past is a tense only in name; in reality it is a participle whose endings vary not according to person, but according to number and gender. The future in form is exactly the same as the present. The conditional in form is exactly the same as the past and serves also as a subjunctive. There is no passive of any part of the verb except the participles, and when a passive idea has to be expressed in Russian, it must be done by means of a participle, a reflexive verb (see § 110), or a periphrasis employing an active form.

Use of the Personal Pronouns with the Verb

The personal pronouns

я	*I*
ты[1]	*thou*
он, она́, оно́	*he, she, it*
мы	*we*
вы	*you*
они́	*they*

are used in Russian with the verbs very much as in English; in certain cases they are, however, omitted altogether, e.g. when the verb is used, as it frequently is, in an answer to a question, instead of or in addition to да (*yes*) or нет (*no*):

Question: бы́ли ли вы у них вчера́? *did you go to see them yesterday?* (lit. *were you at their house?*)

Answer: был *I did* (lit. *I was*)

Question: бу́дете ли вы у него́ сего́дня? *will you go to see him today?*

Answer: бу́ду *I shall/will*

Question: мо́жете ли вы сде́лать э́то для меня́? *can you do this for me?*

Answer: да, могу́ *yes, I can*

The pronoun оно́ is comparatively rarely used; its place is often taken by э́то *this*, e.g.

э́то бы́ло о́чень давно́ *it was a very long time ago*

---

[1] Used in addressing relatives, intimate friends, children and animals; otherwise replaced by the plural вы for politeness' sake.

or, when it does not refer to a thing or event, it is omitted altogether, e.g.

> сегóдня теплó *it is warm today*

In popular speech онó often has the meaning of *the thing* (or *action*) *we were referring to* or *what you were talking about*, e.g.

> онó, конéчно, неприя́тно [*a thing like*] *that* (sc. *which we have been discussing*) *is, of course, unpleasant*

How to Express the General Pronoun *one*

It is most frequently expressed by the 2nd pers. sing., e.g.

> ничегó не поймёшь *one can't understand a word* (for this use of the perfective future see § 104 (c))

After когдá *when* and éсли *if* in such expressions either the present or the future may be used, e.g.

> когдá подýмаешь . . .   *when one thinks* . . .
> éсли на э́то смóтришь   *if one looks at this*

The perfective future (see § 104 (b)) is frequently used after когдá = *whenever* and éсли = *if ever*.

One can also be rendered by the infinitive, as in

> мнóго желáть, добрá не видáть *if one wishes* [*too*] *much, one is never content* (lit. *sees no good*) (proverb)
> волкóв боя́ться, в лес не ходи́ть *if one is afraid of wolves, one shouldn't go into the forest* (proverb)
> éсли сказáть всю и́стину *if one were to tell the whole truth*

The reflexive verb, the 3rd pers. pl. of the present, future, and past tenses, and the passive participles are also used to express *one*, see § 110.

§ 87. The Present

Old Bulgarian verbs are divided into five classes, and for etymological purposes Russian verbs can be similarly treated. For practical purposes, however, it is best to divide the verbs into only two classes, or conjugations, not according to the infinitive, but according to the personal endings of the present. The few irregular verbs, which in Old Bulgarian formed the fifth class, are in Russian not sufficiently numerous to form a class by themselves, but as they are very important they are given in full in a separate paragraph. For the regular verbs there are two sets of personal endings, which are added to the verb-stem sometimes directly, sometimes with a vowel (-a-, -я-, -e-, -y- -ю-) or a consonant (-н-) inserted between stem and ending.

The first difficulty to be faced is the fact that, although every present may be put in one class or the other, the infinitives are much more difficult to classify, because verbs having various infinitive endings have identical present endings, while others having identical infinitive endings have different present endings. In the lists of verbs below they are arranged alphabetically according to the last letter of the present stem, obtained by removing -ут, -ют, -ат, or -ят from the 3rd pers. pl.

The verbs of conj. I are divided into three lists according to their 1st pers. sing.: those ending in a consonant + y (pp. 226–35), those ending in a consonant + ю (pp. 235–6), and those in a vowel or soft sign + ю (pp. 236–40). The fourth list (pp. 240–45) contains verbs of conj. II.

Another difficulty is that the soft vowels in the personal endings have in many cases affected the last consonant of the stem, so that the present stem differs from the infinitive stem. The personal endings of the present tense of the two conjugations of Russian verbs are the following.

		I	II
Sing.	1	-у (or -ю[1])	-ю (or -у[2])
	2	-ешь[3]	-ишь
	3	-ет	-ит
Pl.	1	-ем	-им
	2	-ете	-ите
	3	-ут (or -ют[1])	-ят (or -ат[2])

Conjugation I comprises all the verbs contained in the first three classes in Old Bulgarian; in that language the endings of class I were: 2nd sing. -еши, 3rd sing. -етъ, 1st pl. -емъ, 2nd pl. -ете, of class II -неши, -нетъ, &c., of class III -юши, -ютъ; &c. In Russian these appear respectively as -ешь, -ет, &c., -нешь, -нет, &c., and -ешь, -ет, &c., viz. the personal endings of 2nd and 3rd sing. and 1st and 2nd pl. all begin with -е-. Of the verbs which originally belonged to class I, those whose stems end in г or к change these letters to ж and ч before the soft vowel of the endings -ешь, -ет, &c., but retain the г and к before the hard -у of the 1st sing. and 3rd pl. The stems of the verbs which insert -н- between the stem and the personal ending undergo no change. Of the verbs which originally belonged to class III, those whose stems end in a vowel take the endings -ю, -ешь, -ет, -ем, -ете, -ют; while those whose stems end in a consonant change the consonant (except л and sometimes р) before the iotated vowels of the personal endings -ю, -ешь, -ет, &c., in such a way as to absorb the _y_-sound contained in them, viz. final к of the stem becomes ч, final т becomes ч or щ, final ск and ст become щ, final г, д, and з all become ж, and final с and х become ш. The personal endings thus appear as -чу, -чешь, -щу, -щешь,

---

[1] Used after a vowel, ь, л, or when infin. ends in -орóть.

[2] Used after ж, ш, ч, or щ.

[3] When the stress falls on them, the personal endings of the 2nd and 3rd sing. and 1st and 2nd pl. of conjugation I become -ёшь, -ёт, -ём, -ёте.

-жу, -жешь, and -шу, -шешь, &c. Similarly, stems ending in б, п, в, ф, and м insert л before the endings -ю, -ешь, &c.

In conj. II the final vowel of the first person singular is often disguised as -у (i.e. apparently the same as in conj. I); the reason is that the -ю of the 1st pers. sing. has changed the final г, к, д, т, з, с, or х of the stem into ч, щ, ж, or ш (as above) and these letters cannot be followed by ю. The ending is also -у when the stem itself ends in ж, ш, ч, or щ. Similarly, the -ят of the 3rd pers. pl. becomes -ат when the stem ends in ж, ш, ч, or щ. In conj. II, those stems which end in б, п, в, ф, and м insert л only before the -ю of the 1st sing.

Another difficulty which the beginner has to face is that of the verbal prefixes. Verbs compounded with one of the prefixes (mostly identical with prepositions) are infinitely more numerous than those without, and this fact makes the beginner think at first sight that the language possesses a far larger number of verbs than it actually does. When reading Russian, the beginner should always try and see the root of each verb and cut off the prefix or prefixes which precede it. For this purpose it is important to learn the verbal prefixes dealt with in § 118, and to compare them with the prepositions given in §§ 79–85. As the prefixes always have an effect on the meaning of each verb, only simple verbs have been given in the following lists: the alteration in meaning effected by the various prefixes is described in § 118.

Many of the verbs included in these lists are rather uncommon, others (preceded by a hyphen) are not used in their simple forms. The student should not attempt to learn the lists, but only use them for reference. The list of conj. I verbs (§ 88a) contains all the difficult primary verbs which belong to this conjugation; the list of conj. II verbs (§ 88b) is far from being exhaustive; it is intended merely to be representative.

Only the 1st and 2nd pers. sing. and the infinitives are given. Whenever the 1st sing. ends in -y, the 3rd pl. ends in -ут (conj. I) or -ат (conj. II); when the 1st sing. ends in -ю, the 3rd pl. ends in -ют (conj. I) or -ят (conj. II). In verbs of both conjugations, the 1st sing. is stressed on the same syllable as the infinitive. In the 2nd sing. the stress will remain on the same syllable unless in the 1st sing. the stress falls on the ending, in which case the stress may shift to the stem in the 2nd sing. The stress on the remaining forms is always identical with that of the 2nd sing.

Verbs marked 'pf.' are perfective. The great majority of the other (imperfective) verbs in the following lists will become perfective if any prefix is added to them. The present tense of a perfective verb always conveys a future meaning (see § 101).

Examples of the present tense:

§ 88a. Conjugation I

The most typical verbs of conj. I in modern Russian end in -ать and -ять and have identical infinitive and present stems. The present tense of such verbs is formed by removing the infinitive suffix -ть and adding the personal endings -ю, -ешь, &c., as:

де́лать *to do*	знать *to know*	гуля́ть *to walk, stroll*
pres. stem де́ла-	pres. stem зна́-	pres. stem гуля́-
де́лаю *I do, am doing*	зна́ю *I know*	гуля́ю *I walk, am walking*
де́лаешь	зна́ешь	гуля́ешь
де́лает	зна́ет	гуля́ет
де́лаем	зна́ем	гуля́ем
де́лаете	зна́ете	гуля́ете
де́лают	зна́ют	гуля́ют

This is the productive type, and all new verbs belonging

to conj. I form their present tense in the same way. Verbs in -ать and -ять following this regular pattern are not included in these lists.

Examples of other types:

име́ть *to possess*	мыть *to wash*
pres. stem име́-	pres. stem мо́-
име́ю	мо́ю
име́ешь	мо́ешь
име́ет	мо́ет
име́ем	мо́ем
име́ете	мо́ете
име́ют	мо́ют

нести́ *to be carrying*	писа́ть *to write*
pres. stem нес-	pres. stem пиш-
несу́	пишу́
несёшь	пи́шешь
несёт	пи́шет
несём	пи́шем
несёте	пи́шете
несу́т	пи́шут

мета́ть *to fling*	ропта́ть *to grumble*
pres. stem меч-	pres. stem ропщ-
мечу́	ропщу́
ме́чешь, &c.	ро́пщешь, &c.

пла́кать *to weep*	иска́ть *to seek*
pres. stem пла́ч-	pres. stem ищ-
пла́чу	ищу́
пла́чешь, &c.	и́щешь, &c.

тяну́ть *to pull*	стать (pf.) *to become*
pres. stem тян-	pres. stem ста́н-
тяну́	ста́ну
тя́нешь, &c.	ста́нешь, &c.

советовать *to advise*   клевать *to peck*
pres. stem совету-   pres. stem клю-
    советую   клюю
    советуешь, &c.   клюёшь, &c.

дремать *to slumber*   давать *to give*   пить *to drink*
pres. stem дремл-   pres. stem да-   pres. stem пь-
    дремлю   даю   пью
    дрéмлешь, &c.   даёшь, &c.   пьёшь, &c.

Special note should be taken of verbs in -чь, as

печь (from пек+ть) *to bake*   мочь (from мог+ть) *to be able*
pres. stem пек-   pres. stem мог-
(but печ- before e)   (but мож- before e)

    пеку́ *I bake*   могу́ *I can*
    печёшь   мóжешь
    печёт   мóжет
    печём   мóжем
    печёте   мóжете
    пеку́т   мóгут

All conj. I verbs with irregular present stems (those not found by removing -ть from the infin.) are given below. Their compounds (formed with prefixes) are conjugated in the same way. The verbs are listed under each heading alphabetically, according to the last letters of the present stem.

(i) present tense ending in -у, -ешь, -ет, -ем, -ете, -ут. stem ending in

-б-		infin.	basic meaning
гребу́	гребёшь	грести́	*row*
скребу́	скребёшь	скрести́	*scrape*
-шибу́[1]	-шибёшь	-шиби́ть	*(hit)*

[1] e.g. ушибу́, infin. ушиби́ть (pf.) *bruise, hurt*.

stem ending in

-в-		infin.	basic meaning
реву́	реве́шь	реве́ть	*roar*
живу́	живёшь	жить	*live*
зову́	зовёшь	звать	*call*
рву	рвёшь	рвать	*tear*
плыву́	плывёшь	плыть	*float, swim*
слыву́	слывёшь	слыть	*be renowned as*

-г- (becomes -ж- before e)

бегу́[1]	——	бежа́ть	*run*
-брегу́[2]	-брежёшь	-бре́чь	*(keep)*
берегу́	бережёшь	бере́чь	*guard*
стерегу́	стережёшь	стере́чь	*watch over*
жгу	жжёшь	жечь	*burn*
стригу́	стрижёшь	стричь	*shear*
лгу	лжёшь	лгать	*lie, prevaricate*
могу́	мо́жешь	(мочь)[3]	*be able*
ля́гу	ля́жешь	лечь (pf.)	*lie down*
-прягу́[4]	-пряжёшь	-пря́чь[5]	*(harness)*

-д-

кладу́	кладёшь	класть	*put, lay*
паду́	падёшь	пасть (pf.)	*fall*
краду́	крадёшь	красть	*steal*
е́ду[1]	е́дешь	е́хать	*ride, drive*
веду́	ведёшь	вести́	*lead*
бреду́	бредёшь	брести́	*wander*
жду	ждёшь	ждать	*(a)wait*
стра́жду[6]	стра́ждешь	страда́ть	*suffer*
жа́жду	жа́ждешь	жа́ждать	*thirst for*

---

[1] See § 89.   [2] e.g. пренебрегу́, infin. пренебре́чь (pf.) *neglect*.
[3] Not used; a purely theoretical form.
[4] e.g. запрягу́, infin. запря́чь (pf.) *harness*.
[5] Pronounced as -пречь.
[6] Note the stress; this form is archaic; usually страда́ю, страда́ешь.

иду́	идёшь	идти́ ⎫	
-йду́[1]	-йдёшь	-йти́ ⎬	go, walk
-ду́[2]	-дёшь	-йти́ ⎭	
бу́ду[3]	бу́дешь[3]	быть	be
блюду́	блюдёшь	блюсти́	observe
гряду́	грядёшь	(pres. only)	draw nigh
пряду́	прядёшь	прясть	spin
ся́ду	ся́дешь	сесть (pf.)	sit down

-ж-			
-кажу́[4]	-ка́жешь	-каза́ть	(show)
ма́жу	ма́жешь	ма́зать	smear
ре́жу	ре́жешь	ре́зать[5]	cut
бры́зжу[6]	бры́зжешь	бры́згать	splash (intr.)
дви́жу[7]	дви́жешь	дви́гать[8]	move
лижу́	ли́жешь	лиза́ть	lick
нижу́	ни́жешь	низа́ть	thread
гложу́	гло́жешь	глода́ть	gnaw
ржу	ржёшь	ржать	neigh
обяжу́[9]	обя́жешь	обяза́ть (pf.)	oblige, bind
вяжу́	вя́жешь	вяза́ть	knit

-з-			
везу́	везёшь	везти́	convey

[1] e.g. пойду́, infin. пойти́ (pf.) go, set off.

[2] in приду́, infin. прийти́ (pf.) arrive.

[3] This is a future tense, meaning I shall be, you will be, &c.

[4] e.g. скажу́, infin. сказа́ть (pf.) say, tell; but the reflexive кажу́сь, infin. каза́ться seem, appear is used in the simple form.

[5] But -реза́ть, forming compound ipf. verbs, is reg.: -реза́ю, &c.

[6] But бры́згаю, бры́згаешь, when transitive (bespatter, besprinkle).

[7] The forms дви́жу, дви́жешь, &c., are used of mechanisms which drive or propel and of emotions which move or impel; the 'regular' forms дви́гаю, дви́гаешь, &c., mean move, shift (from one position to another). The reflexive forms are differentiated as follows: дви́жется it is moving, in motion, дви́гается it is starting to move, starting off.

[8] But -двига́ть, forming compound ipf. verbs, is reg.: -двига́ю, &c.

[9] Really a compound, derived from об + вяжу́.

лéзу	лéзешь	лезть	*clamber*
ползý	ползёшь	ползти́	*crawl*
грызý	грызёшь	грызть	*gnaw*

-к- (becomes -ч- before e)

влекý	влечёшь	влечь	*draw*
пекý	пчёшь	печь	*bake*
-рекý[1]	-речёшь	-рéчь	*(say)*
секý	сечёшь	сечь	*cut, flog*
текý	течёшь	течь	*flow*
толкý	толчёшь	толóчь	*pound*
волокý	волочёшь	волóчь	*drag*

Note:

тку	ткёшь	ткать	*weave*

-м-

жму	жмёшь	жать	*squeeze*
-нимý[2]	-ни́мешь	-ня́ть	
-имý[3]	-и́мешь	-ня́ть	
-ймý[4]	-ймёшь	-ня́ть	*(take)*
-ьмý[5]	-ьмёшь	-я́ть	
-ымý[6]	-ы́мешь	-ъя́ть	

-н-

стáну	стáнешь	стать (pf.)	*become*
гну	гнёшь	гнуть	*bend*
дéну	дéнешь	деть (pf.)	*put*
жну	жнёшь	жать	*reap*
мну	мнёшь	мять	*crush*

[1] e.g. изрекý, infin. изрéчь (pf.) *pronounce, utter.*
[2] e.g. обнимý, infin. обня́ть (pf.) *embrace*; отня́ть (pf.) *take away* has отниму́, отни́мешь, and (colloq.) отыму́, оты́мешь.
[3] in примý, infin. приня́ть (pf.) *accept.*
[4] e.g. займý, infin. заня́ть (pf.) *occupy.*
[5] in возьмý, infin. взять (pf.) *take.*
[6] in изымý, infin. изъя́ть (pf.) *withdraw.*

стону́[1]	сто́нешь	стона́ть	*groan*
-пну́[2]	-пнёшь	-пя́ть	*(stretch)*
-чну́[3]	-чнёшь	-ча́ть	*(begin)*
льну	льнёшь	льнуть	*cling*
кляну́	клянёшь	клясть	*curse*
-стря́ну[4]	-стря́нешь	-стря́ть	*(get stuck)*
тяну́	тя́нешь	тяну́ть	*pull*

Intrans. verbs in -нуть connoting a gradual process:

ги́бну	ги́бнешь	ги́бнуть	*perish*
зя́бну	зя́бнешь	зя́бнуть	*become chilled*
-бе́гну[5]	-бе́гнешь	-бе́гнуть	*(run)*
мо́згну	мо́згнешь	мо́згнуть[6]	*decay, wilt*
-сти́гну[7]	-сти́гнешь	-сти́чь[8]	*(attain)*
дро́гну	дро́гнешь	дро́гнуть	*become chilled*
-ве́ргну[9]	-ве́ргнешь	-ве́ргнуть	*(throw)*
-то́ргну[10]	-то́ргнешь	-то́ргнуть	*(tear)*
-че́зну[11]	-че́знешь	-че́знуть	*(disappear)*
мёрзну	мёрзнешь	мёрзнуть	*become frozen*
вя́зну	вя́знешь	вя́знуть	*sink in*
блёкну	блёкнешь	блёкнуть	*fade*
ни́кну	ни́кнешь	ни́кнуть	*droop*
-ни́кну[12]	-ни́кнешь	-ни́кнуть	*(press)*
мо́лкну	мо́лкнешь	мо́лкнуть[13]	*become silent*

[1] стону́ is rare; 1st sing. usually стона́ю; then сто́нешь, and colloq. стона́ешь, &c.   [2] e.g. распну́, infin. распя́ть (pf.) *crucify*.
[3] e.g. начну́, infin. нача́ть (pf.) *begin*.
[4] e.g. застря́ну, infin. застря́ть (pf.) *get stuck*.
[5] e.g. прибе́гну, infin. прибе́гнуть (pf.) *resort (to)*.
[6] Rare except in the compound промо́згнуть (pf.) *grow dank*.
[7] e.g. дости́гну, infin. дости́чь or дости́гнуть (pf.) *achieve, attain*.
[8] Or (rarer) -сти́гнуть; past: -стиг (rare: -сти́гнул), -сти́гла.
[9] e.g. отве́ргну, infin. отве́ргнуть (pf.) *reject*.
[10] e.g. исто́ргну, infin. исто́ргнуть (pf.) *expel*.
[11] e.g. исче́зну, infin. исче́знуть (pf.) *disappear*.
[12] e.g. прони́кну, infin. прони́кнуть (pf.) *penetrate*.
[13] Rare except in compounds, e.g. умо́лкнуть (pf.) *become silent*.

мо́кну	мо́кнешь	мо́кнуть	*get soaked*
-вы́кну[1]	-вы́кнешь	-вы́кнуть	*(become accustomed)*
мя́кну	мя́кнешь	мя́кнуть	*become soft, weak*
-ся́кну[2]	-ся́кнешь	-ся́кнуть	*(become dry)*
тону́	то́нешь	тону́ть	*sink, drown* (intr.)
слѣ́пну	слѣ́пнешь	слѣ́пнуть	*go blind*
крѣ́пну	крѣ́пнешь	крѣ́пнуть	*grow strong*
га́сну	га́снешь	га́снуть	*die down*
-крѣ́сну[3]	-крѣ́снешь	-крѣ́снуть	*(rise)*
ви́сну	ви́снешь	ви́снуть	*hang* (intr.)
ки́сну	ки́снешь	ки́снуть	*turn sour*
па́хну	па́хнешь	па́хнуть	*smell* (intr.)
ча́хну	ча́хнешь	ча́хнуть	*pine away*
-ти́хну[4]	-ти́хнешь	-ти́хнуть	*(become quiet)*
глóхну	глóхнешь	глóхнуть	*grow deaf*
сóхну	сóхнешь	сóхнуть	*become dry*
бу́хну	бу́хнешь	бу́хнуть[5]	*swell, warp* (intr.)
сты́ну	сты́нешь	стыть[6]	*grow cold*
вя́ну	вя́нешь	вя́нуть	*wither* (intr.)

Verbs connoting a single action:

улыбну́сь[7]	улыбнёшься	улыбну́ться pf.	*smile*
шагну́	шагнёшь	шагну́ть pf.	*stride*
дрóгну	дрóгнешь	дрóгнуть pf.	*shudder*
пры́гну	пры́гнешь	пры́гнуть pf.	*jump*
дви́ну	дви́нешь	дви́нуть pf.	*move* (trans.)
ки́ну	ки́нешь	ки́нуть pf.	*hurl*
кри́кну	кри́кнешь	кри́кнуть pf.	*shout out*
трóну	трóнешь	трóнуть pf.	*touch*

[1] e.g. привы́кну, infin. привы́кнуть (pf.) *be used* (*to*).
[2] e.g. исся́кну, infin. исся́кнуть (pf.) *dry up* (intr.).
[3] e.g. воскрѣ́сну, infin. воскрѣ́снуть (pf.) *rise from the dead*.
[4] e.g. прити́хну, infin. прити́хнуть (pf.) *become quiet*.
[5] ipf. Past: бу́х[нул], бу́хла, &c.; for бу́хнуть (pf.) *thump* (past бу́хнул, бу́хнула, &c.) see p. 232.   [6] or сты́нуть; past стыл, сты́ла.   [7] See § 100.

шепну́	шепнёшь	шепну́ть pf.	*whisper*
косну́сь[1]	коснёшься	косну́ться pf.	*touch*
ду́ну	ду́нешь	ду́нуть pf.	*blow*
пахну́	пахнёшь	пахну́ть pf.	*waft*
бу́хну	бу́хнешь	бу́хнуть pf.	*thump, bang*
ру́хну	ру́хнешь	ру́хнуть pf.	*collapse*
вы́ну	вы́нешь	вы́нуть pf.	*take out*
кольну́	кольнёшь	кольну́ть pf.	*prick, stab*
плю́ну	плю́нешь	плю́нуть pf.	*spit*

-р-

вру	врёшь	врать	*prevaricate*
беру́	берёшь	брать	*take*
деру́	дерёшь	драть	*tear*
жру	жрёшь	жрать	*devour*
мру[2]	мрёшь	мере́ть	*die*
ору́[3]	орёшь[3]	ора́ть	*bawl*
пру	прёшь	пере́ть	*push*
тру	трёшь	тере́ть	*rub*
-стру́[4]	-стрёшь	-стере́ть	(*stretch*)

-с-

пасу́[5]	пасёшь	пасти́	*guard, pasture*
несу́	несёшь	нести́	*carry*
сосу́	сосёшь	соса́ть	*suck*
трясу́	трясёшь	трясти́	*shake*

-т-

цвету́	цветёшь	цвести́	*blossom*
плету́	плетёшь	плести́	*plait*
мету́	метёшь	мести́	*sweep*

[1] For -сь/-ся see § 100.
[2] Rare; usually with prefix, as умру́, умрёшь, infin. умере́ть (pf.) *die*; ipf. умира́ю, &c., infin. умира́ть.
[3] Also used in dialect for орю́, о́решь (see p. 236).
[4] e.g. простру́, infin. простере́ть (pf.) *extend*, ipf. простира́ть.
[5] Including the compound спасу́, infin. спасти́ (pf.) *save*.

гнету́	гнетёшь	гнести́	*press, oppress*
-рету́[1]	-ретёшь	-рести́	(*find*)
расту́	растёшь	расти́	*grow* (intr.)

рассветёт (3rd sg. impers. only) рассвести́ *dawn*

-чту́[2]	-чтёшь	-че́сть	(*reckon, read*)

-ч- (< к or т before ю or e)

скачу́	ска́чешь	скака́ть	*leap, gallop*
мечу́	ме́чешь	мета́ть[3]	*fling, cast*
а́лчу[4]	а́лчешь	алка́ть	*hunger for*
щекочу́	щеко́чешь	щекота́ть	*tickle*
хлопочу́	хлопо́чешь	хлопота́ть	*busy oneself*
хочу́ (see	хо́чешь	хоте́ть	*wish, want*
§ 89)			
топчу́	то́пчешь	топта́ть	*tread*
тычу́[5]	ты́чешь	ты́кать	*poke, thrust*
пря́чу	пря́чешь	пря́тать	*hide* (trans.)

To this type belong several verbs denoting noises:

(*a*) With infinitives of two syllables —

пла́чу	пла́чешь	пла́кать	*weep*
кли́чу	кли́чешь	кли́кать	*cry out*
шепчу́	ше́пчешь	шепта́ть	*whisper*
хны́чу[6]	хны́чешь	хны́кать	*whimper*

(*b*) Three syllables with stress on the last—

щебечу́	щебе́чешь	щебета́ть	*chirp*
лепечу́	лепе́чешь	лепета́ть	*babble*
гогочу́	гого́чешь	гогота́ть	*gaggle*
клокочу́	клоко́чешь	клокота́ть	*bubble*

[1] e.g. приобрету́, infin. приобрести́ (pf.) *obtain*.
[2] e.g. прочту́, infin. проче́сть (pf.) *read*.
[3] But мета́ть in sense of *tack, baste* (in sewing) is regular: мета́ю, &c.
[4] Note the stress; also алка́ю, алка́ешь.
[5] Also (colloq.) ты́каю, ты́каешь; ты́кать meaning *use* ты *to, address familiarly* has only ты́каю, ты́каешь, &c.
[6] Also (colloq.) хны́каю, хны́каешь.

рокочу́	роко́чешь	рокота́ть	*rumble, roar*
бормочу́	бормо́чешь	бормота́ть	*mutter*
лопочу́	лопо́чешь	лопота́ть	*mutter*
грохочу́	грохо́чешь	грохота́ть	*roar, rumble*
хохочу́	хохо́чешь	хохота́ть	*laugh loud*

(c) Three syllables with penultimate stress —

| куда́хчу | куда́хчешь | куда́хтать | *cluck* |
| мурлы́чу[1] | мурлы́чешь | мурлы́кать | *purr* |

-ш- (< х or c before ю or e)

машу́[2]	ма́шешь	маха́ть	*wave*
пашу́	па́шешь	паха́ть	*plough*
брешу́	бре́шешь	бреха́ть	*yelp; fib*
тешу́	те́шешь	теса́ть	*hew, trim*
чешу́	че́шешь	чеса́ть	*scratch, comb*
пишу́	пи́шешь	писа́ть	*write*
пы́шу	пы́шешь	пы́хать	*glow*[3]
колы́шу[4]	колы́шешь	колыха́ть	*sway*
пляшу́	пля́шешь	пляса́ть	*dance*
-поя́шу[5]	-поя́шешь	-поя́сать	*(girdle)*

-щ- (< т, ст, or ск before ю or e)

клевещу́	клеве́щешь	клевета́ть	*slander*
скрежещу́	скреже́щешь	скрежета́ть	*gnash*
блещу́	бле́щешь[6]	блесте́ть	*shine, sparkle*
плещу́[7]	пле́щешь	плеска́ть	*splash*
хлещу́	хле́щешь	хлеста́ть	*lash*
трепещу́	трепе́щешь	трепета́ть	*tremble*

[1] Also (colloq.) мурлы́каю, мурлы́каешь.
[2] Also (colloq.) маха́ю, маха́ешь.
[3] With *heat* or *health*; in the sense of *puff, pant* the present is пы́хаю, пы́-хаешь. [4] Note the stress; also (colloq.) колыха́ю, колыха́ешь.
[5] e.g. опоя́шу, infin. опоя́сать (pf.) *gird*.
[6] Now more commonly блести́шь, &c. (conj. II); the forms блиста́ю, блиста́ешь, infin. блиста́ть *shine*, are now generally confined to the fig. sense *stand out (because of), be conspicuous (for)*.
[7] Also (colloq.) плеска́ю, плеска́ешь.

ищу́	и́щешь	иска́ть	*look for*
свищу́	сви́щешь	свиста́ть	*whistle*
полощу́[1]	поло́щешь	полоска́ть	*rinse; flap*
ропщу́	ро́пщешь	ропта́ть	*murmur, grumble*
ры́щу[2]	ры́щешь	ры́скать	*roam, lurk*

(ii) Present tense ending in -ю, -ешь, -ет, -ем, -ете, -ют.
(a) Stems ending in a consonant:

-л-

мелю́ (see § 89)	ме́лешь	моло́ть	*grind*
стелю́	сте́лешь	стлать	*spread*
колю́	ко́лешь	коло́ть	*pierce*
полю́	по́лешь	поло́ть	*weed*
шлю (see § 89)	шлёшь	слать	*send*

-бл- (< б before ю or е)

колéблю[3]	колéблешь	колебáть	*rock*
зы́блюсь[4]	зы́блешься	зы́биться	*surge, swell*

-мл- (< м before ю or е)

внéмлю[5]	внéмлешь	внимáть	*heed*
дремлю́	дрéмлешь	дремáть	*slumber*

-пл- (< п before ю or е)

кáплю[6]	кáплешь	кáпать	*drip, leak*
кра́плет[7] (3rd sg. only) (rare)		кра́пать	*spot (of rain)*
клеплю́	клéплешь	клепáть[8]	*slander*
треплю́	трéплешь	трепáть	*tousle*

[1] Colloq. also often полоска́ю, полоска́ешь; but never thus in the sense [*cause to*] *flutter, flap*, as in ве́тер поло́щет зна́мя, зна́мя поло́щется.

[2] Also (colloq.) ры́скаю, ры́скаешь.

[3] Note the stress.   [4] For -сь/-ся see § 100.

[5] Poetic: note the stress; also внима́ю, внима́ешь (archaic).

[6] Usually кáпаю, кáпасшь, esp. in sense of *pour* (*drop by drop*).

[7] More often кра́пает, as [дождь] кра́пает *it is spotting with rain.*

[8] But клепáть meaning *rivet* is usually regular: клепáю, &c.

щеплю́[1]	ще́плешь	щепа́ть	*split*
щиплю́[2]	щи́плешь	щипа́ть	*nip*
сы́плю	сы́плешь	сы́пать[3]	*scatter*

-р-

борю́сь[4]	бо́решься	боро́ться	*struggle*
порю́	по́решь	поро́ть	*unstitch; cane*
орю́	о́решь	ора́ть	*plough* (dial.)

(*b*) Stems ending in a vowel or -ь:

-а-

Verbs with stems in -a- form the most considerable group in conj. I. Nearly all of them have 'regular' infinitives, in -ать. Typical of such verbs are:

де́лаю	де́лаешь	де́лать	*do, make*
чита́ю	чита́ешь	чита́ть	*read*
встреча́ю	встреча́ешь	встреча́ть	*meet*
зна́ю	зна́ешь	знать	*know*
рабо́таю	рабо́таешь	рабо́тать	*work*
за́втракаю	за́втракаешь	за́втракать	*breakfast*

but the following form their infinitives irregularly:

даю́	даёшь	дава́ть	*give*
ла́ю	ла́ешь	ла́ять	*bark*
ма́юсь[4]	ма́ешься	ма́яться	*pine away, toil*
-знаю́[5]	-знаёшь	-знава́ть	(*know*)
та́ю	та́ешь	та́ять	*melt*
-стаю́[6]	-стаёшь	-става́ть	(*become*)

[1] Also (colloq.) щепа́ю, щепа́ешь.
[2] Also (colloq.) щипа́ю, щипа́ешь.
[3] But -сыпа́ть, forming compound ipf. verbs, is reg.: -сыпа́ю, &c.
[4] For the reflexive suffix -сь/-ся see § 100.
[5] e.g. призна́ю, infin. признава́ть (ipf.) *recognize, admit*.
[6] e.g. отстаю́, infin. отстава́ть (ipf.) *lag behind*.

-e-

Although some verbs with infinitives in -еть belong to conj. II, the majority belong here, having stems ending in -e-. They include many verbs indicating a process or condition, as:

болею	болеешь	болеть¹	*be [often] ill*
имею	имеешь	иметь	*possess*
смею	смеешь	сметь	*dare*
коченею	коченеешь	коченеть	*grow numb*
умею	умеешь	уметь	*know how*
спею²	спеешь	спеть	*ripen*
грею	греешь	греть	*warm*
зрею³	зреешь	зреть	*ripen*

and verbs formed from adjectives of quality, as:

белею	белеешь	белеть	*become* or *appear white*
краснею	краснеешь	краснеть	*turn red, blush*
старею	стареешь	стареть	*grow old, age*

also certain verbs with infinitives in -еять(ся) and -ить, as:

надеюсь⁴	надеешься	надеяться	*hope*
смеюсь⁴	смеёшься	смеяться	*laugh*
рею	реешь	реять	*hover*
брею	бреешь	брить	*shave*
сею	сеешь	сеять	*sow*
затею	затеешь	затеять (pf.)	*plan*

-и-

гнию	гниёшь	гнить	*rot*
вопию	вопиешь	вопиять⁵	*wail, lament*

¹ But болеть *ache* belongs to conj. II.
² Not to be confused with спою, infin. спеть (pf.), from петь *sing*.
³ Not to be confused with зрю, infin. зреть (conj. II) *see*.
⁴ For the reflexive suffix -сь/-ся see § 100.
⁵ Archaic; see also the related verb вопить (conj. II).

почи́ю	почи́ешь	почива́ть[1]	*lie* (*buried*) (arch.)
почи́ю	почи́ешь	почи́ть (pf.)	*rest; die* (arch.)

-о-

во́ю	во́ешь	выть	*howl*
мо́ю	мо́ешь	мыть	*wash* (trans.)
но́ю	но́ешь	ныть	*ache*
пою́	поёшь	петь	*sing*
ро́ю	ро́ешь	рыть	*dig*
кро́ю	кро́ешь	крыть	*cover*

-у-

-у́ю	-у́ешь	-у́ть[2]	(*shoe, boot*)
ду́ю	ду́ешь	дуть	*blow*
жую́	жуёшь	жева́ть	*chew*
кую́	куёшь	кова́ть	*forge*
сную́	снуёшь	снова́ть	*weave; scurry*
осную́	оснуёшь	основа́ть (pf.)	*found*
се́тую	се́туешь	се́товать	*grieve*
чу́ю	чу́ешь	чу́ять	*scent*
по́тчую	по́тчуешь	по́тчевать	*treat*
бушу́ю	бушу́ешь	бушева́ть	*rage*

and many thousands of other verbs, including a great many technical terms, formed from either Russian or non-Russian words by the addition of the suffixes -овать/-евать, -вовать, -ствовать, -и́ровать (sometimes -ирова́ть), -изова́ть, and -изи́ровать, e.g.

сове́тую	сове́туешь	сове́товать	*advise*
жа́луюсь[3]	жа́луешься	жа́ловаться	*complain*
форму́ю	форму́ешь	формова́ть	*mould* (tech.)

---

[1] But почива́ть (archaic) *sleep* has present: почива́ю, &c.
[2] e.g. обу́ю, infin. обу́ть (pf.) *put shoes* (or *stockings*) *on* (trans.).
[3] For the reflexive suffix -сь/-ся see § 100.

танцу́ю	танцу́ешь	танцева́ть	*dance*
линчу́ю	линчу́ешь	линчева́ть	*lynch*
существу́ю	существу́ешь	существова́ть	*exist*
свире́пствую	свире́пствуешь	свире́пствовать	*rage*
меблиру́ю	меблиру́ешь	меблирова́ть	*furnish*
формиру́ю	формиру́ешь	формирова́ть	*form*
молни́рую	молни́руешь	молни́ровать	*wire*[1]
опери́рую	опери́руешь	опери́ровать	*operate*
аплоди́рую	аплоди́руешь	аплоди́ровать	*applaud*
советизи́рую	советизи́руешь	советизи́ровать	
			sovietize
нейтрализу́ю	нейтрализу́ешь	нейтрализова́ть	
			neutralize

-ь-

бью	бьёшь	бить	*hit*
вью	вьёшь	вить	*twist*
лью	льёшь	лить	*pour*
пью	пьёшь	пить	*drink*
шью	шьёшь	шить	*sew*

-ю- (all with infin. in -ева́ть)

блюю́	блюёшь	блева́ть	*spew*
штемпелю́ю	штемпелю́ешь	штемпелева́ть	*stamp,*
			mark
клюю́	клюёшь	клева́ть	*peck,*
			nibble
плюю́	плюёшь	плева́ть	*spit*
воюю́	воюешь	воева́ть	*wage war*
горю́ю	горю́ешь	горева́ть	*mourn*

---

[1] *by express telegram* (« мо́лния »).

-я-

A large number of conj. I verbs have stems in -я-; they are mostly compound (prefixed) imperfective counterparts of compound perfective verbs belonging to conj. II and are regular. The unprefixed verbs in this group are:

ва́яю	ва́яешь	ва́ять	*sculpt*
гуля́ю	гуля́ешь	гуля́ть	*walk*
ка́шляю	ка́шляешь	ка́шлять	*cough*
кла́няюсь	кла́няешься	кла́няться	*bow*
меня́ю	меня́ешь	меня́ть	*change* (trans.)
теря́ю	теря́ешь	теря́ть	*lose*

§ 88b. Conjugation II

To this conjugation belong all verbs in -ить (except the monosyllables бить, брить, вить, гнить, жить, лить, пить, шить, and compounds of -шибить), some verbs in -еть, most verbs in -жать, -шать, -чать, -щать, and the verbs гнать, спать, and their compounds.

The present stem of regular verbs of conj. II is formed by removing the last three letters from the infinitive and adding the personal endings -ю (-у after ж, ш, ч, щ), -ишь, -ит, -им, -ите, -ят (-ат after ж, ш, ч, щ). Characteristic types:

говори́ть *to speak*	смотре́ть *to look*
говорю́ *I speak, am speaking*	смотрю́ *I look, am looking*
говори́шь	смо́тришь
говори́т	смо́трит
говори́м	смо́трим
говори́те	смо́трите
говоря́т	смо́трят

плати́ть *to pay*

   плачу́
   пла́тишь
   пла́тит
   пла́тим
   пла́тите
   пла́тят

ви́деть *to see*

   ви́жу
   ви́дишь
   ви́дит
   ви́дим
   ви́дите
   ви́дят

кра́сить *to paint*

   кра́шу
   кра́сишь
   кра́сит
   кра́сим
   кра́сите
   кра́сят

вози́ть *to convey*

   вожу́
   во́зишь
   во́зит
   во́зим
   во́зите
   во́зят

учи́ть *to teach*

   учу́
   у́чишь
   у́чит
   у́чим
   у́чите
   у́чат

лежа́ть *to lie*

   лежу́
   лежи́шь
   лежи́т
   лежи́м
   лежи́те
   лежа́т

люби́ть *to love, like*

   люблю́
   лю́бишь
   лю́бит
   лю́бим
   лю́бите
   лю́бят

спать *to sleep*

   сплю
   спишь
   спит
   спим
   спи́те
   спят

The list below contains some common 'regular' verbs (with infin. in -ить), besides all the 'irregular' verbs of conj. II. They are arranged alphabetically, according to the last letters of their present stems:

-б- (becomes -бл- before -ю)

скорблю́	скорби́шь	скорбе́ть	*sorrow*
люблю́	лю́бишь	люби́ть	*love, like*
сверби́т, свербя́т (3rd sg., pl.)		свербе́ть	*itch*

-в- (becomes -вл- before -ю)

ловлю́	ло́вишь	лови́ть	*catch*

-г- became -ж- in all forms of conj. II.

-д- (-дю becomes -жу)

гла́жу	гла́дишь	гла́дить	*stroke*
(no 1st sing.)	бди́шь	бде́ть	*watch*(arch.)
ви́жу	ви́дишь	ви́деть	*see*
сижу́	сиди́шь	сиде́ть	*sit*
(no 1st sing.)	галди́шь	галде́ть	*make a row*
вожу́	во́дишь	води́ть	*lead*
хожу́	хо́дишь	ходи́ть	*walk*
гожу́сь[1]	годи́шься	годи́ться	*be of use*
(no 1st sing.)	смерди́шь	смерде́ть	*stink*
горжу́сь[1]	горди́шься	горди́ться	*be proud*
гляжу́	гляди́шь	гляде́ть	*look, glance*
зужу́	зуди́шь	зуде́ть	*itch, pester*

-ж-

—— (see § 89)	бежи́шь	бежа́ть	*run*
лежу́	лежи́шь	лежа́ть	*lie, recline*
дребезжу́	дребезжи́шь	дребезжа́ть	*clatter*
визжу́	визжи́шь	визжа́ть	*screech*
брюзжу́	брюзжи́шь	брюзжа́ть	*grumble*
дрожу́	дрожи́шь	дрожа́ть	*tremble*

[1] For the reflexive suffix -сь/-ся see § 100.

| держу́ | де́ржишь | держа́ть | *keep, hold* |
| жужжу́ | жужжи́шь | жужжа́ть | *buzz* |

-з- (-зю becomes -жу)

| ла́жу | ла́зишь | ла́зить | *clamber* |
| вожу́ | во́зишь | вози́ть | *convey* |

-к- became -ч- in all forms of conj. II

-л-

велю́	вели́шь	веле́ть[1]	*command*
молю́сь[2]	мо́лишься	моли́ться	*pray*
боли́т, боля́т (3rd sing., pl.) боле́ть[3]			*ache*

-м- (becomes -мл- before -ю)

| шумлю́ | шуми́шь | шуме́ть | *make a noise* |
| ломлю́ | ло́мишь | ломи́ть | *break* (trans.) |

-н-

| виню́ | вини́шь | вини́ть | *blame* |
| гоню́ | го́нишь | гнать | *chase* |

-о-

бою́сь[2]	бои́шься	боя́ться	*fear*
сто́ю	сто́ишь	сто́ить	*be worth*
стою́	стои́шь	стоя́ть	*stand*

-п- (becomes -пл- before -ю)

воплю́	вопи́шь	вопи́ть	*wail, howl*
тороплю́	торо́пишь	торопи́ть	*hurry* (trans.)
соплю́	сопи́шь	сопе́ть	*wheeze*
терплю́	те́рпишь	терпе́ть	*tolerate*
сплю	спишь	спать	*sleep*

[1] Either ipf. or pf.; hence велю́ is present or future.
[2] For -сь/-ся see § 100.
[3] But боле́ть *be [often] ill* belongs to conj. I.

-р-

зрю	зришь	зреть	*look, see* (archaic)
говорю́	говори́шь	говори́ть	*speak, say*
горю́	гори́шь	горе́ть	*burn* (intr.)
смотрю́	смо́тришь	смотре́ть	*look*
курю́	ку́ришь	кури́ть	*smoke* (trans.)

-с- (-сю becomes -шу)

кра́шу	кра́сишь	кра́сить	*paint, dye*
вишу́	виси́шь	висе́ть	*hang* (intr.)
зави́шу	зави́сишь	зави́сеть	*depend*
ношу́	но́сишь	носи́ть	*carry, wear*

-т- (-тю becomes -чу or -щу)

плачу́	пла́тишь	плати́ть	*pay*
свечу́	све́тишь	свети́ть	*shine*
лечу́	лети́шь	лете́ть	*fly*
посещу́	посети́шь	посети́ть (pf.)	*visit*
——	хоти́м (see § 89)	хоте́ть	*wish, want*
верчу́	ве́ртишь	верте́ть	*turn, twist*
чту	чтишь[1]	чтить	*respect, honour*

-ст- (-стю becomes -щу)

блещу́	блести́шь[2]	блесте́ть	*shine, sparkle*
свищу́	свисти́шь	свисте́ть	*whistle*
пущу́	пу́стишь	пусти́ть (pf.)	*allow, let go*

-ф- (becomes -фл- before -ю)

тра́флю	тра́фишь	тра́фить	*hit the mark*

-х- became -ш- in all forms of conj. II

---

[1] 3rd pl. чтят or чтут.
[2] Also (but now less commonly) бле́щешь, conj. I.

-ч-

кричу́	кричи́шь	крича́ть	*shout*
молчу́	молчи́шь	молча́ть	*keep silent*
мчу	мчишь	мчать	*rush along*
бренчу́	бренчи́шь	бренча́ть	*jingle*
ворчу́	ворчи́шь	ворча́ть	*growl*
торчу́	торчи́шь	торча́ть	*protrude*
урчу́	урчи́шь	урча́ть	*rumble*
бурчу́	бурчи́шь	бурча́ть	*mutter*
журчу́	журчи́шь	журча́ть	*babble*
учу́	у́чишь	учи́ть	*teach, learn*
звучу́	звучи́шь	звуча́ть	*sound, ring*
стучу́	стучи́шь	стуча́ть	*knock*
мычу́	мычи́шь	мыча́ть	*low, moo*
рычу́	рычи́шь	рыча́ть	*snarl*

-ш-

дышу́	ды́шишь	дыша́ть	*breathe*
слы́шу	слы́шишь	слы́шать	*hear*

-щ-

верещу́	верещи́шь	вереща́ть	*chirp*
трещу́	трещи́шь	треща́ть	*crackle*
пищу́	пищи́шь	пища́ть	*squeak, cheep*

§ 89. Irregular Present Forms

Most of these are not really irregular at all, but merely the remains of an old conjugation.

The forms   есть   (3rd sing.)   *is*
суть   (3rd pl.)   *are*

are all that is left of the present tense of the verb быть *to be* (see §§ 81, 112).

ем *I eat, am eating*

(Infin. есть)

$$\text{Sing.}\begin{cases} 1 & \text{ем} \\ 2 & \text{ешь} \\ 3 & \text{ест} \end{cases} \qquad \text{Pl.}\begin{cases} 1 & \text{еди́м} \\ 2 & \text{еди́те} \\ 3 & \text{едя́т} \end{cases}$$

N.B. The imperative of this verb (ешь, е́шьте) is less polite than that of ку́шать (ку́шай, ку́шайте).

дам *I shall give*

(Infin. дать, pf.)

$$\text{Sing.}\begin{cases} 1 & \text{дам} \\ 2 & \text{дашь} \\ 3 & \text{даст} \end{cases} \qquad \text{Pl.}\begin{cases} 1 & \text{дади́м} \\ 2 & \text{дади́те} \\ 3 & \text{даду́т} \end{cases}$$

N.B. Besides the true compounds of дать, the unrelated verb созда́ть (pf.) *to create* is also conjugated in this way.

вем *I know* (old pres. of ве́дать, now reg.)

is obsolete except in the phrase Бог весть *God knows*, still sometimes used; the imperative still survives in the very common particle ведь *for; then; of course; you know*.

The following two presents are mixtures of conjugations I and II and, as they are common, deserve special attention:

хочу́ *I want, wish*

(Infin. хоте́ть)

$$\text{Sing.}\atop\text{(conj. I)}\begin{cases} 1 & \text{хочу́} \\ 2 & \text{хо́чешь} \\ 3 & \text{хо́чет} \end{cases} \qquad \text{Pl.}\atop\text{(conj. II)}\begin{cases} 1 & \text{хоти́м} \\ 2 & \text{хоти́те} \\ 3 & \text{хотя́т} \end{cases}$$

бегу́ *I am running*
(Infin. бежа́ть)

Sing. { 1 бегу́ 2 бежи́шь 3 бежи́т }   Pl. { 1 бежи́м 2 бежи́те 3 бегу́т }

Three common verbs with regular endings have un-expected present stems which should be noted:

éхать *to be riding, driving* has ед- (pres. éду, éдешь, &c.);

моло́ть *to grind* has мел- (pres. мелю́, мéлешь, &c.);

and, owing to the sound changes caused by a following 'soft' vowel, слать *to send* has шл- (pres. шлю, шлёшь, &c.; imperative шли, шли́те).

§ 90. The Past

As mentioned in § 86, the past in Russian is a tense only in name. In reality it is a past participle active which formerly was used, with the help of the present of the verb быть *to be*, as a compound perfect tense like the German *ich bin gewesen*. When the present of быть became obsolete, the past participle came to be used alone as the past tense and is now not felt to be a participle at all. It is formed from the infinitive, the general rule being to cut off the last two letters (-ть or -ти) and add:

-л   for the masc. sing. ⎫
-ла   for the fem. sing.   ⎬ all three persons
-ло   for the neut. sing. ⎭

and -ли   for the plural, all three persons and genders.

In the singular it must always agree in gender with the subject of the sentence, whichever person it be, except, of course, that the neut. sing. form in -ло is used only for the 3rd person.

The personal pronouns must be prefixed as required, e.g. я, ты, он, она́, оно́ for the singular, according to the gender, and мы, вы, они́ for the plural; but they may be omitted when the subject can be quite clearly understood from the context.

There is no difficulty in forming the past from any verb with infinitive in -ать, -ять, -еть,[1] -ыть, -ить,[2] -оть, or -уть.[3] This covers all the verbs in conj. II and most of those in conj. I. The only difficulty is the stress: it sometimes falls on the ending and sometimes not and is best learnt by observation and practice.

Examples are given of the past of verbs in conj. II, and of those in conj. I whose infinitives end as indicated above:

	1, 2, 3 pers. sing.	*1, 2, 3 pers. pl.*	*Infinitive*
M.	знал		
F.	зна́ла	зна́ли	знать *know*
N.	зна́ло		
M.	гуля́л		
F.	гуля́ла	гуля́ли	гуля́ть *walk*
N.	гуля́ло		
M.	говори́л		
F.	говори́ла	говори́ли	говори́ть *speak*
N.	говори́ло		
M.	ви́дел		
F.	ви́дела	ви́дели	ви́деть *see*
N.	ви́дело		
M.	мыл		
F.	мы́ла	мы́ли	мыть *wash* (trans.)
N.	мы́ло		
M.	пил		
F.	пила́	пи́ли	пить *drink*
N.	пи́ло		

[1] But not those in -ереть.   [2] But not those in -шибить.
[3] But not those in -нуть.

	1, 2, 3 *pers. sing.*	*1, 2, 3* *pers. pl.*	*Infinitive*
M.	боро́лся		
F.	боро́лась	боро́лись	боро́ться *struggle*
N.	боро́лось		
M.	дул		
F.	ду́ла	ду́ли	дуть *blow*
N.	ду́ло		

In the case of conj. I verbs with stems ending in a consonant and infinitives ending in -ти, -зти, -зть, -сти, -сть, -ереть, -шибить, -чь, and some verbs with infinitives in -нуть, the formation of the past tense is a little more difficult.

One reason is that the infinitive sometimes disguises the end of the stem, and it is to the present stem (ending in a consonant) that the endings of the past have to be added; and another is that some of the stems undergo phonetic changes when followed by the -л of the past. The stem can always be found in the 1st pers. sing. of the present by cutting off the ending -у, -ю, or -ну.

Stems in -с-, -з-, -к-, -г-, -б-, and -р-[1] lose the -л of the masc. sing. in the past tense, e.g.

M.	нёс		
F.	несла́	несли́	нести́ *carry*
N.	несло́		
M.	вёз		
F.	везла́	везли́	везти́ *transport*
N.	везло́		
M.	лез		
F.	ле́зла	ле́зли	лезть *climb*
N.	ле́зло		

---

[1] The past tenses of those in -р- are formed from stems with an inserted -е-, e.g. in the case of тере́ть, from тер- and not from тр- (cf. present тру *I rub*).

M.	тёк			
F.	текла́	}	текли́	течь *flow*
N.	текло́			

M.	мог			
F.	могла́	}	могли́	мочь *be able*
N.	могло́			

M.	грёб			
F.	гребла́	}	гребли́	грести́ *row*
N.	гребло́			

M.	тёр			
F.	тёрла	}	тёрли	тере́ть *rub*
N.	тёрло			

Stems ending in -д- and -т- lose these consonants before all the past endings beginning with л, e.g.

M.	вёл			
F.	вела́	}	вели́	вести́ (stem вед-) *lead*
N.	вело́			

M.	клал			
F.	кла́ла	}	кла́ли	класть (stem клад-) *put*
N.	кла́ло			

M.	мёл			
F.	мела́	}	мели́	мести́ (stem мет-) *sweep*
N.	мело́			

Of the verbs whose infinitives end in -нуть, the majority form their past in the ordinary way,[1] e.g.

M.	тро́нул			
F.	тро́нула	}	тро́нули	тро́нуть *touch* (pf.)
N.	тро́нуло			

---

[1] Note: дви́нуть *to move* (and its compounds) has past tense дви́нул, &c., but воздви́гнуть *to erect* has past воздви́г, воздви́гла, &c.

but those verbs in -нуть which denote a process of any
sort lose the syllable -ну- and add the terminations of the
past direct to the root unless (as in тонуть *sink*) the
infinitive suffix is stressed. When the root ends in -х-, -к-,
-с-, or -з-, the -л is absent in the masc. sing. of the past:

	Singular	*Plural*	*Infinitive*
M.	сох[1]		
F.	сóхла	сóхли	сóхнуть *become dry*
N.	сóхло		
M.	кис[1]		
F.	кúсла	кúсли	кúснуть *turn sour*
N.	кúсло		
M.	мок[1]		
F.	мóкла	мóкли	мóкнуть *get wet*
N.	мóкло		
M.	стыл		
F.	стыла	стыли	стынуть[2] *grow cold*
N.	стыло		
M.	исчéз		
F.	исчéзла	исчéзли	исчéзнуть *disappear*
N.	исчéзло		(pf.)

The pasts of the following verbs of conj. I must be mentioned individually, being somewhat unexpected; to them
are added those of the irregular verbs.

M.	-чёл		
F.	-члá	-члú	-чéсть (*reckon, read*)
N.	-члó		

---

[1] There is a strong tendency to avoid such monosyllables (apart from
стыл), unless they are compounded with a prefix, and to prefer the forms
сóхнул, кúснул, мóкнул, &c., for the masc. sing. (but просóх, скис, про-
мóк, &c.).   [2] Or стыть.

M.	сел			
F.	сéла	}	сéли	сесть *sit down*
N.	сéло			

M.	рос			
F.	рослá	}	рослú	растú *grow*
N.	рослó			

M.	клял			
F.	клялá	}	кля́ли	клясть *swear*
N.	кля́ло			

M.	лёг			
F.	леглá	}	леглú	лечь *lie down*
N.	леглó			

M.	жёг			
F.	жглá	}	жглú	жечь *burn*
N.	жглó			(trans.)

M.	толóк			
F.	толклá	}	толклú	толóчь *pound*
N.	толклó			

M.	-ши́б			
F.	-ши́бла	}	-ши́бли	-шиби́ть (*hit*)
N.	-ши́бло			

Notice especially:

M.	шёл			
F.	шла	}	шли	идти́ *go* (*on foot*)
N.	шло			

The verbs which are irregular in the present tense form the past tense quite regularly:

быть	*be*	has был	былá	бы́ло	бы́ли
есть	*eat*	has ел	éла	éло	éли
дать	*give*	has дал	далá	дáло	дáли
хотéть	*wish*	has хотéл	хотéла	хотéло	хотéли

бежа́ть	*run*	has	бежа́л	бежа́ла	бежа́ло	бежа́ли
éхать	*travel*	has	éхал	éхала	éхало	éхали
моло́ть	*grind*	has	моло́л	моло́ла	моло́ло	моло́ли
слать	*send*	has	слал	сла́ла	сла́ло	сла́ли

§ 91. The Future

In form the future is exactly the same as the present and has no special endings of its own. It is a peculiarity of Russian that the present tense of any so-called perfective verb has future meaning. This will be explained amply in §§ 101, 104.

The only imperfective verb with a simple future tense is быть *to be*: бу́ду *I shall be*, бу́дешь *thou wilt be*, &c. All other imperfective verbs have a compound future tense, composed of the future of быть and the infinitive, e.g. он бу́дет говори́ть *he will be speaking*, *he will speak*. The difference in meaning between the simple future of perfective verbs and the compound future of corresponding imperfective verbs will be explained in § 104.

§ 92. The Conditional

This is formed by adding the enclitic particle бы (often contracted to б) to the past of any verb.

This particle is really a part of the verb быть *to be*, which originally possessed a complete conditional tense, long since quite obsolete.

This particle бы can be placed after the verb:

	Singular	*Plural*
M.	хоте́л бы	
F.	хоте́ла бы	хоте́ли бы
N.	хоте́ло бы	

all of which forms can, of course, be preceded by the requisite personal pronouns; or бы can precede the verb:

	Singular	*Plural*

M. ⎧ я́ бы хоте́л   мы́ ⎫
   ⎨ ты́ бы хоте́л   вы́ ⎬ бы хоте́ли
   ⎩ о́н бы хоте́л   они́ ⎭

F. ⎧ я́ бы хоте́ла   мы́ ⎫
   ⎨ ты́ бы хоте́ла   вы́ ⎬ бы хоте́ли
   ⎩ она́ бы хоте́ла   они́ ⎭

N.   оно́ бы хоте́ло   они́ бы хоте́ли

in which case, since бы is an enclitic, the personal pronouns are essential when бы would otherwise be the first word of a clause.

The conditional can refer to present, future, or past time, according to the context, see § 105 (a):

    хоте́л бы *would like* or *would have liked* (infin. хоте́ть)

The Russian conditional also serves as a subjunctive, see § 105 (b).

§ 93. The Imperative

The endings of the imperative are:

2nd sing.	-и	-ь	-й
2nd pl.	-ите	-ьте	-йте

The endings -и, -ите are added to the present stems of all those verbs in conj. I which end in a consonant and have the stress on the ending of the 1st sing. present (future if the verb is perfective); the endings are stressed:

1st sing. pres.	*Imperative*	
иду́	иди́! иди́те!	*go!*
пишу́	пиши́! пиши́те!	*write!*

1st sing. pres.	*Imperative*	
пеку́	пеки́! пеки́те!	*bake!*
берегу́[1]	береги́! береги́те!	*watch [it]!*

When the stress does not fall on the ending of the 1st sing., then -ь, -ьте are added, e.g.

бу́ду	будь! бу́дьте!	*be!*
ся́ду	сядь! ся́дьте!	*sit down!*
пла́чу	плачь! пла́чьте!	*weep!*

When, however, the present stem ends in two consonants, the endings -и, -ите are added,[2] even if the stress falls on the stem, e.g.

кри́кну	кри́кни! кри́кните!	*shout!*

No matter where the stress falls, the endings -й, -йте are added to all those present stems which end in a vowel, thus forming a diphthong, e.g.

де́лаю	де́лай! де́лайте!	*do!*	пою́	пой! по́йте!	*sing!*
кро́ю	крой! кро́йте!	*cover!*	дам	дай! да́йте!	*give!*
	сове́тую	сове́туй! сове́туйте!	*advise!*		

---

[1] The common reflexive береги́сь! (pl. береги́тесь!) means *take care!*
[2] But note: from сы́плю — сыпь(те)! *scatter!*; from ка́плю — ка́пай(те)! *drip!*; and from внемлю — вне́мли(те)! or внемли́(те)! *heed!*

Notice that the imperatives of the five verbs бить, вить, лить, пить, and шить are somewhat different, viz.:

бей! } *hit!*
бейте!

пей! } *drink!*
пейте!

Verbs of conj. II take the endings -и, -ите when the stress falls on the ending of the 2nd sing. of the present, and the endings, -ь, -ьте when the stress falls on the stem, e.g.

2nd sing. pres.	Imperative	
спишь	спи! спите!	*sleep!*
сиди́шь	сиди́! сиди́те!	*sit!* (i.e. *don't get up!*)
отве́тишь (pf.)	отве́ть! отве́тьте!	*reply!*
бро́сишь (pf.)	брось! бро́сьте!	*throw it! stop it!*

When the stem ends in a vowel, it takes -й, -йте, e.g.

стои́шь	стой! сто́йте!	*stand! stop!*

Note that verbs with the stressed prefix вы- normally have in the imperative the same ending as the unprefixed form, e.g. пиши́! — вы́пиши!, пеки́! — вы́пеки!, брось! — вы́брось!

The following imperatives are irregular:

from ля́гу, ля́жешь, infin. лечь (pf.)

imper. ляг! ля́гте! *lie down!*

from ем, ешь, infin. есть

imper. ешь! е́шьте! *eat!* (N.B. ку́шай(те) is more polite)

from дава́ть, -знава́ть, -става́ть

imper. дава́й(те)!, -знава́й(те)!, -става́й(те)!

from (по)éду, (по)éдешь, infin. (по)éхать

imper.   поезжáй!   ⎫
         поезжáйте! ⎬ *start! go! drive away!*
               ⎭

The 1st pl. of the imperative (*let us . . .*) is expressed, as a rule, by the 1st pl. of the future (perfective or imperfective) and also of the present in the case of verbs of 'actual' motion (see § 116):

кýпим нóвый дом!	*let's buy a new house!*
посидúм ещё нéсколько минýт!	*let's sit a few minutes longer*
бýдем читáть газéту кáждый день!	*let's read the paper every day!*
пойдём (or идём) домóй!	*let's go home!*

All the above forms except идём may be preceded by давáй(те), see § 106 (a).

In colloquial speech an anomalous 1st pl. of the imperative is sometimes formed by adding the ending -те to the 1st pl. of the future (also present of verbs of 'actual' motion); such a form should be used only when addressing two or more people or a person to whom one uses вы:

поговорúмте!	*let's have a little chat!*
бýдемте рабóтать прилéжно!	*let's work hard!*
пойдёмте (or идёмте)!	*let's go!*

The 3rd sing. and 3rd pl. of the imperative are expressed by the word пусть (from пустúть *to let*) or пускáй (2nd sing. imperative of пускáть *to let*) followed by the future (perfective) or present (imperfective):

пусть [он] скáжет!	*let him tell!*
пусть [онú] стоя́т!	*let them stand!*
пускáй [онá] придёт!	*let her come!*

§ 94. The Infinitive

The infinitive ends in -ть, -ти, or -чь, preceded by various vowels and consonants; when the stress falls on the infinitive ending itself (which it does in a small minority of Russian verbs), then the ending is -ти, otherwise it is -ть (-чь).[1]

As examples of all possible varieties of infinitives have been given in § 88, it is unnecessary to repeat them here.

§ 95. The Gerunds

THE PRESENT GERUND is in most cases formed from the third person plural of the present by cutting off the last two letters, viz. -ут, -ют, or -ят, and adding -я, e.g.

неся	*carrying*	from несу́т
чита́я	*reading*	from чита́ют
говоря́	*speaking*	from говоря́т
си́дя	*sitting*	from сидя́т
сто́я	*standing*	from стоя́т
гля́дя	*looking*	from глядя́т

The following are formed somewhat irregularly:

дава́я	*giving*	but даю́т (from дава́ть)
-знава́я	(*recognizing*)	but -знаю́т (from -знава́ть)
-става́я	(*standing*)	but -стаю́т (from -става́ть)

N.B. The present gerund хотя́ (from хотя́т *they wish*) has acquired the meaning *although* and is now used only as a conjunction.

The present gerund form of a perfective verb has the sense of a past gerund, e.g. принеся́ (or принёсши) *having brought*.

---

[1] A verb compounded with the stressed prefix вы́- usually has the same infinitive suffix as the unprefixed verb, e.g. бить — вы́бить, нести́ — вы́нести, сечь — вы́сечь.

When the 3rd pl. of the present ends in -ут or -ат preceded by ж, ш, щ, or ч, the present gerund ends not in -я,
but in -a, e.g.

плáча	*weeping*	from плáчут
ищá	*seeking*	from йщут
мóлча[1]	*without speaking*	from молчáт
лёжа[1]	*lying down*	from лежáт

There is another form of the present gerund which is
formed by cutting off the last letter of the 3rd pl. present
(-т) and adding -чи. This form is used in dialect and in
folk-poetry, but in the literary language it is rarely found;
from the verb быть *to be*, however, it is the only form of the
present gerund ever used, viz.

бýдучи   *being*   from бýдут

No present gerund in -я/-а is formed from conj. I verbs
(i) with present stems that have no vowel or only a 'mobile'
o/e (e.g. ждать, мять, пить, терéть, звать), (ii) in which
-с-/-з- become -ш-/-ж- throughout the present (e.g.
писáть, рéзать), or (iii) with present tense in -ну, -нешь,
&c. (e.g. гáснуть); nor do the verbs мочь, петь, гнить,
лезть, бежáть, and éхать have a gerund in -я/-а.

THE PAST GERUND is formed from the masc. sing. of the
past tense by cutting off the -л and adding -в or -вши,
e.g.

прочитáв (or прочитáвши)	*having read*	from прочитáл
вспóмнив (or вспóмнивши)	*having remembered*	from вспóмнил
прибы́в (or прибы́вши)	*having arrived*	from при́был

---

[1] Used as an adverb.

Those verbs that have no -л in the masc. sing. of the past form their past gerunds with -ши, e.g.

лёгши   from лёг (infin. лечь)
пресе́кши   from пресе́к (infin. пресе́чь)

From most perfective verbs in -сти/-зти the present gerund form with past meaning is now preferred: принеся́ (or принёсши) from принести́.

Those verbs in which a final -т-/-д- of the stem has dropped before the -л in the masc. sing. of the past tense, replace the dental and add -ши in the past gerund, but this form is archaic, and the present form (with past meaning) is preferred when the verb is perfective, e.g.

ве́дши   from вёл (infin. вести́, ipf.)
приведя́ (or приве́дши) from привёл (infin. привести́, pf.)

Notice especially:

ше́дши   from шёл (infin. идти́, ipf.)
пройдя́ (or проше́дши) from прошёл (пройти́, pf.)

Reflexive verbs take the suffix -вшись, e.g.

умы́вшись   from умы́лся (infin. умы́ться)

The Participles

§ 96. The present participle active is formed, like the present gerund, from the 3rd pl. of the present tense. For the participle, cut off only the last letter (-т), add -щий, -щая, -щее, and decline exactly like хоро́ший, хоро́шая, хоро́шее (p. 114), e.g.

from лю́бят (infin. люби́ть), pres. part. act. лю́бящий *loving* (sc. *who/which loves*)

from веду́т (infin. вести́), pres. part. веду́щий *leading* (sc. *which/who leads*) from зна́ют (infin. знать), pres. part. зна́ющий *knowing* (sc. *who/which knows*)

It must be noticed that the participle, present in form, of the verb бу́ду *I shall be*, viz. бу́дущий, has imperfective future meaning, and commonly means *next*, or *the next*; the neuter бу́дущее is also used substantivally with the sense of *the future*.

Only imperfective verbs form a present participle active.

§ 97. The past participle active is formed, like the past gerund, from the masc. sing. of the past tense, by cutting off -л and adding -вший, -вшая, -вшее; the word so formed declines exactly like хоро́ший,

e.g. from люби́л (infin. люби́ть), past part. люби́вший, &c., *who/which loved, has loved*, or *had loved*

from съел (infin. съесть), past part. съе́вший, &c., *who/ which ate, has eaten*, or *had eaten*

from был (infin. быть), past part. бы́вший, which is also used to express *former* or *late* (though, N.B., not *the late* [i.e. *deceased*] which is поко́йный)

Those verbs which lose the -л in the masc. sing. of the past tense add -ший, -шая, -шее.

e.g. from у́мер (infin. умере́ть), past part. уме́рший, &c., *who died, has/had died*

Those verbs in which a final -д-/-т- of the stem has fallen out before the -л in the masc. sing. of the past tense replace the dental and add -ший, &c.

e.g. from вёл (infin. вести́), past part. ве́дший, &c., *who/ which was leading, led, had led*

from шёл (infin. идти́), past part. ше́дший, &c., *who/ which was going, went, had gone*

from пал (infin. пасть) there are two forms: па́вший and
па́дший *who/which fell, has fallen*; па́вший is used literally, and is applied to those who fall in battle, while
па́дший is used figuratively.

§ 98. The present participle passive is formed from
the 1st pl. of the present tense of imperfective verbs by
adding the ending -ый, -ая, -ое, the word thus formed
being declined like бе́лый.

> e.g. from чита́ем (infin. чита́ть), pres. part. pass.
> чита́емый, &c., (*being*) *read*

> from ви́дим (infin. ви́деть), pres. part. pass. ви́димый,
> &c., (*being*) *seen, visible*

> from лю́бим (infin. люби́ть), pres. part. pass. люби́мый,
> &c., (*being*) *loved, favourite*

A few verbs of the 1st conjugation with stems ending in
consonants form the pres. part. pass. irregularly, in -о́мый,
&c.

> e.g. from несём (infin. нести́), pres. part. pass. несо́мый,
> &c.

> from ведём (infin. вести́), pres. part. pass. ведо́мый, &c.

> from иска́ть *to seek*, pres. part. pass. иско́мый, &c.

Like the present gerund, the present participle passive
is not formed from many verbs and those of others are
rarely used.

§ 99. The past participle passive is formed from
the infinitive in two different ways. One is by cutting off
the -ть of the infinitive and adding -н, -на, -но for the short
or predicative, and -нный, -нная, -нное for the long or

attributive form. The short form has the nominative case only and is used only in the predicate; its plural form for all genders ends in -ны. The long form declines like the adjective бе́лый.

Past part. pass. are generally formed from perfective verbs: simple imperfective verbs are rarely used in the past part. pass., and those compounded with a prefix — almost never.

e.g. from	сде́лать *to make*
past part. pass.	сде́лан, -а, -о; -ы; сде́ланный, &c.
from	потеря́ть *to lose*
past part. pass.	поте́рян, -а, -о; -ы; поте́рянный, &c.
from	дать *to give*
past part. pass.	дан, дана́, дано́; даны́; да́нный, &c.
from	осмотре́ть *to inspect*
past part. pass.	осмо́трен, -а, -о; -ы; осмо́тренный, &c.

Verbs with infinitive in -ить form the past part. pass. as follows:

from	обвини́ть *to accuse*
past part. pass.	обвинён, -ена́, -ено́; -ены́; обвинён- ный, &c.
from	ужа́лить *to sting*
past part. pass.	ужа́лен, -а, -о; -ы; ужа́ленный, &c.
from	ра́нить *to wound*
past part. pass.	ра́нен, -а, -о; -ы; ра́ненный,[1] &c.
from	учи́ть *to teach, learn*
past part. pass.	у́чен, -а, -о; -ы; у́ченный,[2] &c.

[1] Spelt ра́неный when used purely as adjective or noun = *wounded* [*man*].
[2] But учёный when used purely as adjective or noun = *learned* [*man*].

The past part. pass. of those verbs of conj. II whose 1st person sing. present is affected by the following soft vowel (see § 87), is formed from the 1st pers. sing. of the present in the following way:

from	заплати́ть *to pay*
1st sing. pres.	заплачу́ (-чу < -т + ю)
past part. pass.	запла́чен; запла́ченный
from	посади́ть *to set, plant*
1st sing. pres.	посажу́ (-жу < -д + ю)
past part. pass.	поса́жен; поса́женный
from	скоси́ть *to mow*
1st sing. pres.	скошу́ (-шу < -с + ю)
past part. pass.	ско́шен; ско́шенный[1]
from	купи́ть *to buy*
1st sing. pres.	куплю́ (-плю < -п + ю)
past part. pass.	ку́плен; ку́пленный

Notice especially:

from	оби́деть *to offend*
past part. pass.	оби́жен; оби́женный, &c.
but from	[у]ви́деть *to see*
past part. pass.	[у]ви́ден; [у]ви́денный

A few verbs of this class which have presents in -щу form their past part. pass. with -щ-.

e.g. from	обрати́ть *to turn*
past part. pass.	обращён, -ена́, &c.; обращённый
from	просвети́ть *to enlighten*
past part. pass.	просвещён, -ена́, &c.; просвещённый

---

[1] But скошён, -ена́, &c.; скошённый from скоси́ть (глаза́) *to squint*.

from	посети́ть *to visit*
past part. pass.	посещён, -ена́, &c.; посещённый
and from	отомсти́ть *to avenge oneself*
past part. pass.	отомщён, -ена́, &c.; отомщённый

Many 1st conjugation verbs whose stems end in a consonant form their past part. pass. from the 2nd pers. sing., by cutting off the ending -ешь and adding -ён, &c., for the predicative, -ённый, &c., for the attributive form.

| e.g. from увести́ *to lead away* |
2nd sing. pres.	уведёшь
past part. pass.	уведён, -ена́, &c.; уведённый
	прочéсть *to read through*
2nd sing. pres.	прочтёшь
past part. pass.	прочтён, -ена́, &c.; прочтённый
	стричь *to shear, cut (hair)*
2nd sing. pres.	стрижёшь
past part. pass.	стри́жен, -а, &c.; стри́женный (note stress)
	сжечь *to burn* (trans.)
2nd sing. pres.	сожжёшь
past part. pass.	сожжён, -ена́, &c.; сожжённый

and others.

The other way of forming the past participle passive is by cutting off the -ь of the infinitive; this gives the masculine short or predicative form, the long or attributive form being obtained by adding -ый (declined as бéлый). Few verbs form their past passive participle in this way.

e.g. from	мыть *to wash*
past part. pass.	мыт, -а, -о, -ы; мы́тый
from	бить *to hit*
past part. pass.	бит, -а, -о, -ы; би́тый

from	гре́ть *to heat*
past part. pass.	грет, -а, -о, -ы; гре́тый

Other common verbs which form their past part. pass. in this way are:

нача́ть	*to begin*	жать	*to reap*
нажи́ть	*to earn*	мять	*to crush*
заня́ть	*to occupy, borrow*	оде́ть	*to dress*
покры́ть	*to cover*	петь	*to sing*
жать	*to press*	брить	*to shave*

and all verbs in -уть

e.g. from	протяну́ть *to stretch out*
past part. pass.	протя́нут, -а, -о, -ы; протя́нутый

Notice also:

from	прокля́сть *to curse*
past part. pass.	про́клят, -а́, -о, -ы; про́клятый[1]
from	тере́ть *to rub*
past part. pass.	тёрт, -а, -о, -ы; тёртый
from	запере́ть *to shut, lock up*
past part. pass.	за́перт, -а́, -о, -ы; за́пертый

§ 100. The Reflexive Verb

This is formed by the addition of -ся (or -сь), a reduced form of the reflexive pronoun себя́, to all parts of the verb, as follows:

купа́ться *to bathe* (imperfective and intransitive)

Present

я	купа́юсь
ты	купа́ешься
он, она́, оно́	купа́ется

[1] In purely adjectival use as a term of abuse (= *accursed, damned,* &c.) this word has the stress on the second syllable.

мы   купа́емся
вы   купа́етесь
они́   купа́ются

Past

M.   купа́лся

Sing. F.   купа́лась   } Pl. купа́лись

N.   купа́лось

Future

бу́ду купа́ться, &c.

Conditional	*Imperative*
купа́лся бы, &c.	купа́йся
	купа́йтесь

Present Gerund	*Past Gerund*
купа́ясь	купа́вшись

Present Participle	*Past Participle*
купа́ющийся, &c.	купа́вшийся, &c.

-ся is added whenever the part of the verb ends in a consonant or in -ь or -й; -сь when it ends in a vowel. -ся is added in the participles throughout, whether preceded by vowel or consonant.

§ 101. The Uses of the Verb

In order to use the verb correctly it is necessary to know not only the way it is conjugated but also what aspects it possesses.

This is where the real difficulty begins. It will have been noticed that, compared with other languages, Russian possesses very few tenses in the grammatical sense of the word; this want is supplied by the aspects.

The aspects are ways of looking at an action; the same verb acquires different forms and a different meaning according to its aspect. The aspects are formed by altering the verb itself either by adding a prefix or by lengthening or otherwise altering the stem itself; the personal endings remain unaltered and each aspect of the verb has a more or less complete set of forms, i.e. present, imperative, infinitive, &c. (see pp. 270–1).

There are two main divisions of the aspects of the Russian verb:

(1) imperfective

and (2) perfective.

The verbs themselves are called imperfective or perfective according to the aspect which they express; every Russian verb must necessarily belong to one aspect or the other.

The difference in meaning between these two aspects is that when one uses an imperfective verb the action described by that verb is, in the mind's eye of the speaker, HABITUAL, REPEATED, INCOMPLETE, or (in the past or future) of UNCERTAIN DURATION.

When, on the other hand, someone uses a perfective verb, then either he is speaking of a single COMPLETED action, or if it is in the future, the speaker must have its completion in his mind's eye.

In English there is of course also variety of aspect, but it is expressed not by altering the verb itself, but by the use of auxiliary verbs or adverbs; for instance, *I go, I am going, I used to go, I often went, I was going, I shall go every day* are imperfective, whereas *I once went, I have gone, I shall go tomorrow* are perfective actions.

The majority of simple Russian verbs, i.e. those which are not compounded with a prefix, are imperfective, but from the fact that a given verb is compounded with a prefix it by no means follows that that verb is perfective. Nevertheless, it is true that the commonest way of turning a simple imperfective into a perfective verb is by prefixing to it a preposition or one of the other verbal prefixes (§ 118).

Now the curious thing is that when a prefix is used merely to make a perfective out of an imperfective verb, that prefix loses its original meaning. The prefixes which are used in this way include по-, с-, о-, у-, на-, про-, вы-, and из-.

Further, while there is always one prefix in particular which, when prefixed to a verb, both makes the verb perfective and loses its own original meaning, all the other prepositions when prefixed to the same verb make it perfective and, at the same time, retain their original meaning, thus altering the meaning of the verb as well.

The difficulty is to know in each case which is the particular prefix that merely makes a given verb perfective. The only thing for the beginner to do is to make a list of the commonest verbs and learn them by heart, putting down the simple (imperfective) verb and the form of the same verb compounded with that prefix which makes the verb perfective without altering its meaning.

The prefix most frequently used for transforming an imperfective into a perfective verb is the preposition по, which in the process quite loses its meaning of *along* or *over*, and merely limits the space of time during which the action took place or will take place, e.g.

смотрéть (imperfective)	*to look, be looking (at)*
посмотрéть (perfective)	*to have a look (at)*
спать (imperfective)	*to sleep, be asleep*
поспáть (perfective)	*to sleep a while, have a nap*

It has already been indicated that not all simple verbs are imperfective and, conversely, that not all verbs compounded with prefixes are perfective; these categories of verbs will be examined later.

There follow now paradigms of one or two very common verbs in pairs, first the simple (imperfective) and then the compound (perfective) verb. It will be noticed that the two aspects of the same verb do not have an equally complete paradigm. This, as will be explained, is in the nature of things and is invariably the case.

First the paradigms are given, then remarks on the use of the various parts of the two aspects:

де́лать (ipf.) ⎫
сде́лать (pf.) ⎭ *to do, to make*

	Imperfective	*Perfective*
present	де́лаю	— cf. § 102 (*c*)
past	де́лал	сде́лал
future	бу́ду де́лать	сде́лаю
conditional	де́лал бы	сде́лал бы
imperative	де́лай	сде́лай
infinitive	де́лать	сде́лать
pres. gerund	де́лая	—
past gerund	де́лав	сде́лав
pres. part. act.	де́лающий	—
past part. act.	де́лавший	сде́лавший
pres. part. pass.	де́лаемый	—
past part. pass.	де́ланный	сде́ланный

писа́ть (ipf.) ⎫
написа́ть (pf.) ⎭ *to write*

	Imperfective	*Perfective*
present	пишу́	— cf. § 102 (*c*)
past	писа́л	написа́л
future	бу́ду писа́ть	напишу́
conditional	писа́л бы	написа́л бы
imperative	пиши́	напиши́
infinitive	писа́ть	написа́ть

	Imperfective	*Perfective*
pres. gerund	— cf. § 95	—
past gerund	писа́в	написа́в
pres. part. act.	пи́шущий	—
past part. act.	писа́вший	написа́вший
pres. part. pass.	— cf. § 98	—
past part. pass.	пи́санный	напи́санный

§ 102. (a) The Present (imperfective)

Russian possesses only one present, while English has two: я пишу́ = (1) *I write* (sc. *it is my custom or profession to write*) and (2) *I am writing* (sc. *at this moment*). Both these meanings are of course imperfective; when one says я пишу́ *I write* or *I am writing*, the speaker does not naturally envisage the termination of his activity. Examples of the use of the imperfective present:

что вы де́лаете?	*what are you doing?*
я пишу́ письмо́	*I am writing a letter*
пти́цы лета́ют	*birds fly*
он хо́дит в шко́лу	*he goes to school*

The imperfective present is frequently used instead of the future in Russian, as in English, to express a future action (usually motion) firmly decided on or expected; such a present is always accompanied by an adverb of future time:

он приезжа́ет за́втра *he is arriving tomorrow* (приезжа́ет is an imperfective present)

ле́том мы е́дем в СССР *in summer we are going to the U.S.S.R.*

The historic present is often used in narration instead of the past.

The present combined with быва́ло may indicate habitual action in the past.

(b) Use of the Present in Subordinate Clauses

After verbs of *declaring, feeling,* &c., the imperfective present is used in all cases where the present is used in English. The subordinate clause is introduced by что, e.g.

я говорю́, что он врёт	*I say that he is lying*
я ду́маю, что он лю́бит её	*I think he loves her*
ты зна́ешь, что я тебя́ люблю́	*you know I love you*

In this connexion it should be noticed that after the verb ви́деть the so-called paratactic construction is very common in Russian; this is especially frequent in narration. By omitting the что (or как) two principal clauses are formed instead of a principal and a subordinate clause, e.g.

ви́дят: лети́т к ним пти́ца *they see a bird flying towards them* (lit. *they see — a bird is flying towards them*)

Russian is more logical than English in the expression of time, and the present and future are often used in Russian in subordinate clauses where in English we use the past although referring to present or future time:

he told me he was writing a book он сказа́л мне, что пи́шет кни́гу (lit. *is writing,* cf. '*I am writing*')

I asked him why he was there я спроси́л его́, почему́ он там (lit. *why he* [*is*] *there,* cf. '*Why are you here?*')

he informed me he was leaving shortly он мне сообщи́л, что вско́ре уе́дет (lit. *will leave,* cf. '*I shall leave shortly*')

After verbs of oral communication (saying, asking, informing, &c.) it would be a very bad mistake to use the past in the subordinate clause, as this would indicate a preceding action, e.g.

он сказа́л мне, что он писа́л кни́гу *he told me he had been writing a book*

я спроси́л его́, почему́ он был там *I asked him why he had been there*

In the third example above it would be nonsensical to use the past in the subordinate clause.

A similar construction is regularly used after verbs of thinking:

> *she thought he loved her* она́ ду́мала, что он её лю́бит (lit. *loves her*, cf. her thought: '*He loves me*')
>
> *we believed he was ill* мы ве́рили, что он бо́лен (cf. our thought at the time: '*He is ill*')

After other verbs introducing 'indirect speech', the past *may* be used in the subordinate clause instead of the imperfective present without involving a change in the time relationship, but the present is usual and more vivid:

> *I didn't know that that was so* я не знал, что э́то [бы́ло] так
>
> *he suddenly realized that she was lying* он вдруг по́нял, что она́ лжёт (or лгала́)

In conditional clauses the imperfective present is used whenever the condition refers to the actual present; the subordinate clause is introduced by е́сли (sometimes е́жели) *if*, and the antithesis in the principal clause is often expressed by the conjunction то, e.g.

> е́сли вы хоти́те, [то] скажи́те ему́ *if you waut to, tell him*
>
> сде́лайте э́то для неё, е́сли вы её лю́бите *do this for her if you love her*

When the condition refers to the future, the perfective future is usual, though in the cases of some verbs the imperfective present is used for the future, as in English, e.g.

> е́сли мо́жете, [то] приходи́те за́втра *if you can, [then] come tomorrow*

In concessive clauses the imperfective present is used, as

in English; the subordinate clause is introduced by хотя́ *although* (sometimes reduced to хоть), несмотря́ на то, что *in spite of the fact that*, and the antithesis in the principal clause is expressed by но *but*, одна́ко *nevertheless*, всё-таки *all the same*, or by the enclitic -таки *yet*.

> хотя́ все говоря́т, что э́то пра́вда, я им всё-таки не ве́рю *although everybody says* (lit. *all say*) *that this is true* (*the truth*), *all the same I don't believe them*

In relative clauses — *whoever*, in sentences where the present is necessary, is expressed by the simple relative кто, e.g.

> кто говори́т э́то, врёт *whoever says so, is lying*

Whoever, whatever, and *however* are also expressed by the relative with the particle ни, which is here emphatic, not negative.

> что он ни де́лает, всё ему́ удаётся *whatever he does, he succeeds* [*in everything*]
> как вы ни стара́етесь, вы не суме́ете э́то сде́лать *however much you try, you will not be able to do this*

If the relative clause is negative, the ordinary negative particle не is used and not ни.

> кто не зна́ет э́того челове́ка, тот не мо́жет поня́ть, почему́ его́ так уважа́ют *whoever does not know this man, cannot understand why people respect him so*

In causal clauses the imperfective present is very common; the subordinate clause is introduced by потому́ что *because* or та́к как *since* (in letter-writing the latter is often abbreviated to т. к.).

> она́ целу́ет его́, потому́ что она́ его́ лю́бит *she kisses him because she loves him*
> та́к как вы э́того не хоти́те сказа́ть мне, я спрошу́ его́ *since you do not wish to tell me this, I'll ask him*

In consecutive clauses the imperfective present is used as in English; the subordinate clause is introduced by что:

он так бо́лен, что я не могу́ его́ оста́вить *he is so ill that I cannot leave him*

Temporal clauses are introduced by когда́ *when* (often followed by тогда́ *then* in the main clause), пока́ *while*, мѐжду те́м как or в то вре́мя как *while, whereas*:

когда́ я пишу́, я не люблю́, что́бы со мной говори́ли *when I'm writing I don't like people talking to me*

посиди́те со мной, пока́ я одева́юсь *sit with me while I am dressing*

Comparative clauses are introduced by как *how*, followed by так or так и *thus* in the main clause:

как ду́мает, так и говори́т *as he thinks, so [too] he speaks*

(c) The Present Form of Perfective Verbs

It is one of the greatest peculiarities of the Russian verb that the present form of every perfective verb has future meaning. This tense is accordingly dealt with under the heading of Future (perfective) (see § 104).

§ 103. (a) The Past of Imperfective Verbs

The imperfective past is the equivalent of the imperfect, and its use denotes that the action was more or less habitual or that the period of time during which it lasted is, in the mind's eye of the speaker, indefinite.

я писа́л *I was writing*, or *I used to write*

Examples of the use of this tense:

что вы де́лали, когда́ я вошёл в ко́мнату? *what were you doing when I entered the room?*

я писа́л письмо́ *I was writing a letter*

пре́жде она́ писа́ла мно́го *formerly she used to write a lot*

The use of the imperfective past in subordinate clauses is common in temporal, concessive, and comparative clauses but presents no difficulties.

It is important to remember that in Russian the present is often used in a subordinate clause where in English we use the past.

The word быва́ло with the past tense of an imperfective verb stresses the habitual nature of the past action.

For the use of быва́ло with the perfective future see § 104 (b); for its use with the imperfective present see § 102 (a).

For the use of бы́ло with the imperfective past see § 103 (b).

(b) The Past of Perfective Verbs

This is the equivalent of the aorist and its use denotes the completion (sometimes the commencement) of an action; it can never be used for any action that is habitual, frequentative, or indefinite:

я написа́л *I wrote,* or *I have written,* or *I had written*

я сде́лал э́то наро́чно *I did this on purpose*

что вы сде́лали? *what have you done?*

я написа́л письмо́ *I have written a letter*

она́ вдруг запла́кала *she suddenly began to cry*

There is one use of the perfective past which, owing to its prevalence and peculiarity, deserves special mention. The perfective past of any verb can be combined with the enclitic word бы́ло (orig. the neuter singular of the past of быть) to convey the notion that an action was on the point of being done and was only just prevented; it is the Russian way of saying *was on the point of, was just about to* ... This unstressed бы́ло may also stand beside an imperfective past, the most common combination being хоте́л бы́ло *was about to, was on the point of*, which is followed by an infinitive; бы́ло may also be combined in a similar function with a past participle or gerund.

Examples of бы́ло:

он на́чал бы́ло приподнима́ться на посте́ли, чтоб встать . . . *he was on the point of beginning to raise himself on the bed, in order to get up* (sc. *when someone addressed him and he stayed where he was*)

не дожида́ясь отве́та, он ушёл бы́ло, когда́ . . . *without waiting for an answer he was just going to leave the room when* . . . (sc. *he was stopped*)

Алёша ста́л бы́ло от ликёра отка́зываться, но . . . *Alesha was about to refuse the liqueur, but* . . .

я хоте́л бы́ло сказа́ть ему́ об э́том, но переду́мал *I was just going to tell him about it, but changed my mind*

Although this construction usually implies an unfulfilled intention, it is sometimes used when the action was really accomplished, but was interrupted at the very moment of completion.

Another idiomatic construction with much the same meaning is чуть бы́ло не or чуть не with the perfective past, e.g.

он чуть бы́ло не вста́л с посте́ли *he almost got up from the bed* (sc. *but didn't*)

я чуть [бы́ло] не упа́л *I very nearly fell, almost fell*

This is the usual way of saying *nearly* followed by a verb: the adverb почти́ *nearly* is almost exclusively used with nouns and adjectives.

(c) The use of the Imperfective Past where the Perfective Past is to be expected

This is very common and, for the foreigner, greatly increases the difficulty of correct expression. It is most frequent in negative sentences; negation of an action seems to the Russian to demand the use of an imperfective verb if possible, e.g.

> я не писа́л ему́ may mean *I was not writing to him*; but it may also mean, and usually does, *I have not written to him*

Common phrases are:

> вы мне давно́ не писа́ли (imperfective) *you haven't written to me for a long time*

> я никогда́ не вида́л его́ (imperfective) *I have never seen him*

> я не слыха́ла её (imperfective) *I have not heard her* (sc. *never*).

But where the negation refers to one particular event or to any part of the sentence other than the verb, the perfective may be necessary, e.g.

> я не узна́л вас *I didn't recognize you*

> не я э́то сдела́л *it was not I [who] did this*

In interrogative sentences where the question covers a long period of time, the imperfective is also frequently used (ли is the interrogative particle):

писа́ли ли вы		*written?*
де́лали ли вы	когда́-нибудь? *have you ever*	*done?*
вида́ли ли вы		*seen?*
слыха́ли ли вы		*heard?*

In general it may be said that in negative and

interrogative sentences the imperfective is, in the nature of things, more usual than the perfective aspect.

A most unexpected use of the imperfective past is made in some cases where the action is quite definite and the most obvious aspect to use would seem to be the perfective. These are cases in which the speaker who uses the imperfective instead of the perfective aspect wishes by so doing to give a slightly indefinite tone to what he is saying; by using the imperfective instead of the perfective he makes a suggestion, as it were, instead of a statement. To the beginner this seems a gross inconsistency, but it is really a very subtle refinement.

For example, one often hears Russians say:

он мне писа́л об э́том

when one definite letter is referred to and the meaning can only be: *he wrote to me about this*, or *he did write to me*, &c.; in this case the use of the imperfective may connote hostility or incredulity on the part of the speaker, or it may be merely intentional vagueness.

Another very common instance is:

он говори́л мне, что … *he told me, that* …

where a perfective verb would be natural; in this case there is an English equivalent, for we often say *he was telling me* when we mean *he told me* (*once*).

The imperfective past of verbs of motion is used with particular frequency where an English-speaking person would expect the perfective past. The past tense of the *potential* imperfective verbs of motion and of many *compound imperfective* verbs formed from them (e.g. ходи́л, приходи́л, носи́л, приноси́л) has two main functions:

> either (1) to indicate that the action was repeated or habitual,

or (2) to indicate motion to a destination and imply that the subject has already returned to the place of departure after a short stay.

For example, in the majority of contexts он е́здил will mean *he used to go* (*travel, drive*), but in the sentence он е́здил в Ита́лию ле́том it means *he went* (sc. *once*) and implies that he returned after a short stay, while it was still summer. Similarly, она́ приходи́ла in most contexts means *she used to come*, but она́ сейча́с приходи́ла с письмо́м indicates that *she came* (sc. *once*) *just now with a letter* and implies that she has already gone away again; whereas она́ пришла́ с письмо́м may mean *she has come with a letter* and imply that she is still here.

It should be noted that only the past tense of these verbs can be used to imply return to the point of departure after a *single* journey. Compare this 'double' action with Ива́н хо́дит в шко́лу *Ivan attends* (*goes to*) *school* and Ива́н бу́дет ходи́ть в шко́лу *Ivan will attend school*, in which the present and future tenses always imply Ivan's regular return to his point of departure — a *habitual* action.

A similar 'double' action may be expressed by the past tense of some ordinary imperfective verbs denoting a movement.

Compare

я взял (pf.) в библиоте́ке « Войну́ и мир » *I have taken* (*borrowed*) '*War and Peace*' *from the library* (implying that I still have it out)

with

я брал (ipf.) в библиоте́ке « Войну́ и мир », which may mean (1) *I used* (*often*) *to take* '*War and Peace*' *from the library*, or (2) *I took* '*War and Peace*' *from the library* (*once*) (implying that I have already returned it)

Compare

это напи́сано в той кни́ге, кото́рую я вам дал (pf.)
that is in the book I have given (or *gave*) *you* (implying that you now have the book)

with

это напи́сано в той кни́ге, кото́рую я вам дава́л (ipf.)
that is in the book I lent you (implying that you have already returned the book to me)

Compare also

здесь бы́ло жа́рко, и я откры́л окно́ (pf.) *it was hot in here, so I [have] opened the window* (implying that the window is still open)

with

здесь бы́ло жа́рко, и я открыва́л окно́ (ipf.) *it was hot in here, so I opened the window* (implying that I closed it again and that, as the window has been open, the room is no longer too hot)

(d) The use of the Perfective Past as an Imperative

In the case of two verbs the perfective past is used as a peremptory imperative; these are:

пошёл, &c., from infin. пойти́ *to go* (*on foot*) and пое́хал, &c., from infin. пое́хать *to go* (sc. *in any way except on foot*)

It must be noticed that the verb of course agrees with the object addressed, e.g.

пошла́, соба́ка! *go away! be off!* (addressing a dog)

In colloquial style the plural forms пошли́ and пое́хали are used with the meaning '*let's go*', '*let's be off*', '*let's get started*'.

Notice also the idiomatic use of the plural past of нача́ть *to start* as an imperative in starter's orders:

пригото́вьтесь — внима́ние — на́чали! *ready—set—go!*

(e) The use of the Perfective Past in Subordinate Clauses

The perfective past is used in subordinate clauses after verbs of *declaring*, &c., when the event really refers to the past, e.g.

> я ужé сказáл вам, что написáл письмó *I have already told you that I have written the letter*

but it is important to remember that whenever the action is still going on, even though the principal clause contains a perfective past, the verb in the subordinate clause must be in the present or the future (see § 102).

> я емý сказáл, что не люблю егó *I told him that I didn't like him*

In relative, concessive, temporal, comparative, and consecutive clauses the imperfective and perfective past are of course both common, but their use presents no difficulties; the perfective past is common in temporal clauses beginning with *as soon as* (как тóлько), *before* (préжде чем, péред тéм как, до тогó как), *after* (пóсле тогó как), *hardly . . . when . . .* (тóлько что . . ., как . . .), *as soon as ever* (чуть, едвá), *until* (покá не):

> я захворáл, как тóлько приéхал *I fell ill as soon as I arrived*

> он сдéлал э́то, préжде чем я емý написáл *he did this before I wrote to him*

> он написáл э́то пóсле тогó, как получи́л моё письмó *he wrote this after he had received my letter*

> тóлько я пришёл, как он вдруг у́мер *I had hardly (only just) arrived when he suddenly died*

> вы едвá вошли́, как я вас узнáла *you had no sooner entered than I recognized you*

§ 104. (a) The Future of Imperfective Verbs

The imperfective future presents no difficulties; it is a compound tense consisting of бу́ду (*I shall be*) and the imperfective infinitive. It is always used when referring to any future action whose completion is not envisaged by the speaker, or to a future action that is to be habitual or repeated.

It must be remembered that it is only the imperfective infinitive which can be used after бу́ду; to use a perfective infinitive after бу́ду is one of the worst mistakes a foreigner can make. An example of the tense is given in full:

я	бу́ду писа́ть
ты	бу́дешь писа́ть
он, она́	бу́дет писа́ть
мы	бу́дем писа́ть
вы	бу́дете писа́ть
они́	бу́дут писа́ть

= *I am going to write* (sc. *indefinitely*), *I shall write* (sc. *more than once*), &c.

Examples of the use of the imperfective future:

что вы бу́дете де́лать по́сле за́втрака? *what are you going to do after lunch (in the afternoon)?*

я бу́ду писа́ть, чита́ть *I am going to write, read*

вы бу́дете мне писа́ть? *you will write to me?* (sc. *more than once*) — бу́ду *I will*

ста́ну, ста́нешь, &c. (from стать *to become*) is also used followed by an imperfective infinitive to form this same tense, instead of бу́ду, but it is much commoner in the written than in the spoken language. It is particularly common in negative sentences.

The use of the imperfective future in subordinate clauses does not present any difficulties, but see § 102.

(b) The Future of Perfective Verbs

This is, in form, the present tense of the perfective aspect, but it nearly always has a future meaning. It is used when the completion of any future action is in the speaker's mind. The use of this tense is at first the most puzzling for the English-speaking beginner.

Examples:

> я напишу́ ему́ тепе́рь   *I shall write to him now*
>
> я сде́лаю э́то за́втра   *I shall do it tomorrow*

The perfective future and the imperfective present can of course be used together, e.g.

> я посмотрю́, что́ он де́лает там *I shall have a look* [*and see*] *what he is doing there*

while

> я смотрю́, что́ он де́лает *I am watching what he is doing*

There is one use of the perfective future which is very idiomatic and requires special notice. The perfective future of any verb can be combined with the neuter singular of the past of быва́ть (the imperfective frequentative form of быть *to be*), viz. быва́ло, to convey the idea of an action which used to take place often or customarily in the past:

> зайдёт она́ быва́ло ко мне чай пить *she used to look in on me to have tea* (зайдёт *she will look in, call*, perfective)
>
> он быва́ло ска́жет мне: «Принеси́ стака́н воды́» *he would often say to me: 'Bring me a glass of water'*

Быва́ло can also be used with the imperfective present or past to express an imperfective habitual action in the past, but these constructions are not so common.

The perfective future is also used in narration to describe a repeated, habitual, or generalized action in the past or present, e.g.

Татья́на то вздохнёт, то о́хнет *at one moment Tatyana would sigh, at the next she would groan*

всё бы́ло во мра́ке, то́лько и́зредка папиро́са мелькнёт *everything was in darkness, broken only by the occasional glow of a cigarette*

то́нкий язы́к пла́мени лизнёт су́чья и ра́зом исче́знет *a thin tongue of flame would lick the tree-stumps and immediately disappear*

всё в лесу́ молчи́т. Вы прохо́дите ми́мо де́рева, оно́ не шелохнётся *everything in the forest is silent. You walk past a tree and it doesn't stir*

как постéлешь, так и поспи́шь *as you make your bed, so you must lie*

In the colloquial style the perfective future preceded by как is occasionally used, for the sake of greater vividness, instead of the perfective past. It describes a sudden or unexpected action in the past, e.g.

он как вско́чит да как сту́кнет кулако́м по́ столу *he suddenly jumped up and thumped on the table with his fist*

It is also frequently used where one would expect *I cannot* followed by a perfective infinitive, e.g.

не разберу́ ничего́, всё вздор *I can't make out a word, it's all nonsense* (lit. *I shall not be able to make out, understand*)

(c) Use of the Future in Subordinate Clauses

The future is often used in Russian in subordinate clauses where in English we use the past or *would, should,* e.g. after verbs of *declaring,* &c.:

he said that he would be there, or *that he was going to be there* он сказа́л, что бу́дет там (cf. his own words: '*I shall be there*')

I knew that he would do it, or *that he was going to do it* я знал, что он э́то сде́лает (cf. my thought: '*He will do it*')

she did not know that I would (was going to) write a letter она́ не зна́ла, что я напишу́ письмо́

&c.

In relative clauses the perfective future is used after кто ... ни *whoever* and что ... ни *whatever*:

что вы ни ска́жете, я вам не пове́рю *whatever you say, I shall not believe you*

The use of the perfective future is especially common in temporal clauses with the meaning of the future perfect, where we in English illogically use the present, e.g.

напиши́те, как то́лько прие́дете *write as soon as you arrive* or *have arrived* (lit. *will arrive*)

поду́майте хороше́нько, пе́ред те́м как сде́лаете э́то *reflect well before you do* (lit. *will do*) *this*

ска́жем вам всё, по́сле того́ как вернёмся *we shall tell you everything after we return* or *have returned*

N.B. как is often used alone with the meaning *when*. *Until* is usually expressed by пока́ не + pf., e.g.

я не напишу́, пока́ не получу́ от него́ письма́ *I shall not write until I have a letter from him*

пока́ translates *until* after verbs of *waiting*; elsewhere пока́ + pf. fut. means *by the time that*.

The future is often used in conditional clauses where we use the present illogically:

е́сли он сде́лает э́то, я закричу́ *if he does* (lit. *will do*) *that I shall scream*

§ 105. (a) The Conditional (**Imperfective and Perfective**)

The conditional, as already explained in § 92, is composed of the past tense and the particle бы. It can be formed from the imperfective as well as from the perfective past, but it is far more commonly formed from the latter. It serves also as the Russian equivalent of the subjunctive, see § 105 (b).

The peculiarity of the Russian conditional mood is that it has no tenses: its one form is timeless and may refer to the past, present, or future, according to the context, e.g.

он бы сделал это вчера *he would have done it yesterday* (sc. *if they had come*)

он бы сделал это теперь *he would do it now* (sc. *if they came*) or *he would have done it now* (sc. *if they had come*)

он бы это сделал завтра *he would do it tomorrow* (sc. *if they came*) or *he would have done it tomorrow* (sc. *if they had come*)

что вы бы написали? *what would you write* or *what would you have written?*

это было бы невозможно *that would be impossible* or *that would have been impossible*

The conditional is used in unfulfilled conditional sentences, both in the principal and in the subordinate clauses:

если бы она хотела, она бы написала *if she had wished [to], she would have written* or *if she wanted [to], she would write*

However, бы is normally omitted from a principal clause containing a verb of possibility referring to past time:

Compare

если бы вы хотели, я мог бы это сделать *if you wished (were to wish) it, I could do it* with

> е́сли бы вы хоте́ли, я мог э́то сде́лать *if you had wished it, I could have done it*

and

> ему́ (бы́ло) ничего́, что кто́-то мог пло́хо поду́мать о нём *he doesn't (didn't) care that somebody may (might) have thought badly of him*

If the condition is still capable of fulfilment, either the future tense or the conditional may be used; the use of the conditional in such a case indicates that the speaker considers that the fulfilment of the condition is unlikely or is not taken for granted.

Compare

> я бу́ду о́чень рад, е́сли вы э́то сде́лаете *I shall be very glad if you do* (lit. *will do*) *it*

with

> я был бы о́чень рад, е́сли бы вы э́то сде́лали *I should be very glad if you did* (or *were to do*) *it*

Of course, the latter sentence could also mean *I should have been glad if you had done it*, since the conditional may also refer to an imagined situation in the past.

Compare

> е́сли мы откро́ем окно́, здесь бу́дет хо́лодно *if we open* (lit. *shall open*) *the window, it will be cold here*

with

> е́сли бы мы откры́ли окно́, здесь бы́ло бы хо́лодно *if we were to open the window, it would be cold here*

The conditional also serves to express a more polite request or question than the present tense:

> я проси́л бы вас не крича́ть *I would* (=*do*) *beg you not to shout*

что́ бы вы э́тим хоте́ли сказа́ть? *what would (=do) you mean by that?*

or a milder form of command (more a suggestion) than the imperative:

вы́ бы отдохну́ли немно́го *you should rest a while*

вы́ бы [лу́чше] записа́ли мой а́дрес *you should [had better] write down my address*

The particle бы is sometimes used by itself in certain expressions elliptically, e.g.

во́т бы хорошо́! *there, wouldn't that be nice!*

For the use of бы with the infinitive see § 107 (c).

(b) Use of the Conditional as a Subjunctive

The conditional is very common in concessive clauses beginning with *whoever, whatever, wherever,* &c., expressed in Russian by кто, что, где, &c., followed by the бы of the conditional and the particle ни:

кто́ бы э́то ни написа́л, я ему́ скажу́ ... *whoever wrote this, I shall tell him* . . .

что́ бы вы ни сде́лали, ничего́ не помо́жет *whatever you do, nothing will help*

чего́ бы э́то ни сто́ило, на́до э́то сде́лать *whatever it costs, we must do it*

что́ бы ни случи́лось, пое́дем *whatever happens, we shall go*

The conditional is used in clauses denoting *purpose* unless the subject of the subordinate would be the same as that of the principal clause; the бы of the conditional is always joined to the conjunction что which introduces the subordinate clause, e.g.

я пишу́ ему́ с тем, что́бы он узна́л пра́вду *I am writing to him in order that he may learn the truth*

он де́лает э́то, что́бы мы заме́тили его́ *he is doing this so that we shall notice him*

она́ помогла́ ему́, что́бы он пото́м помо́г ей *she helped him in order that later he might help her*

The conditional is used in *concessive* clauses if the sense is hypothetical, e.g.

хотя́ бы я и знал, что вы там, я бы не пришёл *even if I had known you were there, I should not have come*

The conditional is required after verbs of *wishing, commanding,* and *requesting,* both affirmative and negative, unless the subject of the subordinate would be the same as that of the main clause. The subordinate clause is introduced by что́бы (or чтоб).

я хочу́, что́бы он э́то сде́лал *I want him to do this* (lit. *I wish that he would do this*)

она́ хо́чет, что́бы я ей написа́л *she wishes me to write to her* (sc. *once*) (N.B. ...что́бы я ей писа́л would denote *to write to her* sc. *often, regularly*)

он приказа́л, что́бы к ве́черу всё бы́ло гото́во *he ordered everything to be ready by evening*

она́ проси́ла, что́бы мы э́то сде́лали *she asked us to do it*

and in such expressions as:

жела́тельно, что́бы он лежа́л в посте́ли *it is desirable that he should stay in bed*

It must be carefully noted that a verb of *wishing* must not be followed by a что́бы clause if the subjects of both clauses would be the same; the infinitive must be used instead:

я хочу́ сде́лать э́то (never: я хочу́, что́бы я сде́лал э́то) *I want to do this*

она́ хо́чет написа́ть вам *she wishes to write to you*

The conditional is used similarly after verbs of *liking* and *disliking*:

она́ лю́бит, что́бы её хвали́ли *she likes being praised (likes people praising her)*

The conditional is often used in expressions of *doubt* or *denial* (e.g. *negatived* verbs of *declaring, thinking*); the subordinate clause is introduced by что́бы. For example:

мы сомнева́емся [в том], что́бы он их при́нял *we doubt whether he will accept them*

никто́ не ожида́л, что́бы она́ ушла́ *no one expected her to go away*

я не говорю́, что́бы э́то бы́ло так *I do not say that this is so*

я не ду́маю, что́бы он э́то сде́лал *I do not think he did it*

она́ не ве́рит, что́бы э́то бы́ло опа́сно *she does not believe that it is (would be) dangerous*

However, что + present, past, or future tense (as appropriate) may be used instead of что́бы + conditional; the future is especially common, e.g.

не сомнева́юсь, что вы ко́нчите э́ту рабо́ту *I don't doubt that you will finish this work*

я не ду́маю, что бу́дет хо́лодно *I don't think it will be cold*

я не говорю́, что э́то непра́вильно *I don't say that it is wrong*

The conditional is usual after сомни́тельно *it is doubtful*, нельзя́ and невероя́тно, and generally after negative expressions, e.g.

невозмо́жно, что́бы э́то была́ пра́вда *it is impossible that this is true* (lit. *the truth*) там нет никого, кто мог бы ему помочь *there is nobody there who can (could) help him*

The conditional, with an expletive не, is found after verbs of *fearing* when they express the fear that something positive may possibly happen; in this case the subordinate clause may be introduced by чтобы or как бы. When the feared event will probably happen, что should be used with the future, *without* не. For instance:

я боюсь, как бы он не пришёл	*I am afraid he may (may have) come*
я боюсь, что он придёт	*I am afraid he will come*
я опасался, чтобы вы не простудились	*I was afraid you might catch or might have caught cold*
я опасался, что вы простудитесь	*I was afraid you would catch cold*

When the fear is of something negative (i.e. a fear that something desirable will fail to happen), then only что + не + *future* is possible:

я боюсь, что он не придёт	*I am afraid he won't come*
я боялся, что он не придёт	*I was afraid he wouldn't come*

When the fear is connected with a definite past or present event, the appropriate tense is used:

мы боимся, что он отстаёт в работе *we fear he is lagging behind in his work*

я боюсь, что я не выдержал экзамена *I am afraid I did not pass the examination*

A fear of a rather remote possibility may also be expressed by an interrogative clause:

она боялась, не оскорбила ли она его *she was afraid that perhaps she had hurt his feelings*

In indirect speech, the conditional with чтобы replaces an imperative of direct speech:

Compare

> я ему́ сказа́л: «Приди́ ве́чером!» *I said to him 'Come round in the evening'*

with

> я ему́ сказа́л, чтобы он пришёл ве́чером *I told him to come round in the evening*

The conditional may sometimes express a *wish, desire,* or *fear* without an introductory verb of wishing or fearing:

> я́ бы купа́лся здесь ка́ждый день! *I should like to bathe here every day!*

> уда́лось бы! *may it succeed, I hope it'll be a success*

> не провали́лся бы ты! ⎞
> ка́к бы ты не провали́лся! ⎠ *I hope you won't fail*

§ 106. (a) The Imperative (Imperfective and Perfective)

The imperative is used in Russian as in English. The basic difference between the aspects in 'affirmative' commands (not prohibitions) is that the imperfective generally implies that an action is to continue indefinitely or be repeated, whereas the perfective implies a single action and usually points to some result.

Compare

> пиши́! пиши́те! *write!* (sc. *start writing! go on writing!* or *write often!*)

(in which no limit is set to the duration of the action and no result is envisaged)

with

> напиши́! напиши́те! *write [it]!* (sc. *get [the letter, &c.] written!*)

(which implies some such result as *and then you can post it* or *and then they will be informed*).

As can be seen from these examples, the ipf. command is often general in nature, whereas the pf. refers to a particular object.

Compare also

смотри́, смотри́те! *look out* (sc. *take care*) *!*
посмотри́, посмотри́те! *look here! look at this!*
слу́шайте меня́! *listen to me* (sc. *take my advice*) *!*
послу́шайте! *listen* (sc. *to this*) *!*

Often the imperfective imperative is used when it is a question of a polite request rather than of a peremptory command; this is especially so in the case of the verbs брать (imperfective) and взять (perfective) *to take*, e.g.

бери́те э́то! *take this!*

is more polite than

возьми́те э́то!, though the latter is often used.

The same holds good of the verbs подава́ть (imperfective) and пода́ть (perfective) *to hand, to serve*, e.g.

подава́й(те) обе́д! *serve the dinner!*

is more polite than

пода́й(те) мне счёт! *give* (lit. *hand*) *me the bill!*

Compare

приходи́те (ipf.) к нам   *come and see us* (invitation)

with

приди́те (pf.) сейча́с же!   *come at once!* (command)

The particles пусть (orig. an imperative of пусти́ть pf. *to allow, let*) and, in colloquial style, пуска́й (sing. imperative of пуска́ть ipf.) are followed by the 3rd pers. of the present or future to express the 3rd pers. of the imperative (see § 93), e.g.

пусть (or пуска́й) ска́жет   *let him tell you*
   вам

| пусть ма́льчик напи́шет | *let the boy write* [*it*] |
| пусть пи́шут | *let them write* (sc. *go on writing*) |

The imperative дава́й(те), followed by the imperfective infinitive or by the 1st pl. of the future (perfective or imperfective), is commonly used colloquially with the meaning *let's*, e.g.

| дава́й(те) игра́ть в ка́рты | *let's have a game of cards* |

to which the answer usually is: дава́й(те)! *yes, let's!*

дава́й(те) не [бу́дем] спо́рить	*let's not argue*
дава́й(те) [бу́дем] говори́ть по-ру́сски	*let's speak Russian*
дава́й(те) пойдём домо́й	*let's go home*

The imperative да́й(те) is often used with the meaning *let, allow*; it is followed by the imperfective infinitive or the 1st sing. or pl. of the perfective future, e.g.

| да́й(те) нам говори́ть! | *let us speak!* (sc. *don't interrupt!*) |
| да́йте я вам спою́ пе́сню | *let me sing you a song* |

In prohibitions the imperfective is used, followed by the infinitive, e.g.

| не дава́й(те) ей говори́ть! | *don't let her speak!* |

In negative commands the imperfective imperative is almost invariably used, even when the prohibition only covers a definite act or period of time, e.g.

не пиши́те ему́!	*don't write to him!* (sc. either *now* or *at any time*)
не смотри́те!	*don't look!*
не говори́те ему́!	*don't tell him!*
не говори́те!	*don't talk about it!*

(For the use of the infinitive in commands see § 107.)

An exception is the verb *to forget*, забыва́ть (imperfective), забы́ть (perfective), of both of which the imperative is quite common, e.g.

не забыва́йте меня́! *don't forget me!* (sc. *always remember*)
but не забу́дьте, что́ я вам сказа́л! *don't forget what I told you!*

не забу́дьте! *don't forget!* (sc. *to do one thing once*)
не забу́дьте написа́ть мне письмо́! *don't forget to write me a letter!*

(Cf. незабу́дка *forget-me-not*.)

The negative imperative of other perfective verbs is used to express a warning, not a command, e.g.

не урони́те! (from урони́ть, pf.) *now, don't drop it* (warning)
не упади́те! (from упа́сть, pf.) *mind you don't fall* (warning)

The imperative смотри́(те) *watch, take care* may precede a negative warning or command, as:

смотри́те, не упади́те! *watch you don't fall* (warning)
смотри́, не говори́ об э́том! *mind you don't talk about it!* (command)

The particle -ка, placed after the imperative, imparts an air of informality to a request:

запиши́те-ка мой а́дрес *just jot down my address*

Notice the following idiomatic uses of the imperative:
пожа́луй (from пожа́ловать) *by all means, I expect, I dare say, perhaps, I shouldn't wonder* (used as an interjection in conversation and in such sentences as пожа́луй, вы пра́вы *I dare say you're right, you're probably right*)

The plural form пожа́луйте is used with the meaning

be so good in polite invitations like пожа́луйте сюда́ *please step this way*.

поми́луйте! (from поми́ловать) is used as a remonstrance in conversation, with the meaning *good gracious! I say, look here! no, really!*

скажи́те (often followed by пожа́луйста)! *you don't say so! well, I never!*

расска́зывайте! *tell me (us) another! it's a good story!*

извини́те!⎫
          ⎬*excuse me! I beg your pardon! I'm sorry!*
прости́те!⎭

сде́лайте одолже́ние! *by all means! please do!*

(b) Use of the Imperative in Conditional Clauses

The imperative is frequently used in Russian in unfulfilled conditional clauses; in this construction the imperative (always the singular form) can be combined with any noun or pronoun, e.g.

бу́дь э́тот дом деше́вле, я бы купи́л его́ *if this house had been cheaper, I should have bought it* (lit. *be this house cheaper*)

In fulfilled conditions which, if not fulfilled, would have caused the result expressed in the principal clause, the perfective imperative is always used, despite the associated не:

не случи́сь там ло́дка, я бы утону́л *if a boat hadn't happened [to be] there* (sc. *but it was*), *I should have drowned*

не сде́лай они́ э́того, она́ бы пришла́ *if they had not done this* (sc. *but they did*), *she would have come*

скажи́ я сло́во, он бы и написа́л *if I had said the word, he would have written*

There is an idiomatic use of the imperative which is especially common in narration and deserves mention. This is a combination of the imperative of the perfective verb взя́ться *to appear* (lit. *to take oneself*), viz. возьми́сь, with the words отку́да ни *from wherever*, e.g.

вдруг, отку́да ни возьми́сь, за́яц! *suddenly, as if from nowhere, a hare appeared!*

Notice also the following idiomatic uses of the imperative:

того́ и смотри́, он упадёт! *I am afraid that* (sc. *at any moment* or *before we know where we are*) *he will fall*

помина́й, как зва́ли! *you'll never see* [*him*] *again* (lit. *remember, how they called him*)

кажи́сь (uneducated equivalent of ка́жется) *it seems*

Another idiomatic use of the imperative is with the conjunction хоть (pronounced *khət′*), when it acquires the meaning (*you*) *may as well . . .*

éсли вы не помо́жете нам, то уж не зна́ем, как и быть: про́сто хоть в пе́тлю полеза́й! *if you don't help us, we simply shan't know what to do: we may as well go and hang ourselves!* (lit. *climb into the noose*)

ничего́ нельзя́ с э́тим поде́лать, хоть брось *nothing can be done with this, you may as well fling it away*

Sometimes хоть means *even though* (хотя́) in this same construction:

хоть убе́й, не скажу́ *even though you kill me, I shall not tell*

§ 107. (a) The Infinitive (**Imperfective and Perfective**)

The difference in meaning between the two aspects of the infinitive has already been explained; it remains to give some examples of the various uses of the infinitive.

In expressing a general activity the imperfective infinitive is always used, e.g.

писа́ть кни́ги неприя́тно *writing books is unpleasant*

while if a single event is referred to, the perfective is of course necessary, e.g.

ско́лько у него́ де́нег? — тру́дно сказа́ть *how much money has he? — it is difficult to tell*

The following idiomatic use of the infinitive should be noticed:

не́чего де́лать *there is nothing to be done*

он пьёт от не́чего де́лать *he drinks because he has nothing [else] to do*

говори́ть не́чего! (or не́чего и говори́ть!) *there's nothing more to be said!* (sc. *that goes without saying*) (see § 51)

уж так и быть *so be it*, or *well, let's make the best of it!*

ста́ло быть *consequently* . . . or *in that case, I suppose* . . .

After verbs of *beginning, continuing, ceasing, finishing,* &c., the imperfective must be used, e.g.

уже́ на́чали игра́ть	*they have already begun to play*
я сел и стал ждать	*I sat down and waited*[1]
он продолжа́л чита́ть	*he continued to read*
они́ переста́ли говори́ть	*they ceased talking*
я ко́нчил писа́ть	*I have finished writing*

After the verbs уме́ть (imperfective) and суме́ть (perfective) *to know how to* the imperfective and perfective infinitives respectively are used, e.g.

он уме́ет де́лать фо́кусы *he knows how to do tricks*

суме́ете ли вы э́то сде́лать? *will you know how (manage) to do this?*

---

[1] N.B. An English past may denote the start of an action of indefinite duration. In this example *waited* can only be rendered by стал (or на́чал) ждать; neither ждал (ipf.) nor подожда́л (pf.) has this denotation.

After the verbs успевáть (imperfective) and успéть (perfective) *to have time to* the perfective is always used, e.g.

успéете ли вы э́то сдéлать сегóдня? *will you have time to do it today?*

я кáждый день успевáю написáть пять пи́сем *every day I find time (manage) to write five letters*

After the verbs мочь (imperfective) and смочь (perfective) *to be able* either aspect may be used, depending on the sense, e.g.

мóжете ли вы э́то сдéлать? *can you do this?*

он не мóжет говори́ть (imperfective) *he can't speak* (sc. *is physically unable*)

я не могу́ сказáть (perfective) *I can't say* (sc. *am not allowed* or *don't know*)

я не мог писáть *I could not write* (sc. *was physically unable*)

я не мог написáть *I could not write* (sc. *just then, that once*), or *I have been unable to write* (sc. *till now*)

The imperfective future of мочь is not used; its place is taken by the phrase

бу́ду в состоя́нии + infin. *I shall be in a position to . . .*

or by the imperfective present or perfective future.

The perfective future смогу́ (*I shall become [physically] able to*), &c., is often avoided, particularly in literature, the present могу́, &c., being used with future meaning, just as in English:

я могу́ прийти́ зáвтра *I can* (sc. *shall be able to*) *come tomorrow*

In colloquial style the perfective past and future tenses of смочь (*to become [physically] able to*) are sometimes replaced by those of the perfective verb сумéть (*to contrive, to find a way to*), but this practice cannot be recommended.

After the verbs хотѣть (imperfective) and захотѣть (perfective) *to wish* either aspect can be used, e.g.

я хочу́ писа́ть	*I wish to write* (sc. *be an author*)
я хочу́ написа́ть письмо́	*I want to write a letter*
я не хочу́ говори́ть (imperfective)	*I don't want to talk*
я не хочу́ сказа́ть (perfective)	*I don't want to say*
я хотѣ́л говори́ть	*I wanted to speak*
я хотѣ́л сказа́ть	*I wanted to say, I meant*

After verbs such as люби́ть *to like*, предпочита́ть *to prefer*, не люби́ть *to dislike*, the imperfective infinitive, implying an activity, is the more usual.

After verbs of *refusing, agreeing*, &c., either aspect can be used, though the perfective is the commoner.

(b) Use of the Infinitive instead of the Future

This is common in such phrases as the following. Note that with an infinitive the logical 'subject' of the action is expressed in the dative, but may often be omitted.

что́ же дѣлать?	*what are we to do?* (*what is to be done?*)
написа́ть ли ему́?	*shall I write to him?*
что [мнѣ] написа́ть?	*what shall I write?*
пойти́ и сказа́ть ему́	*I'll go and tell him* (or *let us . . .*)
как нам быть?	*how are we to manage?*
зачѣ́м [вам] продава́ть?	*why [are you going to, should you] sell?*
сказа́ть вам?	*shall I tell you?*
как вам сказа́ть?	*how shall I put it?*
не вам рѣша́ть	*it's not for you to decide*
быть дождю́	*it's going to rain*
помо́чь тебѣ́?	*shall I help you?*

(c) Use of the Infinitive with the Conditional Particle бы

This construction may express a wish, suggestion, reproach, or warning, e.g.

посмотре́ть бы, как . . . *I'd like to look and see how* . . .
не опозда́ть бы нам! *I hope we shan't arrive late*
ка́к бы ему́ не забы́ть! *I hope he won't forget*
не упа́сть бы вам в во́ду! *mind you don't fall into the water*
ва́м бы сего́дня уе́хать! *I think you ought to leave today*

Combined with бы́ло this construction may express a suggestion referring to the past:

ему́ бы об э́том бы́ло поду́мать! *he ought to have thought about that*

Often it is merely that the verb бы́ло has been omitted:

хорошо́ [бы́ло] бы пое́хать! *it would be nice to go*

(d) Use of the Infinitive instead of the Past

In popular narrative the infinitive, by itself, may describe vividly a sudden past action; preceded by дава́й, ну, or пошёл (пошла́, &c.), the infinitive denotes the beginning of an intense or violent action in the past, e.g.

пле́нник бежа́ть, и мы за ним *the prisoner [suddenly] ran away, and we ran after him*

они́ дава́й его́ бить, а я дава́й бежа́ть *they started to beat him, and I took to my heels*

он бро́сил его́ на́ землю и ну топта́ть нога́ми *he threw it on the ground and began stamping on it*

(e) Use of the Infinitive instead of the Imperative

This is especially common in public notices and military commands, e.g.

éхать ша́гом! (imperfective) *dead slow! drive at walking speed!* (cf. *aller au pas!*)

никого́ не пуска́ть! (imperfective) *don't let anyone go!*

разверну́ть зна́мя полка́! *unfurl the regimental colours!*

на часа́х не разгова́ривать! *no talking on sentry-go!*

наплева́ть! *spit!* (sc. *take no notice of it! it doesn't matter!*)

cf. мне наплева́ть на твоего́ учи́теля! *I don't care a damn about your teacher!*

(f) Use of the Infinitive in Subordinate Clauses

In final clauses the infinitive is used when the subject of the subordinate is the same as that of the principal clause (cf. § 105 (b)), e.g.

я пишу́ ему́, что́бы узна́ть пра́вду *I am writing to him in order to find out the truth*

он де́лает э́то, что́бы помо́чь мне *he is doing this [in order] to help me*

In conditional clauses the infinitive is very common, e.g.

е́сли ему́ написа́ть, он э́то сде́лает сейча́с же *if we write to him, he will do it at once*

сказа́ть вам (or е́сли вам сказа́ть), вы не пове́рите *if I tell you, you won't believe [me]*

Sometimes the infinitive is used in the principal as well as in the subordinate clause, in which case е́сли is omitted:

мно́го жела́ть — добра́ не вида́ть (proverb) *if you wish too much, you'll never be content*

идти́ — так идти́! *if we are going, then let's go! come on, then, if we're going!*

There is a curious idiomatic use of the infinitive that is at first extremely puzzling to the foreigner; it is often, though not always, in the form of an answer to a question and consists of the infinitive followed by the past or present of the same verb. It always implies dissatisfaction or the non-fulfilment of a possibility, e.g.

Question:

слыха́ли ли вы про э́то? *have you heard about this?*

Answer:

слыха́ть[-то] слыха́л, но не ве́рю *oh yes, I* have *heard about it, but I don't believe it*

Question:

вида́ли ли вы мини́стра? *have you seen the minister?*

Answer:

вида́ть-то вида́л, но . . . *oh yes, I've* seen *him, but* (e.g. *never spoken to him*)

говори́ть-то она́ говори́т, а ничего́ не де́лает *she talks a lot but does nothing*

уме́ть-то я уме́ю, но я не хочу́ *I* know *how to* [*do it*], *but I don't want to; I can, but I won't*

писа́ть он всё равно́ не писа́л и не занима́лся *in any case he wasn't* writing (sc. *his novel*), *nor was he studying*

§ 108. The Gerunds (Imperfective and Perfective)

The gerunds in Russian are verbal adverbs, used to avoid the complication of an explanatory clause (usually subordinate) of time, manner, reason, &c. They are not declined and may refer only to an action performed by the subject of the main verb.

The present gerund is naturally formed only from imperfective verbs: it expresses an action which is simultaneous with that denoted by the main verb, e.g.

игра́я в саду́, де́ти ча́сто ссо́рятся *playing (while they play) in the garden, the children often quarrel* бу́дучи в го́роде, мы зашли́ к вам *being (as we were) in the town, we looked you up*

Whenever a perfective verb has the ending of the present gerund (-я), it has the meaning of a past gerund, e.g. уви́дя, from уви́деть (pf.) *to perceive*, has the same meaning as the past gerund forms уви́дев, уви́девши *having perceived*.

The past gerund is formed from both aspects, but mainly from perfective verbs. The perfective past gerund describes an action that preceded (or will precede) the action of the main verb, e.g.

проговори́в три часа́, он сел на своё ме́сто *having spoken (after speaking) for three hours, he sat down in his place*
прочита́в письмо́, он знал, что оте́ц у́мер *having read (since he had read) the letter, he knew that his father had died*

The imperfective past gerund (rare) describes an action that was taking place simultaneously with that of the main verb; this function is now usually performed by the present gerund.

The negative gerund often renders English *without —ing*:

without saying a word, he got up and went away не сказа́в ни сло́ва, он встал и ушёл

Some gerunds are very commonly used to express attitude, e.g.   говори́ть лёжа   *to speak while lying down*
писа́ть си́дя   *to write while sitting*
петь сто́я   *to sing standing up*

The following idioms should be noticed:

мо́лча   *in silence, without speaking*
не́хотя   *unwillingly*

немно́го погодя́ *after a while* (lit. *having waited a little*)
не говоря́ уже́ о + loc. *not to speak of, let alone*

Some gerunds are used as prepositions, and as such do not always refer to the action of the subject, e.g.

комитéт состоя́л из десяти́ члéнов, не счита́я председа́-
теля *the committee consisted of ten members, not counting the chairman*

егó поздра́вили все, исключа́я егó проти́вника *he was congratulated by everyone except(ing) his opponent*

Other gerunds used in this way include: благодаря́ (+ dat.), включа́я, спустя́, несмотря́ на(+ acc.), конча́я (+ instr.), начина́я(+ instr. or with c+ gen.).

Some gerunds have quite lost their original meaning and are used as adverbs or conjunctions:

from хотéть *to wish*
    хотя́ *although* (N.B. *willingly* is охóтно)

from зреть *to look*
    зря *at random, without reflection, to no purpose*

from смотрéть *to look*
    несмотря́ на + acc. *in spite of*
    смотря́ *all according, depending,* e.g.

        смотря́ когда́ *it all depends [on] when [it is]*
        смотря́ по погóде *according to the weather*

and from умéть *to know how to* the popular form умéючи *having the knowledge,* e.g.

э́то на́до сдéлать умéючи *you must have the knack to do this*

§ 109. The Participles (Imperfective and Perfective)

The participles are little used in conversation but are very common in literature.

As it has been pointed out above, perfective verbs have no present participles. Past participles active are formed from almost all verbs of both aspects; past participles passive are formed from all perfective transitive verbs and from a considerable number of imperfective transitive verbs.

As regards the use of the participles it may be mentioned that some of them are used as nouns, e.g.

для куря́щих	*for smokers*
для некуря́щих	*for non-smokers*
бу́дущее	*the future*
в бу́дущем	*in the future*
подлежа́щее	*the subject* (gram.)
сказу́емое	*the predicate* (gram.)
насеко́мое	*insect*

while in general it may be said that the present participles, both active and passive, are far more commonly used as pure adjectives without being considered as participles at all, e.g.

сле́дующий *following* is used for *the next*
   в сле́дующий раз *next time*
све́дущий (по+dat.) *knowing, learned* (*in*)
настоя́щий (1) *present* (of time), (2) *real, genuine*
бу́дущий *future, next*
   в бу́дущем ме́сяце *next month*
люби́мый *favourite*
зави́симый *dependent*
незабыва́емый *unforgettable*

Notice the adverb:

по-ви́димому   *apparently*

Adjectival passive pres. participles of this type can also be formed from perfective verbs; they are often compounded with не- and correspond to English adjectives in *in—able*, e.g.

непобеди́мый	*invincible*
неоцени́мый	*invaluable*

From several verbs two forms of participle are in use, the regular present participle in -щий (which is phonetically of Old Bulgarian, not Russian, origin) and the purely adjectival form in -чий (which is the original Russian form of the present participle); e.g.

from	горе́ть	*to burn* (intrans.)
	горя́щий	*burning*
	горя́чий	*hot* (esp. of *water, food,* &c.)

Notice the following pres. participles which are used in letter-writing:

уважа́емый (or -ая)... *respected, dear* . . .
глубòкоуважа́емый (or -ая)... *deeply respected* . . .
уважа́ющий (or -ая) Вас *yours respectfully*
глубо́ко уважа́ющий (or -ая) Вас *yours very respectfully*
люби́щий (or -ая) Вас *your loving, yours affectionately*

The past participle active, too, is only rarely used as a participle. One or two forms are very commonly used as adjectives or nouns, e.g.

| | бы́вший | *former* |
| | проше́дший | *past*[1] |

Notice

| | сумасше́дший | *madman* |
| from | сойти́ с ума́ | *to go mad* (lit. *to go off one's mind*) |

The past part. pass. is by far the most commonly used of all the participles, and is not rare even in conversation. This participle also often takes the place of the passive, e.g.

[1] Now seldom used except in the grammatical term проше́дшее вре́мя *the past tense*; far commoner are

про́шлый *last*
про́шлое *the past*
(cf. the perfective past прошёл).

кем эта книга была переведена? *who was this book translated by?*

кем эта пьеса написана? *who has this play been written by?*

она одета в чёрное (note acc.) *she is dressed in black*

In this case also many participles are almost entirely used as adjectives, e.g.

уверенный	*assured, confident, sure*
вышеупомянутый	*above-mentioned*

Notice the idioms:

занято	*[it is] occupied* (of seats, &c.), *engaged*
заперто	*locked, shut*
закрыто	*closed, shut*
открыто	*open*
битком набито	*chock-full*
распродано	*sold out*
запрещено	*it is forbidden*

§ 110. The Reflexive Verb and the expression of the Passive

A reflexive verb is sometimes used, instead of a passive participle, to express the passive, e.g.

он родился в мае   *he was born in May*
(cf. она родила сына *she gave birth to a son*)

but phrases which in other languages are in the passive are in Russian most often expressed in the active (see also § 111 (iii)), e.g.

he is very much liked would always be translated by его очень любят (lit. *people like him very much*)

he is hated is его ненавидят

that is not done may be этого не делают

though the phrase это не делается is also common.

that is not said is так не говорят

this paper is little read is э́ту газе́ту ма́ло чита́ют or э́та
газе́та ма́ло чита́ется

Reflexive verbs in Russian are often merely the intransitive forms of otherwise transitive verbs, e.g.

мыть	*to wash* (trans.)
мы́ться	*to wash* (intr.)

For example: мыть посу́ду и́ли ребёнка *to wash dishes or a child*, but он мо́ется *he is washing*, i.e. *washing himself*. Similarly:

одева́ть	*to dress (somebody)* (trans.)
одева́ться	*to dress (oneself)* (intr.)
продолжа́ть	*to continue* (trans.)
продолжа́ться	*to continue* (intr.)
руга́ть	*to abuse, call (somebody) names* (trans.)
руга́ться	*to swear, use bad language* (intr.)
куса́ть	*to bite (something)* (trans.)
куса́ться	*to bite* (intr.)

(e.g. э́та соба́ка куса́ется *this dog bites, is vicious*)

укла́дывать	*to pack (things)* (trans.)
укла́дываться	*to pack, do one's packing* (intr.)

Some reflexive verbs denote a reciprocal or mutual type of action:

мы ре́дко ви́димся	*we seldom see one another*
они́ проща́ются	*they are taking leave [of one another]*
друзья́ обняли́сь	*the friends embraced [one another]*
они́ встре́тились	*they met* (intr.)

Such verbs may also have as subject only one party to the possible reciprocal action, the other party being expressed in the instrumental after с, e.g.

они́ здоро́ваются с на́ми *they greet (exchange greetings with) us*

она́ встре́тилась с ним *she met him*

Occasionally the reflexive form of a verb has a more particularized or personalized meaning than the non-reflexive:

стуча́ться в дверь *to knock at the door* (i.e. *to announce one's presence by knocking*)

проси́ться куда́-нибудь *to request permission to go somewhere*

пла́каться* (кому́ на что) *to complain* (*to somebody about something*)

беле́ться *to stand out white in the distance*

Some transitive verbs when used intransitively require the complete reflexive pronoun себя́ instead of -ся, e.g.

чу́вствовать	*to feel* (trans.)
чу́вствовать себя́	*to feel* (intr.)
я себя́ чу́вствую нехорошо́	*I don't feel well*
как вы себя́ чу́вствуете?	*how do you feel?*

Many reflexive verbs which are intransitive have no corresponding transitive form, e.g.

стара́ться	*to try*
улыба́ться	*to smile*
смея́ться	*to laugh*
станови́ться	*to become*
наде́яться	*to hope*
боя́ться(+ gen.)	*to be afraid (of)*
боро́ться	*to struggle*
каза́ться	*to seem*
остава́ться	*to remain*
случа́ться	*to happen*
очути́ться	*to find oneself, be*
очну́ться	*to regain one's senses*

The verbs

нра́виться	*to please*
каса́ться	*to touch, concern*
любова́ться	*to admire*
наслажда́ться	*to enjoy*

are intransitive in Russian, the first taking the dative, каса́ться the genitive, and the last two the instrumental case.

A few reflexive verbs are used only impersonally:

смерка́ется *it is growing dark*

мне хо́чется(+infin.) *I feel like* (doing something)

мне ничего́ не хоте́лось де́лать *I didn't feel like doing anything*

мне нездоро́вится *I don't feel well*

мне не спи́тся *I can't get to sleep, I don't feel sleepy*

здесь мне хорошо́ спи́тся *I sleep well here*

(у меня́) че́шется (*I*) *have an itch*

разуме́ется *it is understood, of course*

Note the curious impersonal verb

прихо́дится (lit. *it comes itself*)

which has many uses, two of the most common being:

1. + dat. and infin. *one has to*

прихо́дится рабо́тать	*one has to work*
(мне) пришло́сь заплати́ть	(*I*) *had to pay*
что придётся нам сде́лать?	*what shall we have to do?*

2. + dat. and adverb *life treats* (*one*) . . .

ему́ тру́дно прихо́дится (or живётся) *he has a hard time of it*

For прихо́дится expressing relationship see p. 197.

§ 111. **Impersonal Statements**

The formal 'it' and 'there' of English impersonal sentences are not expressed in Russian; and since the present tense of the verb быть *to be* is seldom used, many Russian impersonal statements contain no verbs either:

it was (will be) cold бы́ло (бу́дет) хо́лодно *it is cold* [*here*] [здесь] хо́лодно	хо́лодно is the neut. sing. of the predicative (short) form of the adj.
there will be no rain *it will not rain* не бу́дет дождя́	(gen. after neg. verb)
there are many such (*like that*) [есть] мно́го таки́х *it was winter* была́ зима́ *there will be rain* *it is going to rain* бу́дет дождь	N.B. In Russian these are personal sentences, with subjects мно́го, зима́, дождь

Russian impersonal statements are of the following types:

(i) Containing one of the small number of verbs that can be used only impersonally; apart from the infinitive, these verbs possess only two forms: 3rd pers. sing. present (or future) and neut. sing. past.

ужé светáет	*day is already breaking*
мою́ рýку сáднило	*my hand was raw and painful*
меня́ тошни́т	*I feel sick, want to vomit*

(ii) Containing a personal verb used impersonally (in 3rd sing. or neut. sing.), often with a special idiomatic meaning; the action described is generally that of natural forces or fate.

вечерéет *evening is setting in*
совсéм стемнéло *it is* (*has grown*) *completely dark*

сего́дня подморо́зило *there was a touch of frost today*
бу́дет мороси́ть *there will be some drizzle*
меня́ знобит *I feel shivery, chilled*
мне повезло́ *I had a stroke of luck*
меня́ вдруг потяну́ло(+ infin.) *I had a sudden urge (to . . .)*
в окно́ сквози́т *there's a draught from the window*
здесь па́хнет ро́зами *there's a smell of roses here*
от неё па́хнет духа́ми *she smells of scent*
доро́гу замело́ (or занесло́) сне́гом *the road has been covered by snow*
ло́дку кача́ло [волна́ми] *the boat was tossed about [by the waves]*
ребёнка уби́ло бо́мбой *the child was killed by a bomb*
он закры́л дверь, что́бы не ду́ло *he closed the door so that it wouldn't be draughty (to stop the draught)*
сто́ит *it's worth while*
хва́тит *that will suffice, that's enough*
сле́дует + infin. *it is proper to, one should . . .*
вам сле́довало бы + infin. *you ought to . . .*
как и сле́довало ожида́ть *as was to be expected*
мне остаётся + infin. *it remains for me to . . .*

For examples of other reflexive verbs used impersonally see § 110.

Notice the impersonal use of the verb начина́ть/нача́ть *to begin* + infin.:

начина́ет темне́ть *it is beginning to grow dark*
(cf. когда́ он начина́ет петь *when he begins to sing*)
but когда́ конце́рт начина́ется? *when does the concert begin?*

After negatived impersonal verbs any complement is expressed in the genitive:

но Ле́ны среди́ них не́ было *but Lena wasn't amongst them*
у нас не достава́ло де́нег *we hadn't enough money*

не хвата́ет ему́ това́рища *he misses his friend*

о́сенью там не быва́ет мо́шек *there are no midges there in autumn*

не оказа́лось возмо́жности *there was no opportunity*

с тех пор не прошло́ и ме́сяца *not even a month had passed since then*

ему́ не́ бы́ло жаль сестры́ *he wasn't sorry for his sister*

(iii) Containing a personal verb used impersonally in 3rd person pl. without a subject pronoun (see also § 110):

говоря́т, что он бо́лен *it is said* (lit. *they say*) *he is ill*

тут, говори́ли, жа́рко *it was said to be hot here*

меня́ задержа́ли *I was held up, people delayed me*

ему́ меша́ют *he is being disturbed* (меша́ть is intr.)

(iv) Containing a personal verb in the 2nd person sing. without a subject pronoun:

здесь не отдохнёшь *one can't get any rest here*

ти́ше е́дешь, да́льше бу́дешь *the slower one travels the further one will get* (i.e. *more haste, less speed*)

(v) Containing a past participle used impersonally (neut. sing.):

там у́брано *it's tidy there* (lit. [*it*] *has been tidied up there*)

в ко́мнате наку́рено *the room is full of smoke*

везде́ бы́ло закры́то *everywhere was closed* (lit. *it was closed*, i.e. *the doors were shut*)

об э́том ничего́ не бу́дет упомя́нуто *nothing will be mentioned about this*

сего́дня не доста́влено това́ров *no goods have been delivered today*

(vi) Containing an infinitive (+ 'subject' in the dative). For examples see § 107 (b).

(vii) Containing a verb of condition (быть, быва́ть

стать, станови́ться, &c.) combined with a neuter predicative adjective or some other impersonal predicative word. This is the most common impersonal construction in Russian. If it is affirmative, any complement will usually be in the accusative (rarely genitive); if it is negative, any complement will of course be in the genitive.

мне жа́рко	I am (feel) hot (lit. to me [it] is hot)
ему́ бы́ло ве́село	he was gay (happy)
ей бу́дет легко́ (тру́дно)	she will find it easy (hard)
в ко́мнате хо́лодно	the room is cold
мне ста́ло доса́дно на него́	I got vexed with him
как вам не сты́дно!	you ought to be ashamed!
мне со́вестно за вас	I am ashamed of you
нам нело́вко пѐред ни́ми	they make us feel embarrassed
как вам уго́дно	as you wish
не ну́жно мне э́тих книг	I don't need these books
нам ну́жно останови́ться	it is necessary for us to stop
доста́точно, or дово́льно	that is enough
с горы́ ви́дно озёра	lakes can be seen from the hill
мне не слы́шно му́зыки	I can't hear any music

Notice the following:

мо́жно (never negatived, see нельзя́) one may, it is possible

мо́жно?	may one? may I?
мо́жно кури́ть?	is smoking allowed?
когда́ мо́жно бу́дет?	when will it be possible (permitted)?
как мо́жно лу́чше	in the best way possible
мо́жно сказа́ть	one may say, it may be said . . .
cf. мо́жно говори́ть	talking is permitted

нельзя́ (neg. of мо́жно)   one may not, it is impossible

нельзя́ мне бе́гать	I am not allowed to run
на него́ нельзя́ полага́ться	he can't be relied upon

| нельзя́ сказа́ть | *one cannot (may not) say* |
| but N.B. неизве́стно | *one cannot tell (know)* |

| возмо́жно ⎫ мо́жет быть ⎭ | *it is possible, perhaps* |

возмо́жно, что он отка́жется *it is possible that he will refuse*

мо́жет быть, он зна́ет   *perhaps he knows*

он, мо́жет быть, знал   *he may have known*

мо́жет быть is sometimes transposed (быть мо́жет) and in popular speech often abbreviated to мо́жет alone.

невозмо́жно *it is impossible*

    невозмо́жно, что́бы он не знал *it is impossible for him not to know* (lit. *that he should not know*)

до́лжно + infin. *it is fitting, one should* (literary)

должно́ быть *it is probable, I expect* (lit. *it must be*)

    он, должно́ быть, зна́ет *I expect he knows, he must know*

    должно́ быть, он знал *he must have known*

ста́ло быть *and so, then I suppose* (lit. *it has become to be*)

    ста́ло быть, вы его́ не лю́бите? *then I take it you don't love him?*

    ста́ло быть, так! *I suppose it is so!*

на́до *it is necessary*

    на́до его́ проучи́ть *he needs to be taught a lesson*

    мне не на́до бы́ло ва́ших де́нег *I didn't need your money*

    ей на́до ру́сскую газе́ту *she needs a Russian newspaper*

    не на́до! *don't!*

жаль (or жа́лко) (in the affirmative the object goes into the acc. case when it denotes a definite person; when not, and always in the negative, the object is in the genitive), as:

> как жаль! *what a pity!*
> ему́ станови́лось жаль сестру́ *he was becoming sorry for his sister*
> мне жаль свое́й мо́лодости *I regret my youth*
> не́ было жаль ему́ сестры́? *wasn't he sorry for his sister?*

пора́ (+infin.) *it is time (to . . .)*

> пора́ бы́ло идти́ *it was time to go*

Just as жаль and пора́ (both originally feminine nouns) are treated as neuter when used impersonally, so too may be the impersonal охо́та, неохо́та, лень, found mainly in the colloquial style:

> охо́та (or хо́чется) обе́дать (*I*) *feel like dinner*
> нам неохо́та бы́ло рабо́тать *we didn't feel like working*
> нам бы́ло лень отпра́виться *we didn't want (we were too lazy) to set off*

Note a few of the English impersonal sentences that are translated into Russian by a personal construction:

it is raining, it rains	дождь идёт (lit. *rain is going*)
it was raining, it rained	дождь шёл
it began to rain	пошёл дождь
it has stopped raining	дождь переста́л or прошёл
it is snowing, it snows	идёт снег
there's been a heavy snowfall	мно́го сне́гу вы́пало
it was hailing, it hailed	шёл град
there is lightning	сверка́ет мо́лния
it is thundering	греми́т гром

It is freezing is usually expressed merely by the noun мороз *frost* (sc. *there is a frost*), e.g.

сегодня мороз   *it is freezing today*

similarly, вчера была оттепель *it was thawing yesterday*

§ 112. How to Express the Verb *to be*

The present tense of the verb быть *to be* has long since become obsolete; it is either omitted altogether or, in cases of potential ambiguity, its place is taken in writing by a long dash and in speaking by a slight pause, e.g.

я англичанин	*I am an Englishman*
сын мой — учитель	*my son is a teacher*
сын — мой учитель	*the son is my teacher*

A pause is also made if the speaker wishes to put special emphasis on the subject of the sentence.

Notice the fact that the phrases *this is, that is, it is, these are, those are, they are* are usually expressed by это, irrespective of the number and gender of the predicate, e.g.

это моя жена	*this is my wife*
это мои дети	*these are my children*

unless, of course, special emphasis is laid on the pronoun:

те книги — его, а эти — мои *those books are his, but these are mine*

Here is and *here are*, used when pointing to something, are expressed by вот, e.g.

вот мой дом *here is my house*

вот can also mean [*over*] *there is*; when something in the far distance is pointed to, вон [там] can be used. вон is also used in pointing out the more remote of two objects.

The 3rd sing. of the present is still commonly used in certain cases, e.g.

> то́ есть   *that is* (*to say*)
> т. е.   *i.e.*

Combined with у and a noun or pronoun it is the commonest way of saying *to have* [*got*], e.g.

> у меня́ есть   *I have*
> у него́ есть   *he has*

though as often as not the verb есть may be omitted in general statements and also in questions, unless the answer expected is *yes* or *no* (see pp. 188–9). In shops, restaurants, &c., when asking a question, есть must be used, e.g.

Question:

> есть у вас икра́?   *have you* [*got*] *any caviare?*

Answer:

> есть   *we have*

the negative answer is always

> нет (or colloq. не́ту)   *we haven't*

нет is really a contraction of не есть, and has come to be the ordinary word for *no*; it also means *there is not* and thus *have not*, e.g.

> у меня́ нет + gen.   *I haven't* [*got*] . . .
> у меня́ нет отца́   *I have no father*

The interrogative particle ли is sometimes added after есть, though есть by itself, if the voice is inflected accordingly, is quite sufficient to indicate the question.

е́сть ли is apt to sound like е́сли (*if*), and е́сли is in fact a corruption of есть ли.

не́т ли у вас + gen.? is another common way of saying *have you* [*got*] . . . ?

найдётся ли у вас + nom.? from найти (*to find*) is also much used to express the same thing.

есть is also used for *there is*, *there are* in the sense of *there exist(s)*, as:

есть такие люди, которые не любят икры *there are [such] people who don't like caviare*

есть много вещей, о которых я бы хотел с вами поговорить *there are many things I should like to talk to you about*

в этой книге есть много хорошего *there is much that is good in this book*

The 3rd sing. есть and the 3rd pl. суть are also used in emphatic declarations or definitions; it should be noted, however, that суть is very little used, and that есть can be used for any of the three persons singular or plural, e.g.

что есть истина?   *what is truth?*

она любит вас, как вы есть *she loves you as you are*

Owing to the fact that есть is so seldom used, single neuter adjectives (short form) may acquire the meaning of whole sentences, e.g.

хóлодно	*it is cold*
теплó	*it is warm*
жáрко	*it is hot*
возмóжно	*it is possible*
нýжно	*it is necessary*
мне хóлодно	*I am cold*, &c.

The 3rd sing. of the present of бывáть, the imperfective frequentative of быть, is often used:

это чáсто бывáет	*that often happens*
это никогдá не бывáет	*that never happens*
он у нас бывáет	*he sometimes comes to see us*

The past tense of быть does not call for special mention. It is often used to express the idea of a visit, e.g.

вы бы́ли в Москве́?   *have you been to Moscow?*

я был у них вчера́   *I went to see them yesterday*

The neuter is often used impersonally:

вчера́ бы́ло хо́лодно   *it was cold yesterday*

For other uses of бы́ло and быва́ло see §§ 103, 104.

The future (бу́ду, бу́дешь, &c.) presents no difficulties. Notice the idioms:

бу́дет! *enough!*

де́сятью оди́ннадцать бу́дет сто де́сять *ten elevens are a hundred and ten*

For uses of the future, conditional, imperative, and infinitive of быть see §§ 104–7.

Notice that состоя́ть and явля́ться are also used sometimes with the meaning *to be*, e.g.

я состою́ чле́ном э́того о́бщества *I am a member of this society*

он явля́ется председа́телем о́бщества *he is the president of the society*

э́то яви́лось после́дствием его́ поведе́ния *that was the consequence of his behaviour*

For the use of the instrumental after these verbs see pp. 211–12.

§ 113. Various forms of Imperfective and Perfective Verbs

It has already been remarked (§ 101) that most perfective verbs are formed from imperfective verbs by adding a prefix (mostly a preposition) to the latter, and that the prefix used for this purpose loses its original meaning. It is impossible to tell which prefix will be used in each particular case for the purpose of making the imperfective verb perfective, as various prefixes are thus used, e.g.

Imperfective		*Perfective*
смотрѣ́ть	*to look*	посмотрѣ́ть
писа́ть	*to write*	написа́ть
дѣ́лать	*to do*	сдѣ́лать
знать	*to know*	узна́ть
	and others	

The only thing that can be said is that по is used for this purpose in an infinitely greater number of cases than any other prefix. But it must be remembered that while one prefix merely makes the imperfective verb perfective and loses its own original meaning, all the other prefixes when compounded with the same verb *make the verb perfective and at the same time endow it with their own special meaning.* For instance:

рассмотрѣ́ть	*to examine closely*
осмотрѣ́ть	*to inspect*
приписа́ть	*to ascribe; to add in writing*
списа́ть	*to copy*
передѣ́лать	*to do over again; to alter*
отдѣ́лать	*to trim; to put the finishing touches to*

These verbs, as has been remarked, are perfective; the imperfective verbs corresponding to them are combinations of the same prefix and the frequentative forms of the verbs. Frequentative verbs are a subsidiary category of imperfective verbs which seldom occur in Modern Russian in their simple forms, but whose compounds are common. Frequentative verbs are formed by lengthening the stem of the root-verb, during which process the vowel preceding the infinitive ending may change (o often changes into a).

The only simple frequentative verb in common use is

бывáть (from быть)	*to be* (sc. *often, usually*)
э́то бывáет	*that sometimes happens*
я у них бывáю	*I am in the habit of going to see them*

Others are found occasionally, mostly in popular speech, e.g.

говáривать[1] (from гово-р́ить)	*to be in the habit of saying*
он так говáривал	*he often used to say so*
сúживать[1] (from сидéть)	*to sit (often, regularly)*
он сúживал у пéчи	*he used to sit by the stove*

These simple verbs are truly frequentative in meaning. When they are compounded with a prefix, they remain imperfective but lose their special frequentative force. The compounds are quite ordinary imperfective verbs corresponding to perfective verbs of the type which we formed above by adding to an ordinary simple verb a prefix which made it perfective and at the same time altered its meaning; they may have frequentative meaning, but normally this has to be specially expressed by the addition of some such word as чáсто *often*. For example, the compound imperfective corresponding to забы́ть (pf.) *to forget* is забывáть; я забывáю may mean *I often* (or *always*) *forget*, but on the other hand it may mean *I am forgetting, I forget* (*at the present moment*). Similarly, я разговáривал с ним may mean either *I used to talk to him* or *I was talking to him* (*once*).

---

[1] Colloquial; used only in past tense.

It is now time to examine the various ways in which these compound imperfective verbs are formed.

In a large number of cases they are formed by the insertion of the syllable -ыв- or -ив- between the stem of the verb and the infinitive ending. Compound imperfectives from almost all verbs ending in -ать and from many others besides are formed in this way. Verbs of this formation which, in their original form, contain the vowel o in their root, usually (but not always) change this vowel to a in the compound imperfective. The verbs are arranged below in series of four, e.g.

1. писáть *to write*—simple imperfective.

2. написáть *to write*—compound perfective in which the prefix loses its own meaning and merely indicates the aspect.

3. приписáть *to ascribe*—compound perfective in which the prefix retains its meaning.

4. припи́сывать *to ascribe*—compound imperfective in which the prefix retains its meaning. *It must of course not be imagined that in each of the examples given here the particular compound perfective in which the prefix retains its meaning is the only such compound perfective formed from that verb.* In the case of some verbs such compounds are very numerous; the examples have been chosen at random, but they include only verbs that are commonly used:

Imperfective		Perfective
писáть	*to write*	написáть
припи́сывать	*to ascribe*	приписáть
дéлать	*to do*	сдéлать
передéлывать	*to alter*	передéлать
смотрéть	*to look*	посмотрéть
рассмáтривать	*to examine*	рассмотрéть

Imperfective		*Perfective*
чита́ть	*to read*	прочита́ть (or прочéсть)
дочи́тывать	*to finish [reading]* something	дочита́ть
слу́шать	*to listen*	послу́шать
подслу́шивать	*to eavesdrop [on]*	подслу́шать
лома́ть	*to break*	слома́ть
прола́мывать	*to break through*	проломáть
стро́ить	*to build*	постро́ить
устра́ивать	*to arrange*	устро́ить
смея́ться	*to laugh*	засмея́ться
осмéивать	*to deride*	осмея́ть
кра́сть	*to steal*	укра́сть
обкра́дывать	*to rob*	обокра́сть
тяну́ть[1]	*to pull*	потяну́ть
стя́гивать	*to tighten, close*	стяну́ть

Those second conjugation verbs which, in the 1st sing. present, have a stem affected by the personal ending -ю (which changes into -у, see §§ 87, 88), are similarly affected in their compound imperfective forms, though no longer belonging to the second conjugation, e.g.

Imperfective		*Perfective*
проси́ть	*to request*	попроси́ть
спра́шивать	*to ask (a question)*	спроси́ть
топи́ть	*to heat*	истопи́ть
зата́пливать	*to kindle, light*	затопи́ть
дави́ть	*to squash*	подави́ть
зада́вливать	*to throttle*	задави́ть

---

[1] from тяг + нуть.

From a number of perfective verbs the compound imperfectives are formed by inserting -ва- between the stem and the infinitive ending, e.g.

Imperfective		*Perfective*
бить	*to hit, beat*	побить[1]
убива́ть	*to kill*	уби́ть
петь	*to sing*	спеть
запева́ть	*to strike up a song*	запе́ть
пить	*to drink*	вы́пить
пропива́ть	*to spend on drink*	пропи́ть
крыть[2]	*to cover*	покры́ть
раскрыва́ть	*to uncover, open, discover*	раскры́ть
мыть	*to wash* (trans.)	вы́мыть
умыва́ться	*to wash* (intr.)	умы́ться

Notice especially the following verbs (for other simple perfective verbs see § 114):

Imperfective		*Perfective*
дава́ть	*to give*	дать
pres. даю́		fut. дам
дева́ть[3]	*to put* (colloq.)	деть
pres. дева́ю		fut. де́ну

and быва́ть *to be often, to happen* (from быть *to be*).

---

[1] Meaning *to beat, hit a little*; *to strike, hit* (*once*) is уда́рить.

[2] More usual is the compound imperfective покрыва́ть.

[3] The past has either imperfective or perfective sense.

Some verbs of this category cannot be formed in complete series in this way, e.g.

Imperfective		Perfective
знать	*to know*	
узнава́ть	*to learn (news),*	узна́ть
	to recognize	
pres. узнаю́, узнаёшь		fut. узна́ю, узна́ешь
(станови́ться)	*to* [*take one's*] *stand*[1]	стать
		fut. ста́ну
устава́ть	*to grow tired*	уста́ть
pres. устаю́		fut. уста́ну

(and many other common compounds)

Those verbs which, both in their imperfective and perfective aspects, have no prefix, can of course also be compounded with a prefix in both aspects, the prefix always retaining its meaning, e.g.

Imperfective		Perfective
дава́ть	*to give*	дать
подава́ть	*to hand, serve*	пода́ть
продава́ть	*to sell*	прода́ть
придава́ть	*to add*	прида́ть
передава́ть	*to transmit*	переда́ть
предава́ть	*to betray*	преда́ть
издава́ть	*to publish*	изда́ть
раздава́ть	*to distribute*	разда́ть
воздава́ть	*to reward*	возда́ть
выдава́ть	*to hand out, give away*	вы́дать
поддава́ться	*to submit*	подда́ться
удава́ться	*to be a success*	уда́ться
сдава́ть	*to hand over*	сдать

[1] For its other meanings see pp. 229, 299, 332.

Imperfective		Perfective
задава́ть	*to set (task, questions)*	зада́ть
додава́ть	*to add (the rest)*	дода́ть
also создава́ть	*to create*	созда́ть

(N.B. Many of these compounds have other meanings besides those given here, and of course the same applies to other verbs.)

Imperfective		Perfective
дева́ть[1]	*to put (colloq.)*	де́ть
одева́ть(ся)	*to dress*	оде́ть(ся)
надева́ть	*to put on*	наде́ть
раздева́ть(ся)	*to undress*	разде́ть(ся)
переодева́ть(ся)	*to change (dress)*	переоде́ть(ся)
задева́ть	*to brush against*	заде́ть
(-става́ть)	*to [take one's] stand*	стать
перестава́ть	*to cease*	переста́ть
застава́ть	*to find (a person)*	заста́ть
достава́ть	*to obtain*	доста́ть
остава́ться	*to remain*	оста́ться
встава́ть	*to get up, stand up*	встать
расстава́ться	*to part (intr.)*	расста́ться

Verbs with infinitives in -чь, -зть, -сти form their compound imperfectives by adding -ать to their stem, e.g.

Imperfective		Perfective
мочь	*to be able*	смочь
помога́ть	*to help*	помо́чь
влечь	*to drag*	повле́чь
привлека́ть	*to attract*	привле́чь

[1] The past has either imperfective or perfective sense.

The verb есть forms its compound imperfective as follows:

Imperfective		Perfective
есть	*to eat*	поéсть
съедáть	*to eat up, consume*	съéсть
надоедáть(+ dat.)	*to bore*	надоéсть(+ dat.)

The cognate verb обéдать (ipf.) *to dine* is from the noun обéд *dinner* and has the perfectives пообéдать and отобéдать.

Verbs with stems containing two adjacent consonants insert ы or и between these in the compound imperfective, e.g.

Imperfective		Perfective
слать[1]	*to send*	послáть
pres. шлю		
высылáть	*to banish, send out*	вы́слать
жать	*to press*	пожáть
pres. жму		
сжимáть	*to squeeze*	сжать
		fut. сожму́
звать	*to call*	позвáть
pres. зову́		
называ́ть	*to name*	назвáть
жечь	*to burn* (trans.)	сжечь
pres. жгу		fut. сожгу́
зажигáть	*to light, kindle*	зажéчь

---

[1] More common is the compound imperfective посылáть.

Imperfective		*Perfective*
ждать	*to wait (for)*	
pres. жду		подождáть
ожидáть	*to expect*	
поджидáть	*to wait for*	
дожидáться	{ *to attain by waiting* / *to wait until (arrival)* }	дождáться

Notice verbs with infin. in -ереть:

терéть	*to rub*	потерéть
pres. тру		
обтирáть	*to wipe*	обтерéть

There are several verbs of this kind which are rarely or never used without a prefix, e.g.

Imperfective		*Perfective*
умирáть	*to die*	умерéть
		fut. умрý
начинáть	*to begin*	начáть
		fut. начнý

The verb -ять (only used in composition with prefixes, see § 88) forms its compound imperfectives as follows:

Imperfective		*Perfective*
[-имать]		[-ять]
внимáть	*to hearken* (archaic)	внять (fut. not used)
занимáть	*to occupy, to borrow*	занять fut. займý займёшь
нанимáть	*to hire*	нанять fut. наймý, &c.
понимáть	*to understand*	понять fut. поймý поймёшь, &c.

Imperfective		*Perfective*
поднима́ть (or подыма́ть)	*to lift*	подня́ть fut. подниму́ подни́мешь, &c.
принима́ть	*to accept*	приня́ть fut. приму́ при́мешь, &c.
снима́ть	*to take off* (*remove*), *to photograph*	снять fut. сниму́ сни́мешь
—— (§ 117)	*to take*	взять
[взима́ть[1]	*to levy* (*money*)]	fut. возьму́ возьмёшь

In the case of this verb, the roots of which are -им- and -ьм-, the н between the prefix and the root is explained by the fact that the preposition-prefixes с and в originally ended in a nasal, which was dropped after such forms as снять had become crystallized. On the analogy of these forms, the н was inserted between the prefix and the root in some other compounds of this verb (поня́ть, понима́ть, &c.). The compound пойма́ть *to catch* is perfective, see § 117.

The pasts of all these perfectives are за́нял, заняла́, за́няло; за́няли: по́нял, поняла́, по́няло; по́няли, &c., i.e. they are, as was to be expected, formed from the infinitives.

§ 114. Perfective Simple Verbs

Not all perfective verbs are compound. There are a fair number of simple verbs which are perfective in themselves.

Such verbs are

дать	*to give*
деть	*to put*
стать	*to* [*take one's*] *stand, to become, to begin*

---

[1] There is no perfective verb from the same root with this meaning.

Besides these, there are two categories of simple verbs which are perfective; the first contains verbs of various classes, most of them very common:

Imperfective		*Perfective*
бросáть	*to throw*	брóсить
кончáть	*to finish*	кóнчить
ложи́ться	*to lie down*	лечь
лишáть	*to deprive*	лиши́ть
пáдать	*to fall*	пасть[1]
прощáть	*to forgive*	прости́ть
прощáться	*to say goodbye*	прости́ться
пускáть	*to let, let go*	пусти́ть
решáть	*to decide*	реши́ть
станови́ться	*to become, stand*	стать
ступáть	*to step*	ступи́ть
сади́ться	*to sit down*	сесть
хватáть	*to seize*	хвати́ть
являться	*to appear*	яви́ться

One verb in this category has in the imperfective aspect a prefixed form while the perfective aspect is a simple verb, viz.

покупáть	*to buy*	купи́ть

These verbs, being perfective when they are simple, are no less perfective when compounded with a prefix. Of the corresponding simple imperfective verbs, some when prefixed become perfective and require the formation of a compound imperfective, others remain imperfective.

Imperfective		*Perfective*
ступáть	*to step*	ступи́ть
поступáть	*to act, behave* / *to enter (an institution)*	поступи́ть

---

[1] More common is упáсть.

Imperfective		*Perfective*
реша́ть	to *decide*	реши́ть
разреша́ть	to *permit*	разреши́ть
явля́ться	to *appear*	яви́ться
объявля́ть	to *declare*	объяви́ть
	but	
броса́ть	to *throw*	бро́сить
выбра́сывать	to *throw out*	вы́бросить
станови́ться	to *become, stand*	стать
остана́вливаться	to *stop*	останови́ться
сади́ться	to *sit down*	сесть
переса́живаться	to *change* (*trains, &c.*)	пересе́сть

The other category contains a number of verbs ending in -нуть, which by means of this ending connote a single instantaneous (perfective) action and are termed *semelfactive*, e.g.

Imperfective		*Perfective*
гляде́ть	to *look*	гляну́ть
дви́гать	to *move* (*something*)	дви́нуть
крича́ть	to *cry out*	кри́кнуть
кида́ть	to *fling*	ки́нуть
маха́ть	to *wave*	махну́ть
плева́ть	to *spit*	плю́нуть
сова́ть	to *shove*	су́нуть
тро́гать	to *touch*	тро́нуть
шепта́ть	to *whisper*	шепну́ть

It is important not to confuse these with other simple verbs ending in -нуть which are imperfective, e.g. тяну́ть to *pull* and кре́пнуть to *grow strong*, which are made perfective in the ordinary way, viz. by a prefix: потяну́ть, окре́пнуть. These verbs in -нуть, being perfective, are naturally also perfective when compounded with a prefix; the corresponding simple imperfective verbs are usually lengthened by the already familiar process (insertion of -ыв- or -ив-) to form the corresponding compound imperfective, e.g.

Imperfective		*Perfective*
глядѣ́ть	*to look*	гляну́ть[1]
взгля́дывать	*to look up*	взгляну́ть
сова́ть	*to shove*	су́нуть
высо́вывать	*to shove out*	вы́сунуть
тро́гать	*to touch*	тро́нуть
дотра́гиваться	*to come into (physical) contact with*	дотро́нуться
крича́ть	*to cry out*	кри́кнуть
вскри́кивать	*to scream*	вскри́кнуть
Notice		
кида́ть	*to fling*	ки́нуть
прики́дываться	*to pretend to be*	прики́нуться
but		
покида́ть	*to abandon*	поки́нуть

Some verbs, only used in composition with prefixes, cannot be formed in complete series, e.g.

Imperfective		*Perfective*
обма́нывать	*to deceive*	обману́ть
вздыха́ть	*to sigh*	вздохну́ть
исчеза́ть	*to disappear*	исчѣ́знуть
достига́ть	*to reach*	достигнуть
привыка́ть	*to grow accustomed to*	привы́кнуть
отвыка́ть	*to get out of practice*	отвы́кнуть

[1] A perfective verb поглядѣ́ть also exists.

§ 115. Compound Imperfective Verbs

Conversely, not all compound verbs are perfective. We have already seen that adding a prefix does not necessarily make a verb perfective, e.g. разговáривать *to converse*, убивáть *to kill*, покупáть *to buy*, поступáть *to act, behave*. Besides these there are very many compound imperfective verbs which form a class by themselves. These correspond in meaning to a series of compound perfective verbs ending in -ить and belonging to conj. II. The corresponding compound imperfectives are formed not by lengthening the stem with additional syllables, but by altering the infinitive ending from -ить to -ять (-ать after ж, ш, ч, or щ), thus making them verbs of conj. I. In the course of this alteration the phonetic changes observable in the 1st sing. of the present of verbs of conj. II (palatalization of the last consonant of the stem and substitution of the ending -у for -ю, e.g. вижу from видеть, or insertion of л, e.g. люблю from любить) are reproduced throughout the whole of the compound imperfective owing to the influence of the 'soft' vowel я (which in certain cases itself becomes a, e.g. -т + ять, -т + яю, &c., become -чать, -чаю, &c.).

Imperfective		*Perfective*
встречáть	to meet	встрéтить
воображáть	to imagine	вообразúть
выражáть	to express	вы́разить
навещáть	to visit	навестúть
объяснять	to explain	объяснúть
ошибáться	to be mistaken	ошибúться[1]
отвечáть	to answer	отвéтить
переменять	to change	переменúть
повторять	to repeat	повторúть
получáть	to receive	получúть

[1] For future tense see p. 226.

Imperfective		Perfective
позволя́ть	*to permit*	позво́лить
посеща́ть	*to visit*	посети́ть
ударя́ть	*to strike* (trans.)	уда́рить
убежда́ть	*to convince*	убеди́ть
употребля́ть	*to use*	употреби́ть

and many others.

Notice ве́шать   *to hang* (trans.)   пове́сить

In the case of a few verbs which are used in their simple forms it is possible to form the already familiar complete series of four, e.g.

Imperfective		Perfective
ста́вить	*to put*	поста́вить
оставля́ть	*to leave*	оста́вить

and many other common compounds.

Compound Imperfectives formed by Change of Stress

In the case of a few verbs the form of the compound imperfective differs from that of the simple imperfective (apart from the addition of the prefix) only in the position of the stress, e.g.

Imperfective		Perfective
па́дать	*to fall*	пасть[1]
пропада́ть	*to get lost*	пропа́сть

Notice also the very common verbs:

попада́ть	*to get [into], catch, hit*	попа́сть

---

[1] The compound perfective упа́сть, pres. упаду́, is more commonly used than пасть.

Imperfective		*Perfective*
сы́пать	*to scatter*	посы́пать
pres. сы́плю		fut. посы́плю
сы́плешь		посы́плешь
просыпа́ть	*to spill (not liquids)*	просы́пать
pres. просыпа́ю		fut. просы́плю

Notice also:

просыпа́ть	*to oversleep*	проспа́ть
засыпа́ть	*to fall asleep*	засну́ть
просыпа́ться	*to awake*	просну́ться

дви́гать	*to move* (trans.)	дви́нуть
pres. дви́гаю and дви́жу (see p. 228)		
отодвига́ть	*to move away* (trans.)	отодви́нуть
pres. отодвига́ю		

Note воздвига́ть   *to erect*   воздви́гнуть

бе́гать	*to run*	побе́гать
избега́ть	*to avoid*	⎰ избежа́ть ⎱ избе́гнуть

§ 116. Verbs with Two Simple Imperfective Forms

Fourteen simple verbs of motion have two imperfective forms which are distinct, though related, in meaning. They are both equally imperfective, but one describes an action that is actually in progress and involves motion in one direction only, while the other connotes potentiality, habit, or an action in progress involving motion in more than one direction. The former are called *actual simple imperfectives* (sometimes called *concrete* or *determinate*), the latter *potential simple imperfectives* (sometimes called *abstract* or *indeterminate*).

A good example is the Russian for *to go* (sc. *on foot*); to express this there are two distinct imperfective verbs:

1. идти́ (*actual*)
2. ходи́ть (*potential*)

The first is usually rendered by *to be going* (sc. *in one direction and at a particular moment*); the second is usually translated by *to go, be in the habit of going* (sc. *and returning in the opposite direction after each trip*), or *to go, be going* (sc. *in more than one direction*). Examples:

куда́ вы идёте? *where are you going?* (sc. *now*)

хо́дите ли вы в теа́тр? *do you go to the theatre?* (sc. *ever* or *often*)

я иду́ гуля́ть *I am going for a walk*

я уже́ хожу́ *I can now walk* (sc. *after an illness*)

я его́ встре́тил, когда́ он шёл домо́й *I met him* (sc. *once*) *when he was going home*

когда́ он жил у нас, он ходи́л в шко́лу *when he lived with us he went (used to go) to school*

она́ шла по у́лице *she was walking along* (*up* or *down*) *the street*

она́ ходи́ла по ко́мнате *she was walking about* (*up and down*) *the room*

The verb *to fly* is:

1. лете́ть (*actual*)
2. лета́ть (*potential*)

вот лети́т самолёт! *there's an aeroplane flying!* (sc. *in one direction*)

пти́цы лета́ют *birds fly* (sc. *can fly, do fly*) or *birds are flying about* (sc. *in many directions*)

The verb *to carry* is:

1. нести́ (*actual*)
2. носи́ть (*potential*)

почтальо́н несёт вам письмо́ *the postman is bringing you a letter*

носи́льщики но́сят бага́ж *porters carry luggage* (sc. *that is their job*)

носи́ть can also mean *to wear* (habitually):[1]

я всегда́ ношу́ ша́пку *I always wear a cap*

она́ но́сит бе́лое пла́тье по воскресе́ньям *she wears a white dress on Sundays*

The fourteen verbs in question are:

	Actual		*Potential*
infin.	бежа́ть	*to run*	бе́гать
pres. {	бегу́		бе́гаю
	бежи́шь		бе́гаешь
	брести́	*to trudge*	броди́ть
	бреду́		брожу́
	бредёшь		бро́дишь
	везти́	*to convey*	вози́ть
	везу́		вожу́
	везёшь		во́зишь
	вести́	*to lead*	води́ть
	веду́		вожу́
	ведёшь		во́дишь
	е́хать	*to go* (*in any way except on foot*)	е́здить
	е́ду		е́зжу
	е́дешь		е́здишь

---

[1] Actual wearing on one occasion cannot be expressed by носи́ть or нести́; resort must be had to periphrasis: *he is wearing a blue suit* = на нём си́ний костю́м or он в си́нем костю́ме.

Actual		*Potential*
гнать гоню́ го́нишь	to drive, chase	гоня́ть гоня́ю &c.
идти́ иду́ идёшь	to go (on foot)	ходи́ть хожу́ хо́дишь
кати́ть качу́ ка́тишь	to roll, bowl, push along	ката́ть ката́ю &c.
лете́ть лечу́ лети́шь	to fly	лета́ть лета́ю &c.
лезть ле́зу ле́зешь	to climb, clamber	ла́зить ла́жу ла́зишь
нести́ несу́ несёшь	to carry	носи́ть ношу́ но́сишь
плыть плыву́ плывёшь	to float, swim, sail	пла́вать пла́ваю &c.
ползти́ ползу́ ползёшь	to crawl	по́лзать по́лзаю &c.
тащи́ть тащу́ та́щишь	to drag	таска́ть таска́ю &c.

In addition two verbs belonging to this category do not connote motion; they are colloquial and defective, viz.

Actual		Potential
ви́деть	*to see*	вида́ть
ви́жу		вида́ю
ви́дишь		&c.
слы́шать	*to hear*	слыха́ть
слы́шу		——
слы́шишь		

The present of слыха́ть is not used and that of вида́ть is rare; their infinitives and pasts are, on the other hand, quite common, especially in negations and questions, e.g.

я его́ давно́ не вида́л *I haven't seen him for ages*

его́ не вида́ть *he is not to be seen* (sc. *I can't see him*)

слыха́ли ли вы э́того певца́? *have you ever heard this singer?*

When these verbs are compounded with prefixes it is the *actual imperfective* which combines with по- to form the normal *perfective* without change of meaning. It is also the *actual imperfective* which, when compounded with any other prefix, forms a *compound perfective* with meaning affected by the prefix. The corresponding *compound imperfective* is formed from the *potential imperfective*, the prefix imparting its full meaning to the action of the simple verb. Occasionally, the potential imperfective is used to make a compound *perfective* verb: examples of this are given later in this section.

Imperfective		Perfective
лете́ть (*actual*) ⎫	*to fly*	полете́ть
лета́ть (*potential*) ⎭		
перелета́ть	*to fly over*	перелете́ть

Imperfective		Perfective
вести } водить }	to lead	повести
проводить	{ to lead through } { to spend (time) }	провести
везти } возить }	to convey, cart	повезти
привозить	to bring (in a conveyance)	привезти
нести } носить¹ }	to carry	понести
приносить	to bring (by hand)	принести
идти } ходить }	to go (on foot)	пойти
приходить	to come (on foot)	прийти
находить	to find	найти
проходить	to pass	пройти

Needless to say, both forms of all these verbs have many other compounds besides those given here.

The two verbs видеть and слышать have the following perfectives:

Imperfective		Perfective
видеть } видать }	to see	{ увидеть { увидать
слышать } слыхать }	to hear	{ услышать { услыхать

¹ носить has no perfective with the meaning *to wear*; instead, the verb надеть or some periphrasis must be employed, e.g. я надену новый костюм *I shall wear a new suit* (sc. on a particular occasion); вчера он надел шапку or вчера на нём была шапка *yesterday he wore a cap*.

The futures of увидеть and услышать are very common, being the ordinary perfective futures of видеть and слышать, e.g.

> я увижу его завтра *I shall see him tomorrow*

The futures of увидать and услыхать are never used by educated speakers. Their pasts are quite common in colloquial speech, and it is to be noticed that there is no essential difference in meaning between

> увидал and the more common увидел

or between

> услыхал and the more usual услышал.

Notice the compounds:

Imperfective		*Perfective*
завидовать	*to envy*	позавидовать
ненавидеть	*to hate*	возненавидеть
предвидеть	*to foresee*	(no perfective)

Two verbs deserve special mention, viz. бежать and ехать; these form their compound perfectives from the *actual imperfective*, but the corresponding compound imperfective is formed not from the *potential imperfective* but from yet a third imperfective form of the word, only used in composition with prefixes:

Imperfective		*Perfective*
бежать (*actual*)	*to run, flee*	побежать
бегать (*potential*)	*to run, flee*	——
перебегать	*to run across*	перебежать
избегать	*to avoid*	{ избежать and избегнуть

Imperfective		Perfective
убега́ть	*to run away, flee*	убежа́ть[1]
прибега́ть	{ *to run to*	прибежа́ть
	{ *to have recourse to*	прибе́гнуть
е́хать[2] (*actual*)	*to go* (*not on foot*)	пое́хать
е́здить (*potential*)	*to go* (*not on foot*)	———
приезжа́ть	*to arrive*	прие́хать
уезжа́ть	*to depart*	уе́хать

плыть and лезть have the same peculiarity, forming their compound imperfectives not with the verbs пла́вать and ла́зить but with -плыва́ть and -леза́ть; they are not given in full here, because they are of much less common occurrence.

It has already been mentioned that the *potential imperfectives* are sometimes used to form *compound perfectives*. For example, по- may be prefixed to any *potential imperfective* to form a *perfective* verb with the connotation that the action is of *limited duration*, as поноси́ть (pf.) *to carry for a while*, походи́ть (pf.) *to do a bit of walking*, побе́гать (pf.) *to run about for a short time*, &c.

The *potential imperfectives* may be compounded with the prefix с- to form *perfective* verbs that imply motion to a destination, a brief stay, and a speedy return to the point of departure, e.g. сходи́ть as a *perfective* verb means *to go and return again quickly*, hence я схожу́ на по́чту *I'll just slip (pop along) to the post* (sc. *and will be back soon*); similarly, я сбе́гаю за у́гол за хле́бом *I'll run round the corner for some bread*.

---

[1] In the sense of *to flee*, убежа́ть is replaced by бежа́ть in a special perfective use; hence, он бежи́т *he is fleeing* or *he will flee*.

[2] е́хать and е́здить form parallels to идти́ and ходи́ть, e.g.
я е́ду в Ло́ндон *I am travelling to London*
я ка́ждый год е́зжу в СССР *I travel to the U.S.S.R. every year.*

Besides these there are numerous instances of the use of the *potential imperfectives* to form *compound perfectives*; in such cases the corresponding *compound imperfective* is formed not from the *actual imperfective* but by the suffix -ива-, or by some other form. It is to be noticed that several *potential imperfectives* which are themselves intransitive become transitive when compounded with a prefix. For the sake of lucidity the verbs are repeated in full, followed by examples of their compounds:

Imperfective		*Perfective*
нести́ (*actual*)	to carry	понести́
носи́ть (*potential*)	to carry, wear	——
——	to carry, wear for a while	поноси́ть
——	to take (carrying) (and bring back soon)	сноси́ть
сноси́ть	to carry down, away	снести́
приноси́ть	to bring (carrying)	принести́
выноси́ть	to carry out, endure	вы́нести
изна́шивать	to wear out (clothes)	износи́ть
заноси́ть	to bring (when passing)	занести́
зана́шивать	to soil (by constant wear)	заноси́ть
вести́ (*actual*)	to lead, bring (someone) (on foot)	повести́
води́ть (*potential*)	to lead, bring (someone) (on foot)	——
——	to take, lead for a while	поводи́ть
——	to take (and lead back soon)	своди́ть
своди́ть	to lead down, &c.	свести́

Imperfective		*Perfective*
приводи́ть	to bring (leading)	привести́
проводи́ть	to lead through; spend (time)	провести́
провожа́ть	to see off, accompany	проводи́ть
идти́ (actual)	to walk, go (on foot)	пойти́
ходи́ть (potential)	to walk, go (on foot)	——
——	to walk about for a while	походи́ть
походи́ть (на + acc.)	to resemble	——
——	to slip round, pop along	сходи́ть
сходи́ть	to walk down, descend	сойти́
приходи́ть	to arrive (on foot)	прийти́
уходи́ть	to go away (on foot)	уйти́
уха́живать (за + instr.)	to look after; court; toady to	——
——	to exhaust; squander; get rid of (pop.)	уходи́ть
заходи́ть	to call (for or on), pop in	зайти́
——	to begin walking	заходи́ть
е́хать (actual)	to travel, go (not on foot)	пое́хать
е́здить (potential)	to travel, go (not on foot)	——
——	to ride about for a while	пое́здить
——	to pop round (not on foot) and return quickly	съе́здить
съезжа́ть	to descend (not on foot)	съе́хать
приезжа́ть	to arrive (not on foot)	прие́хать
уезжа́ть	to go away (not on foot)	уе́хать
заезжа́ть	to call, pop in (while travelling)	зае́хать

Imperfective		*Perfective*
разъезжа́ть	to travel round (from —— place to place)	
разъезжа́ться	to depart in various directions	разъе́хаться
разъе́зживать	to wear out (road with constant use)	разъе́здить

and somewhat anomalously

| изъезжа́ть | to travel through all parts of, cover the length and breadth of | изъе́здить |

and many others.

Notice also the causative verbs

	выра́щивать	to rear, grow (trans.)	вы́растить
from	расти́	to grow (intr.)	вы́расти
and	пои́ть	to water (animals), give drink	напои́ть
from	пить	to drink	вы́пить

§ 117. Anomalous Verbs

A few simple imperfective verbs have, as compound perfectives corresponding to them in meaning, verbs from other stems; these are:

	Imperfective			*Perfective*
	брать	to take		взять
pres.	беру́		fut.	возьму́
	берёшь			возьмёшь
	бить	to hit		уда́рить
pres.	бью		fut.	уда́рю
	бьёшь			уда́ришь
	класть	to put		положи́ть
pres.	кладу́		fut.	положу́
	кладёшь			поло́жишь

Imperfective		Perfective	
	ловить	*to catch*	поймать
pres.	ловлю́	fut.	пойма́ю
	ло́вишь		пойма́ешь
	говори́ть	*to say, tell*	сказа́ть
pres.	говорю́	fut.	скажу́
	говори́шь		ска́жешь

Several of these verbs have compound perfectives or imperfectives formed from the same stem as well as those given here, but it has so happened that, e.g., the verb сказа́ть has come to be the regular perfective corresponding in meaning to говори́ть; there is a perfective verb поговори́ть, but it means *to have a little talk*, while сказа́ть and говори́ть both mean *to say* or *tell* (говори́ть can also mean *to talk*). It is thus possible to form fuller though incomplete series of these verbs, e.g.

Imperfective		Perfective	
брать	*to take*		
собира́ть	*to collect*	собра́ть	*to collect*
взима́ть	*to levy (money)*	взять	*to take*
бить	*to hit*	поби́ть	*to hit a little*
убива́ть	*to kill*	уби́ть	*to kill*
ударя́ть	*to strike*	уда́рить	*to hit (once), strike*
класть	*to put*		
укла́дывать	*to pack* (trans.)	уложи́ть	*to pack* (trans.)
укла́дываться	*to pack* (intr.)	уложи́ться	*to pack* (intr.)
полага́ть	*to suppose*	положи́ть	{ *to put* / *to suppose* }

Notice the idioms:

полага́ется	*it is customary, fitting, proper*
поло́жим	*let us suppose*

Imperfective		*Perfective*	
лови́ть	*to [try to] catch←*		
нала́вливать	*to catch a lot*	нaлови́ть	*to catch a lot*
	*→*пойма́ть	*to catch*

Cf. the cognate verb:

понима́ть	*to understand*	поня́ть	*to understand, grasp (meaning)*
говори́ть	*to say, tell, talk←*	поговори́ть	*to talk a little*
разгова́ривать	*to converse*		
угова́ривать	*to try to persuade*	уговори́ть	*to persuade*
отгова́ривать	*to try to dissuade*	отговори́ть	*to dissuade*
пригова́ривать	*to sentence*	приговори́ть	*to sentence*
ука́зывать	*to point out*	указа́ть	*to point out*
отка́зывать(ся)	*to refuse*	отказа́ть(ся)	*to refuse*
ока́зываться	*to turn out to be*	оказа́ться	*to turn out to be*
прика́зывать	*to order (action)*	приказа́ть	*to order*
зака́зывать	*to order (goods)*	заказа́ть	*to order*
нака́зывать	*to punish*	наказа́ть	*to punish*
дока́зывать	*to seek to prove*	доказа́ть	*to prove*
пока́зывать	*to show*	показа́ть	*to show*
расска́зывать	*to relate*	рассказа́ть	*to relate*
ска́зывать[1]	*to relate, tell*	*→*сказа́ть	*to tell, say*

[1] Archaic.

Imperfective   *Perfective*

[Cf. ка́жется $\begin{cases} \textit{it seems} \\ \text{sc. } \textit{I think} \end{cases}$

казáлось *it seemed*   показáлось *it seemed, began to*
                                        seem]

Certain verbs have only a perfective aspect, e.g.

очути́ться   *to find oneself suddenly somewhere*
очну́ться   *to regain consciousness; wake up*
состоя́ться   *to take place*

Others have only an imperfective aspect, e.g.

зави́сеть	*to depend*
знáчить	*to mean*
недоумевáть	*to be perplexed, to hesitate*
нуждáться	*to need*
повиновáться	*to submit to*
подлежáть	*to be open to* (e.g. *doubt*)
подражáть	*to imitate*
покрови́тельствовать	*to protect*
предстоя́ть	*to be imminent*
предчýвствовать	*to have a presentiment of*
пресле́довать	*to persecute*
принадлежáть	*to belong*
содержáть	*to contain, maintain*
сожале́ть	*to regret*
состоя́ть	*to consist*
сочýвствовать	*to sympathize*
стóить	*to cost*

Others have only one form, which can be used either
as an imperfective or as a perfective, e.g.

велéть[1]   *to order, command*
жени́ться   *to marry* (with male subject)

[1] Note that не велéть means *to forbid*, e.g. дóктор мне не вел́ел вставáть
the doctor forbad me to get up, ordered me not to get up.

обеща́ть[1]	to promise
ра́нить	to wound
телефони́ровать	to telephone
содéйствовать[2]	to help, further

and many others in -овать.

Some verbs with prefixes, which look perfective, are derived from compound nouns and are simple imperfectives, e.g.

Imperfective		Perfective
разумéется (ра́зум)	it is understood	——
забóтиться (забóта)	to see to, look after	позабóтиться
наслéдовать (наслéдие)	to inherit	унаслéдовать

PREFIXES

§ 118. The following is not intended to be a complete list of all the various meanings and shades of meaning conveyed by the prefixes of verbs, nouns, &c.; an exhaustive list would fill a whole book.

Here only the most important meanings are given, to help the beginner, who is often puzzled by the apparently countless compound words in Russian. It is important to remember that some of the prefixes can be used merely to form the perfective aspect of a simple imperfective verb and that, in many cases besides this, the original idea conveyed by the prefix is barely apparent. On meeting an unfamiliar Russian word it is helpful to cut off the prefix or prefixes; the root (and the meaning) will then often be clear.

---

[1] The form пообеща́ть (pf.) is colloquial.
[2] The perfective is содéйствовать or посодéйствовать.

The majority of Russian verbal prefixes (like those of Latin, German, &c.) are cognate with prepositions expressing closely related notions, but вз-, воз-, вы-, низ-, пере-, пре-, and раз- never occur as prepositions.

без-

(spelt бес- before a voiceless consonant, and безъ- before е, ё, ю, я)

This prefix is cognate with the preposition без *without* and corresponds to the English suffix -*less* and the prefixes *un-*, *in-*, *dis-*, *non-*; it is used in forming adjectives, nouns, and their derivatives, e.g.

безусло́вно	*unconditionally*
бесси́льный	*powerless* (cf. без си́лы)
бесчелове́чность	*inhumanity*
беспарти́йный	*non-party* (in Soviet usage: *not belonging to the Communist Party*)
безде́льничать	*to idle* (cf. без де́ла)
небезуспе́шный	*not [entirely] unsuccessful*

After без- (and the other prefixes ending in a consonant, except меж-, сверх-, and those of foreign origin, like контр-, пан-, транс-, &c.) и becomes ы, e.g.

безымя́нный *anonymous* (cf. и́мя *name*)

The simple prefix без- is mainly used in adjectives; it is very seldom used to form verbs (see обез-) and never forms the perfective of an imperfective verb.

в-

(въ- before е and я; во- in all forms of войти́, before о, before a consonant + ь, and usually before a group of consonants)

1. Indicates motion *into*, e.g.

входи́ть (ipf.), войти́ (pf.) *to walk in, enter*
вход в дом *the entrance to the house*
въезжа́ть (ipf.), въе́хать (pf.) *to drive in, ride in*
ввози́ть (ipf.), ввезти́ (pf.) *to convey in, import*
ввоз са́хара *the importation of sugar*
вставля́ть (ipf.), вста́вить (pf.) *to put in, insert*
влюбля́ться (ipf.), влюби́ться (pf.) *to fall in love*
всма́триваться (ipf.), всмотре́ться (pf.) *to look closely*

Nearly all verbs with в- which express an action are construed with в + acc., e.g.

мы вхо́дим в теа́тр	*we are entering a theatre*
он влюби́лся в неё	*he fell in love with her*
она́ всмотре́лась в карти́ну	*she took a good look at the picture*

The prefix with the opposite meaning is вы-.

2. A limited number of verbs in в- indicate either motion *into* (as in 1, above) or motion *up, on to*. In the latter use they are construed with на + acc., e.g.

ко́шка вле́зла на де́рево *the cat climbed up the tree*

(whereas ко́шка вле́зла в я́щик means *the cat got into the box*).

Such verbs are вбежа́ть *to run up* (or *in*); влезть *to climb up* (or *get in*); втащи́ть *to drag up* (or *in*). These forms are preferred in everyday Russian to взбежа́ть, взлезть, and встащи́ть, which sound bookish. Notice also встава́ть (ipf.), встать (pf.) *to get up* (after lying or sitting).

ВЗ-

(вс- before a voiceless consonant; взо- before й and before some groups of consonants; взъ- before е, ю, я)

1. Indicates motion *up*:

вздёрнуть   *to hitch up*
вздуть   *to blow up, inflate*
всходи́ть   *to ascend* (pf. взойти́)
взлезть   *to climb up*

The verbs взлезть, взбежа́ть *to run up*, встащи́ть *to drag up* are frequently replaced by the forms влезть, вбежа́ть, втащи́ть.

2. This prefix may also denote an *intense* or *thorough* action, as in:

вскрича́ть   *to cry out, shriek*
взмоли́ться   *to beseech, implore*
взбудора́жить *to work up, agitate*
взбеси́ться   *to go mad, get frantic*
вскипе́ть   *to come to the boil*

3. Sometimes its force has been lost, as in:

взять (fut. возьму́) *to take*
вздор   *nonsense*

In roots beginning with и, и changes to ы after вз-, e.g. взыска́ть *to exact* (*a debt*, &c.) from иска́ть *to look for*.

Care must be taken not to confuse this prefix with в- (or во-) in composition with roots beginning with з-, с-.

See also the prefix воз-.

вне- and внутри-

are adverbs used as native prefixes corresponding to Latin *extra-* and *intra-* respectively; they are added to adjectives, as:

внеочередно́е заседа́ние *extraordinary meeting*
внебра́чный   *extra-marital*
внеевропе́йский   *non-European, outside Europe*

вневре́менный	*timeless*
внутри́ве́нная инъе́кция	*intravenous injection*
внутри́заводско́й тра́нспорт	*transport within the factory*

воз-

(вос- before a voiceless consonant)

This prefix, cognate with вз-, is no longer productive. Words with this prefix tend to be bookish or even archaic.

1. Basically, it denotes motion *up*, but it is usually more figurative than вз-:

возводи́ть	*to raise, lift up*
возника́ть	*to arise, crop up*
восхо́д со́лнца	*sunrise*
восто́к	*the east*
воскресе́ние	*resurrection*
воспита́ние	*upbringing, education*
возбужда́ть	*to stir up, rouse*
восста́ние	*uprising, revolt*

2. It may indicate an *intense* action, e.g.

возгоре́ться	*to flare up*
восклица́ние	*exclamation*
восхвали́ть	*to extol*

3. Often it expresses the notion of *restoration* or *return*, and is equivalent to the English *back, again, re-*:

воздержа́ться	*to refrain, abstain*
возвраща́ть	*to give back, return*
возрази́ть	*to retort, reply*
возме́здие	*retribution*
возобнови́ть	*to renew*

4. Sometimes воз- merely makes an imperfective verb perfective, as возненави́деть (pf.) from ненави́деть (ipf.) *to hate*; and occasionally the force of the prefix has been lost, as in возмо́жно *possibly*.

The prefix воз-, вос- should not be confused with the prefix во- before roots beginning with з- and с-.

After воз- и becomes ы: compare име́ть (ipf.) *to possess*, i.e. *have*, with возыме́ть (pf.) *to conceive*, [*begin to*] *have*.

все-

forms 'learned' adjectives, adverbs, and nouns; it corresponds to English *all-* and Latin *omni-*, e.g.

всезна́ющий	*all-knowing, omniscient*
всемогу́щество	*omnipotence*
всевозмо́жный	*all possible, every kind of*
всево́лновый приёмник	*all-wave radio*
всеми́рный	*world[-wide]*
всесою́зный	*of the whole Soviet Union*
всесторо́нне (adv.)	*from every angle, thoroughly*
во всеуслы́шание	*for all to hear, publicly*

вы-

(corresponds to the preposition из + gen. *out of*)

1. Usually indicates motion *out* (Latin *ex-*), e.g.

выходи́ть (ipf.)	} *to go out* (*on foot*)
вы́йти (pf.)	
вы́ход	*way out, exit*
выставля́ть (ipf.)	} *to exhibit*
вы́ставить (pf.)	
вы́ставка	*exhibition*

Verbs of motion with вы- are construed with the preposition из + gen., e.g.

он вы́бежал из ко́мнаты   *he ran out of the room*

2. вы- sometimes indicates the *thoroughness* or *completion* of an action:

вы́здороветь (pf.)	*to get thoroughly well, recover completely*
вы́печься (pf.)	*to be done (thoroughly baked)*
вы́мыть (pf. of мыть)	*to wash (well)*
вы́сечь (pf. of сечь)	*to whip, flog*
вы́пить (pf. of пить)	*to drink (the whole cupful, glassful, &c.)*

3. It may also indicate *achievement of aim*, as in the perfective verbs:

вы́просить	*to get something out of someone (by asking, soliciting)*
вы́молить	*to obtain by entreaties*
вы́держать	*to pass (an examination)*

while with imperfective verbs compounded with вы- the action is repeated or the *aim has not been attained*.

A peculiarity of this prefix in composition with verbs is that when it makes a perfective verb it attracts and holds the stress throughout all forms, whereas the stress remains on the stem of the verb when the compound verb is imperfective, e.g.

Imperfective		*Perfective*
выраба́тывать	*to work out (a plan)*	вы́работать
выезжа́ть	*to drive out, depart*	вы́ехать
вые́зживать	*to break in (a horse)*	вы́ездить

до-

1. Means basically *as far as*.

Verbs of motion with до- are usually construed with the preposition до + gen.

я дочита́л до середи́ны страни́цы *I have read as far as the middle of the page*
она́ не доживёт до ле́та *she will not live till the summer*
он дое́хал до Москвы́ *he reached Moscow*
дохо́д *income*
догово́р *treaty*

2. It may also indicate the *completion of an action that has been interrupted*, or introduce the *amount to be done before the action will be complete*, e.g.

дописа́ть письмо́ *to finish writing a letter* (*already begun*)
допе́йте во́дку *drink up your vodka*
доли́ть ча́шку ча́ем *to fill up a cup* (*still partly full*) *with tea*
оста́лось доплати́ть сто рубле́й *there were 100 roubles left to pay*

3. It denotes the *achievement of the aim* of the action in such perfective verbs as:

я не дозвони́лся [к вам] *I rang* [*you*] *but couldn't get through*
наконе́ц я её* (gen.) добуди́лся *I finally managed to wake her*
достучи́тесь у две́ри *knock until they open the door*
доду́маться до мы́сли *to hit on an idea*

4. In adjectives, до- may correspond to English *pre-*, *ante-* :

довое́нный	*pre-war* (cf. до войны́)
дореволюцио́нный	*pre-revolutionary*
допото́пный	*antediluvian*

5. A compound of до- is

недо-

which expresses *incompleteness* or *deficiency*, and often corresponds to English *under-*. The prefix with the opposite sense is пере- (*over-*).

недовéс	*underweight; giving short weight*
недооцéнивать (ipf.)	*to underestimate*
недоедáть (ipf.)	*to undereat, to eat too little*
недоплатúть (pf.)	*not to pay in full, not pay up*
N.B. по недосмóтру	*by an oversight*

Verbs with недо-[1] are felt to be in the affirmative and are therefore followed by an object in the accusative, not genitive, case:

онú недооцéнивают нáши знáния *they underestimate our knowledge*

Note the difference between

он не дописáл письмá *he didn't finish off the [already partly written] letter*

in which no action takes place, and

он недописáл письмó *he [started but] didn't complete the letter*

in which the action is started but not completed.

еже-

means *every* and is found in a limited number of adjectives (denoting frequency) and their derivatives, e.g.

ежеднéвная газéта	*daily newspaper*
выхóдит ежемéсячно	*issued monthly*
ежегóдник	*annual, year-book*

---

[1] Except недост(ав)áть (more correctly не дост(ав)áть) *to be lacking*.

за-

1. This prefix, like the preposition за, means basically *behind*:

сóлнце захóдит зá гóру *the sun is setting behind the hill*
захóд сóлнца *sunset*
заложи́ть рýки зá спину *to put (cross) one's hands behind one's back*
он запусти́л свои́ делá *he neglected his affairs*
запи́ть пилю́ли водóй *to wash down pills with water*

за- conveys many diverse notions not obviously, but indirectly, connected with this meaning. The most important are:

2. *Beyond, far away, to the wrong place*:

забежáть вперёд   *to run on ahead*
кудá же ты нас завёл?   *where have you brought us?*
мы заéхали сли́шком далекó *we've gone too far*
заслáть письмó   *to misdirect a letter*

3. *To excess, until destruction, exhaustion, or death*:

заки́дывать вопрóсами *to overwhelm with questions*
засéчь   *to flog to death* (cf. вы́сечь *to flog*)
захвали́ть   *to praise to the skies* (cf. похва-ли́ть *to praise*)

Reflexive verbs with the prefix за- often indicate an action that is indulged in *to excess* or until *exhaustion* or a *state of oblivion* is reached:

зарабóтаться *to wear oneself out with work, to work too long*
забéгаться   *to tire oneself out with running*
засидéться   *to sit up very late, sit too long, overstay one's welcome*
замечтáться *to get lost in thought or reverie*
заговори́ться *to lose all sense of time while talking*

4. The action is continued until the object is *covered, closed, filled, stopped up*, or *driven home* (fig.):

зарыть	*to bury*
засыпать	*to* *cover* (surface), *fill up* (hole), *by strewing something*
закрыть	*to close, shut up*
захлопнуть	*to close with a bang, to bang to*
запечатать; заткнуть	*to seal up; to stop up, plug*
забить гвоздь	*to drive a nail home*
забить окно досками	*to board up a window*

The opposite notion (*uncover, open*, &c.) is expressed by от- or раз-.

5. A *short stay* on the way to one's destination:

я зашёл в библиотеку по пути домой *I called* (*stopped*) *at the library on the way home*

он едет в город, завезёт сундук к вам в контору *he's driving to town. He'll drop* (*deliver*) *the trunk at your office*

она зашла к нам вчера *she called* (*dropped in*) *on us yesterday*

or a short stay *in order to collect, fetch*:

заезжай за мной в семь часов *call for me at seven*

This notion of a *quick and brief* action is also to be found in:

записать	*to note, jot down* (cf. писать *to write*)
зарисовать	*to sketch* (cf. рисовать *to draw*)

6. Action *in advance, for the future*:

запас	*stock, store*
заготовить	*to lay in a stock of, stock-pile*
запродажа	*forward sale, advance sale*
заказ	*order* (for goods)
запланировать	*to plan [ahead]* (pf. of планировать)

7. *Gain* as the result of the action:

завоева́ть	*to conquer, win*
за́работок	*earnings, wages*

8. *The start* of the action (with inchoative perfective verbs):

заговори́ть	*to break silence, begin speaking*
закрича́ть	*to start shouting*
засмея́ться	*to burst out laughing*
запла́кать	*to burst into tears*
он заходи́л по ко́мнате	*he began walking up and down the room*

9. *Completion*:

зако́нчить	*to complete, finish*
заверши́ть	*to complete, conclude*
заключи́ть	*to conclude*

10. *Intensifying* the action (used mostly in conversation and becoming more frequent):

запримéтить (pf.)	*to notice, spot*
засня́ть (pf.)	*to film, 'shoot' (a scene)*

11. за- is also used in adjectives and nouns based on the combination of the preposition за (*beyond*) + noun, e.g.

зарубéжный	*foreign* (cf. за рубежо́м *beyond the frontier*)
закули́сный	*back-stage, secret* (cf. за кули́сами)
Закавка́зье	*Transcaucasia* (cf. за Кавка́зом)

из-

(ис- before a voiceless consonant; изъ- before е, ё, ю, я; изо- in all forms of изойти́, before др-, лг-, рв-, гну-, гне-, and before a consonant + ь)

Now mainly used figuratively, из- meant originally *out* and often corresponds to the prefixes *ex-*, *e-* of English

words. Actual motion outwards is usually expressed by
вы-. The prefix with the opposite sense is в- (*inwards*).

1. The original meaning of *out, away* is still easily discerned in:

исхо́д	*outcome, result*
изда́ние	*edition*
исключи́ть	*exclude*
изгна́ть	*drive out, expel*
издо́хнуть	*expire, die*
исте́чь	*run out, expire*

2. из- may indicate *an intense action* that is carried out *all over an area*, as in:

я исходи́л весь лес *I have wandered through every part of the wood*

он изъе́здил весь мир *he has travelled all over the world*

исколо́ть *to prick* (*stab*) *all over*

or is *carried to the highest degree*, as in:

измя́ть	*to crumple thoroughly* (cf. смять)
изби́ть	*to beat up, beat unconscious*
изукра́сить	*to adorn lavishly*
изруга́ть	*to revile* (cf. вы́ругать *to abuse*)
изно́шенный	*worn out, threadbare*

or *until the object is exhausted*, as in:

изму́чить	*to wear out, exhaust* (someone)
исписа́ть	*to use up* (paper, ink, &c.) *by writing*
исписа́ться	*to write oneself out, exhaust inspiration* (colloq.)
измота́ться	*to wear oneself out, be fagged out* (colloq.)

3. It is found in many verbs denoting *distortion*:

искриви́ть	*to bend, distort*
искале́чить	*to cripple*
изуро́довать	*to disfigure*

исказ́ить	to *distort*
изув́ечить	to *maim*
изврат́ить	to *pervert*

4. Certain reflexive verbs with из- are used in colloquial speech to indicate the *degeneration* of the subject into an antisocial mode of life:

излен́иться	to *grow incorrigibly lazy*
исхулиѓаниться	to *become a rowdy*
изворов́аться	to *turn to stealing, become a confirmed thief*

5. Sometimes из- merely makes a perfective out of an imperfective verb:

| расх́одовать, израсх́одовать | to *spend, expend* |
| нас́иловать, изнас́иловать | to *coerce, rape* |

After the prefix из-, и becomes ы:

| Compare | исќать | to *seek* |
| with | изысќать | to *seek out, find* |

лже-

corresponds to the Greek prefix *pseudo-* and English *false, mock*; it forms adjectives and nouns and their derivatives:

лжѐна́учный	*pseudo-scientific*
лжѐсвид́етель (*m.*)	*false witness*
лжѐприс́яга	*perjury*

меж- (межъ- before e, ё, ю, я) and между-

are prefixed mainly to adjectives and are equivalent to *inter-*:

междунар́одный	*international*
междуц́арствие	*interregnum*
мѐжплан́етный	*interplanetary*
мѐжзаводсќой	*inter-factory*

на-

1. Indicates motion *on to* something:

нае́хать на сте́ну, на ма́льчика	*drive into a wall, run over a boy*
находи́ть(+ acc.)	*to find* (lit. *to come upon*)
напа́сть на врага́	*to fall on, attack the enemy*
накле́ить ма́рку на конве́рт	*to stick a stamp on an en-velope*
накры́ть [на] стол	*to lay a table*
наде́ть костю́м	*to put on a suit*
насле́дник	*heir, successor*
настоя́щий	*present, actual, real*

or an action taking place *on* something:

на стёклах намёрз лёд *ice formed on the window-panes*

2. In a verb followed by the genitive, на- can convey the idea of *much, many* of the object(s):

мы нарва́ли цвето́в	*we picked a great many flowers*
я накупи́л ма́сла	*I bought a great deal of butter*
ты наде́лал оши́бок	*you made a lot of mistakes*

3. на- may also point to the fact that the action has been *indulged in to a high degree*, until the subject is *satisfied* or *weary*:

нае́сться	*to eat a lot, to eat one's fill*
ненасы́тный	*insatiable*
нарабо́таться	*to work a great deal, until weary*
ненагля́дный	*that one cannot feast one's eyes on long enough, enchantingly beautiful*

or that the action has been done *thoroughly* or *excessively*:

натопи́ть	*to heat (stoke) well* (cf. потопи́ть *heat a little, for a while*)
насоли́ть	*to salt [too] well* (cf. посоли́ть *to salt*)

4. A few verbs with the prefix на- denote an action which is *done lightly, incompletely, not properly*, as:

    напева́ть   *to hum, sing softly*
    наи́грывать *to strum out a tune*

5. Like many other prefixes, на- may simply make an imperfective verb perfective without otherwise adding to the meaning:

писа́ть, написа́ть	*to write*
рисова́ть, нарисова́ть	*to draw*
проро́чить, напроро́чить	*to prophesy*
бедоку́рить, набедоку́рить	*to cause trouble*

6. In a few adjectives на- has full prepositional force, as e.g.:

насто́льный те́ннис (cf. те́ннис на столе́) *table tennis*
назе́мные войска́ (cf. войска́ на земле́) *ground forces*

над-

(надъ- before е, ё, ю, я; надо- before рв-, and before a consonant+ ь)

1. The primary meaning of *over* (Latin *super-*) is found in only a few words, e.g.

надсма́тривать(+ над/за + instr.)	
надзира́ть(+ за + instr.)	*to supervise, control*
надсмо́тр, надзо́р	*supervision*
на́дпись *(f.)*	*inscription, sign-board*
надгро́бие	*epitaph*
надзе́мный	*above ground, elevated*

2. An extension of this meaning is found in certain transitive verbs, where над- adds the idea of increasing the size of the object by *adding an extra piece*:

надстро́ить дом	to extend a building (upwards)
надстро́ить эта́ж	to build on an extra storey
надстро́йка	superstructure
надда́ть	to add, increase
надши́ть простыню́	to sew an extra piece on to a sheet

3. над- may also indicate that the action is *slight* and affects only the surface of the object:

| надкуси́ть | to nibble (cf. покуса́ть to bite) |
| надломи́ть | to crack, fracture (cf. сломи́ть to break) |

небез-

see без-

недо-

see до-

низ-

(also низо-, нис-)

is an unproductive prefix, found in rhetorical, archaic, and obsolescent words only. Its meaning (*down*) is now expressed by the prefix c-.

низве́ргнуть	to cast down; overthrow
(cf. modern све́ргнуть)	
нисходи́ть	to go down, descend
(cf. modern сходи́ть)	

The only widely used words with this prefix are:

| снисходи́ть | to condescend |
| (pf. снизойти́) | |

and its derivatives, which have the two prefixes c- (*with*) and низ-.

o- and об-

(обо- before й; объ- before e, ё, ю, я; о-, об-, or обо- before groups of consonants)

This prefix, with primary meaning *round*, imparts many shades of meaning to the action of the root verb:

1. Motion *round* the outside of the object, or the *encirclement* of the object by something:

проводни́к обвёл нас вокру́г боло́та *a guide led us round the marsh*

мы обошли́ препя́тствие *we went round (avoided) the obstacle*

она́ обвяза́ла го́лову платко́м *she wrapped a kerchief round her head*

он обсади́л дом дере́вьями *he planted trees round his house*

необходи́мый *essential, unavoidable*

Extensions of this sense are (*a*) that of forming an *envelope* or *coating* round or on something:

оку́тать ребёнка одея́лом	*to wrap (envelop) a child in a blanket*
окле́ить ко́мнату обо́ями	*to paper a room*
обледене́ть	*to become covered with ice, ice over*
обрами́ть карти́ну	*to frame a picture (cf. ра́ма frame)*

(*b*) that of *removing the outer surface* of the object:

очи́стить апельси́н	*to peel an orange*
ободра́ть себе́ ко́жу	*to graze one's skin*

and (*c*) that of the *waste* that remains when the best has been taken away:

оку́рок	*cigarette-end, cigar stub*
огры́зок (я́блока)	*core (of an eaten apple)*
очи́стки, опи́лки, обре́зок	*peelings, filings, a scrap*

2. o- and об- with verbs of motion may stress the fact that the action covers *the whole* of the object, e.g.

молвá обошлá весь гóрод	*the rumour went round the town*
он объéздил странý	*he has toured the whole country*
я обéгал мнóгих друзéй	*I called on (ran round to) many friends*

Some verbs of motion with об- (or обо-) can indicate the action of *overtaking*:

обогнáть	*to overtake*
обскакáть	*to overtake at a gallop, gallop by*

This prefix may also correspond to English *over-* in the sense of doing an action *to excess*:

обкормúть	*to overfeed*
объéсться	*to overeat*
опúться	*to drink to excess*

3. A word with the prefix o- or об- may denote a *mistaken, wrong* action (reflexive verbs):

оговорúться	*to make a slip of the tongue*
опечáтка	*a misprint*
обсчитáться	*miscalculate*

or a *fraudulent* action (transitive verbs):

обсчитáть покупáтеля	*to cheat a customer* (in calculating)
обвéс *short weight*	обмáн *deception, fraud*

4. A verb formed from a noun and having this prefix (usually in the form o- unless a vowel follows) may denote that the object is equipped with something:

оборýдовать фáбрику	*to equip a factory* (cf. орýдие *tool*)
остеклúть окнó	*to glaze a window* (cf. стеклó *glass*)

5. Verbs formed from nouns and adjectives by means of this prefix (usually in the form o-) denote the actions of *making* the object (with transitive verbs) and *becoming*

(with reflexive verbs) imbued with a certain quality or characteristic:

обогати́ть	*to enrich* (transitive)
обогати́ться	*to become rich* (reflex.)
освободи́ть	*to set free, liberate*
объясни́ть	*to make clear, explain*
олицетвори́ть	*to personify*

6. Many simple verbs form their perfective aspects by adding о-, as

бедне́ть, обедне́ть	*to become poor*
сле́пнуть, осле́пнуть	*to go blind*

Note: (1) after the prefix об- и becomes ы; compare иска́ть *to seek* with о́быск *search*.

(2) The form обо- is used in all parts of обойти́ and usually before groups of two or more consonants.

(3) The form объ- is used before roots beginning with е, ё, ю, я.

обез-

(обес- before a voiceless consonant)

This is a compound prefix, made up of о + без-; it is used to make verbs, participles, and verbal nouns from nouns. The resulting compounds often correspond to English words with the prefixes *dis-* and *de-*. The stress is always on the root.

Verbs with the suffixes -ить (pf.) and -ивать (ipf.) are transitive and denote that their object is deprived of the thing indicated by the root; whereas verbs with the suffix -еть (pf.) are intransitive and denote the loss by the subject of the thing indicated by the root. For example:

from си́ла *strength* are formed:

обесси́ли(ва)ть	*to deprive of strength, make weak, weaken*
обесси́леть	*to lose strength, grow weak, weaken*

from оружие *weapon*, cf. вооружить *to arm*, are formed:

      обезоружи(ва)ть   *to disarm (someone)*

but *disarmament* is разоружение;

from вода *water* are derived:

      обезвоживать (ipf.) ⎱
                      ⎰ *to dehydrate*
      обезводить (pf.)

от-

(отъ- before е, ё, ю, я; ото- in all forms of отойти, before certain groups of consonants, and before a consonant + ь)

1. Indicates *departure*, motion *away* from a position near or at an object (compare the prefix у-, which connotes complete removal and disappearance), e.g.

он отошёл в сторону *he moved [away] to one side, aside*
она отходила от окна *she was walking away from the window*
перед нашим отъездом *before our departure, before we left*
отложить *to put off, postpone*
он в отставке *he is retired (in retirement)*
отказ *refusal*, отказаться *to refuse*

2. Indicates motion *back*, usually figuratively, and often corresponds to *re-* in English words, e.g.

    отобьём атаку   *we'll repel the attack*
    отвергнуть предложение *to reject a proposal*
    отражать свет   *to reflect light*
    ответить на письмо   *to reply to a letter*

3. Denotes the action of *opening, undoing,* or *detaching,* e.g.

    открыть дверь   *to open a door*
    откупорить бутылку   *to uncork a bottle*
    отвинтить гайку   *to unscrew a nut*

оторва́ть часть от . . .   *to tear [off] a piece from . . .*
отде́л, отделе́ние   *division, department*

4. May sometimes indicate the *completion* of the action, as

дере́вья отцвели́ *the trees have finished blossoming*
я отобе́дал *I have had (finished) dinner*

or may merely turn an imperfective verb into its perfective counterpart, e.g.

отомсти́ть (pf. of мстить) врагу́ *to take vengeance on an*
enemy

5. In some words the force of от- has been more or less lost, e.g.

отва́га   *bravery, daring*
отчёт   *report*
отноше́ние *relation, attitude*

6. от- is used in 'learned' adjectives based on the combination of preposition от + noun, as:

отглаго́льное существи́тельное *deverbal noun* (i.e. *formed from a verb*, cf. от глаго́ла)

N.B. In roots beginning with и, this vowel changes into ы after от-, as:

отыгра́ться (from игра́ть) *to win back one's losses*

пере-

This prefix closely corresponds to the preposition чѐрез and indicates:

1. Motion *across* or *through* an object, or *from one (place, &c.) to another* (English *trans-*); in the sense of *across* it may be followed by the direct acc. or by чѐрез + acc.:

переходи́ть [чѐрез] у́лицу   *to walk across, to cross the street*
перепры́гнуть [чѐрез]   *to jump over a rope*
верёвку

перепилить бревно	*to saw through a beam*
пересесть	*to change* (seats, trains, &c.)
перенести на другое место	*to transfer to another place*
перевод на русский язык	*Russian translation*

2. An action *repeated* (English *re-*):

передержать экзамен	*to re-sit an examination*
перестройка	*reconstruction*
перечитать письмо	*to re-read a letter*

or an action performed by or on *many objects in turn*:

я перечитал все эти книги *I've read through all these books*
они все переболели гриппом *they all caught 'flu* [*in turn*]

3. An action *excessive* in length or intensity (English *over-*):

пережарить мясо	*to overcook meat*
переутомиться	*to overtire oneself, overwork*
переоценить	*to overestimate*
передержать	*to keep too long*
он всех перекричал	*he shouted them all down*

4. A *reciprocal* action (in reflexive verbs):

мы регулярно переписываемся *we correspond regularly*
мы перессорились с ними *we have fallen out with them*
они переглянулись *they exchanged glances*

5. An action continued *over a fixed period*:

он переночевал у нас *he spent the night at our house*
мы переждали дождь *we waited till the rain stopped*

по-

по- as a true prefix is linked in meaning not with the preposition по, but with the по- of the comparatives, like поменьше *just a little less* (see § 58); it limits the action in

some way and is thus a very common way of forming a
perfective from an imperfective verb. Its main uses are:

1. To show that the action is completed *at one go*:

посмотре́ть *to take a look [at]*
постуча́ть *to knock (give several raps on one occasion)* (cf.
  сту́кнуть *to rap once*)

2. To emphasize the *result* of the action:

я пообе́дал *I have had (some) dinner*
они́ побели́ли потоло́к *they have whitewashed the ceiling*
его́ похорони́ли вчера́ *he was buried yesterday*
она́ погаси́ла свет *she put out the light*

3. To indicate the *commencement* of the action:

мы пошли́ домо́й *we set off home*
я карти́ну наконе́ц полюби́л *I've at last got to like ('taken
 to', 'fallen for') the picture*

4. To denote that the action is done only *for a while*:

мы порабо́тали и пото́м легли́ *we worked for a while
 and then lay down*
поговори́ть *to have a chat*
он походи́л в саду́ *he walked about for a while in the
 garden*

or done only a little, *slightly*:

 попу́дрить   *to powder lightly* (cf. напу́дрить)
 поцара́пать *to scratch slightly* (cf. исцара́пать)

5. To indicate that the action is *repeated at intervals* (verbs
with the suffix -ыва-/-ива-):

 поку́ривать   *to smoke from time to time*
 пои́грывать в ка́рты *to play cards now and again*

6. To show that the action affects separately several objects or subjects:

он побросáл монéты на стол *he threw the coins on the table* (sc. *one at a time*)

гóсти порассказáли о своих переживáниях *the guests told about their experiences* (sc. *spoke one after another*)

7. по- is also used in forming words based on the combination of preposition по + noun, as

посильный	*feasible, within one's ability* (cf. по силам)
почáсная оплáта	*payment by the hour* (cf. по часáм)
поминýтно (adv.)	*frequently, by the minute*
побережье	*coastal area, seaboard* (cf. по берегу)
Повóлжье	*Volga region, land along the Volga*
посмéртный	*posthumous* (cf. по смéрти (loc.) *after death*)

под-

(подъ- before е, ё, ю, я; подо- in all forms of подойти, before most groups of consonants, and before a consonant + ь)

This prefix corresponds partially to the preposition под *under*; it denotes:

1. The placing of one thing *under* another:

подстáвить	*to place underneath; substitute*
подписка	*subscription*
подóшва	*sole of shoe* (lit. *sewn under*)
подчеркнýть	*to underline, emphasize*
подозрéние	*suspicion*

sometimes no motion is implied:

подразумевáть	*to imply*

Note that in по́длый (по́длость) *base* (*baseness*), под is the root.

2. Motion *upwards*:

поддержа́ть	*to hold up, support*
подня́тие	*raising, lifting up*
подорва́ть	*to blow up, demolish*

3. *Approach*:

подходи́ть, подойти́ [к + dat.] *to approach, draw near* [*to*]
он подбежа́л ко мне   *he ran up to me*

4. *Supplementation* (followed by the gen. of the thing added):

поддли́ть воды́ в стака́н   *to pour more water into the glass*
подбро́сить у́гля в пе́чку   *to put more coal on the fire* (*stove*)
подвинти́ть га́йку   *to screw a nut up tighter*

5. An action affecting *only a part* (usually the lower part) of an object, or affecting the whole object *only slightly*:

подгоре́лый	*slightly burnt; burnt underneath*
подмо́кнуть	*to get wet underneath*
поды́гривать	*to play lightly, accompany*

6. An action done *in secret*:

подслу́шивать	*to eavesdrop, overhear*
подкарау́лить	*to lie in wait for*

or *in imitation*:

подража́ть(+ dat.)	*to imitate*
подде́льный	*counterfeit, forged*
подкра́сить	*to dye, tint*

7. The name of a *subdivision*:

подотде́л, подразде́л	*subdivision, subsection*
подкомите́т	*subcommittee*
подполко́вник	*lieutenant-colonel*

8. Used to form words based on the combination of preposition под + noun, e.g.

подво́дная ло́дка	*submarine*
подру́чный	*any available* (cf. под руко́й *at hand*)
подборо́док	*chin* (lit. *thing under beard*)
Подмоско́вье	*environs of Moscow* (cf. под Москво́й near Moscow)

N.B. In roots commencing with и, и changes into ы after под-, e.g. подыто́жить *to sum up* (cf. ито́г *total*).

после-

means *after*, e.g.

по̀слереволюцио́нный	*post-revolutionary*
послеобе́денные ре́чи	*after-dinner speeches*
послесло́вие	*epilogue*
послеза́втра	*the day after tomorrow*

пра-

This prefix is used mostly with nouns of kinship:

праба́бушка	*great-grandmother*
прапра́внук	*great-great-grandson*
пра́деды	*forefathers, ancestors*
праязы́к	*parent language, Ursprache*
прароди́на	*original homeland*

пре-

This prefix is the Old Church Slavonic equivalent of the Russian пере- and is no longer used to form new compounds. It is found in numerous Russian words, mostly of a literary nature, in which its basic meaning of *across* is employed in figurative senses.

It is used chiefly to indicate:

1. A change of state (*across*, *trans-*) or a *barrier*:

превратить во́ду в лёд	*to turn (change) water into ice*
преобразова́ние	*transformation*
преда́ть	*to hand over; to betray*
преступле́ние	*transgression, crime*
препя́тствие	*obstacle, hindrance*
преде́л	*limit*

2. An excessive action (*beyond*):

преувели́чить	*to exaggerate*
превы́сить	*to exceed*
преиму́щество	*advantage, priority*

or a high degree of a quality (*most, very*):

прекра́сный	*beautiful, fine*
преспоко́йно	*very calmly, imperturbably*

compare also престо́л *throne* (from стол, formerly *seat*).

For the use of пре- to intensify adjectives see § 59.

3. An action cutting short another action (*off, through*):

прерва́ть	*to interrupt*
прекрати́ть	*to stop, cut short*

4. The force of пре- has often become greatly weakened or lost, as in:

презира́ть	*to despise*
пре́лесть (*f.*)	*charm*

пред-

(предъ- before е, ё, ю, я)

1. As a pure prefix, пред- is no longer productive but is still found in many rather bookish words, with the meaning

before, in front of, or *in advance* (cf. Latin *pre-*), e.g.

предсказа́ть	*to foretell, predict*
предста́вить	*to present*
предупреди́ть	*to forewarn*
предопределе́ние	*predetermination*
предго́рье (sing.)	*foothills*

2. пред- is still a productive prefix in literary adjectives based on the combination of the preposition пѐред+noun:

предвы́борная речь [*pre-*]*election speech* (cf. пѐред вы́борами)

предобе́денная прогу́лка *a stroll before dinner* (cf. пѐред обе́дом)

N.B. In roots beginning with и, и changes into ы after пред-, e.g.

предыду́щий	*foregoing, previous*
предысто́рия	*pre-history*

при-

corresponds to the preposition при+loc. (*near*); but since verbs with при- usually express motion, this prefix is closer in sense to the preposition к + dat. (*towards*), which in fact often follows such verbs. It often corresponds to the Latin prefix *ad-* (*ac-, ap-, ar-, at-,* &c.) in English words.

при- may denote:

1. *Arrival* at a destination, or motion *in the direction of the speaker*:

он прие́хал в Москву́ вчера́	*he arrived in Moscow yesterday*
она́ ча́сто прихо́дит к нам	*she often comes to* [*see*] *us*
прибы́тие, прихо́д, прие́зд	*arrival*
пришли́те мне кни́гу	*send me the book*
прибли́зиться (к + dat.)	*to approach, draw near* (*to*)
приглаше́ние	*invitation*
привлека́тельный	*attractive*

also figuratively:

прибе́гнуть к + dat.   *to resort to*
при́быль (*ʃ*.)   *gain, profit*

2. The action of *attaching* one thing to another:
приба́вить [к + dat.] *to add [to]*
приши́ть пу́говицу к ку́ртке *to sew a button on a jacket*
приписа́ть кни́гу не тому́ а́втору *to ascribe a book to the*
wrong author
note also: при́город *suburb*

3. That the action is *incomplete* or of *short duration*:
привста́ть   *to raise oneself* (*a little* or *for a while*)
прихва́рывать *to feel rather unwell*
приумо́лкнуть *to become silent for a short time*

4. That the action *accompanies the main activity*; such verbs
usually have the suffix -ыва-/-ива-.
притáптывать   *to beat time to something with one's*
feet
он шёл, присви́стывая *he whistled as he walked along*
note also: при́вкус   *after-taste, tang*

5. при- is found also in adjectives based on the combination of the preposition при + noun, e.g.
примо́рский   *maritime, seaside* (cf. при мо́ре)
привокза́льная пло́щадь *station square* (cf. при вокза́ле)
придво́рный шут   *court jester* (cf. при дворе́ *at court*)

6. In many words the force of при- has been lost or
weakened:
при́говор   *sentence, verdict*
прибау́тка *facetious saying*
прибо́р   *device*

про-

is nearer in sense to the prepositions сквозь and чѐрез than to the preposition про. The basic meaning (*through*) can be detected in most of its uses, the chief of which denote:

1. Motion *through* (including the idea of making *a hole through*):

со́лнце проглянýло из-за туч *the sun peeped through the clouds*

он проре́зал дырý в коро́бке *he cut a hole in the box*

она́ прошла́ в кýхню *she went [through] to the kitchen*

мы прошли́ э́ту кни́гу *we have gone through (studied) this book*

мы прое́хали по́ мосту (по́д мостом) *we went over (under) the bridge*

мы прошли́ 15 киломе́тров *we covered (walked) 15 km.*

часы́ проби́ли пять часо́в *the clock has struck five*

прока́шляться *to clear one's throat*

промо́кнуть до после́дней ни́тки *to get wet through (soaked to the skin)*

провари́ть (промы́ть, пропе́чь) *to boil (wash, bake) thoroughly*

2. The expenditure of *a definite time* on some activity:

он простоя́л це́лый час на углý *he stood a whole hour at the corner*

она́ проспала́ всю ночь *she slept the whole night through*

3. *Loss* or the expenditure of money:

проигра́ть [10 рубле́й] *to lose [10 roubles]* (at a game, &c.)

он про́пил всю зарпла́ту *he spent all his wages on drink*

4. Motion *past* an object:

я проходи́л ми́мо теа́тра *I was walking past the theatre*

бо́ли ско́ро пройдýт *the pains will soon pass (be over)*

мы прое́хали ва́шу ýлицу *we missed your street (drove past by mistake)*

5. A *mistaken* action:

> просчита́ться *to miscalculate*
> промахну́ться *to miss the mark*

6. The *unintentional disclosure* of a secret:

> проговори́ться *to let the cat out of the bag*

7. The *completion* of the action (forming perfective):

> я прочита́л кни́гу *I have finished reading the book*
> он продиктова́л письмо́ *he has dictated the letter*

N.B. про- in such words as про̀англи́йский *pro-British*, про̀неме́цкий *pro-German* has, of course, been borrowed from Latin; see the paragraph on borrowed prefixes (pp. 390–1).

противо-

This prefix, corresponding to the preposition про́тив *against*, is found mostly in adjectives, which frequently correspond to English words with *anti-*, *contra-*, and *counter-*, e.g.

противозако́нный посту́пок	*illegal act* (cf. про́тив зако́на)
противообще́ственное поведе́ние	*antisocial behaviour*
противоде́йствовать(+ dat.)	*to counteract*
противоре́чие	*contradiction; opposite*
противога́з	*gas-mask*

раз-

(рас- before a voiceless consonant; разъ- before е, ё, ю, я ; разо- in all forms of разойти́, before most groups of consonants, and before a consonant + ь; ро́з-/ро́с- when stressed)

1. The basic idea expressed by this prefix (to which there

is no corresponding preposition) is that of *scattering*, i.e. motion in various directions from one point; the thing(s) over which the object is thus distributed is (are) often found in the dative case after по. For example:

он разбросáл вéщи пó столу *he scattered the things about (all over) the table*

я развéшал картúны по стенáм *I have hung pictures on the walls*

онá расстáвила кнúги по пóлкам *she arranged (put) the books on their [correct] shelves*

разлéйте чай по чáшкам *pour out the tea into the cups*

раздáть (он рóздал) *to distribute (he distributed)*

распространúться (на + acc.) *to spread (to), affect*

расхóды *expenses, outgoings*

2. Natural extensions of use 1 are the ideas of *splitting*, or otherwise *dividing* (English *dis-*), and of *taking apart, untying, disclosing* the contents, *removing* (English *un-*), &c.:

разделúть	*to divide, share*
разбúть	*to smash, break to pieces*
разорвáть	*to tear apart*
развязáть ýзел	*to untie a knot* (cf. связáть *to tie*)
разгрузúть	*to unload* (cf. нагрузúть *to load*)
развернýть пакéт	*to unwrap a parcel* (cf. завернýть *to wrap*)
раздé(вá)ться	*to undress* (intr.)
развúтие	*development* (lit. *unwinding*)
рóспуск парлáмента	*dissolution of parliament*
разочарóванный	*disappointed*

3. раз- may also stress the *intensity* of the action:

разобúдеть *to offend greatly* (cf. обúдеть *to offend*)

разгорéться *to flare up* (cf. горéть *to burn*)

compare also рáзум *intellect* with ум *mind*,

and раскрасáвица моя́ *my beauty* (used in folk-songs and popular language) with красáвица, the normal word for *beautiful woman*; or it may stress the *thoroughness* of the action:

рассмотрéть	*to examine, scrutinize*
расспрóс	*interrogation*
расслы́шать	*to make out (catch) what was said*

N.B. In stems beginning with и, и changes into ы after раз-, e.g.

разы́скивать	*to make a thorough search for*
рóзыск	*investigation* (cf. искáть *to look for*)

с-

(съ- before e, ё, ю, я; со- in all forms of сойти́, before most groups of consonants, before a consonant+ь, and usually in uses 7, 8, and 9, below)

This prefix corresponds both to the preposition с+gen. (*from*) and to с+instr. (*with*); it can indicate:

1. Motion from being at a position 'на', i.e. motion *off* a surface, or else *down* to a lower position, as:

сходи́ть/ сойти́	*to go down, descend*
сбрить бóроду	*to shave off a beard*
стерéть мел с доски́	*to rub chalk off the blackboard*
слезáть/ слезть [с]	*to get (climb) down [from]*

2. Abstract (or indeterminate) simple verbs of motion can take the prefix с- and become perfective; they then indicate *motion to a place followed by a speedy return* to the point of departure, e.g.

он сбéгал в магази́н за винóм *he popped along to the shop for some wine*

я схожу́ навéрх за перчáтками *I'll slip upstairs for my gloves*

3. The action of *copying*:

| спи́сывать/ списа́ть | *to copy (by writing)* |
| срисо́вывать/ срисо-ва́ть | *to copy (by drawing)* |

4. The action of *joining, bringing together*:

скрепи́ть (скле́ить)	*to fasten (stick) together*
связа́ть (сшить)	*to tie (sew) together*
соедини́ть	*to unite*
сосредото́чить	*to concentrate*

or of *coming together*:

| собра́ться, съе́хаться | *to assemble, meet* |
| стече́ние | *confluence* |

5. A *reciprocal* action:

сговори́ться [с] *to come to an arrangement [with]*
мы спи́шемся об э́том *we'll settle that by letter*
они́ созвони́лись *they arranged it by 'phone*
мы снесли́сь друг с дру́гом *we got in touch with one another*

6. *Completion* of the action (forming pf. from simple ipf. verb):

мы э́то сде́лали	*we have done it*
они́ соста́рились	*they have grown old*
она́ сжа́рит мя́со	*she will roast the meat*

7. A *contention* (usually со-):

| соревнова́ние, состяза́ние | *competition* |
| сопротивля́ться+dat. | *to resist* |

8. A *comparison* (usually со-):

сравне́ние	*comparison*
соизмери́мый [с]	*commensurable [with]*
соотве́тствовать+dat.	*to correspond to*

9. An action *accompanying* that of another (usually co-):

сопровождáть	*to accompany, attend*
сочýвствовать+dat.	*to sympathize with*
сосуществовáние	*co-existence*
соáвтор	*co-author*
сослужи́вец	*colleague, fellow employee*

N.B. In roots commencing with и, и becomes ы after с-, e.g.

сыгрáть (pf.) *to play* (cf. игрáть, ipf.)

само-

is derived from сам *oneself* and corresponds to the English *self-*, Latin *auto-*; it is found in hundreds of Russian nouns and adjectives and their derivatives, as :

самозащи́та	*self-defence*
самовнушéние	*auto-suggestion*
самодовóльный	*self-satisfied*
самоцéль (*f.*)	*an end in itself*
самохóдный	*self-propelled*
самолёт	*aeroplane, aircraft*
самоýчка	*self-taught person*
самоувéренно	*self-confidently*
самоуправлéние	*self-government*
самодéржец	*autocrat*
самобы́тность	*originality*
самовóлие	*licence*
самогóн	*home-made spirits*

сверх-

(сверхъ- before е, ё, ю, я)

The adverb сверх is used as a prefix corresponding to Latin *super-*, e.g.

сверхъесте́ственный	*supernatural*
сверхзвуковы́е ско́рости	*supersonic speeds*
сверхмо́щный генера́тор	*high-power generator*
сверхчелове́к	*superman*
сверхпла́новое произ- во́дство	*production in excess of what was planned*

у-

This prefix is closer in sense to the prepositions из and от than to the preposition у; it may indicate:

1. Motion *away*, including the notion of complete removal or disappearance:

он ушёл от отца́ *he left (went away from) his father* (or
 his father's house)
они́ уе́дут из Москвы́ *they will go away from Moscow*
мы улете́ли во Фра́нцию *we flew off to France*
меня́ увели́ в теа́тр *they took (led) me off to the theatre*

also figuratively:

указа́ть	*to indicate, point out, point (to)*
уговори́ть	*to persuade*

2. *Reduction* in size (*down*):

уре́зать (pf.)	*to cut down, curtail*
мя́со ужа́рилось	*the meat has shrunk (in the roasting)*

3. *Exhaustion, fatigue*:

утоми́ть(ся)	*to tire, fatigue (oneself)*
уста́ть	*to get tired, to tire (intr.)*
уе́здить (ука́тать) ло́- шадь (popular)	*to tire out a horse*

4. Action performed *despite difficulties*:

удержа́ть	*to retain, hold on to*

он устоя́л пе́ред искуше́нием *he stood firm against (resisted) temptation*

он не усиди́т мину́тки *he can't sit still a minute*

5. The action of *settling*:

улёчься *to lie down, settle, subside*
устро́иться *to establish oneself, settle down*

6. *Accommodation*:

уложи́ть, упакова́ть *to pack* (trans.)
умести́ть *to find room for, get in* (trans.)
уписа́ться *to go in (word on line or page)*

7. The *fullness of scope* of the action:

уста́вить по́лку кни́гами *to set out (fill) a shelf with books*
уста́вить все кни́ги на по́лку *to set out (put) all the books on a shelf*
луг усе́ян маргари́тками *the meadow is dotted [all over] with daisies*

8. y- forms verbs from adjectives, with the meaning *to make*+adj.:

улу́чшить *to make better, improve* (cf. лу́чше)
уме́ньшить *to reduce* (cf. ме́ньше)
упрости́ть *to simplify* (cf. просто́й)

9. y- turns some verbs (mainly verbs of perception) perfective:

уви́деть (pf. of ви́деть) *to catch sight of, begin to see*
узна́ть (pf. of знать) *to find out, get to know*

10. The force of y- has often weakened or been lost, as in:

ухо́д за больны́ми *care of the sick*
умере́ть *to die*
удо́бный *convenient, comfortable*
узнава́ть (pf. узна́ть) *to recognize*

чрез- and через-

(before a voiceless consonant: черес-, чрес-)

correspond to the preposition че́рез (*across, beyond*); they are used mainly in adjectives, as:

чрезвыча́йный	*extraordinary*
чрезме́рный	*excessive*
чересчу́р (adv.)	*excessively, too* . . .

BORROWED PREFIXES

Just as suffixes of foreign origin, like -ист and -ация, form new words with purely Russian stems, so some internationally used prefixes of Latin, Greek, and French origin are now sometimes combined with Russian words to form new nouns, adjectives, adverbs, and verbs, in which these prefixes bear, or may bear, a secondary stress. As their meaning is generally quite clear, a few examples will suffice:

а̀виапо́чта	*air-mail*
а̀виасъёмка	*aerial survey*
авиано́сец	*aircraft carrier*
автомаши́на	*motor vehicle*
а̀вторучка	*fountain pen*
антисове́тский	*anti-Soviet*
а̀нтинау́чный	*unscientific*
архиплу́т	*arch-rogue, thorough scoundrel*
а̀рхиопа́сный	*highly dangerous*
дешифрова́ть	*to decipher*
ѝнфракра́сный	*infra-red*
ква̀зиучёный	*quasi-scientist*
кѝноплёнка	*cine-film*
кѝнозвезда́	*film star*
ко̀нтрразве́дка	*counter-espionage service*
ко̀нтрга́йка	*lock-nut*

мо̀толо́дка	*motor boat*
мо̀топехо́та	*motorized infantry*
па̀нславя́нский	*pan-Slav*
про̀сове́тский	*pro-Soviet*
псѐвдонау́чный	*pseudo-scientific*
ра̀диово́лны	*radio waves*
сỳперобло́жка	*book wrapper, dust-cover*
ỳльтракоро́ткий	*ultra-short*
э̀кс-коро́ль	*ex-king*
э́кстренный	*special, extra*

INTERJECTIONS

§ 119.

(*a*) Sounds

a! *ah! oh!* (pain, surprise, horror), *oh, well!* (resignation)

o! *oh!* (address, wish, reproach, surprise, regret)

y! *oh!* (reproach, threat, fear)

э! *oh! well, then!* (objection, disbelief, determination)

ax! àx-áx! *ah! oh!* (surprise, joy, regret, reproach)

ox! òx-óx! *oh! ah!* (regret)

yx! *ugh!* (disgust, relief), *ouch! ow!* (pain), *bang!*

эx! *eh! oh, what a . . . !* (disgust)

ай! àй-àй-áй! *ow! oh!* (pain, fright), *tut-tut* (reproach)

áй да [молоде́ц]! *there's a [fine fellow]!* (admiration)

айда́! *come on! let's go!* (colloq., dialect)

ой! òй-òй-óй! *oh!* (fright)

эй! *hey there! ahoy there! I say!* (attracting attention)

ѐй-éй! ѐй-же-éй! ѐй-Бо́гу! *really, really and truly, by God* (asseveration)

ará! oró! (r sounds as *h*) *aha! oho!* (triumph)

ará (r as *h*) *aha, mhm* (lazy man's *yes*)

эгé (r as *h*) *I say!* (colloquial, introducing an important or unexpected statement) алло́! *hello!* (on telephone)

ау́! *hallo! cooee!* (used to keep contact with someone out of sight, as in a wood or in darkness)

ба! *oh! hullo!* (surprise)

бррр... *brrr* . . . (from cold)

брысь! *shoo!* (to a cat)

гм! *h'm! ahem!* (doubt, insinuation)

ни гугу́! *keep it dark! mum's the word!*

ки́с-ки́с! *puss-puss*

кукареку́! *cock-a-doodle-doo*

мм... *er* . . . (hesitation)

мя́у! мя́у-мя́у! *miaow*

на! на́те! *here you are, take it!* во́т тебе́ [и] на́! *well, fancy that!*

но! *gee-up!*

ну, ...! *now* (in commands), *now, now!* (warning), *now, then!* (indignation), *there, there!* (calming), *come along!* (encouragement), *well* (concessive)

ну? *well, what of it? so what?*

ну! да ну́! *well! well, I like that!* (surprise, irritation)

ну̀-ну́! ну̀ и ну́! *well, well!*

ну и...! *what a...!*

ну [во́т] *well [then]* (in telling a story)

ну так что́ же? *so what? well, what if I* (*he,* &c.) *did?*

ну тебя́! *go away! I can't be bothered with you!*

тпру! *wo! whoa!* (to horses)

тсс! тшш! *sh! hush!*

тьфу! (imitative of spitting) *pooh! pah! ugh!* (disgust)

тьфу, про́пасть! *confound it! bother!*

тя́в-тя́в! *bow-wow!*

увы́! *alas!*

ура́! *hurray! hurrah!*

уф! *phew! heigh-ho!* (fatigue)

фи! *fie! bah!* (contempt)

фу! фу́-ты! *fie! ugh! pooh!* (reproach, annoyance, disgust)
фу́-ты, ну́-ты! *fancy that! well, well!*
xà-xá! xà-xà-xá! *ha-ha!* (laugh)
xѝ-xѝ! xѝ-xѝ-xѝ! *he-he! te-he!* (giggle, snigger)
чу! *listen! hark!*
чур! *pax! fains!* (in children's games)
чур молча́ть! *mum's the word! keep it dark!*
ш-ш! *hush! sh!*

There are many onomatopoetic interjections which may be used instead of verbs, e.g. бац! *crack! bang!* may be used colloquially as a forceful verb with the same meaning as ба́цнул: он его́ бац по лицу́ *he slapped him across the face*; other such words include бах! *boom! bang!* бух! *knock! plop!* щёлк! *crack! tinkle!* булты́х! *plop! splash!* and шмыг *off he dashed!*

(b) WORDS FREQUENTLY USED AS INTERJECTIONS

ба́ста! *enough! that'll do!*
ба́тюшки [мой]! *good gracious!*
беда́! *that's bad! oh, dear!*
бис! *encore!*
Бог [его́] зна́ет! *God knows! Goodness knows!*
Бог с ним! *forget about him! never mind!*
не дай Бог! *God forbid!*
сла́ва Бо́гу! *thank goodness! thank God!*
Бо́же [мой]! *my goodness! my God!*
бра́во! *bravo! well done!*
брось(те)! *stop it!*
была́ не была́! *better risk it! here goes!*
вали́(те)! *go on, do it!*
вон! *go away! get out!*
вот...! *there's a ... for you!* (sarcasm)
во́т тебе и...! *there's your ... for you!* (sarcasm)
вот не знал *well, you see, I didn't know*

во́т так [исто́рия]! *there's a nice [mess] for you!* (sarcasm)

во́т так сде́лал! *there's a nice thing for him to do!* (sarcasm)

во́т так та́к! *well, I never!* (astonishment)

во́т та́к! *that's right! that's the way!* (approval)

во́т-во́т! *that's it! that's just the thing!*

во́т еще́! *indeed! fancy that!* (astonishment)

во́т что́! во́т ка́к! *so that's how it is! really? you don't say so!*

Го́споди! *good gracious! Good Lord!*

до́брое у́тро! *good morning!*

до́брый день! *good afternoon! good day!* (on meeting only)

доло́й(+acc.)! *down with . . .! off with . . .!*

ду́дки! *not on your life! nothing doing!* (refusal)

еще́ бы! *I should think so! rather! of course!*

здоро́во! *hullo! how do! hi!*

здра́вствуй(те)! *how do you do? good morning/afternoon/evening!*

да здра́вствует . . .! *long live . . .!*

ка́к же! *of course!*

как зна́ть? *who knows?*

ка́к бы не та́к! *not likely! nothing of the sort!*

и ка́к еще́! *and how!*

капу́т! *finished! bust!* тут ему́ и капу́т (*or* кры́шка)! *that's finished him! he's done for!* (popular)

карау́л! *help!*

марш! *march! clear off!*

ма́тушки [мои́]! *good gracious!*

ми́лости про́сим! *welcome! come in! come and see us!*

молоде́ц! *well done! good lad!*

не на́до! *don't! you mustn't!*

неуже́ли! *is it possible? really? surely not!*

и не поду́маю! *I wouldn't dream of it!*

поду́маешь... *just imagine . . .!* (introducing sarcastic remark)

поду́мать то́лько, . . .! поду́май(те) то́лько,. . .! *just think!* (introducing matter for consideration) пожа́луйста! *please! don't mention it! not at all!*

добро́ пожа́ловать! *welcome! come in! come and see us!*

пойди́[те]! поди́[те]! *I don't believe it! not really!*

по́лно[те]! *enough! stop it! you don't say so!*

на по́мощь! *help!*

прокля́тие! *damn! blast! curse it!*

прочь! *go away! clear off!*

ра́зве! *really?*

до свида́ния! *good-bye! au revoir!* проща́й(те)! *farewell!*

спаси́бо! *thanks! thank you!*

споко́йной но́чи! (gen. governed by implied verb жела́ть, see § 81 (8) above) *good night!*

сто́й(те)! *stop! stay! halt!* стоп! *stop!*

то́-то! то́-то же! *there you are! what did I tell you! mind you don't!* (popular)

то́-то и оно́! то́-то и есть! *yes, that's just it!*

то ли [ещё] бу́дет! *what will things be like then? you haven't seen anything yet!*

чёрт возьми́! чёрт побери́! *confound it! my goodness!*

что за чёрт! *what a nuisance!*

чёрта с два! *nothing of the sort! not likely!*

че́стное сло́во! *honestly! word of honour!*

да что́ вы! что́ вы говори́те! *you don't say so! go on!* (incredulity)

RELATIONSHIPS

§ 120.

пра́дед *great-grandfather*	пр아ба́бушка *great-grand-mother*
дед (де́душка) *grandfather*	ба́бушка *grandmother*
дя́дя (дя́дюшка) *uncle*	тётка (тётя, тётушка) *aunt*
оте́ц (па́па, тя́тя, &c.) *father* (cf. p. 63)	мать (ма́ма, мама́ша, &c.) *mother* (cf. p. 78)
роди́тели *parents*	де́ти *children* (cf. pp. 77, 80)

сын (сынóк) *son* (cf. p. 65)

дочь (дóчка) *daughter* (cf. p. 78)

брат (брáтец) *brother* (cf. pp. 65, 84)

сестрá (сестрúца) *sister* (cf. pp. 70, 85)

племя́нник *nephew*

племя́нница *niece*

внук (внýчек) *grandson*

внýчка *granddaughter*

двою́родный брат *cousin* (male)

двою́родная сестрá *cousin* (female)

тесть[1] (отéц жены́) *father-in-law* (wife's father)

тёща[1] (мать жены́) *mother-in-law* (wife's mother)

свёкор[1] (отéц мýжа) *father-in-law* (husband's father)

свекрóвь[1] (мать мýжа) *mother-in-law* (husband's mother)

зять[1] (муж дóчери) *son-in-law* (of a man or woman) (pl. зятья́)

снохá[1] (женá сы́на) *daughter-in-law* (of a man)

невéстка[1] (женá сы́на) *daughter-in-law* (of a woman)

зять[1] (муж сестры́) *brother-in-law* (sister's husband)

невéстка[1] (женá брáта) *sister-in-law* (brother's wife)

шýрин[1] (брат жены́) *brother-in-law* (wife's brother)

своя́ченица[1] (сестрá жены́) *sister-in-law* (wife's sister)

дéверь[1] (брат мýжа) *brother-in-law* (husband's brother)

золóвка[1] (сестрá мýжа) *sister-in-law* (husband's sister)

The husband of a man's wife's sister is his своя́к[1] (муж сестры́ жены́).

The husband of a woman's husband's sister is her зять[1] (муж сестры́ мýжа).

---

[1] Russians themselves often confuse these terms, some of which can denote more than one relationship. The use of the unambiguous terms contained in the brackets is becoming more and more frequent, especially in the towns.

óтчим *step-father*

пáсынок *step-son*

сват *match-maker* (male)

женúх *bridegroom; fiancé*

муж *husband* (cf. p. 65)

кум (pl. кумовьá) *godfather of one's child; co-godparent*

крёстный отéц *godfather*

крёстный сын *godson*

мáчеха *step-mother*

пáдчерица *step-daughter*

свáха *match-maker* (female)

невéста *bride; fiancée*

женá *wife*

кумá *godmother of one's child; co-godparent*

крёстная мать *godmother*

крёстная дочь *goddaughter*

MEASURES AND WEIGHTS

§ 121.

In the following tables the sign = should be read as равня́ется (*is equal to*), which takes the dative case of the following numeral and noun (except that after ты́сяча, миллио́н, &c., the noun must always be in the genitive, see pp. 136–7).

MONEY

1 рубль (about 8*s*. 4*d*. = 100 копéйкам at official rate)

1 копéйка (cf. p. 70) = approximately 1 penny

LENGTH AND DISTANCE

1 киломéтр (км) = 1 000 мéтров = $\frac{5}{8}$ *mile* (1094 *yards*)

1 гектомéтр (гм) = 100 мéтрам

1 декамéтр (дкм) = 10 мéтрам

1 метр (м) = 100 сантимéтрам = 39·37 *inches*

1 децимéтр (дм) = 10 сантимéтрам

1 сантимéтр (см) = 10 миллимéтрам

1 миллимéтр (мм) = 1 000 микрóнов (μ) (микрóн *micron*)

Some of these units are found only in technical literature; for everyday purposes only км, м, см, and мм are used.

Old measures of length

1 ми́ля	= 7 вёрстам	= *about 4½ miles*
1 верста́	= 500 сажёням	= *⅔ mile (1,167 yards)*
1 сажёнь (*m.*)	= 3 арши́нам	= *7 feet*
1 арши́н	= 16 вершка́м	= 28 дю́ймам = *2 feet 4 inches*
1 фут	= 12 дю́ймам	= *1 foot*
1 дюйм	= *1 inch*	1 вершо́к = *1¾ inches*

AREA

1 квадра́тный киломе́тр (кв. км ог км²)	= 100 гекта́рам
1 гекта́р (га)	= 100 а́рам = *2·47 acres*
1 ар (а)	= 100 кв. ме́трам = *120 sq. yards*
1 квадра́тный метр (м²)	= 10 000 кв. сантиме́тров = *1·2 sq. yards*
1 кв. дециме́тр (дм²)	= 100 кв. сантиме́трам
1 кв. сантиме́тр (см²)	= 100 кв. миллиме́трам (мм²)

For everyday purposes the usual units are га and м².

Old measures of area

The old measures of length preceded by the adjective квадра́тный *square*, and in addition:

1 десяти́на = 2 400 кв. сажёням = *2·7 acres*

VOLUME AND CAPACITY

Solid or cubic measures

The measures of length preceded by the adjective куби́ческий *cubic*. The usual unit is the куби́ческий метр or кубоме́тр (м³) (= *1·3 cubic yards*) containing 1 000 000 куб. сантиме́тров (см³). One см³ = *0·061 cubic inch*.

Litre measure

1 килоли́тр (кл)	= 1 000 ли́тров	= *220 gallons*
1 гектоли́тр (гл)	= 100 ли́трам	= *22 gallons*

1 декалитр (дкл) = 10 литрам   = *17·6 pints*
1 литр (л)   = 10 децилитрам = *1¾ pints*
1 децилитр (дл)   = 10 сантилитрам = *3½ fluid ounces*
1 сантилитр (сл) = 10 миллилитрам = *2·8 fluid drachms*

Note: 1 литр = 1 000 см³ = *61 cubic inches*
      1 кл   = 1 м³   = *35·3 cubic feet*
      1 мл   = 1 см³   = *0·061 cubic inch*

Old liquid measures

1 бочка   = 40 вёдрам = *492 litres*
1 ведро   = 10 кружкам = *2 7 gallons*
1 кружка *or* штоф = 10 чаркам = *1·23 litres*
1 полуштоф   = 5 чаркам = *approx. 1 pint*
1 чарка   = *0·12 litre* = *0·22 pint*

Old dry measures

1 чёрверть (*f.*) = 2 осьминам   = *approx. 5¾ bushels*
1 осьмина   = 4 четверикам = *105 litres, 11½ pecks*
1 четверик   = 8 гарнцам   = *nearly 3 pecks*
1 гарнец   = *3·28 litres* = *5·78 pints*

Weight

1 тонна (т)   = 10 центнерам   = *2204·6 lb.*
1 центнер (ц)   = 100 килограммам = *almost 2 cwt.*
1 мириаграмм (мрг) = 10 килограммам   = *over 1½ stone*
1 килограмм (кг)   = 1 000 граммов   = *2·2 lb. avdp.*
1 гектограмм (гг)   = 100 граммам   = *approx. 3½ oz.*
1 декаграмм (дкг)   = 10 граммам
1 грамм (г)   = *0·56 dram or 15·4 grains*

also дециграмм, сантиграмм, миллиграмм, микрограмм.

The everyday units are т, ц, кг, г. In speech the usual genitive plural of грамм is грамм, and килограмм is abbreviated to кило (indecl.).

Old measures of weight

1 бе́рковец	= 10 пуда́м	= *360⅔ lb. avoirdupois*
1 пуд	= 40 фу́нтам	= *approx. 36 lb.*
1 фунт	= 32 ло́там	= $\frac{9}{10}$ *lb.*
1 [в]осьму́шка	= 4 ло́там	= *almost 2 oz.*
1 лот	= 3 золотника́м	= *0·45 oz.*
1 золотни́к	= 96 до́лям	= *65·8 grains*

COMMON ABBREVIATIONS

§ 122.

до Р. Х. (до Рождества́ Христо́ва) ⎫
до н. э. (до на́шей э́ры) (in the U.S.S.R.) ⎬ *B.C.*

по Р. Х. (по Рождестве́ Христо́вом) ⎫
н. э. (на́шей э́ры) (in the U.S.S.R.) ⎬ *A.D.*

в. (век) *century*

вв. (века́) *centuries*

г. (год) *year*

гг. (го́ды) *years*

п. м. (про́шлого ме́сяца) *ult.*

с. м. (сего́ ме́сяца) *inst.*

б. г. (бу́дущего го́да) *of next year*

н. ст. *or* н. с. (но́вого сти́ля) *new style* ⎫
ст. ст. (ста́рого сти́ля) *old style* ⎬ see pp. 199–200

ч. (час) *hour(s)*

м. (мину́та) *minute(s)*

г. *or* г-н (господи́н) *Mr.*

г-жа (госпожа́) *Mrs. or Miss*

гг. (господа́) *Messrs. or Mr. and Mrs.*

гр. (граждани́н) *citizen*

гр-ка (гражда́нка) *citizen* (female)

т. *or* тов. (това́рищ) *comrade*

тт. (това́рищи) *comrades*

и др. (и други́е) *and others, et cetera*

и пр. (и про́чее) *and the rest, et cetera*
и т. д. (и так да́лее) *and so on, and so forth*
и т. п. (и тому́ подо́бное) *and the like, and so on*
т. е. (то́ есть) *that is, i.e.*
напр. (наприме́р) *for example, e.g.*
м. б. (мо́жет бы́ть) *perhaps* ⎫
т. к. (та́к как) *since* ⎬ used mostly in letters ⎭
т. н. (так называ́емый) *so-called*
вм. (вме́сто) *instead of*
см. (смотри́) *see, v.*
ср. (сравни́) *compare, cf.*
стр. *or* с. (страни́ца) *page*
гл. (глава́) *chapter*
ч. (часть) *part, section*
т. (том) *volume*
тт. (тома́) *volumes*
ж. д. (желе́зная доро́га) *railway* (noun)
ж.-д. (железнодоро́жный) *railway* (adj.)
ст. (ста́нция) *station*
обл. (о́бласть) *oblast, region*
р-н *or* р. (райо́н) *rayon, district*
кр. (край) *kray, territory*
пос. (посёлок) *settlement, housing estate*
с. (село́) *village*
г. (го́род) *town, city*
р. (река́) *river*
оз. (о́зеро) *lake*
о. (о́стров) *island*
ул. (у́лица) *street*
Б. (Больша́я) *Great* (in street names)
М. (Ма́лая) *Little* (in street names)
пер. (переу́лок) *pereulok, side-street*
пр. (прое́зд *or* проспе́кт) *proyezd, thoroughfare* or *avenue*
пл. (пло́щадь) *square*

д. (дом) *house, building*
кв. (квартира) *flat*
им. (имени) *named after, to commemorate*
б. (бывший) *former*
р. *or* руб. (рубль) *rouble*(s)
к. *or* коп. (копейка) *copeck*(s)

SELECT BIBLIOGRAPHY

A. ACCENTED TEXTS

In recent years many accented texts have appeared; these generally contain fewer errors of stress and spelling than those published previously. The following are a few of the more reliable editions, chosen for their helpful notes on grammatical and other difficulties.

I. A. Búnin, *Расска́зы* (Selected Stories). With an introduction, notes, and vocabulary by P. Henry. London, Bradda Books, 1962.

Antón Chékhov, *Selected Short Stories*. Edited by G. A. Birkett and Gleb Struve. Oxford, Clarendon Press, 1951. (With notes and vocabulary.)

—— *Дя́дя Ва́ня* (Uncle Vanya). Edited, with an introduction, notes, and a select vocabulary, by David Magarshack. London, Harrap, 1962.

—— *Три сестры́* (Three Sisters). Edited, with an introduction, notes, and vocabulary, by J. M. C. Davidson. Text stressed by L. A. Volossevich. London, Bradda Books, 1962.

—— *Вишнёвый сад* (The Cherry Orchard). Edited with notes and vocabulary by J. M. C. Davidson. London, Bradda Books, 1962.

N. V. Gógol, *Шине́ль* (The Overcoat). With introduction, notes, and vocabulary by J. Forsyth. London, Bradda Books, 1962.

A. S. Púshkin, *Цыга́ны* (The Gipsies). With an introduction, notes, and vocabulary by P. Henry. London, Bradda Books, 1962.

—— *Tales of the late Ivan Petrovich Belkin*. Edited by B. O. Unbegaun, Oxford, Blackwell, 1947. (With an introduction and notes.)

—— *A Pushkin Verse Reader*. Edited by I. P. Foote. London, Allen and Unwin, 1962. (A selection of Pushkin's short and longer poems, with an introduction, excellent notes, and a selective vocabulary.)

I. S. Turgenév, *Муму́* (Mumu). With an introduction, notes, and vocabulary by J. Y. Muckle. London, Bradda Books, 1963.

Russian Short Stories. XIX Century. Edited by J. Coulson and Natalie Duddington. Oxford, Clarendon Press, 1953. (With introduction, notes, and vocabulary.)

Russian Prose Reader I. Edited by S. Konovalov and F. Friedeberg Seeley. Oxford, Blackwell, 1946. (Contains passages from seven XIX cent. authors, with many notes and a detailed vocabulary.)

Russian Prose Reader II. Edited by J. Filitz and N. Wysotzky. Oxford,

Blackwell, 1952. (Passages from 23 authors of the XIX and XX centuries, with many notes and a detailed vocabulary.)

B. BI-LINGUAL DICTIONARIES

Русско-английский словáрь (Russian-English Dictionary). Edited by A. I. Smirnitsky (А. И. Смирни́цкий). Fifth edition, Moscow, 1961 (50,000 words).

Áнгло-рýсский словáрь (English-Russian Dictionary). Edited by V. K. Müller (В. К. Мю́ллер). Seventh edition, Moscow, 1960 (70,000 words).

New Complete Russian–English Dictionary. Edited by Louis Segal. Third edition, London, Lund Humphries, 1958.

New Complete English–Russian Dictionary. Edited by Louis Segal. Third edition, London, Lund Humphries, 1958.

C. GENERAL DICTIONARIES OF RUSSIAN

Словáрь рýсского языкá в четырёх томáх. Published by the Academy of Sciences of the U.S.S.R. Four vols. Moscow, 1957–61. (The best dictionary of modern Russian. 82,000 words.)

Толкóвый словáрь рýсского языкá. Edited by D. N. Ushakóv. Four vols. Moscow, 1935–40. (Offset reprints: Ann Arbor, 1948, and Moscow, 1948.) (Already somewhat out-of-date in definitions, spelling, and stress. 85,000 words.)

Словáрь рýсского языкá. By S. I. Ózhegov. Sixth edition, Moscow, 1963. (A useful one-volume dictionary, 52,000 words.)

Словáрь совремéнного рýсского литератýрного языкá. Published by the Russian Language Institute of the Academy of Sciences of the U.S.S.R. Moscow and Leningrad, 1950– . (The first 15 vols. (A–T) have already appeared.)

Орфографи́ческий словáрь рýсского языкá of the Academy of Sciences of the U.S.S.R. Edited by S. G. Barkhudárov, S. I. Ózhegov, and A. B. Shapíro. Fifth edition, Moscow, 1963. (The correct spelling of some 104,000 words.)

Прáвила рýсской орфогрáфии и пунктуáции. Edited by L. A. Cheshkó. Moscow, 1962. (The rules of Russian spelling and punctuation, together with a list of difficult words.) (The 1956 edition has been translated by T. J. Binyon and published in two parts, Oxford, Pergamon Press, 1962–63.)

D. PRONUNCIATION AND WORD-STRESS

Russian Pronunciation. The Russian System of Speech Habits in Sounds, Stress, Rhythm, and Intonation, together with a Russian Phonetic Reader. By S. C. Boyanus. London, Lund Humphries, 1955. (Uses the symbols of the international Phonetic Association.)

Russian Pronunciation. A practical Course. By Dennis Ward. Edinburgh, Oliver and Boyd, 1958. (A short introduction for English-speaking students in Britain and America. Uses the Cyrillic letters as phonetic symbols.)

Ру́сское литерату́рное произноше́ние и ударе́ние: слова́рь-спра́вочник. Edited by R. I. Avanésov and S. I. Ózhegov. Second edition, Moscow, 1959, or later edition. (Gives the stress of some 52,000 words and indicates irregularities in pronunciation, declension, and conjugation.)

Ру́сское литерату́рное произноше́ние: уче́бное посо́бие для педагоги́ческих институ́тов. By R. I. Avanésov. Third edition, Moscow, 1958.

Слова́рь ударе́ний для рабо́тников ра́дио и телеви́дения. Compiled by F. Ageyénko and M. Zárva. Moscow, 1960.

A Practical Guide to Russian Stress. By J. Forsyth. Edinburgh, Oliver and Boyd, 1963.

E. ETYMOLOGICAL DICTIONARIES

Russisches etymologisches Wörterbuch. By M. Vasmer. Heidelberg, 1950–8.

Этимологи́ческий слова́рь ру́сского языка́. By A. G. Preobrazhénsky, Moscow, 1910–16, 1949. (Offset reprints: New York, 1951, and Moscow, 1958.)

Этимологи́ческий слова́рь ру́сского языка́. Compiled by N. M. Shánsky. To be in ten vols., of which vol. I part 1 (words beginning with A) has already appeared. Moscow University, 1963– .

F. GRAMMAR

Грамма́тика ру́сского языка́. Edited by V. V. Vinográdov, E. S. Istriná, and S. G. Barkhudárov. Published by the Academy of Sciences of the U.S.S.R. Vol. I and Vol. II (in two parts), second edition, Moscow, 1960.

Курс ру́сского литерату́рного языка́. By L. Λ. Bulakhóvsky. Fifth edition, Kiev, 1952.

Рýсский язы́к (*Граммати́ческое уче́ние о сло́ве*). By V. V. Vinográdov. Moscow and Leningrad, 1947.

Russian Grammar. By B. O. Unbegaun. Oxford, Clarendon Press, 1957.

Russische Grammatik. By Ludwig von Marnitz, eleventh edition, revised and enlarged by F. Häusler. Halle, (Saale), 1958.

A Short Russian Reference Grammar. By I. M. Púlkina. Moscow, 1960.

Си́нтаксис рýсского языка́. By A. A. Shákhmatov. Edited, with notes, by E. S. Istriná. Second edition, Leningrad, 1941.

Рýсский си́нтаксис в наýчном освеще́нии. By A. M. Peshkóvsky. Seventh edition, Moscow, 1956.

Russian Syntax: Aspects of Modern Russian Syntax and Vocabulary. By F. M. Borras and R. F. Christian. Oxford, Clarendon Press, 1959.

Emplois des aspects du verbe russe. By A. Mazon. Paris, 1914.

The Russian Verb. By Nevill Forbes. Oxford, Clarendon Press, 1916. (Latest reprint: 1955.)

Die russischen Verben: Grundform. Aspekte. Rektion. Betonung. Deutsche Bedeutung. By E. Daum and W. Schenk. (With a guide to the conjugation of Russian verbs and the formation of the aspects by Rudolf Ruzicka.) Leipzig, 1954.

Irregularities of declension and conjugation are included in Avanésov and Ózhegov's *Рýсское литератýрное произноше́ние и ударе́ние: словáрь-спрáвочник*, mentioned under D.

G. HISTORY OF RUSSIAN

Рýсский язы́к: истори́ческий о́черк. By G. O. Vinokúr. Moscow, 1945. (Reprinted in *Г. О. Виноку́р: И́збранные рабо́ты по рýсскому языкý*, Moscow, 1959.) (A good general outline of literary Russian from the eleventh to the twentieth century.)

Истори́ческая граммáтика рýсского языка́. Крáткий о́черк. By P. Ya. Chernýkh. Third edition, Moscow, 1962.

Истори́ческий комментáрий к рýсскому литератýрному языкý. By L. A. Bulakhóvsky. Fifth edition, Moscow, 1958.

Истори́ческая граммáтика рýсского языка́. By V. I. Borkóvsky and P. S. Kuznetsóv. Published by the Academy of Sciences of the U.S.S.R., Moscow, 1963. (The fullest account in a single volume of the phonetic, morphological, and syntactic development of Russian since the eleventh century.)

Russian and the Slavonic Languages. By W. J. Entwistle and W. A. Morison. London, Faber & Faber, 1949.

Structure and Development of Russian. By W. K. Matthews. Cambridge University Press, 1953.

Russian Historical Grammar. By W. K. Matthews. London, Athlone Press, 1960.

Очерки по истори́ческому си́нтаксису ру́сского языка́. By T. P. Lómtev. Moscow, 1956.

Очерки по исто́рии ру́сского литерату́рного языка́ XVII–XIX веко́в. By V. V. Vinogradov. Second edition, Moscow, 1938. Offset reprint, Leyden, 1949.

Ру́сский литерату́рный язы́к пе́рвой полови́ны XIX ве́ка. By L. A. Bulakhóvsky. Two vols., Kiev, 1941–8.

Очерки по истори́ческой грамма́тике ру́сского языка́ XIX ве́ка. Edited by V. V. Vinográdov and N. Yu. Shvedóva. Five vols. Moscow, 1964.

H. BIBLIOGRAPHIES

A Bibliographical Guide to the Russian Language. By B. O. Unbegaun. Oxford, Clarendon Press, 1953.

Библиографи́ческий указа́тель литерату́ры по ру́сскому языкозна́нию с 1825 по 1880 год. Published by the Academy of Sciences of the U.S.S.R., in 8 vols. Moscow, 1954–9.

Библиографи́ческий указа́тель литерату́ры по языкозна́нию, и́зданной в СССР с 1918 по 1957 год. I. Moscow, 1958.

INDEX OF RUSSIAN WORDS
AND PHRASES

This index also contains prefixes and many suffixes and endings. References to § 118 are confined to the prefixes themselves; the words illustrating their use are not included. Nouns in -ь which are masculine are followed by (m.); the other nouns in -ь are feminine. Words with two acute accents may be stressed on either syllable.

The numbers refer to pages.

пасть 227, 262, 333, 337
пасу́ 232
па́сынок 397
паха́ть 234
па́хнуть 212, 231, 314
пахну́ть 232
пашу́ 234
пе́й(те) 256
пеки́(те) 255
пеку́ 226, 229
пере- 373–4
пе́ред (пе́редо) 32, 38, 177, 214
пѐред тѐм, как 175, 282, 286
перебега́ть 344
перебежа́ть 344
передава́ть 328
переда́ть 328
переде́лать 323, 325
переде́лывать 325
передняя 113
пе́редо, see пе́ред
перелета́ть 342
перелете́ть 342
перемени́ть 336
переменя́ть 336
переодева́ть(ся) 329
переоде́ть(ся) 329
переса́живаться 334
пересе́сть 334
перестава́ть 329
переста́ть 299, 329
пере́ть 232
перо́ 75
пе́сня 70
песо́к 63
Пётр 72
Петро́в 115, 116
Петро́во 115, 116
петь 238, 259, 266, 327
Пе́тя 72

печёшь 229
печь 78, 226, 229
пешко́м 209
писа́тель (m.) 61–62
писа́ть 196, 225, 234, 259, 270–1, 323, 325
письмо́ 74
пить 226, 239–40, 248, 259, 327, 348
пиши́(те) 254, 293
пишу́ 225, 234
пища́ть 245
пла́вать 341, 345
пла́кать 225, 233
пла́каться 311
пла́мя 79
плати́ть 204, 241, 244
пла́тье 73
пла́ча 259
пла́чу 58, 225, 233
плачу́ 58, 241, 244
пла́чь(те) 255
плащ 62
плева́ть 239, 334
пле́мя 79
племя́нник 396
племя́нница 396
плеска́ть 234
плести́ 232
плету́ 232
плечо́ 74
плещу́ 234
пло́ский 122
плохо́й 122, 127
пло́ше 122
пло́ще 122
-плыва́ть 345
плыву́ 227
плыть 227, 341, 345
плю́нуть 232, 334
плюю́ 239
пляса́ть 234
пляшу́ 234

-пну 230
по (prep.) 64, 153–4, 156, 177, 199, 200, 207, 217
по- (prefix) 127, 345, 374–6
по времена́м 151
по кра́йней ме́ре 167
по пятисо́т 139
по слу́чаю 200
по ту́ сто́рону 207
по шестисо́т 139
по-ва́шему 156
по-ви́димому 307
по-мо́ему 156, 199
по-пре́жнему 199
побега́ть 338, 345
побежа́ть 344
поби́ть 327, 349
побли́же 170
побо́льше 166
повезти́ 314, 343
пове́рх 177
пове́сить 337
повести́ 343, 346
повинова́ться 351
повле́чь 329
повсю́ду 157
повтори́ть 336
повторя́ть 336
повы́ше 170
погляде́ть 335
поговори́ть 349–50
погодя́ 305
под (подо) (prep.) 32, 38, 177, 207, 215
под- (prefix) 376–8
под го́ру 207
под руку 207
подава́й(те) 294
пода́й(те) 294
подава́ть 328
подави́ть 326
пода́льше 170

F f

SUBJECT INDEX

PRINTED IN GREAT BRITAIN
AT THE UNIVERSITY PRESS, OXFORD
BY VIVIAN RIDLER
PRINTER TO THE UNIVERSITY